ONE PERSON AND ANOTHER
ON WRITERS AND WRITING

Richard Stern

One Person and Another

On Writers and Writing

Richard Stern

BASKERVILLE
PUBLISHERS, INC.
DALLAS • NEW YORK • DUBLIN

BASKERVILLE Publishers, Inc.
7616 LBJ/Suite 220, Dallas, TX 75251

Library of Congress Catalog Card Number: 93-070997
ISBN: 1-880909-06-5

Manufactured in the United States of America
First Printing

Books By Richard Stern

Golk
Europe, Or Up And Down With Baggish And Schreiber
In Any Case (reprinted as The Chaleur Network)
Teeth, Dying And Other Matters
Stitch
Honey And Wax
1968. A Short Novel, An Urban Idyll, Five Stories And
Two Trade Notes
The Books In Fred Hampton's Apartment
Other Men's Daughters
Natural Shocks
Packages
The Invention Of The Real
The Position Of The Body
A Father's Words
Noble Rot. Stories 1949-1988
Shares And Other Fictions
One Person And Another

ACKNOWLEDGMENTS

Grateful acknowledgment is made to the following publishers for permission to reprint these pieces which appeared in somewhat different form in their publications:

Agni: On Reprinting *Golk; Bostonia:* Gaps;*Chicago Tribune Book World*: After Hemingway Hemingway; The Counterlife; Black Box; Bernhard's Loser; Donald Justice; Racehoss; Darlinghissima; Isak Dinesen; Merwin's Modesty; Kafka; Schweitzer; *Critical Inquiry:* Penned In; Some Members of the Congress; A Poetic Exchange; *London Review of Books:* Derridiary. Some Afternoons with the Grand Jacques; *Los Angeles Times:* On Rushdie's Verses; *Modern Philology:* Ortega y Gasset; *Salmagundi:* Beckett; On Feeling 'This is the Way it Was'; *Virginia Quarterly Review:* Janet Lewis; *World and I*; Scanning American Poetry: 1947-1987; E. P. Dutton, *The Books in Fred Hampton's Apartment* (Forster; Flannery O'Connor; Events, Happenings, Credibility, Fictions: The Writer's Jobs; A Writer's Stray Thoughts on Time; Picaresque Extra Cuvée; Proust and Joyce Underway; Dr. Zhivago; Bellow's Henderson; Pnin; Edgar Bowers; On the Johnson Library; Studs Terkel; Joyce, Pound, Eliot; The Novelist on his Work); Northwestern University Press, *The Position of the Body* (Roth; Hellman; Lowell; Country Fiddlers, City Slickers; Hannah's Ray; Short Stories; The Writer Abroad; Final Words); The University of Georgia Press, *The Invention of the Real* (Pound; Bellow; Mailer; Malraux/DeGaulle; Nixon; Kissinger; That Devilish, Thinning Art; Faulkner in Genoa; Inside Narcissus; The Invention of the Real; Underway; The Past and Future of Literature. A Play in Three Scenes).

...To a son he speaks, the son of his soul, the prince, young Hamlet and to the son of his body, Hamnet Shakespeare, who has died in Stratford so that his namesake may live for ever. . . .

But this prying into the family life of a great man, Russell began impatiently.

Art thou there, truepenny?

Interesting only to the parish clerk. I mean, we have the plays. I mean when we read the poetry of KING LEAR what is it to us the poet lived?

You are late, he spoke hoarsely, eyeing her with a suspicious glare. The beautiful woman threw off her sabletrimmed wrap, displaying her queenly shoulders and heaving embonpoint. An imperceptible smile played round her perfect lips as she turned to him calmly.

Mr. Bloom read again: **The beautiful woman.**
*Warmth showered gently over him, cowing his flesh. Flesh yielded amid rumpled clothes. Whites of eyes swooning up. His nostrils arched themselves for prey. Melting breast ointments (**for him! for Raoul!**). Armpits' oniony sweat. Fishgluey slime (**her heaving embonpoint!**) Feel! Press! Crushed! Sulphur dung of lions!*

Stephen Dedalus and AE (George Russell) on writers
and Leopold Bloom reading

The book's title is taken from this paragraph of Proust's *Le temps retrouvé*.

Il y avait en moi un personnage qui savait plus ou moins bien regarder, mais c'était un personnage intermittent, ne reprenant vie que quand se manifestait quelque essence générale, commune à plusieurs choses, qui faisait sa nourriture et sa joie . . . Comme un géomètre qui, dépouillant les choses de leurs qualités sensibles, ne voie que leur substratum linéaire, ce que racontait les gens m'échappait, car ce que m'intéressait, c'était non ce qu'ils voulaient dire, mais la manière dont ils le disaient, en tant qu'elle était révélatrice de leur caractère ou de leurs ridicules; ou plutôt c'était un objet qui avait toujours été plus particulièrement le but de ma recherche parce qu'il me donnait un plaisir spécifique, le point qui était commun à un être et à un autre.

There was a person in me who knew more or less how to look, but it was an intermittent person who came to life only when some general essence, common to many things, showed itself; that was the source of its nourishment and joy...Like a geometer, who strips things of their perceptible qualities, seeing only their linear substratum, what people said escaped me, because what interested me was not what they wanted to say but the way they said it (to the extent that it revealed their character or their absurdities); even more the aim of my reasearch—which pleased me particularly—was what one person had in common with another.

TABLE OF CONTENTS

NOTE

This book, a selection of essays, reports and reviews of writers, books, writers' activities and literary speculations composed between 1956 and 1993, is intended as a companion volume to Noble Rot. Stories 1949-1988. *It is the critical shadow of the author's fiction. The selections are not arranged in chronological order; the collection is not meant to display critical development or decline.*

I dedicate the book to friends met at the University of Chicago these past thirty-eight years, colleagues, students and neighbors, many still here, too many gone.

[I]

LITERARY PORTRAITS

The most remarkable people are usually those most remarked. Not necessarily better or wiser, those who are called upon for opinions, decisions, and actions are almost always better, wiser, and subtler for their responses. Speaking alters people, as living in sun instead of fog alters them.

Few fiction writers spend much time on "historical characters," the remarkable actors and speechmakers of public chronicles. When they do, the results are rarely triumphs. Such characters are often interesting as versions of "the real originals," known to readers from other sources; seldom do they change the historians' assessment of the originals. Shakespeare's Richards, Dante's popes, and Tolstoy's Napoleon function in special ways; at best, readers acquire interesting notions about them. War and Peace required the vanity, pettiness, and uncertainty of its Napoleon (although Tolstoy is too grand to make him a doll of these traits). For Richard the Third, Shakespeare wanted a lyric ranter, an enchanting rat; the want contrived a Richard out of some of the historical clichés of the day.

In Dante the characters simplify around the traits which place them where they are in the Great Design. In hell they darken around their sin:

> ma giú s'abbuia
> l'ombre di fuor, come la mente e trista
> *Paradiso*, IX 71

Dante meant that they could do little but think about their sin. (In his physical, dramatic version of their mental difficulty they act what they think.) It is true that powerful feeling simplifies us. At least it forces us to deal with experience in one way.

Fictional characters are simpler than the simplest real person; every day contains so many thoughts, impressions, and gestures that the most complicated character in literature can never be given a hundredth of them. (The sacredness of human life is not a casual idea.) The made-up characters of fiction and biography are made to appear complex and complete because they answer every—narrative—question asked of them. In life one can say "What if he'd gone to school?" or "What if we'd made love?" No sensible person asks what Hamlet majored in. One can ask, however, what Napoleon did in those hours his biographers don't treat; and this is the great threat to the grandeur of biography.

[3]

Sometimes, the historian-reporter-biographer takes poetic liberties with "real people." Mailer's versions of the astronauts in Of a Fire on the Moon look licentious. His map is more complicated than the terrain to which it's supposedly a guide.

Fictional complexity also comes under fire, I think illegitimately. Zola said of Stendhal's world more or less what Einstein said of Kafka's: "Life is simpler than that." Yet one of the social jobs of literature is complicating what we think about and experience. Every few years literature creates another model which makes moving sense out of lovely data, and, say—to use the favorite example of literary historians—the provincial housewife realizes she's Madame Bovary and kills herself.

A number of my friends are men and women whose work makes people interested in their lives. I've not written much about any of them. Since portraits are in a sense epitaphs and one wants one's friends around alive, even kicking, one holds back. Anyway, alive, they can digest your version and turn it into something ridiculously inadequate. (The modern saints—Gandhi, Dolci, and the like— seemed to enjoy shaking up the plaster versions of themselves. The most pathetic people are centerless bags of energy who constantly require commentators in order to know where they are.) Another reason for my restraint is fear of retaliation. A man as full of defects as this writer will be cautious.

The miniature portraits in this section made it imperative to conceal the poverty of "supporting data," for what is wanted is a sharp impression.

[1]

A MEMORY OF FORSTER

> He traced his decomposition—his work had been soft, his
> books soft, he had softened his relations with other men. He
> had seen good in everything, and this is itself a sign of decay.
> Whatever occurred he had been appreciative, tolerant, pliant.
> Consequently he had been a success . . . it was the moment in
> civilization for his type.
>
> E. M. Forster, "The Point of It"

Mr. Forster, eighty-four then in 1963, was next to me at table (the
maneuver of my friend, a fellow of King's College). It was summer;
high table was three sides of a rectangle in a small dining room off
the Commons Room. Forster had been invited back to this decorous
Georgian Quadrangle after World War II. It was his home; he was
its jewel, the icon of English literary civility.

A long man, now stooped and rounded, Forster's lined face was
shyly forward, a wise old dog's face. His movements were those of
someone who'd mastered the slow grace of economy and security,
someone who has learned how to live a long time.

A man of old accomplishment and modesty, Forster had perhaps
surrendered too early to self-criticism. Or had he found, as years
passed, that what he'd done survived much that was more flamboyant? The man who had domesticated English mysticism could not
be surprised by odd survivals.

Extremely courteous, he had a tolerance founded in that persistent curiosity which saw his absorption in the newspapers, the new
books. He spoke of a fine review in *The Observer*, of the day's
menu, of Cambridge out of term. A small emanation of the peculiar
worked from the wit-sheathed gentility: there had been a heavy burden of chicken in recent menus; he would scrawl a note about it in
the fellows' commentary book. He was so pleased the other day to
receive a copy of the first book of his to be translated into Italian;
he wondered why they bothered now. He enjoyed Santha Rama

[5]

Rau's dramatization of *A Passage to India*, but again the success was puzzling. It sounded to me as if he felt that his work was a piece of antique family silver, brought out every ten years or so for some special turn in sympathetic nostalgia.

Alert to what went on, inoculated against the familiar gestures and self-willed eccentricity of this snug collegiate galley, the secret Forster was still at work: the Man of Sympathy who had invented unsentimental ways of conveying it.

At an age when most men are alert to others only from fear of being injured by them, Forster's alertness was ceremonious, infected with his own rhythm and bite. Here is an instance: my friend had gone beyond the standard offering and bought a bottle of red wine. I drank, relaxed, conversed, grew jocular, expansive, illustrative, and swept the half-filled bottle onto the white tablecloth. Talk stopped. Forty eyes studied the red lake. I ventured: "I wonder if anyone has ever made so clumsy a debut at your table?" There was a long and, for me, terrible pause. Mr. Forster was visibly reflecting, eyes back researching high-table debuts. Survey concluded, he turned to me, and in the slightly burred precision of his speech, said: "I'm not entirely certain of that."

Ah well, minutes later, in the Commons Room, digesting my clumsiness and my friend's rebuke, I looked up to Mr. Forster holding out a clipping from *The Observer*. "Here's that review," he said. "I hope you'll agree with me about it."

That summer I went up to his rooms two or three times. At least to the long, high-ceilinged room with the blue china, the family portraits, the leather chair and hassock before the fireplace, the cluttered table where he might be found writing notes. If I had a child with me, Forster would move slowly across the room to a cabinet for a box of candy, would offer it with enormous sweetness to the little boy, and then give him some book or trinket. To me he talked of life, letters, and—modestly—himself. He still got around a bit. He had a flat in London on the fifth floor of a walk-up. It had recently been burgled, his first experience of that. He spoke of the young policeman who had become a close friend, of the man's family with whom he loved to stay up in the north "where they make goods, not words." His personal talk had the direct warmth which began flickering in his own work and, in different ways, in Bennett's, Wells', and Virginia Woolf's, and which burned out in the mockery and anger of the postwar years. The men who could "make you see the whole of everything at once" *(A Room with a View)* were hard to believe after 1945.

[6]

In 1969, age ninety, there was a ceremony for him at King's, a concert, a dinner. Forster relished the beauty of it; he was a man who had prepared for celebration as he had prepared for long life.

And apparently for what would come.

The year after I saw him at King's, a friend of mine volunteered to read to him. (His eyes were too weak to read much and, oddly, no one seemed to ask whether he'd like to be read to.) He was most grateful, and the next day my friend found a chair drawn up across from Forster's and a book by the table. "Would you mind reading 'The Death of Ivan Ilyich?'"

"Now I am here, but then I shall be there. Where?" Ivan Ilyich sees it is not his vermiform appendix but death itself that is inhabiting him. He tries to avoid it, goes back to the law courts, tries talking with colleagues, goes through his redecorated house, when suddenly "he saw IT."

In the cold room with the fire lit and the eighty-five-year-old man drinking up the great preview of death, my friend began to cry. Mr. Forster reached over and touched his shoulder. "Don't worry," he said. "Don't worry. It's all right. It'll be all right."

[2]

A MEMORY OR TWO OF POUND

The youngish American sculptress from Hemingway's suburb noticed him across the way in Cici's. "It must be someone." Not the first maker of stone heads who'd remarked that one. Cici's own headshape (and contents) is a Brancusi egg, but he agreed to find out the professore's name. A menu was presented and signed "E. Pound."

That afternoon, the sculptress told the American lecturer at Ca' Foscari. Much excitement: one did not expect to see the pillars of literature fleshed and ambulant.

I wrote Hugh Kenner, who supplied the pretext of a mission: ask him about the letters exchanged with Zukofsky; he'd once suggested they'd make a book and Zuk's interested. Fine, though I felt a slight Protocols-of-Zion discomfort in the particular mission.

One November day I walked the quiet *calli* back of the *Salute* knocking on doors, asking if a somewhat elderly American calling himself Pound lived there. I was pointed to Calle Querini, knocked and drew Olga Rudge's head from a third-floor window. "Who wants him?" "An admirer." The door was opened, I was inspected and passed in as relatively harmless. My five-year-old son, Andrew, followed.

Pound was flat on the bed, a blanket to his chin. The face was thinner, the beard sparser than my expectation, the face lined like no one else's, not the terrible morbid furrows of Auden, not the haphazard crevices of so many benign elders. For me, at least, these lines had the signatory look of individual engagements. Brow and cheeks, arcs and cross-hatches, with spars of eyebrow and beard hair curling out from what the sculptors worked with, the grand ovoid, the looping nasal triangle. Silent handshakes, Andrew at the head of the bed, I facing him. Over the silence, Olga Rudge—the one who misses it most, said it was richer than most talk—and I made talk. We were both reading Aldo Palazzeschi, and I lent her

[8]

one of his novels. She said Pound was reading the *Paradiso* aloud to her and also a book on microorganisms. "Beyond me." She brought tea and asked Pound if Andrew could have one of the initialed candied fruits he'd gotten for his birthday. The assent was slow and reluctant. (A great sweet-lover, he blushed when Miss Rudge joshed him about the gluttony segment of a French film on the seven deadly sins which they'd enjoyed.)

She was clearly the sea in which he existed. She cleaned, she shopped, she stoked the old stove (her thumb was split), she did the domestic medication. I would not, though, add a D to her name. There was always the strong charm, energy, wit, and ease of a person of accomplishment. "Domestic detail bores you, doesn't it, Ezra?" "No. You take care of it, Olga." In his mouth, the "Ol" of "Olga" was very full and protracted. "I shouldn't have let Olga go," he said when she'd left him with Joan FitzGerald (the sculptress) and me to go on an errand. There was the small panic of abandonment and worry in the full syllable.

Not that he wasn't a bit overwhelmed by the extraordinary care. "Eat your fish." "No." "It's not good?" "It's not good."

There was much joshing on both sides. I remember her description of his excruciating attempts to play the bassoon. She'd been a brilliant violinist. "Not that you can be a soloist in Italy. What *Italian* would accompany anyone?"

"Are you working now?" I asked him.

"Five minutes a day."

Now and then, the old hand would scoot to the table, scrabble up pencil and paper and make a note.

It was the beginning of a bad winter. He was as low as I guess he'd ever been. His teeth were bad (they were fixed up later), the cold was the worst since 1888, and he'd not recovered from a prostate operation or adjusted to living with the physical inconvenience. Even so, he read lots—there were new American novels on his table—and his literary judgements were always extraordinary, oblique, and unexpected.

The next time I came, he was sitting up and we talked easily for a couple of hours. He asked me what was going on. I told him what I knew. We disagreed about Eliot's plays—he liked them a lot. He spoke of the coherence in Eliot and Frost ("he wanted to be New England"), men who had their feet planted in one place, a fortunate and enviable thing. Nothing overwhelming, but every sentence clear, complete, and underwritten by thought. Remembering my expectations of what he would be, I thought, "This is exceptional sanity." Now and then, an odd remark fell out of silence: "Don't think pianos waited for the railroad." (Which may have had to do with cultural independence.)

Mostly, one sensed his instinct for occasion. It was not the reverse of simplicity. I think the word is probably *courtesy:* he acted fittingly. Which did not exclude play with social formula. "How are you today?" "Senile." Or to a visitor who said that X and Y asked to be remembered: "They're in no danger of being forgotten."

Memory, though, was the central worry of that year. My one emotional session with him turned on it. Joan had come back from America, and we went over for tea. There was some talk of Peggy Guggenheim, who lived down the way. I was going there for supper (the woman had fastened onto my wife). I repeated something she'd told me about Pound in Paris days. Pound frowned, fretted a while, then said I was testing his memory, he was relieved to know for sure that what I said was fiction. The words froze the room. The two women talked a bit above them, then went downstairs. I told myself, "Well, he's shown his hand at last. I guess the stuff I've heard about him is so." I debated leaving him with a nod but went over to the bed, held out my hand, and said he was probably right, most social talk was a mix of persiflage and fiction, I was sorry to inflict it on him. He held my hand tight, then drew me down to the bed. My face was within a foot of his. The blue eyes were charged with—what? Appeal? Reaching out? "No," he said, in his almost Scotch-burred English. "Wrong. Wrong, wrong. I've always been wrong. Eighty-seven percent wrong. I never recognize benevolence."

It was something, but I managed to say that maybe he'd been wrong but that those who delighted to tell him he was weren't in the same league when it came to verity.

"You don't know what it's like," he said. "To get off on the wrong path. Not to remember."

I tried something comforting. "You've been on the bull's-eye plenty in your time."

"No," he said, "I've only left scattered notes. Haven't made anything clear."

I'd been reading him and mentioned things that were not only clear but radiant.

It was no time for mollification. He quoted something from Dante about imperfection, and there was more, some of which I didn't follow. The old man was touching bottom, holding on meanwhile to something human on the surface. After I don't know how much time, minutes perhaps, I withdrew—though I thought after I should have stayed with him till he came all the way back. I touched his hand for goodby.

I didn't see him much. Occasionally we'd meet by chance in the Piazza—no welcoming smile was sweeter—or have ice cream on the Zattere with one of the children and Miss Rudge. When my wife came with me, he spruced up, throwing the blanket over his feet, sitting up straight in bed. He talked about his version of the *Women of Trachis* ("not much Sophocles there"), of walks in France and Venice. By the time I left in the spring of '63, Joan had made a wonderful bronze of his head (which I now own). He loved it, preferring it to the one she made later (which is in the National Portrait Gallery in Washington).

I'd occasionally send him a card—never answered but supposedly welcomed. A card Miss Rudge said he especially appreciated was a Rossellini Madonna and Child sent at Easter as a bit of "spiritual Esperanto from a skeptic Jew to a skeptic Confucian."

We never talked directly about Jews. His anti-Semitism had been—I think—a wicked rhetorical habit, part populist, part the casual snobbery of upper-middle-class Europe and America. During his worst days, it was reinforced by the slime fury dredged up by the Nazis. It was attached to his historically flawed notions of usury and, now and then, to that nineteenth-century orthodoxy which had a Hebraic cast. Miss Rudge spoke deliberately of his Jewish friends, and I noted the dedication of *Guide to Kulchur* (to Bunting and Zukofsky). I doubt that he had ever prejudged a human being or a work on racial grounds.

But who knows? He welcomed all sorts of things one didn't think he would. A prize that year from *Poetry* was enormously important to him. He told me he'd never received any prizes and that none of his recommendations for them was ever heeded. This was surely exaggerated, but he'd been in bureaucratic toils in a way I hadn't, and isolation and persecution were near and awful facts for him.

I remember all sorts of other things, none earth-shaking. I came back from Rimini full of amazed disgust for the colossal chutzpah of Sigismundo Malatesta, one of his heroes. "I was just trying to set down the other side of the story," he responded. "I don't think there's anything actually wrong in there." ("There" was the *Cantos*.) Later, though, reading from them, he'd occasionally say, "No, that isn't right."

[11]

When I saw him again in the fall of '65, he was much cheerier. More of the world had forgiven him; he was honored here and there. We took a marvelous gondola ride to his favorite places. (Offering the one cushioned seat to Miss Rudge, he heard her quote him: "'They will come no more /The old men with beautiful manners.'") We exchanged stories about Hyde Park Corner speakers. (I'd just come from there with a handful.) He remembered an atheist about 1906 describing Hell, "the walls a mile thick and a mile 'igh, and wot hi wants to know is 'ow they get in." Miss Rudge wondered what presents they should carry to Paris. "I believe lace and handkerchiefs are still considered indispensable." He characterized a few locals: "X is a fool and a charlatan." He walked, drank Scotch, went to operas and concerts.

His last years were, I'm told, even pleasanter. He was in generally good spirits, as he was—Joan told me—the night he died. His last birthday party was first rate: cookies, candies, neighboring children, friends, the works. Shortly after it, he was in some discomfort, and Miss Rudge got him to the hospital near San Zanipolo. She and Joan talked with him for hours. He was restless, saw no reason to be there. Joan went back to Calle Querini for his pajamas and to call his daughter, just in case. (Hospitals are hospitals.) He dozed off and died. One blue eye remained open. The coffin was shut on it. He was taken to San Giorgio and remained that night between four lit tapers. To the brief services—conducted by a priest from San Giorgio and another from San Vio—came not only friends and family but contadini from Rapallo. The coffin went in the black gondola to San Michele, where it lies close to Stravinsky's in one of the few uncrowded sections of the burial island. The stone—lettered by Joan FitzGerald—says only "Ezra Pound."

[3]
BELLOW'S MOVING DAY

I've known Saul Bellow thirty-seven years. Our relationship is rich, complicated, varied. Affection dominates the variety. Although I see little of him now, that does not mean the relationship is attenuated; it is simply different. I think him a great man, but I will not define greatness nor his form of it. Nor will I write more about him in a preface which suggests that there is a great deal more to write. I submit only this small portrait of him written at the request of the Sunday Magazine of the New York Times a few days after he won the Nobel Prize in 1976.

An uninspired day, neither hot nor cold, bright nor murky, a gray, medium October day. Two blue trucks pincer an ivory van long as a small tunnel in front of a dark-glassed, mushroom-colored high-rise on Dorchester Avenue.[1] On the sidewalk, padded tables, armchairs, sofas, chiffoniers. Fetching and hauling heavy loads does not leave much energy for joyous reflection, but Hallett's Gibraltar-shouldered movers seem at least bemused by this morning's job. One tells me, "The cameras was waiting when we got here." Another, boy-cheeked, Genghis-mustached, says the phones have been ringing all morning.

On the thirteenth floor, I walk in the open door with the congratulatory bottle and find the departing proprietor, phone to ear, on a scalloped loveseat by the broad window. The view is terrific: the cheery American Gothic towers of the University of Chicago with all their courts and fields and grassy quadrangles; the coppery knuckles of the Loop down—north—to the right; the stone, El-bound lumps of Woodlawn beyond the green flanks of the Midway Plaisance, where, eighty-odd years ago, Henry Adams derived from the machine displays of the Columbian Exposition the notion that

---

[1] January 1993: Bellow moved back here some years ago; he lives on the eleventh floor with his wife Janis and their cat Moosie (né Nijinsky).

the dynamo was a rough equivalent of the Virgin Mary as far as motive power went.

Bellow is in a turtle-neck the color of the Midway. He's tired; the face, which can alter more and more quickly than any I've seen, is now drawn, and, if not quartered, grooved, pallid, a bit puffy at eyes and throat. ("If I don't look well, I look busted," says Charles Citrine in *Humboldt's Gift.*) The news birds have been flying around for days, conveying rumor, asking to *be there as you hear the news.* He read Stendhal to prepare for the afternoon class; his wife, Alexandra, went about her mathematics; this morning a Reuters man waked him with the actual announcement off the wires; he drove a dozen miles south to open the apartment for the movers, and now, between phone bouts, directs which pieces go into storage, which to her lakeside apartment. He's moving to save her the long drive to Northwestern, where she is professor of mathematics. A month ago, gloomy, briefly out of the stream of invention where he's spent most mornings of the last forty-odd years, he described that view as "beautiful void in front, filthy void behind." And, "Don't let me molder." Genuine—I could tell from the low set of the fedora—but for years I have seen this old friend convert depression, fury, whatever, into marvelous literary comedy. Which doesn't make the feelings easier to feel. Indeed, the problem is holding on to them, getting more of them, until they break open on the understanding and you can find words for at least their fragments.

"Why not?" he says to the unusual—unique?—morning bottle. *"Mumm's* the word," say I. He finds a couple of unpacked highball glasses, and we raise them to the dynamite king's bequest. "Alexandra says there's no prize in mathematics because Nobel's wife's lover was a mathematician." A drop of story juice even in this old rind.

The oldest of his three sons calls from San Francisco. "Thank you, Greg. Now you know why I was after you to be quiet thirty years ago. . . You're a good son, I love you." He speaks to his daughter-in-law, inquires after his granddaughter, "a true Bellow," the great dark eyes, the straight nose.

Earlier, his sister had telephoned and, recalling their father's dismay at Saul's desire to be a writer, wept. Now he says dreamily, "That antique." Ten times a year, Moses Herzog's father recited his chronicle of failure. "Put out at four years old to study, away from home. Eaten by lice. Half-starved in the Yeshivah...worked in Kremenchug for his aunt...had a fool's paradise in Petersburg for ten years, on forged papers...sat in prison with common criminals.

[14]

Escaped to America. Starved. Cleaned stables. Begged. Lived in fear. A *baal-chov*—always a debtor... . Taking in drunken boarders. His wife a servant." Brilliant, learned, half-loony Moses, trying to slip out from the weight of these memories, to make sense of them, thinks, "But all these are antiquities—yes, Jewish antiquities, originating in the Bible, in a Biblical sense of personal experience and destiny. What happened during the war abolished Father Herzog's claim to exceptional suffering. We are on a more brutal standard now, a new terminal standard, indifferent to persons. . . Personalities are good only for comic relief. But I am still a slave to Papa's pain."

Tom Guinzberg, Bellow's American publisher, calls, is reminded the author has been with Viking since '48. "One publisher, two— no, three wives."[2] Like Chicago, Viking is another loyalty, another target. ("*Humboldt* was bound so poorly it wouldn't stand up on a shelf.") And now, "They're used to this. They have the English-language Nobels. Patrick White. Steinbeck. Look what I found." From a delicate, brass-figured, many-drawered mahogany desk, he fetches a white pamphlet: Steinbeck's Nobel Prize lecture, 1962, inscribed to "Saul Bellow. You're next." "He was right. Poor fellow. It was a burden on him. He took it seriously, felt he didn't live up to it. Well, it must mean something. At least I don't have to worry any more about recognition. Not a total loss. *Spurlos versenkt.*" (Sunk, without a trace.)

A few years ago, after some other international award, Bellow said, "All I started out to do was show up my brothers. I didn't have to go this far." The magic third son, the baby, pampered by his mother (whom he watched die when he was fifteen—"Her hands turned blue, she saw me notice them"), today overwhelming his brothers and sister with memories for which they have less use. Brother Morris, greatly loved, and grandly described, redescribed, and recreated in Bellow's books, calls later from Georgia—he too has just moved, to accommodate his wife's horses—he has big plans for Stockholm. A dozen years ago, after the inked galleys of *Herzog* were stolen in a post-office heist by thieves who drove off in a yellow Cadillac and were not difficult to locate, Bellow got a late call from someone who said he'd sell him back the galleys— they should meet at midnight under the El tracks. Then, a horse laugh. "Morris" (who'd seen the newspapers). In his way, too,

---

2 1993. Alexandra—now married to the great mathematician, Alberto Calderon—was his fourth wife. Bellow was "sure" he wouldn't marry again after their divorce. Luckily, he found Janis.

Morris has been a "a slave to Papa's pain." Since boyhood, he has been a lordly manipulator, trader, moneymaker and -loser; occasionally he invests some of his younger brother's money.[3] As does his son, another wizard of currency.

Investments, deals, arrangements, the mean grandeur and farce of business have been no small part of Bellow's fiction. About it, he is almost as knowledgeable as Dreiser, but less awed, and both more amused and more disturbed.

Since *Herzog,* he himself has been well off, which he enjoys as a fact, just as he enjoys the new range it supplies. Generous, even prodigal, he is also careful, alert to genteel swindle, to the harsh equations of money and love. In his story, "The Old System," a dying sister offers to make up with and see her brother if he gives her twenty thousand dollars. Desperate to see her, the religious, memory-drunk old finagler coughs up. "As soon as he handed over the money, he felt no more concern for it. It was nothing." The withered, belly-swollen, tube-tied sister sweeps the money away and tries to embrace him. All this is recalled by Dr. Braun, their young cousin, who wonders about the use of all this love-and-money passion, this "crude circus of feeling" which humans tell themselves makes them human. "Perhaps the cold eye was better." Yet he can't stop going over and over the old stories. Why? Is he a depressive? "Depressives cannot surrender childhood—not even the pains of childhood," thinks Herzog who tries to explain this same peculiar haunting of the past. What can you get from it? Understanding? Hardly. Maybe "an intimation of understanding," a small maybe that humankind might, just might "comprehend why it lived." And Dr. Braun goes out to look at the inhuman stars, those "things cast outward by a great begetting spasm billions of years ago."

Stars and sisters, thugs, thinkers, lawyers, rabbis, thieves, philosophers, morticians, doctors, equities and passions. It isn't by dodging the world's racket that a Bellow lives or writes. By equaling it, yes: "The poet is what he is in himself, because a voice sounds in his soul which has a power equal to the power of societies." At least, this is what Charles Citrine learns from the poet Humboldt. "You don't make yourself interesting through madness, eccentricity or anything of the sort, but because you have the power to cancel the world's distraction, activity, noise, and become fit to hear the essence of things." One lives, things happen, one feels,

---

[3] Morris and the third brother, Sam, died within weeks of each other eight or nine years ago.

understands, puts words on them. The odd process is analogous to the slow conversion of living matter into fuel. (Perhaps Bellow carries on his father's coal business in another mode.) In any case, Bellow does not hole up in a cave with a cat, hanging on to the world with a radio and the mail. His books are the world felt by a very special, continuously exercised, very fervent mentality. Unlike much contemporary fiction, his books are not worked out as scores for critical orchestras to turn into sound. Nor is he a fictional factory, a graphomaniacal rambler discharging narrative seizures in annual volumes.

His books are slow in coming because each contains a clearing of a mental and emotional forest. The clearance is done by a central character for whom Bellow has had ever-greater requirements. He is discontented with his early heroes who had "no real appetite for high life, only scorn of low life." "All my books are about education and have therefore a somewhat boyish spirit. Bring characters to the conclusions of their errors and leave them prepared to take the first step." So each book leaves him at the threshold of the next, which must go deeper, further, be less fuzzy-minded. No easy assignment.

Humboldt's Gift was eight or so years in the actual works. It began as most of the books do, out there, with an event, a feeling about an event. Bellow's old friend, the poet Delmore Schwartz, had died in squalor. Bellow had seen him on the street some weeks earlier and could not face him. He began a memoir—so Delmore would not be *spurlos versenkt?*—which, in a month, turned fictional, became a subject, a story: it was important who remembered and why, who survived, how, and why. But the central sensibility, the survivor, was unsatisfactory. The book was written over and over with different centers, once or twice without them.

Meanwhile—luckily, I think—Humboldt and Humboldt's world grew. (He is the largest second banana in Bellow's fiction.) Yet Bellow did not want to make the "mistake" he'd made with *The Adventures of Augie March.* "Augie was excited by the memory of someone I knew in childhood who disappeared and whom I never saw again. I thought I'd imagine what his life might have been like.

"What happened was that I drew on a lesson I learned from Sherwood Anderson and other American innocents and pseudo-innocents. Having adopted the role of the innocent, I couldn't doff it. So the book remained ingenuous. I couldn't introduce a shrewd contrast without surrendering the original given. Therefore, as I went on, I felt trapped in an affectation of innocence." Stymied by

[17]

the Humboldt book, Bellow tried other things. One was a story begun after hearing that his old pal from Tuley High, Oscar Tarkov, had spotted a pickpocket working the Broadway trolleys and didn't know what to do about it. Something here linked up with the lives of some Polish Jews Bellow met in New York and Cracow, and Mr. Sammler, who looks like one of them, came into existence to control and express Bellow's feelings about such things as the violence-hunger and civil rot which were conspicuous facts of the late sixties. Or was it Sammler who needed such feelings, and such events, and was more likely to have them? Perhaps there was a confusion here which led to or resulted from rushing the book.

Bellow is dissatisfied with *Mr. Sammler's Planet*, feels that "like *Augie,* it dealt with a new state of mind but wasn't under control. I should have gone all out with it." As disciplined as anyone I know, as conscious of the longer perspective, Bellow is subject, like every author, to extra-literary pressures, need for response, need to know if his "illusions" catch fire.

Bellow had also worked on another book, "an easy, funny book," based somewhat on the life and stories of his old pal, paddleball partner, and sometime traveling fellow, David Pelz, a Gary contractor, health freak, and bon vivant. They went off to Africa on some sort of industrial diamond hunt, and ended up—with Saul Steinberg—cruising toward Murchison Falls, Bellow euphorically—and rarely—high on hashish, enchanted with the beautiful crocodiles, green and white under the water. Pelz's character and misadventures melted into the book about Humboldt, and another, deeper Bellovian narrator came along to connect the two worlds.

Charles Citrine—a sharpening of the name of Louis Sidrin, another old friend—shuttles between New York and Chicago, past and present, takes his instructions and his lumps from the poet Humboldt and such reality-professors as divorce attorneys, fragrant ladies, and fastidious thugs. Like the Bellow heroes since Augie, Charley is a Columbus of the Absolute (Augie was a "Columbus of those near-at-hand") whose ear is cocked for its supernal music, that is, for a cosmic guarantee of permanent significance, permanent enchantment. In *Humboldt's Gift*, this music is largely supplied by the books of Rudolf Steiner, about whom Bellow had read in a book by the English critic Owen Barfield. (Most intelligent literary critics are unreceptive to such telegraphy; they regard Steiner as a cosmic four-flusher, but Bellow thinks he was an authentic visionary, and he attends Steiner

[18]

Society meetings in Chicago today.)[4]

The final push *Humboldt* needed came from the happiness Bellow found in meeting, courting and marrying Alexandra, the beautiful brown-eyed Rumanian mathematician. Not that Bellow had lived like Saint Anthony in the years since his last, endlessly protracted divorce. "What a woman-filled life I always led," says Citrine. Bellow is ravished by Alexandra's exotic, mathematic celebrity and trails her on the lecture and conference circuit— Berkeley, the two Cambridges, Austin, Jerusalem. Though once, marooned among topologists for a rainy week in the Black Forest, he did not think her world made for ideal society. "Since I've never understood women anyway, I finally married one who's really mysterious."

In a way, Bellow himself is not mysterious. Not now, anyway, after he has spelled out versions of himself on several thousand public pages. He is said to be exceptionally sensitive to criticism, but his books at least are full of what amounts to self-accusation, some of it put into the slanging mouths of enemies, friends, wives. Naturally he surmounts his created alter egos; perhaps he is simpler than any of them, because certain essential reactions and decisions were made very early. Like Bellow, Citrine spent some of "my eighth year in the public ward of a TB sanitarium. ...I became very thoughtful there and I think that my disease of the lungs passed over into an emotional disorder so that I sometimes felt, and still feel, poisoned by eagerness, a congestion of tender impulses together with fever and enthusiastic dizziness."

The eagerness and the tenderness persist, the openness to sensation, to the new and uncatalogued. They are part of the delicate machinery inside a Bellow fortress which is manned by learning, skepticism, comparison, and an extraordinarily sensuous memory for experience and for literature. Bellow is not particularly proud of this gift, but he can be defensive about it. He cited Nietzsche one night; Hannah Arendt challenged the citation. Bellow went home, spent hours hunting it down, copied and mailed it to her the same night.

American literary history is full of writers who for one reason or

---

4 1993. In 1911, Franz Kafka was impressed enough by Steiner to pour out his troubles to him. Kafka writes (*Diaries* I.59. Schocken Books): "He listened very attentively without apparently looking at me at all, entirely devoted to my words. He nodded from time to time, which he seems to consider an aid to strict concentration. At first a quiet head cold disturbed him, his nose ran, he kept working his handkerchief deep into his nose, one finger at each nostril." (This is Kafka's last word about the visit or about Steiner.)

another—isolation, philistinism, celebrity rapidly made and rapidly pulverized, and the pressure of constant invention—have thrown in the literary towel after five, ten, or fifteen years. There is, as well, an insecurity built into the lives of fiction writers and poets. It has to do with confusing the intensity and logic of their stories and poems with the inertness and drift of so much life. The writer often puts excessive pressure on his experience: breakfast tables become theaters, the casual encounter isn't so casual. It makes for trouble, but then trouble makes for books—or for drink, evasion, break-down, suicide. How many American writers have published first-rate imaginative books over a thirty-year period?[5] Perhaps three: Henry James, Faulkner, and now Bellow.

So here is the white-haired, compact, handsome prince of American literature strolling through Hyde Park, Chicago, in one of Armando's splendid suits, candy-striped shirt from the Burlington Arcade, Hermès tie, his velvety fedora jaunty with a Patagonian eaglet's feather in the braid. The slightly hooded eye is taking in the street, the tongue is ready to greet or to annihilate. (Part of the fortress? Part of the static between broadcasts?) A woman complains an old lover came on her like a steamroller. Bellow: "Did you have to lay down the asphalt?" A young waitress sullenly slaps down his hamburger at The Eagle: "Puberty and menopause hit her at the same time." A celebrated poet goes off to Caracas with a pride of critics: "They carry him around like a piece of the true cross." On eminent friends or former colleagues: "the Bettelheim of the Republic"; "Tillich the Toiler." On Bloomsbury: "that Himalaya of molehills." After trying to moderate a difficult meeting with his gifted, sensitive colleagues on the Committee on Social Thought: "All those prima donnas and not one song." Back from one of the fifty-odd lectures given over the globe these past years, he describes the small town: "In *Fontemara,* the priest explains what it's like to be a peasant: 'First, there's the king, then the nobili-ty, then the gentry, then the merchants, the tradesmen, the laborers. Then there's nothing, and again nothing, and once more nothing. Then there's the peasants.' DeKalb's the third nothing."

Always new books, old books, high talk and intimate talk, not so much gossip as the marrow of lives. "The first time I met Saul," said Angus Wilson, the English novelist, "We walked all around

---

[5] 1993. Bellow published the marvellous story "Something To Remember Me By" more than *forty* years after the publication of *Dangling Man.* And one could add a few other first-rate writers to the thirty-year list, Updike and Roth, for instance.

Rome talking about ourselves. I told him everything about myself, things I'd never told my closest friends. When we got back to the hotel and said goodby, he said, 'That was nice, but next time, we'll really have to let our hair down.'"

Bellow's talk is full of opinion as well as wit and observation, but he has not published his opinions—his lectures—in book form. "I was influenced by Schopenhauer's 'Essay on Style'—'You can debate opinion, not imagination.' Why publish opinion?" His book, *To Jerusalem and Back*, is mostly a heap of other people's fascinating opinions beating themselves against the facts of the city, its people, and their own beings and behavior. There is also, though, straight opinion, and it may be that now Bellow feels he should speak out about certain things without submitting them to the canons of imagination. "Tolstoy," he says, "was forced by art to be fair to Karenin. Then he threw art out." It's not likely that Bellow will become a Tolstoyan reformer or even a persistent advocate. Still, he has led a civic life, a social life, a reasonably public one[6] as well as the life which counts most for him and what makes him count most. He thinks of doing a Jerusalem-type book on Chicago (another beleaguered treasure?).[7]

Does he now feel the need to declare himself directly? And does that mean that the maker of Herzog, Henderson, Humboldt (all those *h* 's, "as if I'm getting my breath") has completed his education? I doubt it.

In any case, on this moving day, as he directs the beautiful desk to the North Side, he says, "Maybe now, I can write something really good for a change."

---

[6] 1993. He spoke at the inaugural of Chicago's second Mayor Daley. A year or so later the Daleys gave him a wonderful seventy-fifth birthday party at the Art Institute.

[7] This turned into a novel, *The Dean's December*.

[4]

PHILIP ROTH

Philip Roth is one of my closest friends. We have spoken about almost everything we know and much we don't. The conversations are among the richest and most amusing of my life. I've watched Roth become a finer, deeper and more powerful writer with almost every book. In this small iceberg-tip of a portrait, I suggest the emptiness of the old charge that he is a narrow writer. (After Patrimony, *one didn't hear that charge.)*

I dictated the piece over the phone to an editor who needed it for a twenty-four-hour deadline. A writer who was to do a long piece had done a hatchet job, crude, mean and—what counted for the editor—boring. The writer was one of those critics who—like a man Yeats mentions in The Trembling of the Veil—*conceals spite behind stupidity and always interrupts to deform or silence intelligence. (Naturally, he's on many committees, has much power and is known as a failed this, a one-time that, a something-else manqué. This makes a reasonable dossier for a man who decides the monetary and critical fate of others.) All right, now that's out of the way. As for Roth, he's too good a friend to write about in detail. Yet an intelligent editor, a young, rather naive but literature-loving man, and, therefore, one after my heart, begged to know some of the inside dope about Roth's writing habits. "You just say, 'The manuscript came back. He'd done it again.' What had he done? How had he done it?"*

It's not a miracle, but it looked like that to a reader of Roth's early drafts, one who'd argued for one sort of coherence, one way of doing a scene, an excision here, a presence there. Wonderfully easy to advise when you don't have to follow the advice yourself. Roth invites several readers to hammer at his early drafts. He's a great worrier about his narrowness, though by now he understands he isn't narrow in the way his harsher critics say but only severe about staying within his competence. The danger in his early drafts

[22]

*is Jamesian qualification. His intelligence is engaged, and charac-
ters fight with brilliant primness about this difficulty or that. The
wildness of his greatest characters comes harder now. That's an act
that once came so easily he began to distrust it. Yet if you force
wildness, it shows, and nothing smells worse.*

*Roth's a great master of form, and that saves many a day. He
knows when to break off a scene; his transitions are large and
unexpected. Much of the formal beauty is of absence. Then too there
is the beauty of persistent treatment of rich —"inexhaustible"—
material.*

*Roth separates his own life from lives he creates around similar
characters and events. "Was Jack Benny really a skinflint?" he
asks. "So why should I be a Zuckerman?"* [1] *Right. As for
Roth/Zuckerman and the way one brings musical comedy out of the
other, I can't tell the young editor very much. Omission, reduction,
sharpening, that's what an editor himself does all the time. Roth
also knows how to add, to invent. The rest is finding the true center
of a book and leaving out the rest. That's why my little piece quotes
Michelangelo's most famous technical remark. As for the treatment
of self—whatever that is, as Roth worries it in* The Counterlife—*the
Kierkegaard citation will serve as well as psychiatric treatment of
the subject.*

"Roth."

"Schtoin."

"I took the wrong turnoff."

Every other year, I miss it. Roth is patient with his pals' lesser
idiocies. For those of out-and-out fools and the laser—brained
fanatics around whom his art puts bars, he's positively hungry.
They're out there *living.* (Living: that heap of groans and gestures
out of which he has to make sense.)

Finally, the river, the village, the hill, the turnoff into Connecticut
forest, the flat rocks, the right turn, and the beautiful double house,
the eighteenth-century kitchen stocked for a weight-watcher—for-
merly a gourmet—siege. If you're one of the regulars, you get
told—instead of shown—which upstairs room you're in. You pass
the comic posters of the host: submarine-nosed, thimble-head, leaking a few black wires (done by his late pal, Philip Guston). By your

---

[1] Twenty-odd years ago an actress friend of mine, fulsomely introduced by Jack Benny at a
dinner, said, "Shit, Jack," into the microphone and was left stranded by his infuriated snub; so
perhaps old Benny was a skinflint after all, but in the heart, not the wallet.

bed, a pile of new books. Out of the window—lawns, apple trees, a hay field—the hostess, more beautiful than the pictures that have celebrated her since her teenage Juliet and debut with Chaplin, hanging the wash. She'll be driving to get the night's vegetables and returning for forty laps in the pool.

Sometimes there's another house guest, sure to be someone who's read and been around enough not to drop too many stitches (some of which will be in your side).

This is no vacation retreat. It's a house in which vocation and vacation fuse. The point is that there's no vacation. Not that the atmosphere doesn't alter when a book's being started instead of finished or a play's getting prepared rather than recovered from. But Roth and Bloom, to give the hosts their names, don't store their heads with their winter clothes. They're in—as Roth says—"the same line of work," depicting human beings clearly, forcefully, beautifully.

You don't feel inspected here, though in a house of observers, there's a certain kind of sport about this matter. Now and then something you've said or a trait you thought you'd concealed shows up on a page (or a stage). "I didn't know my head was that small."

"It's not *your* pinhead. It's mine."

People *are* noticed here, but not by reporters. This is a house of fiction-makers. Human beings in and out of the house, in and out of books, are analyzed, magnified, felt with and against so that more interesting ones can get invented. During the day, everyone's at a different typewriter; groans over misplaced commas are bouncing off every wall. We assemble at meals, breakfast and lunch at the kitchen table, Roth and Bloom squeezing oranges, cutting bread, pouring coffee. In late afternoon, it's the pool under birch trees, the trim hostess keeping trim, the rest of us on lounge chairs between the smoking insect-repellers. There may be a wrap-up seminar on the misplaced commas or a homemade routine: Roth as Olivier's Othello—"Now doan you say dat, Yago man, Ah doan *wanna* ring dat hawnky's naik"—Bloom finding Blanche DuBois in Desdemona.

Dinner, candlelit and silvery, is at the table in the barn. The hostess, who's cooked it—unless the host has barbecued something—is in a long dress like some queen's dream of herself. Art doesn't stop at the typewriter here. There's no snorting down burgers and Kool-Aid.

[24]

Now and then guests come from around the county or up from New York. Most are artists (playwrights, musicians, actors, sculptors, poets), people who know what it is to spend life amusing, exciting, judging, and deepening the lives of lots of other people. There's usually one conversation star per evening, seldom the same—though Roth, with a little booze in him, is hard to stop. Or rather, one wants him never to stop: There's a gas shortage, the local gas station gauleiters are rendered to the wart; then the customers get theirs, tanks and bodies open to the pump, mouths and rear ends leaking repletion. The scatological aria spins, frantic, wild, the diction lit with genial mania. Someone breaks in, there's another tack, and *whoosh,* Paganini's whirling again.

The guests are off for their own beautiful acres, the home folk move to the living room for Vivaldi or *Guys and Dolls,* for a final drink and a postmortem. Or we slide back to the day's work, ten minutes become fifty, a hundred. How to get X to Y, how Conrad would do it, where James muffed it. Or where we are, what we were back in Chicago twenty-five years ago, what we're about now, what it's all about. Sometimes, despite fatigue, invention: How about this? how about that? The book's in the air. For a time it only belongs to itself. It's trying to get made; it doesn't matter who feeds it.

One summer it was *Zuckerman Unbound.* I: "Roth. To the woodshed." His workplace, two rooms across the lawn from the main house, desk, chair, couch, a picture of Kafka, the great Czech alter ego, black eyes lighting up the earth. Roth cushions his troubled back, gets out the yellow pad. "Go."

"You've messed it. The book belongs to Pepler, not the brother." Roth writes. "More."

Speech, debate, excitement, analysis, invention, the yellow pad fills. Fifty, sixty, a hundred murderous minutes. "Don't stop. Keep going. Suppose *Pepler's* the kidnapper?"

Finally, I get out. Roth stays.

Like the great writer on the wall, he is deeply a writer. And like him also, a son (of a Herman), deeply, a brother, a friend—the best—a lover, a citizen and, with heavy decision, not a father. Above, beneath, and through all, a writer (whose chief subject is that). Not for self-fingering narcissism though. If anything, there's the special modesty of high intelligence, ever surer of what it can and can't do.

Eight months later, the galleys arrive. Roth, in the middle of his half-year in London—the social part of his life—has somehow done it again. You can hardly spot a seam—who would have guessed the pounding it took?—though that's the book's subject.

"It's simple," said Michelangelo. "Just hammer off everything that doesn't belong on the sculpture."

Or, for Roth, a more fitting quotation from one of his hundred favorite writers: "The majority of men are subjective toward themselves and objective toward all others, terribly objective sometimes—but the real task is to be objective toward oneself and subjective toward all others" (Kierkegaard, *Journals*).

[5]

LILLIAN HELLMAN

This piece was written shortly after the playwright's death in the spring of 1984. I'd read articles (in Commentary *and the* Chicago Tribune*) which attacked the veracity of her memoirs, and I remembered a similar assault by Martha Gellhorn. The "famous lawsuit" alluded to was Hellman's against Mary McCarthy's public assertion (on national television) that Hellman never wrote the truth, that every word she wrote was a lie. I cared a lot for Lillian Hellman, and I wanted to explain something about her which would be both a defense of her character and a salute to her person.*

I was in New York when Lillian died in Martha's Vineyard, had, in fact, decided to write William Abrams, who'd put a notice in the previous Sunday's *Times Book Review* asking for stories about her. I hadn't seen her since December, 1981, when I'd forgotten her unlisted phone number but done what I'd done several times before, walked the few blocks from my sister's house to hers and called through the house phone. I was with my oldest son's girlfriend, a Hellman fan. Would it be all right if I came up with her for a few minutes? Yes, said Lillian, she was all alone—the cook had gone out—and in deshabille, and she wasn't very well, but it would be good to see me and yes it was all right to bring the girl.

Her peignoir was open at the neck so that the depressed, bony triangle between shoulders and breasts, and the loose, wattled neck flesh struck me harshly. Her hair was grayer than I'd seen it, the nose bulked more than ever. It looked as if nature were sending every sort of signal to tell the flesh to give itself up.

Lillian didn't see herself. There'd been many eye operations, and she said she could see "only shapes. I know more or less where you are."

What wasn't included in the gloomy signal system was her voice and the energy of what it did so marvelously. It began with the famous lawsuit. She'd just received Mary McCarthy's deposition.

"There isn't a single instance of lying cited." What did I think of them apples? I said intelligent people had to stop talking to television interrogators as they did in their living room. The spread of domestic slander through the media would only hasten the transformation of the country into one Great Gossip Machine. This launched a story. It had to do with Norman Mailer, and it pivoted on an old sexual turndown. Many of Lillian's stories dealt with distinguished, handsome, youthful, famous or otherwise attractive men pursuing and being rejected by her and later taking some comic or odd revenge. This one also involved another staple, Lillian's fury. She'd hunted up "Dash's" old revolver and headed out to shoot Mailer. "Dash," the *deus ex intellectu* of many stories, locked the door and wouldn't let her out until she'd cooled off and abandoned the lethal mission.

Fatherless, guideless, Lillian had, I think, invented Hammett at least as much as she'd lived with him (and far more interestingly than he'd invented her, as Nora Charles in *The Thin Man*). Dash was the male lead in a thousand stories. He represented guidance, reason, male mystery, heroism, illness, stoicism, partnership, love.

He was not the only transfiguration in Lillian's continuous story. Those who want to nail her to the straight and narrow have an easy time of it. "I knew early that the rampage angers of an only child were distorted nightmares of reality," she wrote (just before she wrote that her story of Julia would be undistorted). How could such an enchanting storyteller tell anything straight? Aren't her plays all about inventors, liars, distorters, and fantasists? Of the sisters in *Toys in the Attic,* she said, "Neither ever told the truth about anything. Not that they lied. They'd just never seen the truth about anything." Such lies are Lillian-truths: not about fact, but about the minds and temperaments which distort fact.

Many think Lillian had a life that didn't need ornamenting or transfiguring. Yet this small, dumpy woman with the great nose and flame-dyed hair had a hunger bigger than her experience, her success, her friends, her failures. She lived among great storytellers and great drinkers and herself knew drink as a short-cut to what satisfied her hunger. "I drank," she said, "but unlike X, Y and Z, I got off the floor everyday and went to work."

This, I think, was true. Lillian was a fantasist, but the fantasies lived off large chunks of truth. How else not be boring? She hated bores but hated "whacks" and "crazies" even more. If she sentimentalized, it was in the direction of vividness, heroism and passion. One night in Chicago we went out with Nelson Algren. Lillian had read Simone de Beauvoir's account of her affair with him, and this redeemed his contempt for that account and his abuse of the teller. (His sentimentality was never to give women the amorous time of day.) He was also sentimental about Hellman, for he'd read her dispatches from the Spanish War. Those were medals. These two fabricators enjoyed each other immensely.

Lillian loved having men around her. Some of her fiercest critics are the wives, ex-wives, sweethearts, and ex-sweethearts of the men who loved her stories and repeated them around the country. I was at her house one night when a famous Hollywood stud called her twice to report his progress with a celebrated American widow. Lillian claimed to be annoyed—bored—by the stud reports, but the fact that she was their receiver tickled her pink. (Now that I think of it, I better add my belief that the calls were "genuine.")

Lillian respected truth because she knew how hard it was to tell or take it. In fact, I think she was on the side of most of the virtues and tried to practice them. She was loyal to friends—sitting by bedsides, taking people to hospitals—a hard worker, a clear-eyed critic, unafraid to tell people what she felt, prodigal of herself, her talents, and her hospitality. She was proud she'd earned the good life she lived, the beautiful houses, the terrific cooks, the good whiskey drunk in good company. Her compassion was genuine—the sublimation of a maternal, childless woman—and was discharged in ways that have damaged her reputation. She was wiser about politicians than politics, but most of those who call her names aren't fit to be in the same room with her when it comes to giving up time, money, and self to what she believed would rectify unfairness.

If she didn't compose her world successfully, she did compose herself. And the self I knew was pretty terrific. When I met her in 1958, she was having a rough time, didn't know if she could write any more plays, thought she might be out of things altogether. We went to see *Endgame* here in Chicago. She thought it might be a new energy in the theater, one that was beyond her. She really didn't care for plays anymore. Still, she overcame self-doubt, and finished *Toys in the Attic*. It was a hit, and she made the money she needed. Meanwhile, in Chicago, she'd learned she could talk to college classes, and that started another career for her. Then there was the career as memoirist, the one that gave her a totally new celebrity. She became a heroine to women all over the United States. The heroine was the one she was as well as the one she invented. There was the Lillian who was the only woman taken to the front line by the Russians, who went there through Berlin (though when and how remain unclear), who sent despatches from Spain, who wrote the sensational plays and doctored—often anonymously—such other famous ones as *A Streetcar Named Desire*, and the one who told the Congressional committee about her conscience. The Lillian behind this Lillian was Lillian the Rememberer, the Memoirist, the Writer, the grown-up version of the girl with the rampaging anger. Lillian remembered and remade Lillian. When she wrote the stories—or when she told them—you forgot the blind little woman with mottled flesh or the warm, fluent, sometimes innocent Auntie-sort of person who said in her gorgeous voice, "Don't forget me. Come see me soon. I don't have forever."

One night in New York she said, "I thought of a title for my book today. Tell me what you think of it. *Pentimento*."

"I don't know what it means."

"It's the sketch the artist covers up when he's rethought or reseen what he's doing. There's a secondary meaning of penitence, of repentance. Is it too fancy for a title?"

"Yes," I said. "It'll never work for you."

[6]

FLANNERY O'CONNOR:
A REMEMBRANCE AND SOME LETTERS

John Morgan, a philosophy student at the University of Chicago, called me the evening of August 3, 1964, to say that he had just heard from Milledgeville the news of "Mary Flannery's death." John and I would meet occasionally around the campus, and he'd pass on news about Flannery. He told me last spring that she'd been very ill, that he hadn't been able to see her when he'd gone home. I wrote her then and received a letter scarcely different from any other I'd received from her in the five years we'd known each other except that the signature was penciled and shaky.

Milledgeville
[April 14] 1964

Dear Richard,
I'm cheered my Chicago agent is keeping up with his duty to keep you informed on my state of being. It ain't much but I'm able to take nourishment and participate in a few Klan rallies. You're that much better off than me, scrapping Tuesday what you wrote Monday. All I've written this year have been a few letters. I have a little contribution to human understanding in the Spring Sewanee but I wrote that last year. You might read something called Gogol's Wife *if you haven't already—by one of those Eyetalians, I forget which. As for me I don't read anything but the newspaper and the Bible. Everybody else did that it would be a better world.*
Our spring's done come and gone. It is summer here. My muscovy duck is setting under the back steps. I have two new swans who sit on the grass and converse with each other in low tones while the peacocks scream and holler. You just ought to leave that place you teach at and come teach in one or our excellent military colleges or female academies where you could get something good to eat. One of these days you will see the light and I'll be the first to shake your

[31]

hand.

Keep me posted what you publish. Since you've slowed down, I might be able to keep up with you. I'm only one book behind now and once my head clears up I'm going to read it first thing.

Cheers and thanks for thinking of me. I think of you often in that cold place among them interleckchuls.

Flannery

She'd come to the "cold place among them interleckchuls" in February 1959, although she was frightened of Northern winters. As if to certify her fears, there was a blizzard and ice storm which forced her plane down in Louisville. She was in a bus and spent nine hours riding to Chicago. I met her at 2 A.M. in the terminal building downtown. She was off the bus first, her aluminum crutches in complex negotiation with handrails, helping arms, steps. Tall, pale, spectacled, small-chinned, wearily piquant. I was to recognize her, she'd written, by the light of pure soul shining from her eyes. Fatigue, relief and wit-edged bile were more like it.

The streets were studded with ice bits. The walking was worse that I'd ever seen it in Chicago. The difficulties drew from her bitter snorts of fulfilled prophecy.

She was installed as Emily Something-or-Other in Residence at a girl's dormitory. The girls asked her about "Christmas customs in Georgia." "Do they think I'm from Russia?" It didn't go too well.

Out of the girls' lounge, she functioned splendidly. She'd written a fine statement about her work as preface to her public reading; and then she read her stories wonderfully, her voice slightly less inflected than those of her characters and full of wry strength.

She read to an audience of thirty,[1] huddled embarrassed, in the front two rows of a thousand-seated auditorium. "You ought to award them your crutches," said I.

"Lucky I don't flingem atem."

Flannery's idea world was the South, Writing, the Holy Ghost and bilge about all three, but her power was narrative.

Her printed stories were built bit by bit until she felt their form. And their sound, for she was a great ear writer. In fact, she had exceptionally alert eyes and ears, gifts which aren't much talked about but which both irrigate lots of her drier story matter and make her wilder creatures eat out of her hand. (Not that Bible salesmen, German DPs, and escaped "mentals" were less than facts of

---

[1] Robert Coover and Charles Newman were two of the then-young writers there.

Milledgeville life.) Maybe that sensuous alertness was bound up with the disease which got to her so young.

The story she read was "A Good Man Is Hard to Find." Many of the lucky few in that audience remember the sound of her voice and the angry-flamingo look behind her spectacles. Anybody there could tell she was her own element, not a derivative of Welty or Faulkner.

We passed those days at parties, dinners, and drinking coffee around town. It was rather a big social bite for her, but great relief from the sessions in the lounge. She talked some about her own work and about Milledgeville. We discussed the novel she'd just finished and a couple of new stories. I felt that they showed the pressure of trying to get certain things said more directly than she'd said them before. She thought not, but her late stories seem to go back to her earlier manner. Maybe she relaxed after putting down what she was afraid she might not have time to put down. Though we never talked about this, and for all I know she didn't think much about it.

We corresponded off and on till her death. Her letters are usually typed on small sheets of paper, though for writing to Europe she used the airmail blues and sometimes wrote in ink. The first letter I find is headed "Hoover's Birthday 1959." I'd written her about a visit to Mystic, Connecticut, and I think there was a paragraph about the Mystic Power Company. "Dear Dick," she wrote (though from then on she addressed me as "Richard"),

Would I were at the Mystic Wax Works where something could be made of me. There is no place hereabouts to cool off except in my mother's deep freeze which is already occupied by last years turkeys. This is the season at which I pick up peafowl feathers as the dear birds shed. In the cool of the evening I am to be seen out in the pastures, bending painfully from my two aluminum sticks, reaching for some bright feather. I hope that this affecting picture touches you.

. . . Should you be in the region of Providence there is a good writer there name of John Hawkes. If you would be interested in co-authoring with me a book listing where good writers may be found, like Duncan Hines for restaurants, we might make us a little extra money. Since I have got my novel out of the house, my thoughts turn largely to finance.

She sent an envelope of peafowl feathers and renewed them a year or two later from the bird which was, she said, pictured in a *Holiday* magazine.

[33]

Milledgeville
17 May 59

Dear po Richard,
I am cheered to hear that the moths have not got into your peafowl feathers yet. I take this symbollically (sp?) to mean that my memory too is unmotheaten in your head. Your memory is unmotheaten in my head also.
. . . If I said my novel was finished, I was misinformed. I am still working at it madly and madly it needs it. Conversationally, I am untrustworthy.

She'd just won a Ford grant, and she alludes to the amount given her and that given someone else.

I reckon my 4 thousand a year looks to me like 8 thousand to him. Last week I made $50 reading a story at a nearby college and I am going to buy a vacuum cleaner with it and reform my life.

Milledgeville
10 January 60

Dear Richard,
One year it is more or less since I was tempted by you to risk life and limberness to come to that place and be questioned for a week by those creamy dormitory dolls and all them other thangs that happened to me such as riding nine hours on a—. It spoils my syntax to think about it. We will pass on to other things.
. . . If you think it is pleasant to see yr novel in print, it is not pleasant to see your novel in print. I have just seen mine. The jacket: On an evil red-lavender background, the head of the hero, in black wool hat, peers out from behind some clay-colored corn (The School of Southern Degeneracy). The title page: a mess. The contents: as I am responsible for these we will not go into them. Anyway, I have not read the book.
My goose has laid two eggs already since Christmas and I would send you one if I thought for a minute you appreciated the finer things.

In a postscript to a handwritten letter, she alludes to something

[34]

I'd written:

"P.S. You caint finger one out of a rosary neither. Your nurse corrupted you."

And, to my defense:

Milledgeville, Ga. A Bird Sanctuary
2 June 60

Dear po Richard
Yessir, you can finger a decade but somebody is then going to ask you a decade of what and you will have to louse it up with some words. . .
I am never going to Chicago or New York again but am going to spend the rest of my life in Milledgeville.
It seems you are being reviewed exclusively in Catholic magazines. This is what you get for being a Catholic writer. Ha.

She also inked in capital letters an ad for the novel she mentioned: *"READ GOLK AND END UP IN A PEW."*

12 October 60
Me I am on my way to Minnesota but managed to get a plane that I don't have to so much as get off of in Chicago as I wish not to set foot again in that airport. I am going to talk at two Cathlick colleges and read at the University and get back as quick as I can to be with the chickens. . .

4 April 61

Dear Richard G.,
. . . You had better get yrself better established with the post office. This is disgraceful. Address me a letter to F. O'Connor, Milledgeville, Ga. and I get it at once. This of course proves that I am better known than you are, even if I didn't get the Nat'l Bk Award. Who is Conrad Richter?
. . . I ain't done nothing otherwise but write a story called

"Everything That Rises Must Converge" to be in NWW in October. I think about another novel as if it were a trip to darkest Africa.

Me, I am satisfied with politics myself—a president after twelve years, or eight anyway.

Somebody invited me to Chicago this February and I said Ha ha ha ha ha ha ha ha.

Cheers,
Flannery

Milledgeville
21 April 62

Dear Richard G.,

Hooray fr you. Rome or Venice yet. Go to see my friends the Fitzgeralds in Perugia and tell them howdy for me. Are you going to bring culture back to Chicago or what? I am coming to Chicago myself shortly to bring it a little culture from Milledgeville. I am going to talk at Rosary College—the thing you finger, son—in River Forest wherever that is and then I am going on to Notre Dame. If I can find a telephone at Rosary College, you can expect to hear my unformed tones over it enquiring as to your health. However, this may be a medieval institution and they may not have telephones. I just met Eudora W. at the Southern Litry Festival where her and me give a paper along with Andrew Lytle and Cleanth Brooks and then we all discussed Whut Makes Suthen Litratoor Great around a panel table. I hope you get shut of the snow before I get there.

Excelsior,
Flannery

30 November 62

Dear Richard,

You are not the only one that's been somewheres. I just got back from Texas. I talked at East Texas State College, so don't talk to me about any University of Vienna. The first thing they showed me in Dallas was General Walker's house—a battleship grey, two story, clapboard dwelling with a giant picture window in front of which you see a ceramic Uncle Sam with a lampshade on top of him. Texas and U.S. flags flying on the lawn. I also heard a Texas joke, to wit: Texan calls up the White House, says, "Is President Kennedy there?" Voice says, "Nawsuh, he ain't here." "Well is Jackie there?" "She ain't here neither." "Well where is Mr. Lyndon?" "He done gone too." "Well who's running things up there?" "We is." (I am trying to make you homesick before your year is out.)...

> *Milledgeville*
> *Georgia, USA*
> *27 July 63*

Dear Richard

What you ought to do is get you a Fulbright to Georgia and quit messing around with all those backward places you been at. Anyhow, don't pay a bit of attention to the Eyetalian papers. It's just like Cudden Ross says all us niggers and white folks over here are just getting along grand—at least in Georgia and Mississippi. I hear things are not so good in Chicago and Brooklyn but you wouldn't expect them to know what to do with theirself there. Down here is where all the writers come from and if you onct come you would never want to leave it.

What are you fixing to do, publish another novel? Do you want to be known as One-a-year Stern? I am doing my best to create the impression that it takes 7 years to write a novel. The four-hour week. You are not helping the brotherhood. Examine your conscience. Think. Meditate. Shilly-shally.

> *Cheers anyway,*
> *Flannery*

[7]

SAMUEL BECKETT

Beckett was born on a Friday the 13th, the Good Friday of April, 1906, and died with Beckettian symmetry on the Friday before Christmas, 1989.[1] Whether he died, as one of his voices, Malone, hoped to die, "tepid, without enthusiasm," is one of the many questions about him that won't be answered.

Between July 1977 and June 1987 I passed about a dozen happy hours with him in Paris cafés and walking to and from them. What's left of Beckett may be the best of him, but the author of the plays and stories was as remarkable in the ordinary sublunar world as his odd characters were in the world he interpreted or contrived for them.

In a 1987 talk given to students of English at Fudan University in Shanghai, I said a few words about Beckett. I don't remember what they were, only that they roused the pique of the old professor in whose classroom I spoke. He said he hoped I would not mind if he set the class straight about Beckett, then proceeded to do so. The only writers who counted, he said, were those who were sincere, who lived as they wrote. If Beckett had been a sincere writer he would have killed himself. Since it was well known that Beckett was alive and well in Paris, it was clear that he wasn't sincere and that therefore he was not worth reading.

The professor was someone Beckett would have enjoyed: very thin, very old, intense, courteously rude and rationally fanatic. He put the question that Beckett may well have put frequently to himself, but which apparently had been answered off the Irish coast when he was in his late thirties, in a discovery that the darkness he sensed and feared would be his subject matter.

. . . no, not happy, I was never that, but wishing night would never end and morning never come when men wake and say, Come on, we'll soon be dead, let's make the most of it . . . What matter whether I was born or not, have lived or not, am dead or merely dying, I shall go on doing as I have always done, not knowing what

---

[1] A more learned Zeitgeister than I might make something of the fact that Kurt Gödel, the brilliant upsetter of mathematical systems, and the brilliant Irish maker and mocker of absurd human ones, were born in the same year.

it is I do, nor who I am, nor where I am, nor if I am.

The lyric voice, the eccentric behavior, the crazy resilience, the crazy resolution, these are more than enough for even those Beckett characters who try and fail to do themselves in.

As for the symmetry between the author's art and his life, I think there is more than between most art and artistic life. Beckett had more sympathy and tenderness than those about whom he wrote, and perhaps the cost of that was a greater degree of irony. But in every way I knew, he comported himself as a good, if exceptionally prosperous, citizen of the Beckettian world. A few months after his eightieth birthday I asked him if his outlook were different now than it had been twenty years ago. "Yes," he said, with subdued intensity, "It's darker. Much darker."

Which did not stop him from working. On the contrary. Though to me he always complained about the difficulty of working.

"Failed again in new work," he wrote me in 1980. "Beating on the walls for help. I hear it coming." Or in '83: "I squeeze on with scarce a drop to show." In '85 he said that he'd written but one sentence the previous year. He recited it, in English first and then in French, saying of a change of tense, "The French past tense is very difficult." The next year I asked him if he'd added anything to it. No, he hadn't, he said. But on his eighty-third birthday the publisher issued a small piece called *Stirrings Still*, a description of which sounds as if it at least followed from the beautiful sentence, which was about a man who looks up to find himself disappearing.

Beckett read the newspapers and watched the news on television. About Giscard's declaration that if he hadn't become a politician he would have liked to have been a writer like Flaubert, he was fiercely amused. The contrast between the words of politicians and the amount of sheer suffering and pain in the world was not at all amusing to him. Once he said that he'd wasted his life: he'd dealt with nothing but words.

Beckett spoke with unqualified affection for friends, many of whom were his critics, editors, directors and actors. Two days after the director Alan Schneider had been killed in London stepping off a curb into an oncoming truck, Beckett received a letter from him and was anguished by the thought that Schneider had been killed after he'd gone to post it. He was very concerned about the heart attack Rick Clutchy had suffered while staging and acting in Beckett plays on tour. "He took on too much." Clutchy, a favorite of his, had committed an armed robbery as a young man and was serving twenty years in San Quentin when he saw an Actor's

[39]

Workshop production of *Godot,* and was transfigured by it. With Beckett's aid he was paroled, and with Beckett's help he staged productions of Beckett plays all over the world.

Saul Bellow was amazed and delighted that Beckett was a fan of his. A Paris meeting was arranged, and after that Beckett seldom failed to send along his best greetings "to Saul."[2] His loyalties to the dead were as strong as those to the living. When I sent him a biography of Nancy Cunard, who'd first published him in 1929 (his poem on Descartes, "Whoroscope"), he wrote, "I read the book with wonder and sadness, and saw her again in the long defunct d'Harcourt." The first day we met he spoke about the heroic qualities of Joyce's life, and recited in his beautiful voice, and with great intensity, lines from Joyce's poem "The Holy Office."

> *So distantly I turn to view*
> *The shamblings of that motley crew*
> *Those souls that hate the strength that mine has*
> *Steeled in the school of old Aquinas.*

He was seventy-one then, yet like almost every extraordinary man I've met, he seemed in some ways youthful, even childish. Perhaps a sense of himself as Joyce's permanent junior was the reason for that. He'd spent his writing life dealing with old age and incapacity, but the youthful intensity and openness I saw in him never died, though over the years there was less spring in his walk, he was more bent, the hair rose less fiercely from the scalp, the lines in his forehead were more deeply creased—as was the small triangle of flesh above his nose—his eyes were not quite as bright and his face was paler. "Thank God my work is over," he said, and, with a laugh, "My range is two inches from the wall." Like Jane Austen, E. M. Forster and, in a way, Henry James, Beckett did intensive tillage on a small plot. He worked with the peculiarities of compulsion, the orderliness of obsession, the fierceness of chained energy. The farcical symmetry in the actions of his characters was obviously related to the order he imposed in his life. He was always prompt, he gave precise directions, he insisted that his plays be performed exactly as he wrote them—the pauses were timed, the distances measured. The burden of this conscious orderliness was countered by his love for the wild and unconscious. Talking of Jack Yeats's painting one day, shortly after I'd been in Ireland looking at

---

[2] Of Beckett, Bellow remarked—fondly—that he didn't look "constructed" but "twisted" into shape.

lots of it, he told me he'd asked Yeats what he thought the difference between his early and late painting was and that, after he'd thought a while, Yeats answered, "Less conscious." Beckett thought that a wonderful answer. He said his own prose "came out of the dark. I never know where it's going." The plays were different. "They're all up there in the light." Which I suppose is why they had to be measured with such precision.

Coming out of the long dark and silence of the four years he'd spent writing the trilogy and the early plays in French ("the siege in the room," he'd called it) had been the great resolution of the internal war between energy and order, fury and farce. His later work carried his early solutions to finer and funnier extremes of silence and small motion.

His last note to me, seven months before his death, said that he was in "an old crock's home." His wife Suzanne, whom he'd known fifty years, had died in July.

He died of lung trouble. The last time I saw him, in June of 1987, he told me that he had emphysema and had cut down but was not giving up the little brown cigarettes that he smoked. Instead of holding out his hand to say goodbye, he opened both hands at his side, and, to my surprise, I embraced him. He was the least embraceable person imaginable. The bristles on his face were like iron, his shoulders were small and bony, and there was a current of unembraceability flowing in him. Yet loveable the man was, a radiant length of probity, decency, sympathy and affection.

Here are a few journal notes from some of my meetings with him.

Paris. Hotel Récamier. July 8, 1977. 10:15 PM. Still light. As I hit the lobby the dear crone is saying, *"Oui, le numéro douze."* and hands me the phone. *"Pour moi?"*

"This is Sam Beckett." A low Irish tenor, very clear.

"Ah, yes," said I.

"I just got your note. This is the situation. I'm going out of town Saturday, and Friday will be a very full day. The only time I can see you then will be between six and seven."

"Today?" It was 7:10.

Slightly miffed, puzzled. "Tomorrow. I'll call round at your hotel if it's physically possible between six and seven."

"Terrific."

"If I can't come, it's because it's physically impossible."

"I hope it won't be. I'll be here. Thanks for calling. So long."

[41]

July 9, 7:50 PM. Sam Beckett, seen from window in his light tan rain jacket and old pants. He was not wearing the prescription sunglasses he put on later. He carries a soft black zip briefcase, Woolworth quality. In the bistro, after his forearm swept his glass of beer to the floor: *"Je suis désolé."* He asked for *une remplacement.* He said he's had two cataract operations. His voice is a soft, warm tenor. There's a tiny lisp as though he had canker sores. From the first word one felt his directness, simplicity, and sweetness. There's a kind of gentle, kind banality in his remarks and inquiries. "Are you academic?" We wandered around looking for a bar, finally turning back till we were a block from the Luxembourg Gardens. We sat at a small table behind smoked glass and smoked our respective cigarillos. The wonderful, huge, light blue eyes, the hair in a fierce brosse, the depth of the forehead channels, the thin arms, lightly veined, the slimness: a young man of seventy-one. We talked about Rick Clutchy . . . Beckett goes to Berlin so they'll produce Clutchy's version of *Godot* . (He'd just returned from directing the German version). He says I should see Clutchy when he returns to Chicago from exercising "the stipendium" which Beckett helped him get. "He was right off the streets, armed robbery or something." When I told Beckett my *Godot* prison anecdote (that prisoners someplace were mesmerized by the play): "Yes, I guess they saw it as something for them, a play about detention. Endless waiting." We talked much about Joyce. "It was a very great thing knowing him. Such an example of writer's dedication. Of probity. Imagine writing *Ulysses* in Trieste. Teaching at Berlitz: 'This is a table,' 'This is a chair,' going home to squabbling children, poverty, and writing that." I couldn't hold off from indirect praise of *him*. He shook it off, sincerely. No, he had nothing of Joyce's strength.

Perhaps his sense of himself as Joyce's junior is a component in his youthfulness. Except for the simplicity, purity, and probity, I could really make no connection with the genius and his work. He talked of Joyce's life as a singer. When I doubted Joyce's second career, he said "What about Fischer-Dieskau? He's sung twenty years and he conducts, composes." Had he had an alternative profession? Yes, he was to be a teacher, till he realized he couldn't teach. Was assistant to a professor of Romance languages at Trinity, had been assistant at the École Normale Supérieure. Parents had sent him to Florence and Venice. "I haven't looked back. I'm not much of a traveller." (Of course he'd just come back from Stuttgart.) As for his German, "It's not good enough" for him to be a translator: "Not up to that." Doesn't like translating

French/English— "going over work"—but there's no one else. Did try a young man, but it wasn't work for him. (I suppose he meant my old pal from Chapel Hill, Dick Seaver.) He took off his glasses and quoted with marvelous intensity Joyce's "Holy Office." He repeated it, beautifully and with feeling. He talked of Joyce's troubles with Lucia. She still writes Beckett, normal letters. "She has good spells." As for Giorgio, poor fellow—"a tragic family"—"He died last June." As for Nora, he lit up and laughed. "A good sport." Saw Joyce last in a Vichy hotel. "He was very depressed. Trying to get Lucia from the hospital. And then *Finnegans Wake* was swamped by the war. And wasn't a success." I asked him about his being stabbed. "Not far from here. Behind Montparnasse. I was having dinner with Irish friends, Alan Duncan. We walked out, and this fellow—he was a pimp—tried to get us to come with him. He was persistent. Finally, I gave him a sort of shove"—shoved—"and then I felt—plunk. Right here." Hand to ribs on left side. "I still have the scar. Got the pleura. No after-effects, no complication. They got me to the apartment, then called the ambulance and police. They got the fellow. I was unconscious for twenty-four hours, stayed two weeks in the hospital. The first person I saw when I woke up was Joyce." Smile. "Asking me if I was all right."

Beckett liked *Finnegans Wake* from the beginning. The others— Hemingway, Pound—hadn't. Only Jolas and a few others. Joyce had talked with him about Vico and other things.

"Pound, as a young man, was very aggressive. Sort of a literary dictator. I saw him again when he came a few years ago. He asked me around. He was silent then."

Was he ever political? "No, but I joined the Resistance. When the business with the Jews started in '41 or '42. The yellow star and everything. It wasn't politics. Just a human thing. I couldn't stay detached from that." I asked how that worked. "I knew people, they'd bring me information, I'd put it together, type it up, put it in a matchbox, and get it over to the Free Zone. It was all over by '42. And I got out at night." Was your wife along? "The woman who's now my wife wasn't in it, but she came with me." Are you writing now? "I'm always doing something or other." Off tomorrow to the country, fifty miles from Paris, near Meaux, the town where Bossuet was archbishop.

He asked about my books, publishers, etc. He doesn't read much now. "My little library is mostly reference books." He does like Saul's books, hadn't read and didn't remember the title of the last one. I mentioned Nabokov dying. "He was an old man, wasn't he?"

[43]

He was kind, sympathetic, but I sensed distance and a literary lack of sympathy.

Beckett said he made no money till he was fifty and *Godot* was produced. He did commercial translations: there was a UNESCO commission for Latin American poetry. "Though I didn't know Spanish well. It was handsomely paid." He lived from a patrimony. "My father died in '33 and left me a pittance. Two hundred pounds a year, although you could live on it then." We talked about violence in Paris vis-à-vis NYC and Chicago. Growing, but not racial: "No racial feelings here." He talked kindly about Ruby Cohn and Martin Esslin—who worked with Clutchy and his theater; and "give my love to Hugh [Kenner]." He took my hands in his. "Make me a sign when you come back to Paris. Bless you."

An odd beauty in both his English and his French, which he spoke to the waitress—I felt a small lilt that wasn't French. As for the English, or at least the American, he asked me about a few phrases I'd used, such as "mug book." In both languages he writes a classic grammar book, bone-close language turning upon itself, its bite, wit and sad poetry coming from the close quarters. He talks to his wife in French. He has no secretary. "The big problem is mail, which gets forwarded to me. Every letter is some sort of request." His publishers help with business. (He asked if my books had any success, this after laughing about *Watt*'s not finding a publisher.) As for the money, it makes things easier.

Sept. 22nd, 1979
Beckett showed up at eleven-thirty. Rich brown tweed jacket, fine heavy dark brown turtleneck, dark, unpressed pants, a little feebler than last time but still solid. The PLM café is new, reasonably obscure, international, not Parisian; comfortable. B: (after we'd ordered, double express coffees) Just back from Tangiers. Several weeks, swimming all day. Translated ten thousand words of prose into French. I don't want to publish anymore. I just wrote to keep myself company. So I call it *Company*. But I found the company worse than my own. So I stopped . . . I never had a plan, just wrote. Out of the dark . . . The plays were a relief, a game. They had to be in the light. There were rules. I wrote as a relief, but the dark calls one back . . . I hate everything I've written. Nine-tenths of everything. I'm ashamed. The world's so full of misery, suffering, and what's one done? I'm ashamed.

After his walk through the Luxembourg yesterday he'd run into a "manifestation." "At Denfert Rochereau, about Goldman." The old

[44]

Polish radical had been killed by two men not far from his house. "No masks, nothing. Just walked up and killed him. Police, tear gas, batons, the whole thing."

There was more about politics. He'd watched "our literary president on the telly"—a steely smile—"talking about Maupassant and Flaubert. Said if he could have written as well as Flaubert, he would have become a writer."

We talked of Bokassa, emperor of the Central African Republic, a child killer who'd just been refused the right to land at Orly and Charles DeGaulle, but was allowed to land at a Normandy military base. "A friend of Giscard's who paid him many visits. Like the Shah and America. If he had such relations in private life they wouldn't be tolerated." I suggested that the world reserve a satellite for these flesh-eaters: Amin, Bokassa, the Shah and company. "They would have each other's company. That would be their punishment. And they'd circle round and round the earth."

Beckett seemed to relish this. "I saw your president [Carter] collapse while running. He'd better give up this jogging."

I told him of the television anchorman who'd shot himself to death on camera. Beckett said, "That's what you call a 'scoop'." We got on to plays. He said that *Godot* should be played on a big stage, "the bigger the better." He said it had been recently acted in Berlin by the man who played the father of the boy in *Le Tambour, Die Blechtrommel.* (His German accent was excellent.) "He just went through the motions. He's a good character actor, but this didn't go well." I told him I'd just seen *Betrayal* in London, and thought it wonderful. He'd read it and liked it very much as well.

"That going back." He'd recently been over in London and had dinner with Pinter and "Alexandra, no, Antonia."

"I like your hotel. You know who finished her days there? Nancy Cunard. She had a little press, the Hour Press. She published my first poem."

"Whoroscope?"

"She was a great friend of the Negroes. Had a long liaison with Henry Crowder. She was in a bad way. They found her collapsed outside the hospital you pass on the way over here. Cochin.

"Madame Jolas is still alive. Her daughter's a musician here."

He'd be off in two days to his pied-à-terre in the Marne. "I work better there, Paris is full of interruptions."

I apologized for being part of that. He waved it off, asked me what I was doing, remembered my teaching. "I'm always tired," he said. "The work is very laborious, though I write the same thing over and over again."

"Why not try something different?"

He thought for a moment."One does and it comes out the same note."

We talked a little more, then he paid the check and walked me to the Avenue de l'Observatoire. We shook hands. "It was good to see you. Come again soon."

June 26, 1987

Sam came into the hotel café half a minute after eleven o'clock. He seemed a bit more bent and grizzled. He wore beret and raincoat, and was very affectionate. I was at a middle table, and he wanted to sit in the corner, his back to the room. "I thought you were going to be late," he said. I'd come to France from Valencia, and the travel people there hadn't reminded me that Americans needed visas. That hadn't been the case the summer before, but it started in the autumn after a department store bombing. My publisher had arranged an extension of my stay through the Maison des Écrivains, and I'd had to pick up a letter across town, near Metro Kléber. I told him I was settled now, though there was a hole in my permission letter large enough for me to fall through.

Sam's troubles had been with health, not bureaucrats. "With lungs. Emphysema. I can't give up smoking altogether. Suzanne isn't well either. She's very tired."

I asked him what his outlook was compared to twenty years ago. "Darker . . . much darker. Twenty years ago I was still . . . I sense the lowering of mental powers . . . loss of memory."

As for daily life, there's the usual weight of correspondence. "Worse than ever. I don't answer everything. I never respond to registered letters. They get returned."

He'd forgotten that he'd been invited to and declined the Valencia conference. "How was it?" I gave him the blow by blow, which amused him. "Never a dull moment."

He spoke about "Ell-mann," whom he said he knew mostly through a friend, who praised his bravery. He asked about the disease, and mangled Lou Gehrig's name. He knew Ellmann had finished the Wilde book. I told him about meeting Paul Léon's son at Ellmann's house in Oxford.

"I didn't know Léon had one. He was so scholarly, an historian, so helpful to Joyce, a good man. Everyone told him not to go back to Paris. He did and they picked him up. He died in transit. In that place on the edge of Paris, where his wife visited him. No, it was en

[46]

route to Auschwitz or one of those places." He remembered his own exodus from Paris with Suzanne. The first time they left they went to Arcachon, and stayed with Mary Reynolds and Marcel Duchamp. Then they went back into the Resistance. "It was the sort of thing where everyone knew everyone, and then someone informed, and we got out in an hour. Had to warn the others. I went to a Greek photographer, Suzanne to someone else. Knocked on the door of the woman's house, opened by the Gestapo. They brought her back to the flat, saw all these German books around, and thought, 'Well, he must be all right.' A fluke. A miracle."

Then, not knowing where or how, and without any money, they went down to Vichy. "There was Joyce. And Nora. Not Lucia, she was in a home. And Giorgio? Can't remember." Joyce gave them a letter of introduction to Valéry Larbaud, who was in a wheelchair, paralyzed. "He was rich. He gave us 20,000 francs, a lot of money in those days. I have to say I paid it back after the war. We went on, God knows how, to the Vaucluse, worked with farmers." And so on, much of which he'd told me before. But his eyes were lit, and the voice flowed with the old story that meant so much to him.

We went on to the disasters of the world, the Iranian War, "which has killed millions," and all of it.

"What a species," said I.

"It hasn't improved much," said he.

Tomorrow he was seeing another ex-prisoner, "An old timer— no, what do you call them, lifers. I'd like to bring him and Clutchy together." Clutchy had just arrived in Paris.

I asked him if he'd written anything to go with the single sentence he said he'd written a year before. "No," he said, "but I wrote a few pages for Barney." This was Barney Rosset, who'd started another company after selling Grove. "A little trilogy."

As for L'Éditions de Minuit, "They've made a lot of money from that woman. What's her name?"

"Duras." I pronounced it without the "s."

"Yes, Duras. *L'amant.* Love, all about love. When I hear the word 'love,' I wince."

He missed the days when "I was *inconnu*," and went on to what I'd heard before, the two men who'd turned everything around, Jerome Lindon, the editor at Minuit, and Roger Blin, the man who produced *Godot.* One obstacle to the publishing of the trilogy was that he'd insisted they take all three volumes. "I suppose it was presumptuous of me, an *inconnu.* I didn't offer one until all three were finished. Suzanne was hawking them. I was sitting in the café on

[47]

the Boulevard St. Germaine when she came up and told me. It turned my life around. It was the last hope."

"Would you have gone on?"

"I suppose so, yes. Though I told Suzanne, 'If this doesn't go, I'll ditch it.'"

He picked up the change from the plate. "Dick, come back soon." We got up, walked to the door, and he said he was going back to the "loo." To my surprise instead of shaking hands as usual he held out his arms, and I put my cheek on his astonishingly grizzled cheek, my hands on his shoulders, which were hard and bony. It was a little like embracing a charged wire.

[8]

ROBERT LOWELL

"Everything is real until it's published." Lowell wrote this as he was writing sonnets about the breakup of one marriage, the beginning of another, "absolutely writing it as he was living through it" (as a friend said). "We asked to be obsessed with writing and we were. . ." went his obituary for John Berryman, one of the other institutionalized, suicidal poets of our time. In the Soviet Union, it is usually the government which breaks, jails, and kills poets. In our country, the poets do it themselves. Why this slaughter of the comparatively innocent? Does it have to do with poetry itself, with writing down what one thinks and feels accurately and powerfully?

> sometimes everything I write
> with the threadbare art of my eye
> seems a snapshot,
> lurid, rapid, garish, grouped,
> heightened from life, yet paralyzed by fact
> . . . Yet why not say what happened?
> Pray for the grace of accuracy
> Vermeer gave to the sun's illumination
> stealing like the tide across a map
> to his girl solid with yearning.
> We are poor passing facts,
> warned by that to give
> each figure in the photograph
> his living name.

Why not say what happened?

If poets lived with cats in caves, why not indeed? But poets have wives, children, parents, friends; and poets who want to make the sort of impression on the world which will make the labels on their photographs superfluous, often try to obliterate the boundary between the colorful veracity of art and the colorless disorder of life. They swallow and groan, and then they burst. They tell people off, they brawl—a word made for a poet's fights—they drink, they fall in love, they confess, and then they publish. Often their wives and friends are writers, and then there are verbal slugfests, exchanges, repudiations, retractions, reparations, consolations, pardons. Terrific stuff for poems and stories.

Robert Lowell is not the first writer who used the brilliance of his wives and friends in poems. Used, that is, published, after which comes the pain of public exhibition. "I regret the Letters in Dolphin," he wrote the wife who wrote them. He called himself a shark circling his own life,

> a vocational killer
> foretasting the apogee of mayhem
> breaking water to strike his wake.

Wives, girl-and men-friends paid plenty for the companionship of this man, but no one paid the price he paid. Within him were treacherous cells. Year after year, they took arms against the master system and broke it down. First, there'd be brilliant, unstoppable monologues, wicked jokes, then drinking and excursions along the razor's edge, new girls, declarations of new life with new apartments and crazy new purchases. A handsome, powerful, charming, troubled bear, Lowell found new girls till the very end. The end was usually mayhem, and Lowell, persuaded or coerced, entered the hospital. Mania turned into depression, then that leaked away leaving waste and humiliation, humiliation at the pain he'd caused those he most loved.

Obsessed by writing. "I feel I, or someone, wrote everything beforehand. If I had read it at twenty, would I have been surprised, would I have dared to go on?"

By twenty, Lowell was already Lowell. The famous families, the acidulous, tyrannical mother, the amiable, gentle, failed father whom Lowell knocked down after a paternal letter to the father of the boy's first fiancée. He became "a case," under the psychiatric eye of Dr. Merrill Moore. (The Old Fugitive sonneteer.) Lowell was also a leader of boys, a brawler, a reader, a rebel, a poet.[1]

---

[1] Not unlike Edgar Allan Poe, who was described as "an imperious older boy, a capital horseman, fencer and shot and a leader of other boys at his school in Richland. he swam in the river James one day six miles against the tide. Devoted to music, he played a flute, he wrote good Latin verses" and so on. These poets who ended in madness had the sort of youth you'd expect from political leaders like Lyndon Johnson. (Caro's biography of LBJ uncovers a sneaky, cowardly backbiter.) For Poe, see Van Wyck Brooks, *The World of Washington Irving* [New York: Dutton, 1944], P. 265.

Moore suggested he go south to the house of Moore's old friend, the poet Allen Tate, and later, to their old friend and teacher, John Crowe Ransom at Kenyon College. There Lowell met the literary friends of his life, Peter Taylor, Randall Jarrell, and John Thompson. He married beautiful Jean Stafford, slammed their car into a wall, which smashed up her face, went to LSU to study with Cleanth Brooks and Robert Penn Warren, worked for Sheed and Ward in New York, made a "manic statement" to President Roosevelt when he received his draft notice, was jailed, came out and lived on the money Stafford earned from her novel *Boston Adventure*. He wrote, published, won prizes, divorced, remarried, had a daughter, traveled, talked, moved, broke down, moved again, broke down again,[2] and was the most famous American poet of his time. He married a third time, had a son, then died in a taxi, age sixty, at the doorstep of his second wife.

Like many brilliant people, Lowell excited brilliance in others.If you compare his biography[3] with, say, Robert Caro's of Lyndon Johnson, you see the difference between history and archaeology. Unlike Hamilton, Caro worked with muttered obliquities. He had to construct background out of non-literary records. There was very little said or written by Johnson or his friends which in itself is interesting. Johnson's verbal world is a biographical desert. In biographies, at least, the pen is mightier than the sword. Lowell's life was one of recording, expressing and transmuting facts to words. His biography, like his life, shines with the intelligence of such records, his and those of his friends.

A personal word. I knew Lowell fairly well. I met him in 1947 at a Carolina Writers' Conference but really got to know him when he came to teach in the Iowa Writers' Workshop in 1953. I remember classes, dinners, rides, talk, jokes, remember his mistranslating French ("Are you sure it can't mean 'eyeball?'"), playing a private

---

[2] Poetry, rhythmic speech, is, in my view, connected with the body's rhythms. In moments of deep emotion the autonomic nervous system takes over, the pulse of the hematic system dominates the body's rhythms, and there ensues a sense of unreality. The techniques of poetry mimic and express such states. The more frequently the autonomic system is called upon to sustain the organism, the greater its sense of unreality. The discharges of endomorphins into the system to inhibit anxiety and to diminish the firing of the limbic system in the cell are perhaps the physiological equivalent of poetic pleasure.

[3] Ian Hamilton, *Robert Lowell. a Biography* (New York: Random House, 1983).

charade with Elizabeth Hardwick (assigning her to do the first line of *Martin Chuzzlewit*) in the midst of our easy charades, and much else that's unrecorded in Hamilton's book. In Chicago, New York, and London, I saw more of him. (A fragment of one visit is recorded in the biography.) The point here is that a man's life overflows the most minute record of it. Like hundreds of other people, I have impressions and feelings about Lowell which aren't in these or any other pages. They aren't significant—or won't be unless I have the will, energy, and gift to make something of them—but they are a deep part of my sense of him.

Full of trouble himself, Lowell was keen about other people's. He loved gossip and was a first-rate gossiper. He was playful, analytic, allusive. The playfulness could become mean, or perhaps a better word is "wicked," which suggests sport. As a young bully, Lowell controlled with his size and fist. Older, he controlled with his tongue, and, rarely, his position (as famous poet, as a Massachusetts Lowell). Mostly, though, there was sweetness and humor, part of the honey of a nature that adored fine literary, amorous, and dramatic expression. In a life spent with writers, I've never known anyone more absorbed by literature. Books and authors were not only a consuming interest for him, they were anodynes, pacifiers, weapons. Lowell was immensely well read, far more than those whom he regarded as really learned because they'd read books he hadn't. He preferred reading history and criticism to poetry. In his last years, he read very little fiction. With little gift for foreign languages, he was always trying to learn and translate them. This was also true of such things as music. I sat with him once listening to Berg's *Wozzeck,* trying to follow the score. Neither of us could, both pretended to. Lowell's—our—pretense was part vanity, part competitiveness. He was a literary competitor, gamesman, and politician. His competitors were writers who others said were his superiors. He was capable of both paying them tribute and cutting them down.

Because of his intermittent madness, Lowell's life had a quality certain writers who don't suffer it pretend to emulate. I believe most poets of Lowell's exceptional gift feel the disjunction between the world they knew or imagined as children and the one they encountered later and with more pain than the rest of us. Their poetry is a way of repairing the discrepancy. Their verbal world substitutes for the actual one. At least, there is a confusion not present in other people. So they become part of the Tradition of Troubled Genius.

I once asked Lowell if his illness brought compensation in poetic insight or ability. He said that it brought him nothing but humiliation and a sense of waste.

[9]

NORMAN MAILER

I met Mailer in 1958 here in Chicago and saw him off and on for about a decade. (I've seen him three or four times since.) We've swum, played badminton, sparred, smoked pot in an old orgone box, schmoozed, argued in print and out, and lost track of each other. He became more and more a celebrity, I more and more a local burgher, but an exchange here and there testifies to old affection, if no longer intimacy. (A friend of mine overheard him rebuking a woman for not having read my work.) The willed and unwilled craziness, the spunk, challenge, uncertainty, and small sadness in this man beg for a fuller portrait than the one here that's twenty-odd years old. There is a later glimpse of Mailer in "Penned In" (below, page 79).

Norman Mailer is to American mental life what jet planes are to transport: familiar, remarkable, ubiquitous, powerful, rapid, noisy, and not altogether free of hot air.

Mailer's passport reads "novelist," and it's as a novelist he began in 1948 with *The Naked and the Dead*, a marvelous book about the Pacific War that's full of Melvillean rhetoric and specificity, organized by his version of Dos Passos's version of *Ulysses*. If the form is creaky and the men refurbished types, the book still feels accurate, lively, intelligent, comic, and built rather than piled.

Three years later, Mailer hauled in a gloomy political allegory called *Barbary Shore* (whose initials summarize the contents), and four years after that, a fine, quiet, off-Hollywood novel called *The Deer Park* which exhibited a little fatigue with its own method, the setting up and then subversion of stereotypes (of character and situation).

This was Mailer's last good novel,[1] the last of any fiction for a time. His literary stock was low, he fiddled in disconnected Connecticut making nutty wooden constructions in a machine shop, playing badminton, drinking, smoking, and giving up drinking and smoking.

With the founding of the *Village Voice* in 1956, he apparently decided there were other ways to skin the literary cat. He turned out pieces about everything, pieces which got longer, stranger, more apocalyptic, and then, as the magazines and television realized he was a man liable to say and do almost anything, more influential.

In 1959, Mailer stitched the miscellaneous pieces (essays, stories, interviews) with splendid bits of self-analysis into a new kind of autobiography, *Advertisements for Myself.*

The "myself" was plural; that was the book's subject. One self was a Henry Adams-Mailer, a self-deprecating and vaunting critic of civilization; another was commonsensical, a comic knifer of pomposities, a sort of court fool; a third was the Great Reporter who made familiar ground unfamiliar until everyone conceded it to him; and finally, there was the old Demon of the Absolute, a pumping ranter scooping theoretical drool from dried-out Nietzschean waterholes and serving it up in the most debased prose since Faulkner's *Fable* and Cozzens' *By Love Possessed.*

When editors didn't send Mailer to the wars, he made his own. He ran for mayor of New York, once unofficially and wildly, once brilliantly and straight. He stabbed a wife, he knifed old writer friends, he spooked (and thrilled) American gentry (presidential wives, transient heroes), he sent out a monkey self whenever he was bored or angry, often on camera.

His last movie (there are, I think, three) ends with Rip Torn improvising on Mailer's skull with a hammer while Mailer tries to rip off the actor's ear.

What remains are the non-fiction books, some of which are terrific. If Mailer's reportage-maps are more detailed than the terrain mapped, this is what the true lensmen-discoverers of literature do; the terrain will be settled by others.

So if the astronauts in his lunar book, *Of a Fire on the Moon*, were not as complicated as his description of them, they might become so after reading it. (Neil Armstrong seems to have realized

---

[1] 1992. A harsh view based on attempts to read most of them. *Harlot's Ghost* is full of narrative gestures: you can feel the old writer saying, "I do this, then I do that," but it's a shadow-novel. As for *Ancient Days*, I leave that mastodon to fast-thinking, fast-reading critical paleographers like the remarkable Harold Bloom.

[55]

Mailer's description in himself; Frank Borman discarded it as more lunatic than lunar.)

Occasionally Mailer's subject turned back on him. Muhammad Ali said no, Mailer's version of his Liston fights was wrong; and I don't imagine Jacqueline Kennedy accepted his version of her, though rumor has it she enjoyed his version of her late husband. (That featured Mailer's Dental Theory of Heroism: Kennedy, hauling a shipmate to safety with his teeth, a molar sublimation of his life's fury which led to his becoming the cool-to-death existential hero. We'd better take another look at Mailer's dental grip on Torn's ear.)

In the best of the reportage books, *The Armies of the Night* (1968), Mailer came up with his first full character, Robert Lowell. Instead of creating somersaulted stereotypes, Mailer kept looking at what was really there, and the result was a complete man; not a "finished" character, because a living man can't be finished,[2] but someone complicated, explainable, memorable, and noble. In addition, the book supplies wonderful confrontations (the best a triangular glare-out in a paddy wagon).

Able to see, subtilize and render such things, what keeps Mailer from writing a wonderful novel, a fully imagined work?

My guess is that Mailer is without real sensuous power, without a unique—how can this be said?—sense of the flow, arrangement, and rhythm of events, a kind of music of feeling which generates—but isn't—meaning; and perhaps Mailer doesn't have the deep, secret patience, the sometimes clumsy tolerance which makes great novelists seem irrelevant to theory or their own personality, beyond any predisposition but the hunger to get people and scenes into formal, literary arrangements.

I won't swear by any of this. Perhaps it's not right to talk about it. Mailer is a national resource, a rare commodity. Should he go dry, he ought to be subsidized, decorated, given a villa in the country. As much as anyone, he is the Secretary of Defense against National Boredom, and even if he's an occasional bore himself, he's worth a good many of us.

May God (Mailer's—that is, Nietzsche's—poor struggling Uncreature) speed him well.

---

[2] Lowell died in 1977. He said he was at first uneasy about the Mailer portrait, but by 1975—the last time I saw him—he admired it.

[10]

JANET LEWIS

When I was at college at Chapel Hill, in the mid and late 1940s, no literary critic was more influential, either as champion or opponent, than Yvor Winters. When my friend, the poet Donald Justice, married another friend, the fiction writer Jean Ross, in August, 1946, my wedding present to them was Winters' trilogy *In Defense of Reason*. We thought Winters was the knight of literary form, the enemy of the chaos into which the romantic movement had disintegrated. Not for him the mess and imprecision of the great modernists. From his throne in Palo Alto, he emitted powerful edicts about what made literary and human sense and nonsense.

After graduation from Chapel Hill, the Justices went out to study with him, and so did another Chapel Hill friend, Edgar Bowers. I received monthly bulletins from the Winters front. It was rigorous, bracing, difficult.

Among his literary exemplars, Winters singled out his wife, Janet Lewis. I read some of her fine, controlled poems, and her beautiful short novel, *The Wife of Martin Guerre*, the story of a Frenchman who "returns after long absence in the wars" to a town and a wife whose doubts about his identity constitute the novel's tension.

Years later, after I'd come to Chicago, I found in the stacks a small book consisting of poems of the members of the Poetry Club of the University of Chicago. Among the poets were the future novelist and memoirist Glenway Wescott, the Pulitzer Prize winning novelist Elizabeth Madox Roberts, the future foreign correspondent (James) Vincent Sheean, and both Winters and Lewis. When we decided to help celebrate the centennial of the University of Chicago with a book about some of the leading writers who'd gone to school here, I hoped we could locate one or more members of the Poetry Club. None could be less than ninety years of age. I telephoned Professor Gelpi at Stanford and asked if Janet Lewis were alive. He said, "She's giving a poetry reading here next Monday." I wrote to her in Los Altos about the project. She agreed to be interviewed and gave me clear directions to her house from San Francisco, on alternate routes; it included a hand-drawn map.

I'd been to San Francisco a few times, but didn't really know the place. My youngest son, who'd just passed his bar exam in November, worked at a law firm there; his fiancée taught in one of the grim public schools of Oakland. They found a room for me in a motel on 16th and Market Streets, a mile from where they lived.

My wayward typing just inserted an "r" between the "o" and "t" of motel, as if the psychopathology of everyday typing reflected the sense of doom I felt in this Castro District. I drank my morning coffee in the Baghdad Cafe—the name itself a darkness in those nervous pre-war days—among tables occupied by sunken-cheeked, bleak-eyed, black-mustached men, surely in the terrible grip of the HIV virus. In the art store across the street, racks of postcards featured photographs by Robert Mapplethorpe of nude men pressing superb bodies together. (No AIDs symptoms showing here.) The other San Francisco menace, the grinding tectonic plates which, fifteen months earlier, had given the city a crack across its gorgeous face, had left signs here and there: the closed ramp of the Embarcadero Bridge looked like monitory italics under the skyscrapers of the glassy, Christmas-lit Embarcadero Center.

I took to the road the next day with some relief. Route 280, the Junipero Serra Highway, runs between the sea and San Francisco Bay, past San Mateo and Palo Alto. The soft foothills of the peninsula were brown and bare. Now and then fog filled some of the dips in the road, but toward noon the sun came out of the clouds, and there was a crystal brightness on cars, houses and the large grey sculpture of Fra Junipero pointing west toward the Pacific.

The wildest surmise of the eighteenth century Franciscan wouldn't have predicted the replacement of the apricot, persimmon, loquat, walnut, fig and grape orchards by the electronic plants of Silicon Valley. I'd recently read about the serpents in this semi-conductor paradise,[1] the high rates of unemployment, homelessness, mental illness, drug abuse and complexly fractured and extended families. Was this the toxic waste of technological genius? (Almost half a century before the silicon chip, Janet Lewis had written about ecological disaster, "the incoherent civilization emerging from the

---

[1] "Land of Dreams and Disaster: Post-Industrial Living in the Silicon Valley," *Brave New Families*, by Judith Stacey, Basic Books, 1990.

physical wilderness," in *Against a Darkening Sky.*)

I took the El Monte turnoff, then drove along San Antonio Road to West Portola, near El Camino Real. A couple of hundred yards up the east side of the road were a mailbox, a garage, a grape gate and, behind that, the small, tree-shaded cottage to which Janet Lewis and Yvor Winters moved in 1934, seven years after they'd come to California. The door was opened by a tallish, straight-backed, white-haired woman wearing glasses on her large, strong nose; the face was serious, amiable, alert. The initial shock was, "This woman can't be ninety-one years old." In a minute, you forgot age, though Janet Lewis moves and talks with that special economy of the long-lived. Perhaps because I'd read her work, I thought I saw an American Indian quality in its grace.

She offered juice, tea or coffee. The upper half of the refrigerator was covered with color photographs of her daughter Joanna and her children, and her son Daniel, "who teaches French and Spanish and, more and more, English in a high school in Davis." One of the pictures is of a cat, perhaps the "morsel of suavity" about whom she wrote in "Lines to a Kitten":

> Only the great
> And you, can dedicate
> The attention so to one small thing . . .
> Kin of philosophers, and more, indeed . . .
> You by your narrowed thought, maintain your place,
> Pure quality of your great treacherous race.

Some of the photographs belonged to Alva Henderson, the composer for whom she's written three libretti and with whom she shares the house. Alva came in to shake hands, a pleasant-looking, blue-eyed man in—I'd guess—his early forties. On the wall was a poster of one of their operas, *The Last of the Mohicans.*

Janet and I took our mugs into the low-ceilinged, book-lined living room, I set up the small tape recorder (which proved more treacherous than any cat), and sat in what she told me was her husband's favorite chair, a wooden armchair with leather seat and back. He died in January, 1968, in his sixty-eighth year. In *Poems Old and New, 1918—1978*, Chicago: Swallow Press, 1981, her dedication reads, "For Yvor Winters Now as Then."

What was immediately clear was that though Janet's past was rich, and richly remembered, she lives vividly, actively in the present. Though "I haven't written any poems for a year," there is one, "Trophy, 1914," in a recent *Threepenny Review*. It's about a cross found on the neck of a soldier dead at Verdun. "That war became vivid to me when we entered it. My brother went off to camp. Jim Gilbert, who'd been in the Poetry Club, and became a fine painter, also went off. I remember girls in the dorm wailing when they saw a friend's name on the casualty list. Later, in 1920, when I visited Chartres, the stained-glass windows were still in storage.

"I was supposed to go to Vassar like my cousins, but I came down to the University from Oak Park to hear my father read his dedication poem at the inauguration of President Judson, and decided, 'This is the place for me.' My father had come here from the East—he was born in Westerly, Rhode Island—with a PhD in Latin from Syracuse. He got another PhD at the University, in English. I think he was in the first graduating class, in 1894. He taught there, and then went on to Lewis Institute, where he became dean. He loved poetry and knew reams of it by heart. I don't think he regarded himself as a poet. He wrote occasional poems, such as the dedication for the Ryerson Laboratory, and one night, at someone's request, he wrote the Alma Mater, which I read you're planning to replace.[2] He was close to President Harper and admired him greatly. I went to Lewis Institute for two years, and took chemistry and geology—wonderful geology—but I have no aptitude for mathematics, and never thought of becoming a scientist. There was never a doubt about my going to college—the University was always co-educational—unlike Pearl Sherry, whose father didn't believe that women should be educated."

"I've spoken to her," I said. (Janet had sent me her number.) She was one of two Poetry Club survivors in Chicago. The other, Gladys Campbell, lived in Hyde Park, and I'd met her years ago. She's ninety-nine, and recently broke her leg. Said Janet, "She's almost immortal, but you better talk to her soon." I said, "I ran into her in a neighborhood restaurant. She was getting around with a cane and a companion. 'It's healing too slowly,' she said. She also told me Professor George Sherburn had her read Henry James's *The Golden Bowl* in 1916. When I mentioned this to Saul Bellow, he said, "My mother had probably changed my diapers a thousand times before she got through the first chapter of that."[3]

Janet laughed. "We read Henry James then. I don't remember Sherburn. I know Saul Bellow's name, but I haven't read him. We read Pound and Eliot as their poems came out." Her first book of

---

[2] 1993. We didn't.

[3] Gladys died in July, 1992.

[60]

poems, *The Indians and the Woods* (1922), contains the sort of imagist poem Pound was writing and championing. "I liked Eliot until *The Waste Land*. That was too messy for me." Yvor Winters had ridiculed Eliot's shuttle between classic appearance and romantic posturing: he enjoys "both the pleasures of indulgence and the dignity of disapproval."[4]

Did Janet know Harriet Monroe? "Yes, she was a friend of the family, an energetic, feisty woman. I admired her a lot. My father took *Poetry* magazine from the beginning. I can't remember her coming down to the University, but we went to her house. We met Sandburg and others there.

"The Poetry Club was the center of our life. We did all sorts of things together, picnics in the woods along the river, dances in dorms and Ida Noyes. I invited Jimmy Sheean to a Foster Hall dance, and we also danced at Frank Lloyd Wright's Midway Gardens, at 60th and Cottage Grove." I told her that almost the first thing I'd read about the University of Chicago was the first chapter of Sheean's autobiography *Personal History*. "I never read it, but he was a wonderful man. I was closer to Glenway Wescott. After Arthur [Winters], he was our best critic. They're just issuing his memoirs, and I've promised to do something about them. There's next to nothing about the University in them, though Robert Phelps, the editor, says a bit about it."

I asked her about other members of the club. "There's Maureen Smith, a very fine poet who's been neglected. I wrote a little essay about her which the *Chicago Review* is supposed to publish.[5] And Elizabeth Madox Roberts, a great writer."

In *Old and New Poems* there are four lines "For Elizabeth Madox Roberts, Who Died March 13, 1941":

> From the confusion of estranging years,
> The imperfections of the changing heart,
> This hour leaves only tears:
> Tears, and my earliest love, Elizabeth, and changeless art.

How had the club started? "A student came to Robert Morse Lovett complaining about the absence of modern poetry in the curriculum. Lovett said he didn't think it should be part of the curriculum, but

---

4 Yvor Winters, *On Modern Poetry* (NY: 1959), p. 71.

5 It was published in the Winter 1991 issue.

they could hold meetings outside of class and he would act as faculty advisor.[6] I did have a writing class with him, and another with Edith Foster Flint. They were wonderful teachers. My major was French. Myra Reynolds was a wonderful teacher; I can't remember the name of my fine French teacher. Mademoiselle Pelley! When my father gave me a round trip ticket to Europe and four hundred dollars for a graduation present in 1920, I was allowed to go because Mademoiselle Pelley was going, too. She didn't stay long, she went off to Vienna. I got a job with the Passport Office on Rue Tilset, behind the Arc de Triomphe. I kept it till my mother came over in December. We toured and then I went back to Chicago with her. I worked at *Redbook* and taught at Lewis. Then I got tuberculosis."

Her acceptance to the Poetry Club had been signed by its secretary, Arthur Yvor Winters, but they didn't meet there. He got tuberculosis his freshman year and went down to Santa Fe to be cured at the Sunmount Sanitorium. "He kept in touch with us through letters. He was our best and severest critic. He kept up with what was going on, the *Little Review*, the *Hound and Horn*. I think he wrote for that. He read Rimbaud, Corbière and Laforgue, though he didn't know the older French poets whom I'd read in class. He was always on to anything new that counted. He discovered Allen Tate and Morley Callaghan and corresponded with them. When I got ill, I went to the sanitorium and we met there. I was on my back for two years and wasn't cured for seven. You have to be cheerful or die." Winters got his MA at the University of Colorado, and went off to teach French and Spanish at the University of Idaho in Moscow. They'd married in 1926, but Janet was too ill to go to Moscow. She did go to Stanford, where he went for his doctorate.

"We lived on the outskirts of Palo Alto. I felt marooned up there, and wrote a story about some neighbors. The *Bookman* accepted it, and I felt I was a writer again."

I said she wasn't the only writer born in 1899 who grew up in Oak Park.

"Yes, Hemingway. I didn't really know him. He was around, but he dropped out for a year to do newspaper work, then graduated the year after I did. I was in class with his sister Marcelline for three years."

I thought of comparing their short stories about northern

---

[6] An excellent survey of American writers in universities doesn't mention Lovett or the Club. See "From Bohemia to Academia: Writers in Universities," Harry Levin, *Bulletin of the American Academy of Arts and Sciences* XLIV. 4 (Jan. 1991), pp. 28-50.

Michigan—hers low key and a bit rambling next to his—but she took it up in another way. "I became a writer in the country, during summer vacations on Neebish and St. Joseph's Islands. I had a close friend, Molly Johnstone, who was part Indian. Her brother Howard was a wonderful storyteller. I wanted to preserve his stories about the family. I went at it in the wrong way, embroidering a sketch about Molly. It didn't make sense unless you went back and told the stories in back of the stories. These went back to the eighteenth century, to their Ojibway grandmother Neengay and her Irish husband John Johnston." Out of research came *The Invasion: A Narrative of Events concerning the Johnston family of St. Mary's* (New York: Harcourt-Brace, 1932), her first prose book.

Of Janet Lewis's four other novels, three, like *The Invasion*, spring from actual events. "I have this affinity for the circumstantial case. I like to get at the intimate obliquely. Perhaps I'd have been more successful if I'd been more personal. Though my contemporary book, which is more personal, is rather shapeless." This is *Against a Darkening Sky* (Doubleday: 1943), the story of the violent accidents and unhappy love affairs which pound the orderly life of a housewife living in a Santa Clara County orchard.

It's Janet Lewis's historical fiction which has been highly praised, especially her second novel, *The Wife of Martin Guerre* (1941). Albert Guerard Jr., the teacher under whom I read it in 1948, called it "one of the greatest short novels in American literature." Like the others, *The Trial of Søren Qvist* (1947) and *The Ghost of Monsieur Scarron* (1959), the book revolves around the misinterpretation of evidence. The critic Donald Stanford[7] relates the theme to the arrest of David Lamson, Sales Manager of the Stanford University Press, who was accused, indicted, tried and sentenced for the murder of his wife. The Winters were active in his exoneration; Yvor Winters helped with the defense brief and co-authored a book on the case.

Lewis's reliance on circumstantiated cases as the basis of fiction is related, I think, to her reliance on meter and rhyme, the need for an unwavering, authoritative control. In her later poetry, written when she'd stopped writing fiction, meter gives way to free verse, and the pure imagistic presentation is mixed with commentary and exclamation, as if, at last, a self drives through modesty.

As for her narrative bent, it was satisfied by writing librettos. (Music is another form of authority.) Her first libretto, based on

---

7 See his splendid piece on Lewis in the *Dictionary of Literary Biography. Yearbook 1987.*

The Wife of Martin Guerre, to music by William Bergsma, was called (by Richard Goldman in 1956) "the most distinguished libretto in the annals of American opera."

I did not ask Janet if changes in her work related to her husband's death. In his lifetime, she too had championed poetry as the controlled expression of a rational judgement of experience, real or imagined.[8] The poem was a public—so a publishable—celebration of the intimate. "It's an Augustan conception," I suggested. "*Out there*, public, formal."

"I'll go along with formalizing," she said.

Her friend, the English poet and critic Donald Davie, has written[9] that her novels center about dutiful women who, from under the protection of authoritative figures—Martin Guerre, Sr., Søren Qvist, Jean Larcher—enter passionate relationships which threaten the authoritarian order. Much of Lewis's invention in these historical "reconstructions" deals with these passionate women. In the forward to *The Wife of Martin Guerre*, she wrote,

> The rules of evidence may vary from century to century and country to country, and the morality which compels many of the actions of men and women varies also, but the capacities of the human soul for suffering and for joy remain very much the same.

Now she said, "I had to imagine the feelings of these people in these situations. I also had to imagine what things looked like to them." Research didn't scuttle the imagination; it stimulated it. For *The Ghost of Monsieur Scarron*, she studied maps of seventeenth century Paris. "When I got to Paris, I knew the Paris of 1690 better than the Paris of 1951. I'd been thinking of seventeenth century France since I'd done a paper on Mme. de Maintenon at the University."

I praised the beauty of the Danish setting in *Søren Qvist*. "I've never been to Denmark, but I had a friend, an engineer at Stanford, who was from Jutland. He told me about the seasons, the way things looked. I've been accused of plagiarizing Blicke, one of my sources. Twain used the same source. Of course it's all the way you use it."

The modesty of her excursions from the actual seems to me relat-

---

[8] See his *In Defense of Reason* (1946), *passim.*

[9] "The Historical Novel of Janet Lewis," *Southern Review* 12 (Jan. 1966), 40-60.

ed to the modesty and surety of her prose (and, perhaps, her being). It is clear, concise, precise, quiet, lyric.

As Davie sees it, the novels exhibit "the dynamics of historical change from one form of society to another." So, in The Wife of Martin Guerre, Bertrande's love of the impostor who claims to be her returned husband is love for "a new psychological type," whose charm and decency may add the sweetness of deception to their erotic life but "disgraces the honorable family" and the social order on which it rests. My own guess is that Lewis's imagination took fire here and, in that way, she is on Bertrande's side, as—according to Blake—Milton was on Satan's. The passionate intrigues are the core of narrative power in all her novels, which doesn't mean that she doesn't dread the "incoherence" and "moral violence" which they engender. Her empathy only makes their danger more real. The tension between imaginative and, say, moral energy is what makes her a narrator rather than a social critic.

The third component may be her life as an educated, relatively independent woman who, most of her life, has been a responsible housewife and mother. "Battle, murder, and sudden death, she thought, still did not prevent one from having to do the dishes."

Against this dangerous sky, there is the relief of duty; and then there's the relief from relief.

Janet seemed relieved when the doorbell rang. The postman brought a large package. She stripped it open (brushing off my offer to do it), removed an amaryllis bulb, examined it closely and assessed its condition. The doorbell rang again, and again she sprang up with relief to introduce me to a lively-looking woman with frizzy hair, who left after a brief exchange. "She leads our local dance group. Three years younger than I and she can stand on one leg for twenty minutes."

Before lunch, which Alva was preparing in the kitchen, she brought me books of poems by Gladys Campbell, Pearl Sherry and Helen Trimpi, the poet who wrote the forward to her *Old and New Poems* and with whom she was having dinner that night.

In the kitchen, we sat down with Alva to macaroni and cheese. Janet said, "Bless Stouffer's."

I exclaimed over the delicious cold persimmon from her fruit tree. She said, twinkling, "Most people can't bear the texture."

She and Alva talked about driving up to San Francisco a few months ago to see Monteverdi's *The Return of Ulysses*. They

[65]

described the sets, the singing, the singers' gestures and the music. I asked Alva how a composer, even one like himself, who had had two operas performed by the time he was thirty, made a living. He pointed to Janet and there was an exchange about which one helped the other most. He said he'd also taught, but then couldn't compose. Now he was writing an opera about *Tess of the D'Urbervilles*, doing the libretto himself.

Janet, too, had taught occasionally. "I taught Narrative 5 at Stanford."

"Why 5?"

"We skipped 1, 2, 3 and 4."

How about music?

"It always meant a great deal, but I don't play anything. My parents sang, hymns mostly. My grandfather was a Seventh Day Baptist minister. I'd have had two Sundays, but I didn't take to it."

"Are you a believer? I'd guess so from the poems."

"I don't go to church much, but I am sort of Christian. Christ without the Church."

"How about your husband?"

"I guess he was an agnostic. The most religious statement I ever heard him make was, 'I don't think the universe can be an accident.'"

Driving back, the light on the hills was beautiful, and I thought of a line from one of her Indian poems, "The sunlight pours unbroken through the wind."

[11]

DERRIDIARY
OR
SOME AFTERNOONS WITH THE GRAND JACQUES

At five o'clock on Friday, April 19, anniversary of the shot heard round the world, Jacques Derrida gave the first of the four annual Frederick Ives Carpenter Lectures at the University of Chicago. Tom Mitchell, chairman of the English Department and editor of *Critical Inquiry*, the English-language journal in which Derrida most often publishes, introduced him to a crowd that not only filled the seats and aisles of the Max Palevsky Auditorium, but the lobby, where there was a PA system, and the street, where there wasn't. The introduction was graceful, Derrida's acknowledgment of it not only graceful, but an integral part of the talk which, like its successors, dealt with questions of gratitude, gifts, "giving and taking time," existence, narrative, fiction, tobacco, luck, chance, "perhaps," and a few other subjects already part of the Derrida canon.[1]

Derrida is a short, compact, energetic man. His face is tan, roughly triangular, sharp but kindly. His eyes are a fine light blue, his short hair pure white. With glasses, he looks like an upper-level, not absolutely topgrade, French bureaucrat, an administrator in a colonial territory (such as the Algeria in which he spent his early life). Without glasses, he could pass for a French movie star, a mix of Jean Gabin and Alain Delon.[2] His English is forceful, strongly accented but clear. There are only occasional mispronunciations, some of them amusing, a hard-g'd "mangy," a confusion between "annul" and "anneal."

Like sermons, his lectures sprang from *texts*. The first was two sentences in a letter from Mme. de Maintenon: "The King takes all my time. The rest I give to St. Cyr [a foundation]; would that it

---

[1] A canon molded by Mallarmé, Heidegger and Maurice Blanchot.

[2] A witty, local anti-Semite called him the *"der schöne Jude."*

[67]

were all." Derrida took off on "the difficulty of giving more than all," especially of a non-commodity, a "nothing" like time. One's mental hair rose at this treatment—after all, Mme. de Maintenon didn't mean time but herself, her thoughts, her actions—but then Derrida acknowledged this objection and asked us to go along with his interpretation. How could one not assent to so gentle a request by a speaker whose self-deprecating modesty had already won that part of the audience which had not come starry-eyed to the famous presence?

He went on to one of the main texts, Marcel Mauss's famous, brief *Essai sur le don (The Gift)*. Derrida said the gifts Mauss described were really exchanges. A real gift should be something given freely, outside the economic circle of debt, repayment, interest, amortization and so on. A gift that leaves the onus of obligation is no gift. Therefore—a somewhat shaky "therefore"—a gift can't exist, not in the ordinary sense of some thing given.

There followed an excursus on the German phrase for "there is," "*es gibt* (literally, it gives, or *ça donne*)."[3] The implication was that existence is a gift, impersonally brought into existence by an "it." This notion became part of a Heideggerian waterfall about Being *(Sein)*, being *(seiendes)*, and being present *(Dasein)*. The Heidegger-Derrida anti-metaphysical metaphysics, or untheological theology, tries, I think, to derail reader-listeners from ordinary logic and usage to a stage of excited insight. The strategy is to put etymological, semantic and even phonetic pressure[4] on key words, often foreign (usually Greek) ones, moving playfully and poetically, until normal usage is opened up, leaving room—gaps or "traces"—for their True Being, which is an energy of consideration that is not quite the same as uncertainty. I can see it as a humanistic parallel to the physicist's Uncertainty Principle, except that that permits two mutually exclusive states of certainty.

Both Heidegger and Derrida pay homage to poets, Heidegger to Hölderlin, Derrida to Mallarmé and Baudelaire.[5] The second text for these talks was a short prose-poem from Baudelaire's *Paris*

---

[3] From what I gather (cf. Herman Rapaport's *Heidegger and Derrida: Reflections on Time and Language*. University of Nebraska Press 1989 pp 133 ff), this excursus is drawn from Heidegger's *Heraklit*.

[4] The usual word employed for such pressure is "paronomasic."

[5] One of the "suggested texts" for these lectures was Mallarmé's "Gift of the Poem," "*Don du poème*," which is "about" the birth of a poem and/or child, and fulfills a Mallarmé-Derrida formula of being "about itself." Derrida discussed it in the lecture I missed.

Spleen, "Counterfeit Money" *("Faux-monnaie")*, which is narrated by a man who leaves a tobacco shop with a friend. The friend arranges his change in various pockets according to its value. When a beggar holds out his hand imploringly to them, the narrator gives him a few sous; his friend astonishes him and the beggar by giving a silver coin. The narrator tells his friend, "You're right. The next best thing to being surprised is giving one." The friend says that the coin was counterfeit, but he still believes that he's done the right thing: he has created an event, a surprise, for the beggar. The narrator, repelled by this uncharitable "charity," is even more repelled by the candid ease of his friend's expression, and decides that naive, stupid malevolence is worse than its intentional, conscious counterpart.

So the talk went from grateful acknowledgment of what the speaker owed the University of Chicago, his friends, colleagues and publishers here, to the false gift of the false money.

This first day, there was no question period, but the audience was invited to a reception. Tom Mitchell hoped there'd be a "loaves and fishes" multiplication of the wine and cheese. Apparently there was enough to satisfy the crowd which lined up to meet Derrida and ask him to autograph copies—acceptable counterfeits—of his books. (Of signatures, Derrida writes that they always signal an occasion, a time, an event.)

I went home feeling both high and low, delighted and surprised at Derrida's own gifts, charm, intelligence and wit. The talk was far more in the tradition of French *clarté*, elegance and formal symmetry than his writings led me to suspect it would be. The occasionally long-winded excursuses seemed those of a man who wanted to make things clear and used repetition, explanation and translation to do it. I was especially pleased that this deconstructor of texts clearly adored them, that an enemy of the fixity of doctrine was a master of the elegance which solidifies it.

Yet I was also low. For years, I'd translated a distaste for the Derridean writings I'd tried to read into scorn, and had passed this on to others even less aware of his work than I. I'd thought he was a faker—a *fumiste,* a smoke-artist—though even his murky, staccato texts were streaked with brilliant passages which should have alerted me to something else. Then too, I'd been upset by his influence on those disciples whose boring and often bellicose use of Derridean devices debased every story, poem or essay they treated. In person, at least, Derrida's prose and manner were graceful; his disciples seldom had even the ponderous grace of Disney's

elephants.[6] I'd also been taken aback, if somewhat amused, by
Derrida's remarkable response to the revelations that his old friend
Paul de Man had written literary journalism for a Belgian Fascist
newspaper. De Man had erased this part of his past along with the
wife and children of those early days. Derrida constructed an elaborate machine to extract the Fascist stings from De Man's essays,
but the machine ground to a halt before one which declared that the
erasure of Jewish contributions to Western literature wouldn't constitute much of a loss. The machine's inability to digest this morsel
seemed to leave Derrida stunned. Still, there was something
admirable in this act of posthumous friendship, as there'd been in
the response of Saul Bellow to some equally unsavory youthful
comments made by our dear old friend Mircea Eliade: "Mircea
needs his Jewish friends more than ever now."

Sunday, I went to a buffet supper where Derrida, in striped shirt
and tie, looked even more elegant, and once again exhibited his
warmth, openness and amiability. I spoke with him about notions
stimulated by his talk, the invention of Santa Claus and other fictions which allowed people to receive actual gifts without the onus
of indebtedness. He appeared to find everything interesting; he
gave you the sense that if only his own text were not complete and
ready for publication, he'd cite your splendid ideas. Proust writes
that kings are always modest; this academic one certainly was.

I couldn't attend Derrida II, but was told that it centered about a
close reading of Mauss's book. The three people who reported to
me about it said that it went "on and on."[7] An old friend said, "The
man doesn't know the difference between writing and speaking." I
discounted this as junior colleagues discount much that I say, as the
words of a stick-in-the-prelapsarian, pre-postmodernist-mud. My
pal shouldn't be expected to like Derrida. After all, Andrew
Hoberek, my very intelligent assistant, a second year graduate student, said that he and his friends had made very little of the lecture,
and this was the case, as well, of several intelligent colleagues.
One, a distinguished philosopher, said the lecture I heard had made
no sense to him. "Though he's obviously clever." I'd had the
advantage of reading the Mauss book and some Heidegger, as well

---

[6] Wendy Doniger told me later that she'd danced with Derrida and that he was "a fantastic
dancer."

[7] Mitchell compares deconstruction to psychoanalysis: "Both are interminable." The difference is that psychoanalysis is intended to finish, whereas deconstruction—like Mao's notion
of revolution—isn't.

as part of a recent book on Heidegger and Derrida (which dissipated almost as much fog as it generated).[8]

Derrida III was introduced by Françoise Meltzer, a tri-lingual "comparatist" who said that the reading of Derrida's *Dissemination* in 1973 changed her intellectual life and reminded her of another revolutionary book she was then reading, Kant's first *Critique*. In his kindly way, Derrida both thanked her and said that the introductions were too much for him. (I'm told that after Professor Arnold Davidson's introduction on Monday, Derrida said "I could cry . . . but I won't.")

The lecture, clearly built on the previous ones, did not seem to require them. Like an episode of a soap opera, it repeated much of what had preceded it. The focus was the Baudelaire *récit*, which Derrida read again, saying, "It's the best thing in the talks." Now, though, it was to be fine-combed. First the title, "Counterfeit Money." The title was itself a counterfeit: just as the narrator was a fiction of Baudelaire's, the title was not just a naive description of the subject matter, but a counterfeit of a title, being about itself, the appearance of a report. This old Mallarmé notion of self-reflexivity was explored, re-explored and played with linguistically in a way that dismayed me. The dear old fellow in front began to seem like a child, a not quite so delightful as tedious one who had to be watched. Not entirely trustworthy. The words which kept cropping up were "excess," "superfluity," "overabundance" and "self-indulgence." Derrida had said Baudelaire's *récit* was about itself. Was his talk about itself? Was this a strange, conscious or unconscious act of self-deconstruction, modesty carried to a pathological, cancerous, self-destructive stage?

Then there was a breath of air, a new theme, "the poetics of tobacco." He read an excerpt from Mauss on the smoking rituals which accompany ceremonious gift-exchanges and reminded us of the tobacco shop from which the Baudelaire narrator and his friend emerged with pockets of change. Smoking was an unproductive act which left nothing but smoke and ashes, a self-indulgent pleasure, a gift to oneself. (No mention was made of the carcinogenic deposits, the poisonous gift[9] to oneself, though Derrida did say "Now that almost everyone has given up smoking," which brought

---

[8] Cf. Note 4.

[9] *Gift*, German for poison, had been invoked to demonstrate the contradictions built into words. This was one of the largest pot-holes on Rue Derrida.

relieved laughter from a crowd stranded in the linguistic maze.) Derrida cited other Baudelaire allusions to tobacco and its companion, liquor, and then read the first and final drafts of the dedication to the whole book. There Baudelaire said that *Spleen de Paris* was a sort of serpent whose segments, he hoped, had life of their own.

It was clear that Derrida had the same hopes, not only for each of his talks, but for the segmental analyses which he frequently broke off with the phrase, "We shall return to this," just as one was hoping for a breakthrough. Was this the Wagnerian or movie serial trick of refusing promised resolutions till the final moments?

Derrida's dullest segment was a discussion of title—Fr. *"titre"*—and the titration of alloys which "gave title" to money.

Perspiring a little, Derrida seemed to be driving harder than usual, mispronouncing more words. Was he reacting to the audience's uneasiness? Only one person had left Derrida I; there must have been thirty or forty who left Derrida III. Derrida started preparing us for the end: he was "coming to the end soon," this was "almost the end," there was "just one more section," and, a few sentences after "This is the end," he ended.

I left before the fifteen-minute question period, upset, head full of Derridiculous language tricks. The *De-rideau* (Fr. "curtain") had lifted to expose not Derrida *ridens* (Lat. "laughing"), but Derrida derided, the self-mocked mocker. More than upset, I was sad, and more than sad. I felt a whiff of tragedy. This, I thought, is what happens to all of us. The cells which build us turn against us, our inventions become tricks, our gift becomes a burden. Decades before, I'd watched Buckminster Fuller talk extemporaneously, brilliantly, interminably, unstoppably (until someone physically interrupted and stopped him). Bruno Bettleheim had whispered, "He's a megalomaniac." I was surprised at the word then, and didn't want to think of it now in connection with this other brilliant, charming man. I preferred to think of the occasional inability of Schubert to end a piece, of Picasso, driving himself, day after day, decade after decade, to fill more and more of the world's walls and town squares with less and less of his genius. There are writers who cannot bear the thought of not writing about every subject on earth, every person they've met, every thought they've had. The four thousand sarcophageal pages of Sartre's unfinished book on Flaubert exhibit this almost heroic vanity/insanity, this inability to stop.

I decided not to go to Derrida IV on Friday, the finale. I'd "had it." Still, on Thursday I realized there was much I wanted to know about the man, the connections between his ideas and his life.

Mitchell invited me to join them for coffee before the lecture. While we walked over to the Quadrangle Club, where Derrida stayed, Mitchell told me about him. His wife was Czech. They had two sons, one an anthropologist in France, the other a student of philosophy in the States. For twenty years he and Louis Althusser had been the philosophy department of the École Normale Supérieure, where he himself had gone to school. After Althusser's tragic end[10] (he'd gone mad, killed his wife and himself), Derrida had been overwhelmed. Now, at the Quadrangle Club in the long, white raincoat he'd bought in Chicago, Derrida was again concerned about a friend. He'd just spoken to his wife in Paris about him. "He had a transplant six weeks ago, and seemed to be doing fine, going up and down stairs. Now he seems to be having some trouble." Concern deepened the fine face.

We went outside, and in front of the empty tennis courts spoke of our writing habits. For the last three years, Derrida said he'd worked happily with a computer. He found my method of writing and dictating, rewriting and redictating, quite odd. I talked about its problems and advantages. When I mentioned some I'd had with female assistants, his chin tilted and his eyes twinkled in the classic Frenchman's delight in talk of *les femmes*. I told him about Henry James dictating his last novels to a woman named Theodora (Gr. "gift of God") Bosanquet. He said he was very fond of Henry James. I'd just been rereading *The Golden Bowl*, and saw it suddenly as a Derridean cat's cradle of psychological and moral displacements. I asked him questions. Had he ever written poetry? Not really. He'd published a few poems in Algeria before he was twenty. Had he learned Arabic there? No, he was almost pathologically monolinguistic. He stumbled over the word. "You see? I can't even say the word in English." Walking to the auditorium, he asked Tom if this was the way they'd come the other three times. Tom said it was, but now things were in bloom. "Is that the way you arrange your lectures?" I asked. "Begin in frost and end with bloom?"

"Ah yes," he said. "It's the way I like to program them." Meanwhile, he had difficulty lighting his pipe and finally put it back in the raincoat.

I told him that the Palevsky of the auditorium was the inventor of Xerox. Did that tempt him to offer a counterfeit of himself?

"A color copy," he said.

---

[10] 1992. Althusser's sensational confessions of fakery and mendacity in *L'Avenir dure longtemps* hadn't been published yet.

At the auditorium door, we shook hands. He had the warmth which almost all the exceptional people I've known radiate. (I've come to think emotional generosity is as much a part of human brilliance as heat is of flame or whiteness of snow.)

This last lecture was introduced by the theologian David Tracy, who talked briefly about Derrida's influence on Christian, Jewish and Buddhist studies. During the applause, a balding, young man made his way to the stage carrying an enormous potted plant, which he presented to Derrida. While the man said he was protesting the University's cancellation of a meeting to discuss the recent harassment of three gay students, Derrida held it dutifully. The man apologized for the interruption, and as Derrida put the plant on the table and said he shared the man's concerns, the man distributed envelopes containing salt and an article from a local newspaper prefaced with the question, "What if this envelope were filled with neurotoxins intended to kill liberal academics?" (Three gay students had received envelopes with a powder of unknown origin in them.)

Derrida did not make of this unexpected arrival what Baudelaire's narrator and friend had made of the beggar. It rather surprised me that he did not make more of this "chance," this Jamesian *donnée,* this *objet*—this *sujet—trouvé.* In informal exchanges, Derrida was witty and spontaneous. But this was a lecture. He was reading from a text. These were the guns he was sticking to. Suddenly he seemed much more the good bourgeois, the *bon père de famille*, the subtle explicator of the haphazard who is uncomfortable with its actuality.

Derrida IV incorporated and refigured all that had been talked about and everything that had been postponed. The heart of it was a traditional, marvelously subtle, almost word-by-word explication of the Baudelaire *récit.* It was full of role reversals: the beggar became the giver, the narrator the receiver of the event created by the friend, thus the true receiver of the gift. There was also much about the creation of money under industrial capitalism, the ambiguities of credit and belief, destitution and homelessness; there was even a moving sidebar about mangy, homeless dogs and their spoiled, household counterparts. All in all, it was a beautifully intricate Jamesian prose-poem, its protagonists not characters but ideas.

At the two-hour mark, Derrida broke off for a few minutes, "so that those who have to or want to can go home," then went on for another fifty minutes, the last dozen of which he delivered in a rush. His final insight explored the narrator's remark that his "fancy ran riot, lending wings to my friend's imagination and drawing all possible deductions from all possible hypotheses." Derrida transformed this Derridean loan into a Daedalian act, one which turned the friend into Icarus, soaring toward self-exaltation on wings which melted because of his stupidity, the abuse of his native gift, the power of reason given to all human beings. Derrida read this soaring conclusion rapidly as if to remove drama from it, part of his endeavor being to take the starch from received texts, elevated positions and fixed hierarchies. Nonetheless, there was prolonged applause. The Deconstructor had built too well; only that ever-surprising Surprise which deconstructs us all would silence the applause.

[II]

PENNED IN

[12]
PENNED IN

The world has changed much more than it usually does in the seven plus years since the PEN Congress of January, 1986. Many of those reported about are dead; many of the burning issues have been doused.

The idea here was to contrast the rapidly-formed impressions of writers in public with the writers "known" through their stories, essays and poems. Rather than annotate every tenth line of the piece, I print it as it stood—with a few annotations—hoping it can stand on its own small feet.

At least one of those described here objected to the description: Ms. Oates threatened litigation and published a photograph with a denunciatory letter. I responded briefly in print and more extensively in answer to her letter to me suggesting "a truce" that I didn't know we were at war.

1

"Writers don't have tasks," said Saul Bellow in a Q-and-A. "They have inspiration."

Yes, at the typewriter, by the grace of discipline and the Muse, but here, on Central Park South, in the Essex House's bright Casino on the Park, inspiration was not running high.

Not that attendance at the forty-eighth PEN conference was a task. It was rather what Robertson Davies called "collegiality." "A week of it once every five years," he said, "should be enough." He, Davies, had checked in early, Saturday afternoon, and attended every session. In black overcoat and black fur cap, with his snowy beard and silvery specs, one lens of which was black, he had a theatrical, Man-Who-Came-to-Dinner look. (He'd been an actor and worked in Minneapolis with the Guthrie Theater.) In the lobby he made a great impression.

Why not? After all, weren't writers here to be seen as well as to see each other, to make as well as take impressions? A month before, I'd spent a couple of hours at the Modern Language Association convention. There were thousands of scholars and critics there. Some of the most noted make a career of squeezing authors out of their texts. An author, wrote one tutelary divinity, "constitutes the privileged moment of individualization in the history of ideas, knowledge, [and] literature..."[1] Not content with auctoricide, deconstructionist critics went after texts. *"Il n'y a pas de hors-texte."*[2] Since there's nothing that doesn't belong to the text, texts are interchangeable. And it's not that superfluous, mythical being, the author, who decides they are, but his readers, at least those readers capable of erecting on his miserable pedestal—the poem, the story, the novel—a memorable explication.

Ah, well, was my thought, for some people a corpse will serve as well as a person. Indeed, for intellectual undertakers, hit-men, and cannibals, as well as for those who suffer the tyranny of authority, corpses are preferable to their living simulacra.

Few authors at the PEN conference were troubled by these critical corpse-makers. They were here to see the authors behind the books they'd read, to swap stories and opinions, and to make clear to each other what splendid thinkers and noble humans they were outside of the poems and stories which had brought them here in the middle of winter and New York. In this city, more than any other in the history of the world, the word had been turned into gold. If one were going to abandon the typewriter for the podium, what better place to do it?

Seven-hundred-odd writers[3] from forty-odd countries. From Korea came Sang-Deuk Moon, Ki-jo Son, Professor Goonie Bang, and Mr. Beomsin Bark; from Latvia, Juris Krombergs and Guna Ikona; from Italy, Soldati, Duranti, Jacometti, Piovene and Prozio. From Yugoslavia, there were Macedonian, Serbian, Croatian, and Slovenian writers. As for writers in exile, there were many, and, as the week went by, they became almost the heart of things. At the

---

[1] Michael Foucault, "What is an author?" in *Textual Strategies: Perspectives in Post-structuralist Criticism*, ed. Josué V. Harari (Ithaca, N.Y., 1979), p. 141.

[2] See Jacques Derrida, *Of Grammatology*, trans. Gayatri Chakravorty Spivak (Baltimore, 1976).

[3] Newspaper estimates ranged between six hundred and eight hundred.

[80]

beginning, one just read their polylingual names, Nguyen Ngoc-Bich, Larissa M.L. Onyshkevych, Bogdan Raditsa. Could any professional convention in the world have been attended by so many exiles? Throughout this collegial week, the division between the writers who worked in comparative security and those whose imaginations and bodies had been abused by the countries in which they lived became more and more important.

2

Founded by Mrs. Dawson Scott, John Galsworthy, H.G. Wells, and other determined optimists three years after the end of World War I, PEN's chief business is rescuing the world's writers[4] from the political and social consequences of their work. The world is older than the state. Words form and reform states. Those who run states know the power of words and attempt to control them. PEN, as much as any group, not only stands for the liberty of the word but does something about it. It gets international petitions to parliaments and heads of state. Frequently it helps unlock prison doors. Its charter reads:

> 1. Literature, national though it be in origin, knows no frontiers, and should remain common currency between nations in spite of political or international upheavals...

> 4. The PEN stands for the principle of unhampered transmission of thought within each nation and between all nations, and members pledge themselves to oppose any form of suppression of freedom of expression in the country and community to which they belong. The PEN declares for a free press and opposes arbitrary censorship in time of peace. It believes that the necessary advance of the world towards a more highly organized political and economic order renders a free criticism of governments, administrations and institutions imperative. And since freedom implies voluntary restraint, members pledge themselves to oppose such evils of a free press as mendacious publication. deliberate falsehood, and distortion of facts for political and personal ends.

That PEN is itself an organization and, therefore, falls into the

---

[4] The acronym stands for Poets, Playwrights, Essayists, Editors, Novelists.

[81]

kind of official behavior and language its charter rejects would be another development of this New York week which amused and dismayed some of the participants.

Except for anarchists, no group of human beings should care less for official collegiality than writers. A writer exists because he puts into words what has never been put before.[5] He exists only as he separates himself from everyone else who has ever written. Even though much of his work depends on that of his predecessors and contemporaries and will last only as it becomes a part of his successors, his stories and poems count because they are original. Unlike the scientist, he's not part of an interdependence in which proof, experimental confirmation, and replication certify his membership. The truth and beauty of his books must win over his colleagues and his other readers. Although he usually writes about society, his life as a writer is not social.

This may be part of the reason PEN exists. Belonging to PEN satisfies the need for affiliation. Writers who make a living at universities and newspapers or in government and business may be less hungry for collegiality. PEN officers are, usually, writers without other institutional affiliation. Many seem to enjoy their institutional roles. Mailer, the president of American PEN, said, "I always wanted to be President of something." And sure enough, he was an efficient, engaging, and diplomatic bureaucrat until the congressional week lit the Mailerian powder and blew the reputation to bits over the world's newspapers.

Mailer is famous for confrontation. As congress president, he was in an odd role: his pride was in his suavity, diplomacy, and gift for pacification. He was Mr. Bones, moderating and correlating the scat objections of the extremities. Still, the old counter-puncher, hungry for and provoking offense, needed to test himself against the pampered timidity of a repudiated childhood in a programmatic self-expansion. Life was a Hemingway Gym out of which would come not only a strengthened man but a great writer. Mailer's books are full of characters who jeopardize themselves. For Existential Mailer, nothing *is*, everything *becomes*. At PEN, he buttoned this self-propulsive and now white-haired self into diplomatic blue and acted as president. (The key word is *act*.) The stage was the world press.

---

[5] I speak of the writer since the invention of the printing press. Authorship was a different matter before that. See E.P. Goldschmidt, *Medieval Texts and Their First Appearance in Print* (Oxford, 1943).

3

Like most people, the artist is far more sensitive to his own restrictions and self-sacrifices than he is to those of others. Out there is the great undifferentiated public. Between the artist and the public is the middle-man, what we've come to call the *media.* The media-men have some of the same skills as those whose strengths and weaknesses they review and reveal. Their skill is to translate the difficult into the simple, the new into a version or extension of the old. They act as social thermostats. They know when the public is cold and needs a little artistic fuel. They also know how much heat the public can take.

The media also act to provoke. They know that *the public* loves to hate, especially those whom it thinks superior, or whom it thinks think themselves superior. The media express this hatred by searching for imperfections and contradictions in those they themselves have elevated. Their power has immediate financial and social consequences. They are both threat and temptation to the artist. The writers who were most prominent at the conference were usually those most sensitive to media power. No one was more sensitive to it than the president of PEN.

4

This account of the congress is meant to fall somewhere between the reports of the media—the dailies, weeklies, monthlies and quarterlies—and those of historians for whom *total history* and the *longue durée* are coordinates. Many such historians reject narrative and biography, and hold the singular event "in disrepute."[6] The media, along with most of the artists it covered, adore the event, find narrative indispensable and biography the prime cut of Sunday features. This account falls somewhere in between. The historical significance—whatever that means—can be left to students of the *longue durée.* As for the small events of the congress, the speakers, the responders, the off-stage commentators, this reports but a few of them, but the report is shaped by a viewpoint.

The press was originally to be excluded from PEN meetings. It was not. It was there and its reports became ever more important as the week went on. Writers are used to publication. Their only form

---

[6] See the discussion of the Annales historians in the preface to *Biology of Man in History*, ed. Robert Forster and Orest Ranum.

of it here was what appeared in the press, particularly in the *New York Times*, which, as the envious correspondent from Hamburg's *Die Zeit* wrote, "covered the congress day-to-day like the Olympics."[7] Writers' statements, which were often personal, lyric and eccentric, were converted into a commodity which could be distributed. Conceived as wholes, in the rhythms and vocabulary of the writer's special language, they were cut up and parceled for distribution. Writers read these truncated, excessively programmatic accounts and adjusted to them. They became more headline-conscious, striking, apothegmatic. The congress became to some degree a popular show.

5

In this part of the New York, there is a sense that everything is a show. Walking up Central Park South, Fifty-Seventh Street, or Fifth Avenue, you feel you're not only seeing a marvelous spectacle, but that you're part of one. There are camera crews on almost every corner: some are shooting models, some documentaries, some film backgrounds. The willed and unwilled peculiarities of self-exhibition—the panache of Fifth Avenue, the hand-me-downs of Seventh—excite the theatrical sensibility in most people. Everybody is *made up*. For writers who see novels in every other face, a New York crowd is intoxicating, exhausting.

In a way, many of the writers, perhaps most of us, wanted to make this show our own. After all, we may be in a very small business, but it is one in which we are all the stockholders, all the management, all the workers. We need few things: some dead trees, some live money, a printer, an editor, a publicity agent, a mailer—small *m* —strings and stamps. The recipients of our art experience it to the full no matter where they are or in what binding they receive it. Once it exists, it can be reproduced without loss (assuming that the type is readable). The products are portable, and though they may be beautiful in themselves, the essential beauty comes from some lines of print which convey one mind to another with maximum intimacy and power. Not even composers and painters, our fellow artists, can make such claims, though they too can rightly regard themselves as emperors of their small domain.

They also run the risk writers so frequently do of letting this

---

[7] "Der Kongress Zankt," *Die Zeit*, 31 Jan. 1986.

imperial position overflow the narrow domains of art into other parts of their lives. *Roi de l'azure* in art, on the decks of ordinary life the artist often appears foolish and awkward. For some artists, this is unbearable. Students of personality, students of ourselves, alert to the deficiencies beneath the apparent grace of those in power, some of us become exceptionally sensitive to its abuses. (In our small kingdoms, omnipotence is always restrained by art.) The sensitivity becomes a critic's fury. In the post-Renaissance, at least the post-Revolutionary world, our literary ancestors worked out the liberties which restrain power.

American writers have been lectured again and again for not treating men of public power. (Only our popular writers have written novels about the love lives of Presidents and Secretaries of State.) The American theory is "Every man a king," and our kings are Huck Finn, Ishmael, Lambert Strether, and Augie March. The American writers who came out of the great wars of this century saw power as a kind of insanity and the so-called man of power as much a puppet of it as the ordinary Schweiks of the world.

There is, then, an attraction between writers and the topic which PEN vice-presidents Donald Barthelme and Kurt Vonnegut thought up, "The Imagination of the Writer and the Imagination[8] of the State." Its slithery grandiosity would itself challenge writers to challenge it. Which is what happened. Along with rhetorical pomposity, plenty was said which had not been said before or said so well.

6

The Congress was many things—a tournament, a display case, a pulpit, a party, an opportunity for social, sexual, and political advancement. For some, it was a form of self-assessment: "How do I stack up against these guys?" For others, it was itself a subject, a quarry of characters and situations. For those who went largely to observe, who seldom or never had the courage to speak up in a large group, whose security blanket was their pencil and notebook, the congress became the scope in which they could isolate and magnify individuals and the ways they related to each other.

---

[8] It was surprising to me that no one I heard spent much time on the word "imagination" itself. (Mailer and George McGovern did cite dictionary definitions of it.) After all, one of the points of our congress was the visual reinforcement of what had been our literary images of each other: "Why, there's X. So that's what he looks like."

But a writers' convention differs from a convention of leather goods salesmen or scholars and critics. Good writers express what is quintessentially themselves. (This has nothing to do with conventional autobiography.) Consequently there is an interplay between their behavior and their books. Even if rhetorical gestures and poses resemble those of any congress, even if slogans and angers betray language as badly as those of a political or scholarly convention, there must be moments in which the language of assertion, debate, exposition, and argument resembles the inspired language which made the writers writers.

Perhaps it made sense that we were, for the most part, penned in with each other. Most of us stayed at the St. Moritz in the two hundred rooms donated to the congress by the young star of New York real estate, Donald Trump.[9] We woke in the St. Moritz, ate there, and then either stayed in the hotel for meetings or walked a block west on Central Park South for meetings in the Essex House. When we went to parties (at the New York Public Library, Gracie Mansion, or the Metropolitan Museum), buses pulled up and transported us, but for the week, most of us shuttled only a few yards between the two great hotels on Central Park South.

7

An organization, PEN falls like any other into organizational traps it is pledged to reject. *Organization* was the first thing that hit one "signing in." Organization's babies, hierarchy and privilege, hit one next. In the Quadrille Room, I got my packet at the table for Special Guests.[10] (There were five different tables.) In the packet, I learned that I didn't have to pay registration fees, and that I was invited to all the parties but one at Gracie Mansion. (An apologetic note said considerations of space made it necessary to exclude all but PEN officers and Foreign Guests of Honor.) A small twinge, but all right, fair enough. The packet listed the names of PEN delegates and Special Guests. There were biographies of the panelists, schedules of events, invitations to parties, and PEN Newsletters. There was also a notice about a complimentary continental break-

---

[9] Mailer knew the sorts of celebrity which were attracted by his own. That's how he raised more money than any PEN president had ever raised.

[10] I'd let my PEN membership lapse. My invitation came from Mailer.

fast at the Café de la Paix. Those excluded from this breakfast were counseled to eat across the lobby at Rumplemayer's.

Early Sunday morning, I went downstairs to the Café and was stopped by—I won't say "flunkies," because if I'd been admitted, I would have called them "pleasant assistants." In any event, they were policing the sweet rolls, juice glasses, and urns of coffee. To my surprise, my hurt, I was not on the list of honorable recipients of these goodies. This brought the first pinch of anger. All right, no matter, it's just a few steps across the lobby to Rumplemayer's.

There I sat at a table, looked at the large menu, and opted for the continental breakfast, nine bucks; a bit much for coffee, juice, and toast, but here I was, I'll live it up. I asked for brewed decaf. Coming right up. I started the *Times*. The *Book Review* started off with Harold Bloom's reinvention of Iris Murdoch, but its heart was an essay by George Steiner denouncing the "almost meaningless" theme of the congress.

"The Writer's Imagination and the Imagination of the State" is a vacant phrase. Its grammar limps.[11]

Limps. Was this a way of saying "I think it's wrong but I don't know why"? Anyway, the magisterial Steiner smelled a committee behind the topic and "the dead waxen prose which comes of morose compromise."[12] *Dead, waxen, morose compromise.* This was the sort of Mount Sinai banality that made *Times*-heavy breakfasts tough to swallow. Where was my decaf? "Coming right up," said a waiter who'd said the same thing five minutes ago. Was "decaf" infra dig at Rumplemayer's? Five more minutes and I treated myself to a small scene, myself the only actor and spectator: I rose with the *Times,* dropped my napkin on the empty plate and took off.

Around the corner, a block and a half down Sixth Avenue, was Sutton's Café. Clean and light enough, juice, coffee, and toast for two bucks, practically a freebie. And though I'd come to New York to be with writers, maybe half an hour with the people we write about would do me good. One table over sat a blind man with an immense, innocent brow: fortyish, babyish, Irish, his napkin tucked in his collar. He asked a waitress to put syrup on his pancakes. She poured. "Would you put on the butter too?" "Do you like a lot?"

---

11 George Steiner, "Language under Surveillance: The Writer and the State," *New York Times Book Review*, 12 Jan. 1986, p. 12.

12 Ibid.

"I'm sure that's enough." Brow furrowed now with surgeon's intensity, he made great-unsurgical-slices in the cakes, then forked large pieces of the result into his mouth. An unbeautiful sight, but better than Rumplemayer's. Or, for that matter, as long as I was making punch of my sour grapes, better than the Café de la Paix.

8

New York was cold. A born New Yorker living in Chicago these last thirty years, I've learned that Big Apple weather is a temperate version of what Chicago's Big Shoulders have shrugged off the day before. New York weather is sort of a nostalgia trip for me. In fact, nostalgia is the New York note. Of the many cities I love, none moves me more. My parents were born and lived here; my grand-parents lived here. At the New York Historical Society or in the lobbies of such old hotels as the Ansonia I see pictures of the city they saw. Some of it can still be seen, so can much of the New York I walked through fifty-odd years ago. It is a weepy business for me, age's compensation. No wonder the old weep easily: so much moves—shall I say "us" or "them"?—*them.*

A few yards east of my hotel was the office of my favorite of the many eye doctors I'd seen as a child. Astigmatic, the crossed eye I had till adolescence (and have had again for the last five years[13]) upset my mother, who thought it a foolish defect in her pomaded wunderkind. I was seen by the various doctors and did eye exercis-es at home and at the New York Eye and Ear Hospital until puberty strengthened the muscles and the iris. Dr. McDaniel was white-haired, blue-eyed, rosy-cheeked, kindly, wise, his hands soft, as he slipped trial lenses into the slots of the trial frames. His nurse, Miss Sheriff, was also wonderful: southern, capable, six feet tall, dressed in white from low shoes to crescent cap. They tested me on Japanese color charts to determine my red-green blindness. No cure, but Dr. McDaniel told me to stare intensely at green trees, blue sky, flowers and all other rich bins of natural color. I have taken his advice for fifty years, and it has brought me joy. I never fail to think of him and Miss Sheriff when I pass his office. I passed it several times every day that week.

---

[13] 1993. Till an operation last year straightened it.

9

Most of the writers at the congress had a New York support system: publishers here, representatives of their countries, friends from earlier visits. Penned in, there was still leakage from the world. Since I grew up in New York, my support system was large. Self-confined to the congress, I still saw my oldest son, my sister and her husband, cousins, friends, publishers and former publishers.

Sunday, my sister-in-law, Cynthia Rollings, was giving a fiftieth birthday party for her husband, Arthur Karlin. I wanted to go. They are my friends as well as relatives, but the party began as the buses would be pulling away from the St. Moritz for the Library. So, I went uptown after breakfast. The cab driver, a swarthy fellow named Constantin from Romania, had been a civil engineer in Bucharest. In the States five years, he couldn't get engineering work as he had no American engineering experience. Catch-22.[14] Nonetheless, he was happy, he'd saved money, and he'd be a citizen in a few months. The day before, I'd taxied in from LaGuardia with a Pakistani named Khan. He'd been in New York for seven years and he was also happy. The catch in his ointment was not being able to see his mother, who couldn't get a visa because she'd joined some enjoined organization.

These immigrant cab drivers, happy despite what would have killed my happiness, were the right environment for our congress. We writers met in the fellowship and allegiance of our ancient profession. The St. Moritz was our island, an embassy of literature. PEN was our administration. Yet our work was rooted in real countries, at least in their life and language. I told Constantin I was a friend of the Romanian novelist and scholar Mircea Eliade (who'd been in Chicago nearly as long as I).[15] He lit up with pleasure, the name itself an icon of cultural nostalgia. It elevated us to a higher level of fellowship.

Cynthia was stirring vats of dip, so Arthur and I took off for

14 To use—my first time—the expression from the book I had reviewed harshly for the Sunday *Times Book Review* twenty-five years ago. When I met its author, five years ago, he recited sentences from the review: "Do you still believe that?" I could only manage, "You don't criticize the Washington Monument, Joe." In today's *Times*, there was a chapter of his new book about his recovery from the illness that had left him paralyzed and mute.

15 Two months later, my dear old friend died in Chicago. A few weeks before his death, followers of the political freak Lyndon LaRouche paraded in front of his apartment carrying signs which read "Burn Eliade, the Satanist." They should know. But not Eliade, the most merrily and wisely innocent of the world's great scholars. [1993. In a forthcoming book, I write about coming to terms with some of his early, less admirable writing.]

Riverside Park with little Samuel and Daniel, their sons. Exhausting. I'd forgotten. Adjudication and pacification aren't easy. I mentioned Dr. McDaniel to Arthur, who told me that the problem of red-green color blindness had just been solved by a Stanford Ph.D. named Jeremy Nathans who'd isolated the single red and three green genes which picked up the amino acids "expressed" as red and green by the cones. Too late for me. My color blindness was a lifetime amusement to friends and family, an old puzzlement to me. (I believe I distinguish every shade of color and wonder why I just can't put the right names to them.) Nathans couldn't help me, but perhaps my granddaughter's son will be saved from the defect by genetic engineers. Or would "saving" be losing? After all, the fact that the world I *saw* was not the one my friends and family *saw* alerted me early to many things.

10

New York is a great setting, or rather, a hundred thousand great settings. PEN did not need much imagination to set their big events. The first took place in the South Reading Room in the New York Public Library on Fifth Avenue. It began with snafus, a crunch, fury, and wounded feelings. The writers were bussed in big cruisers to Fifth Avenue and walked around the corner to Forty-Second Street, where, bunched in a great wad, they were denied admission by "security men."

Who was being secured?

The Secretary of State, PEN's guest speaker. Outside, a letter of protest to him was distributed.

Dear Sir,

As you probably are aware, there are a number of writers and editors who feel it is inappropriate for you to open the 48th International PEN Congress. The Administration you represent has done nothing to further freedom of expression, either at home or abroad. As E.L. Doctorow has pointed out in the New York Times and in the Nation magazine, your Administration supports governments that silence, imprison, even torture their citizens for their beliefs. Under your leadership the State Department has, in the past, excluded many writers from the United States using the McCarran-Walter Act.

PEN has traditionally protected the writer's independence from the state. For this reason it is particularly distressing that a congress whose theme is "The Writer's Imagination and the Imagination of the State" should begin by compromising that independence.

Xeroxes of Doctorow's piece in the *Nation* were also circulated. Its strongest paragraphs were these:

> It is difficult for me to understand why he was invited. What has Shultz written? What is his connection to the world of letters? Has he ever been on the boards of libraries or publishing houses? Has he ever as Secretary of State championed the cause of universal free expression that so concerns the international community of writers?
>
> At the last international congress held in the United States, in 1966, no member of the Johnson Administration was invited to address the writers. The late Ignazio Silone[16] was heard then to remark what a pleasure it was to go to one of these congresses and not hear from the presiding politicians of the host country. Indeed, America is one of the few nations in the world in which writers don't have to ask for the endorsement of the government. I imagine the looks on the face of the hundreds of foreign guests convened in the public library when they realize that American PEN has put itself in the position of a bunch of obedient hacks in the writers union of an Eastern European country gathering to be patted on the head by the Minister of Culture.[17]

A crowd of writers is not much different from any other crowd, though it may provide an unusual perk or two: the recognition of faces from book jackets and literary pages,[18] more articulate complaints, conversion of cold and indignity into wit.

From the top of the crowded steps, a man announced the order of entry: Foreign Guests of Honor (some of whom could not understand him, nor why they were waiting out here in the cold) fol-

---

[16] At that congress, I had one encounter with the marvelously genial author of *Bread and Wine*: I taught him how to use an American pay phone.

[17] E. L. Doctorow, "Shultz and PEN," *Nation*, 18 Jan. 1986, p. 37.

[18] And from other pages. The literary celebrities were gawked at by other celebrities. Cf. Rhoda Koenig's self-infatuated piece, "At Play in the Fields of the Word," *New York*, 3 Feb. 1986. Koenig reports the actress Faye Dunaway saying "how interesting it was...to see how the famous writers looked" (p. 40).

lowed by American Special Guests and PEN delegates. Crowd-wise negotiators elbowed past more decorous types, got checked off a list at the door, and were waved down a corridor to elevators. Upstairs, at the South Reading Room portal, there was another security beachhead with a few distinguished fish beached on it. Bellow, successful elbower in the street, here stood helpless beside Harriet Wasserman, his motherly agent. He called across the ante-room, "Richard, you can't get in without a badge." Mine, however, was in my pocket; his was back at the St. Moritz. It had been a while since he'd needed a name-tag. He needed it now, though. The security man was no literature major. "I'm doing what I was told," he said. PEN officers were summoned, security yielded to pressure. (Bellow doesn't have the classic terrorist profile.)

Someone else called "Richard," the name that few use and which, for me, means intimacy (or intrusive ignorance). I turned to the caller, a frail, bald, thick-moustached man, beautifully tidy in blue blazer and diplomat's tie. Twenty years since I'd seen him, and as I said "Bern," and went to shake his hand, I felt queasy at how age and illness had worked him over.[19] Much complicated feeling had gone into the two syllables of my name, the one of his. We'd met almost thirty years ago. Howard Nemerov had given me his beautiful novel, *The Assistant,* and I also read a couple of the wonderful stories for which—collected with others in *The Magic Barrel*—he was to receive, weeks later, the National Book Award. Back then, there was no moustache, just a bald, sharp-eyed, shoe-salesman's face—till you watched it in action, an intensity of alert skepticism overhauling naiveté, amusement salting belief. A finicky, sharp, funny, roughly frank, partly innocent, crazily metic-ulous fellow, who carried lists of chores and checked them off as he did them. "To keep myself from going crazy." He'd been living in Oregon for a few years, teaching at Oregon State. There they gave medals each year to faculty members who had done the most for the University and mankind. The year Malamud won the Book Award, he'd gotten the bronze medal. The gold had gone to the inventor of a better breast-cup for cows. The silver had gone to a Professor of Logging. Years and years Malamud had chained him-self to a desk in New York, sweating through the fantastic appren-ticeship that made him a writer. Ten years he'd taught night school at Erasmus High. Then he married a Gentile who "pulled me out of

---

[19] I write this two months later, March 19, 1986, a few hours after I read his obituary in the *New York Times.*

New York, showed me what life was."

Life he encountered with dutiful joy. He was suspicious of anything he could not shape with his pen. His stories were full of uproarious fury, no-baloney fantasy, the poetry of rodents. Transfigured rodents.

Conversion to uncontrollable joy, and the comedy of hatred centered his best work. And Jews, that is, human beings broken or connected by suffering. Jew equaled Sufferer. His Italians aspired toward such Judaism, and, at the Saint Francis level, attained it and submitted their tormented organs to the ritual knife.

I'd not seen Malamud since 1963 when he and Philip Roth took a train up from London to visit me at Cambridge. A few days later, we walked around London, had dinner together and went to the National Portrait Gallery. We wrote a card to John Hollander, who we thought was the image of the gallery's Ben Jonson. Malamud also wrote an instructive, date-filled postcard to his son.

Was it then that he told me his wonderful idea for a novel? It was to be about a man singularly gifted for love, able to gratify the complicated needs of many others, but himself without the ability to love. I had seen Malamud give advice and money to un- or scarcely known petitioners. He wrote them recommendations, answered letters, worked out other people's problems. His generosity was brusque, his sympathy dutiful, skeptical. When his novel, *A New Life,* appeared, I found no trace of the theme (or little else for which I cared). I wrote him to that effect and he wrote back sharply. This wasn't quite the end. That came with my reaction to *The Fixer.* This gloomy work had none of the lyric backspin or brutal farce of the stories. Once again, I made the mistake of telling him what I thought.

There were no more letters. I followed him in the newspapers, or through such friends in common as Roth, Bellow, and Jon Levy. Greetings were banked off such cushions. (I also heard that Malamud had supported me for one thing or another.)

In 1958, Malamud met Bellow in my apartment, and there is a note in my journal about the two of them, Malamud the rock garden, Bellow the orchard. Malamud had just read Bellow's *Henderson the Rain King* and raved about what Bellow was able to do with Henderson's clothes. When critics lumped the two writers with Philip Roth, Bellow dismissed this "Hart, Schaffner, and

Marx" amalgamation. Once again, the clothing business.[20]

A few years ago, Malamud suffered a stroke which, with fierce combativeness, he overcame. Three hours a day, he studied mathematics to activate a portion of unused brain. It worked. (At the end though, he forgot the multiplication table.) Roth had been to see him the summer before his death. In his insecure speech, Malamud read him some pages about a Jewish peddler among cowboys. It was such poor stuff Roth was in agony about what to say. Malamud insisted. Roth said something about it turning into something good. "Today's today, tomorrow's tomorrow," said a furious Malamud. Claire Bloom saved what could be saved of the day by saying that the Jewish peddler was a wonderful subject.[21]

So here at the Library was Malamud, ex-president of American PEN, diminished, pale, but elegant, erect, and still dutiful, attending this crowded function which-it seems in retrospect-could not have done him much good.

11

For generations of scholars and browsers, seekers of truth and warmth, the South Reading Room has been a sacred place. Football-field size, its lofty ceiling glows with bright studs; its high walls are books. A hundred reading tables fill the floor space. Here PEN men and women came in by twos and threes. Photographers and reporters coagulated in flashing knots about literary stars, Malamud, Miller, Grass, and Bellow. A *Wall Street Journal* reporter[22] asked Bellow what he thought of PEN's invitation to Omar Cabezas. Bellow said he didn't know who he was. I'd read *Fire from the Mountain*, Cabezas' remarkable account of his transformation from radical student to Sandinista guerilla, but I didn't know that Cabezas had become a Minister of State (in charge of prisons) and had just been made a commandant of the Nicaraguan

---

[20] Bellow, in London, a couple of weeks after Malamud's death, was staring gloomily out the window of Roth's car. Suddenly, he said, "Well, Schaffner's gone."

[21] 11 May 1986. Roth wrote a beautiful if somewhat tamer version of the incident than the one he had told me. It was printed in the Sunday *Times Book Review* on 27 April 1986 and, under the title "Pictures of Malamud," in the *London Review of Books*, 8 May 1986.

[22] A young woman from Hyde Park whose father was one of George Shultz's successors as dean of the University of Chicago Business School.

Army. "Since they're protesting Shultz," said the reporter, "Don't you think there should be a protest against Cabezas?" Bellow has answered thousands of questions and does not tumble easily. "If attendance depends on pedigree, nobody'd be here."

By five thirty, every seat was taken. My neighbor, Susan Sontag, pointed to a couple of men patrolling the bookstacks above the dais. "Look at the goons."

Leon Wieseltier, who sat between Bellow and me, said, "Maybe they're there to guard the books."

Finally, what they *were* guarding showed up: Secretary Shultz, in blue suit and tie, entered from right behind a navy-blue-suited Mailer and in front of J. Kenneth Galbraith, who was here as president of the American Academy of Arts and Sciences, co-sponsor of the reception. As Shultz stepped to the dais, he stumbled[23] but recovered more quickly than his onetime boss, Gerald Ford, used to recover from his heavy-footed, ex-football-player's mis-steps.

Shultz's speech did not stumble, nor did he interrupt it when people ostentatiously left the room or called out objections from the floor. Unlike the other speakers—Mailer, Galbraith, and Per Wästberg, president of PEN International—Shultz knew how to adjust his voice to the room's inhospitable acoustics. His talk was not only audible and sensible, it was aimed right for the occasion. It began with a response to Doctorow's rhetorical questions: "What has Shultz written? What is his connection to the world of letters?" Shultz was here to tell us he was, in his way, part of PEN, at least of its vowel. He'd recently returned from a foreign ministers' meeting in Cartagena, Colombia. Nothing much of literary interest happened while he was there, but a week later he noticed that Cartagena had hosted a party to launch Gabriel García Márquez's new novel. He quoted from the New York Times account:

> Scantily dressed women danced the rhumba, a local politician made a speech about love and death, proud relatives toasted the author's fortune with rum.[24]

Nothing like this had happened when Stanford University Press

---

[23] "Stumbling means something. Stumbling is an omen." (Günter Grass, *Dog Years* [*Hundejahre*] New York, 1965), p. 92.

[24] Quoted in George Shultz, "The Writer and Freedon," United States Department of State, Bureau of Public Affairs, current Policy No. 782, p. 1; all further references to this work will be included in the text. The punctuation in the printed speech—which the Secretary kindly sent to me—suggests that it was taken down from dictation and not inspected with much care.

had published "my latest book. Nobody in Palo Alto even did the foxtrot." So the congress began with the humorous self-deprecation of confident might. It was also clear that George Shultz wanted his literary credentials on the table.

> A book that tries to explain economic policy beyond the head-lines certainly is not a poem or a novel; it's not far from an essay, though. But I recognize that I'm not standing here today simply because of my achievements as an essayist. Indeed, I can only regard Norman Mailer's invitation to me as another shining example of that charitable spirit for which New York literary circles have long been famous.[P.1]

The secretary's impassive, fleshy face did not leak a twinkle, and there were only a few laughs from the audience. Still, the *Times* reporter Walter Goodman knew a good thing, and this splinter of inside know-how showed up on the next day's front page. "But," Shultz went on,

> it wasn't until I read the New York Times on Friday that I realized that I'd become the latest PEN controversy. In Norman's world

—in five sentences, the insider had become an intimate; behind, Mailer stayed impassive, *plus Shultzien que Shultz*, a head ready for Mount Rushmore—

> that's a high form of flattery—and that's how I take it. And I salute you for taking this decision in favor of free speech.[P.1]

The last was one of the few sentences that smacked of the superior patronage at the heart of Doctorow's objection. It roused a small groan from a large part of the audience.

Then Shultz sounded the note which many writers—and the three statesmen who appeared on the conference's final panel—would sound again: a state is not a person, and, therefore, has no imagination. There are "intellectual and moral hazards of personi-fying the 'state,' of divorcing it from its historical and social partic-ulars." It leads to the erosion of "distinctions between states—dis-tinctions crucial to any meaningful reflections about politics and art." He acknowledged that "relations between the writer and the state may be strained, even hostile," but it is usually the state which "falls short", and then writers and intellectuals become its more articulate and forceful critics—the conscience of society. Shultz did not, however, bow to whatever social conscience sat before him. He preferred to remember "the literary vision of the 1940s and the 1950s—both black and white" and its "indispensable" influence on "the epic political and social achievements of the civil rights movement of the 1960s."

However,

> To declare one's alienation without distinction is to abdicate judgement, analysis, differentiation, wisdom. It is to risk marginality and estrangement from the roots of traditional and community life that nourish the creative imagination. It can be a recipe for irrelevance.[P.2]

Here was the voice of power: rational, decanal, monitory, true but not totally true. What did "alienation without distinction" mean? That one had to be selective about one's hatreds? Did it mean that a Céline or a Pound could not be a great writer? Or was it meant for little Grace Paley calling from the floor to have the petition against the Shultz appearance read aloud?

Shultz went on to the information revolution:

> The creative flow of information requires freedom....Ideology has nothing to do with this; it is just a fact of life....It is impossible to stop technological change by political fiat....Democratic societies understand that cultural vitality springs from individual creativity and not from the state. But[25] information is one thing; knowledge is another. Data and wisdom are not the same....
>
> To me, intellect joined with imagination and creativity is achieved [?] in the situation of "man writing." This means books: novels, poetry, plays, criticism, essays.
>
> In the computer age, reading and writing will not become obsolete...our culture is built upon, and relies upon, the written word....
>
> The awesome power of the writer resides in the fact that it takes only paper and pencil to do it.... The horror...of 1984 is...that tyranny...could deprive the individual...of pen and paper.[P.2]

---

[25] The speaker's "buts" were almost always signs of awkward transitions.

Then came the sentence which earned the loudest groan.

> And that is why I am proud to represent an Administration
> that more than any in this century is committed in philosophy
> and in fact to reducing the intrusion of government into the
> lives, minds, and livelihood of the individual.[P.2]

The Secretary had turned from forceful person into apparatchik, at
least to those who thought that the Administration he was proud to
represent was committed in philosophy and in fact to reducing the
intrusion of government into the lives and livelihood of—prosperous male citizens like himself.

Shultz finished as he began, by saying we were all on the same
team. Yet the vividness and individuality of the beginning, its personal defense and its wit had turned rhetorically sour:

> I am optimistic about the future. [Can one be optimistic else-
> where?] As the world gets smaller, the importance of freedom
> only increases. The yearning for freedom is the most powerful
> political force all across the planet. You are among its cham-
> pions. You can be proud of what you have done for that cause.
> And don't be so surprised by the fact that Ronald Reagan and
> I are on your side.[P.3]

The patronizing tone and the amalgamation with the distant
President lost much of what Shultz had gained. The audience
applauded and yet shivered. It had seen the state in action. The state
had risen like the mud and the sand in Goya's great *estancia* paintings to trap the forceful individual who was responsible for so
much of the speech, the individual who, a few weeks earlier, had
been the only official to resist the outrageous proposition that the
Administration seal its leaks by giving its officials lie-detector
tests.

Galbraith followed with a few remarks both aimed at and protec-
tive of his fellow economist: The writers had one weapon in their
arsenal that all the states dreaded; it was ridicule, and he hoped
he'd hear a lot of it this week. (In his talk, Günter Grass would say
that "hellish laughter" was the writer's only response to the state,
the "hellish laughter" of his hero at the end of *Hundejahre*.)

Now Mailer, his great white head neckless on his bunched shoulders, his deep-set grey eyes making him look like a snow leopard
despite his three-piece banker's suit, took the microphone.

It is in the cards, though, that nothing Mailer does goes smoothly. As he rose, people shouted from the floor, "Read the protest." One clear voice was that of the pretty, solid, motherly protestor of protestors, Grace Paley. No, said Mailer, he'd shown the letter to the Secretary but he had too much sense of the decorum and flow of the meeting to rupture it in this way. Pushed, he uttered a classic Mailerism to the effect that he hadn't brought Shultz here to be "pussy-whipped." Besides, he had a speech. Was he being heard? There were shouts of "No, no" from some who heard at least that much. Mailer asked what he should do. An elderly man rose from a reading table up front and said with great distinctness, *"Bite your con-so-nants."*

Mailer, as ever, a bit too quick on the pickup, said he was afraid he would only bite his tongue.

"Speak slowly" a woman called. But Mailer is incapable of speaking slowly. An aggressive, rushing speaker as he is an aggressive, rushing writer, he trusts in divine guidance. Also, he wishes to overwhelm. With forceful rhythms keyed to rhetorical pegs and lush phrases he poured his almost unhearable speech into the microphone and produced a catatonia of indifference and repugnance. Secretary Shultz, his face impassive in the mode of men obliged to endure much boredom for the sake of their office, may have flickered a bit with the knowledge that he had won the day's literary honors.

Mailer's speech (I got a copy from a friend at one of the networks) was not a negligible one. It made a good case for what had seemed an impossible theme, "The Imagination of the State," and for the next two days he showed up at meetings begging the panelists to discuss it. Part of his disappointment seemed to be that it did not ignite the conference.

> Without depending on Jung, a case can still be made that the state is an organism composed of many human beings striving in concert and in opposition to one another who yet reveal by the sum of their actions such faculties as expectation, anticipation, planning, scheming. Images of future activities are projected, historical desires which require exceptional solutions— for instance sending a man to the moon—are undertaken. Mental concepts of the future are formed which are not actually present to the senses—this is merely another way of saying that every state has a budget. Concepts not available to the senses, such as Capitalism is evil, or Communism is evil, become active premises upon which military-industrial pyramids are built...

I might go so far as to suggest that if the state does not possess imagination, then we are left with no need to write history. A computer can reassemble the available facts better than any of us. An era without a recognizable spirit—which, in fact, our period may indeed be—is naught but an assemblage of human units, computer data. In contrast, can we conceive of the Middle Ages without speaking of the imagination of that Church which was, de facto, the State throughout so much of Europe? Can it be that our intellectual impotence before the Holocaust, our fearful lack of insight into Hitler and the Third Reich, which remains as much of a mystery to us today as in the Thirties, may derive from the assumption that Nazism can finally be comprehended by rational means? No, it cannot. The Third Reich can only be understood on the assumption that it did possess an active imagination, a most debased, horrible, paranoid, and catastrophic imagination, but still it was a state that drew its strength from the intoxication of perceiving itself as a protagonist on the world scale.

Here, perhaps, is the clue. When states begin to perceive themselves as protagonists, that is to say, embodiments of a creative vision, we may be entitled to speak not only of the imagination of the state, but to perceive of such states as actors in a scenario, or characters in a novel.[26]

These were the key sentences, their insights glued by highfalutin' rhetoric, antique diction ("naught"), excess, mis- and overstatement. Still, these were its highlights. After, Mailer drifted into familiar attacks on the deadliness of mass aesthetics and the lethal, suicidal genius of cancer. Then there was a sort of lyric departure on a subject which is of intense interest to him: narcissism, in which "the fundamental relation is always with yourself." Mailer felt that the two superpowers were in a state of paranoic, narcissistic obsession with each other (a note followed up two days later by the German writer Peter Schneider). He then quoted himself, his "still contemporary 1957 essay on the White Negro," and finished with a grotesque burst of lyricism about "enflaming one's self with words" (a miserable phrase, looted from the "Faustian pan-sexualist, fantasist, and mediocre writer," Aleister Crowley).

In the Reading Room, we prisoners of these luckily-unheard words were released to descend in sluggish clumps to the reception in Astor Hall.

---

[26] Norman Mailer, "The Writer's Imagination and the Imagination of the State," *New York Review of Books*, 13 Feb. 1986, p. 23.

12

Astor Hall: Benares with neckties and blouses, waiters, editors, reporters, champagne, clumps of cold crab in sacks of fried grease. It was still Gawk Time. A highbrowed, eyeglassed, pleasantly remote or remotely pleasant Hibernian came up to Bellow, who said "Bill Kennedy, Richard Stern." The Kennedy hand went out: *"Teeth, Dying."* A satisfying greeting to a writer who in three decades has never encountered a book of his being read in a bus, on a bench, over drinks. Bellow had been Kennedy's lifeline from a desperate obscurity to not-yet desperate celebrity. Obscurity itself had been the entrance to celebrity: "A fine writer, unknown outside of Albany and not all that well known there." (I know a bit about that, having been for twenty years almost celebrated for being uncelebrated.) I'd read and liked his Billy Phelan book, had felt a slightly-comprehensibly-uncomfortable pressure toward Celtic-Yeatsian-*Dubliners* poetry in it. There was much to say, but Kennedy and I, alone now by a pillar, didn't say much of it. It was clear he was keeping most of both feet on the ground, running a workshop in Albany, paying back the gods of worldly fortune. "Even the horses I bet on are winning."

Old pals came around: a girl I'd watched grow up; a Swedish publisher; a film of faces so well known I had to think which were known from photographs, which from acquaintance. Tiring.

13

The relief of the street, of cold air. The last writer in sight, a balding youth, sported no PEN badge, but stopped those exiting writers who did; in his hand, a clutch of paper which would show "why I'm banned in Boston." ("Oh," said the old fellow in Oscar Wilde's fable, "I resisted the Devil, I spent forty days in the wilderness. I berated the Philistines. Why didn't they crucify me?")

New York's jewels were lit up: the faint sapphire bulk of the library, the soft-bottomed pyramids beneath the Chrysler Building's lance, the neon junk draping the acned aluminum of the Tishman Building, squirts of Christmas tree light triangled on Trump Tower. I walked north up dark Vanderbilt Avenue, the only other walker a man sifting through trash cans and the stumps of de-trunked street signs. It was brighter but scarcely more populated on Park. (Had the neutron bomb exploded while the Secretary of State was doing his turn in the Reading Room?) The Avenue Christmas trees still lit the center strip: New York wouldn't surrender Christmas. The glass business palaces were dark, and so were the stone cubes where New York wealth went to sleep. I felt grand, out of the crowd, but off to a party.

It was at Saul and Gayfried Steinbergs'. Some of the PENites wondered why a brilliant artist was hosting a Park Avenue dinner for two hundred people. PENites who read business pages know that this Saul Steinberg was another fish, a virtuoso of leverage, arbitrage, and golden parachutes, not linear satire and burlesque topography.

In the foyer, PEN staff members checked names against lists — so many lists, so much checking—before permitting elevation to the fifteenth floor.

There were nineteen floors registered on the panel. "How is it the man doesn't live in the penthouse?" What species of billionaire lives so modestly? (Duplexes we knew about, but quad- and quin-taplexes?)

The doorway was thick with tuxedoed attendants. The smallest, a large-cheeked, pleasant fellow, said timidly, "I'm your host;" and from the other side of the portal came, "And I'm your hostess. Men don't usually pass me by." A tall beauty whose dark hair, arranged in waves à la Knossos' murals, fell to beautiful shoulders. "If there's anything at all you want." One felt that a word would bring the Concorde or Paris itself to the window.

The fifteenth floor—only my overcoat went higher—was a small museum, a lesser Frick or Poldi-Pezzoli, more crowded than the former, its paintings better-lit and labeled than the latter. The message was that of all collectors: What Was There Is Here. What He Invented, I Possess. Look on our works, ye lowly, and eat your hearts out. PEN-heads were bent to the metal plaques of identification: the physiology of homage. It was a relief to suspect the Titian and the Lucas Cranach, but a Degas girl combing her long hair was heartrending, and small Dutch paintings may have tempted a few poets to diversify. There were, as well, Chinese vases, lacquered escritoires, embroidered tabourets, velvet sofas, knick-knacks of porcelain and ivory, enough to make comings and goings perilous. One did come and go, though, if only to ooh and aah. Bar, den, library, dining room, sitting room, study. In the library, a few modern novels—none by me—were transfigured into classics, at least, of look and touch.

The PEN crowd soon adjusted: the pictures were compared with others, the *pied d'or de terre* was ranked, classified, and then turned into background, another setting for interrogation, gossip, complaint, boast, debate.

In the hall, Arthur Miller introduced me to Vasily Aksyonov and the German writer Peter Schneider. Schneider was asking Miller how much money he'd made from the television version of *Death of a Salesman.*

Miller has, in his time, heard almost everything, so it only took half-a-second to come up with "A great deal," and then—his mode being witty gravity—in the manner of Frost's famous repeats, "A great deal." Schneider, a pink-cheeked boy of forty-five, smiled but was clearly not content with artful vagueness. You had the sense that he was gathering intelligence for reports on the vulgar, perhaps criminal prosperity which surrounded him.

German sensitivity was to be a basic component of the congress. Whether it was Hans Magnus Enzensberger's sour amazement at John Updike's version of idyllic America or the constant pressure of the once-volcanic, now grandfatherly Günter Grass, the German writers were here to indict.

And why not? Hadn't their older writers been seduced by tongues of brass into fighting for the forces of darkness? Hadn't the younger ones grown up under nuclear umbrellas, dodging emotional—or aggressively accepting national—guilt? The economic miracle did not conceal the emotional panic of defeat and national fission. Hitler had finished off patriotism and racial pride. Into what receptacle could impersonal love go?

Well, for Grass and Enzensberger, there was the supranational, supratemporal fellowship of art. It was the artists who'd bathed Nazi muck from the language, artists who resisted the slogans, mocked the icons, and countered the opium of bourgeois oblivion.[27] Money—as the playwright Heiner Müller would say—was the American curse as politics was Germany's. Now, in Mammon's Cave, the boyish Schneider tried to skewer the famous American dramatist who'd made his pile skewering that American dream.

I was interested in a German writer who was not here, the novelist Uwe Johnson, who'd died in a mysterious way almost two years ago at the age of forty-nine; I asked Schneider about him. In 1967, Johnson had come to Chicago to speak to my classes about his

---

[27] In his talk, Enzensberger would attack these "middle-class, Western essayists who marveled at Leni Riefenstahl's films."

beautiful novel, *Zwei Ansichten (Two Views).* A cryptic, witty fellow, with a long, fair, mostly bald head and an eyeglassed, owlish, Dr. Cyclops look, Johnson had a strange graveness about him. He always smoked a pipe, but he was no comfortable pipe-smoking fellow. His fist gripped this complicated pacifier and puffed out what concealed him. But what was it? All I remembered was that he was born in Pomerania in 1934, joined the *Hitler Jugend,* and in 1945, age ten, had walked halfway across Germany from his youth camp. After *Gymnasium,* he'd studied literature at Rostock and Leipzig, then, unable to get a university job—he was not in favor with the authorities—he'd lived from hand to mouth. He also couldn't get an East German publisher for his first novel, *Mutmassungen Über Jacob (Speculations about Jacob).* Somehow he got it to a West German publisher who'd accepted it. Then he got himself to West Berlin and settled there. But not for long, and not easily. Günter Grass, with whom he'd gone on a lecture tour of the United States in the early sixties, said that Johnson had "remained a stranger in the West," and that "being a stranger was of great importance to him." I thought I understood that. I've liked being a foreigner myself. But this was not it. Nor was it what Samuel Beckett, the Irish Parisian, had said to me a year or so ago. "I started writing in English again when it was a foreign language to me." Beckett was talking about hatred of literary "automatisms" (his word). I was talking of the pleasure of fresh observation, of the peculiar invisibility of the tourist. For Johnson, it was something else. He lived in England and in America, always apart, even when he got a job at his publisher's and acquired an American social security card. Division was his subject, the two Germanies his setting, the Berlin Wall the objectification of his insight. In *The Third Book About Achim,* Karsch, a West German, tries to write the life of an East German bicycle champion. He can't understand why "the inhabitants of this country [East Germany] had let the government...into their daily life...into their jobs, even into the scented streets, into their evening conversations...making it unrecognizable..."

Yet this is not Johnson's view, only Karsch's. Johnson's "view" was embodied in the broken syntax with which the novel ends:

> The characters are invented. The events don't refer to similar ones but to the border: the difference: the distance and the attempt to describe it.[28]

Johnson was at my house one evening when a Chicago detective came in with mug books to show my nine-year-old son, Andrew. A few afternoons earlier he'd opened the door to a man who'd put a gun in his chest. Coming down the stairs with a basket of laundry, my wife begged the man not to shoot. She went upstairs for money. She found twenty dollars. Not satisfied, the man threatened to take Andrew. My wife said everyone on the street would recognize what was happening and call the police, so the fellow—reason and perhaps decency making their way into his narcotized skull—took off with his poor pickings. Johnson watched the detective run through the book describing the brutal specialties: "This one heists Impalas." "This one douses girlfriends with gasoline and sets them on fire." Johnson took all this in with studious appreciation, but it was not his subject. Here the state helped a burgher with problems caused by an outlaw. The brutality Johnson described was the state.

Or so I thought, and thought that might be the reason the books he set partly in America *(Anniversaries)* were not successful. At least the one I looked at did not have the clinical cool of *Two Views*. I thought it ponderous and full of rifts. It was the last book of his I saw until, recently, I looked at a volume of his journals, the one for 1967. There was nothing there about mug books and home invasion.

Schneider told me that Johnson's last years were a misery of paranoia. He felt there was a conspiracy to prevent his writing. His wife and her lover were the chief conspirators. Johnson believed the lover was the father of Johnson's son. "Who was," said Schneider, "Johnson's image." Schneider said Johnson kept his wife on a rigid schedule. He had to know where she was every moment. It did no good. The tension grew worse. He published a denunciation of her in a newspaper. "Now," said Schneider, *"Sie leben im Elend."* "They live in misery." Johnson left them nothing.

It wasn't till I got back to Chicago and read in two old *Encounters* what happened to Johnson that I realized how much more terrible his life had been. Johnson had lived for years on an island in the Thames estuary. The wife, from whom he had separated, an Englishwoman, lived a few streets away. Johnson had given her a copy of his schedule and a map of his walks to prevent any accidental meetings in the streets. He saw almost nobody, except that every night he went to a pub called The Napier, drank eight or nine pints of ale, smoked half a pack of Gaulois, and finished off

---

[28] Uwe Johnson, *The Third Book about Achim* (New York, 1967)

[105]

with a large vodka. It was the bartender who led to the discovery of his body three or four weeks after his death: Johnson hadn't picked up the case of Spanish red wine which he bought every week, "but then," said the bartender, "Charles"—as Johnson was known—was sometimes gone for weeks at a time." Johnson always wore black: cap, jacket, jeans, boots. He sat apart and read the papers. (In his house were bound volumes of the *New York Times.*) Once, though, he'd joined others at the bar to sing *Lili Marlene* and *Mackie Messer.* The bartender said there were tears in his eyes. Invited to Frankfurt to speak on poetics, he lectured the amazed students about "the counter-intelligence of a certain woman's infidelities in an espionage underground." For an anthology edited by Max Frisch, he wrote an indictment of "a lying wife who had betrayed." Apparently his wife's lover was a Czech intelligence agent. His will was even more stringent than Schneider had said: the wife was to have nothing from his house, "not a book, picture or scrap of paper." A few years before his death, he wrote a premature obituary (for a series commissioned by *Encounter's* editor Melvin Lasky) entitled "Dead Author's Identity in Doubt." This astonishing document, written in English, reports his death in the "meandering hallways" of Orly Airport. There follows a straightforward account of his early life, birth in Pomerania, life in a village on the river Peene, life from 1945 to 1954 in a Mecklenburg country town by the river Nebel, his schooling in Rostock on the river Warnow. At Leipzig, he angered the State Youth organization so that he was "unemployable" everywhere in Germany but the U.S.-occupied zone.

> ...excluded from his type of work, barred from hopes of poetic fame, Mr. Johnson accepted an offer that literally made him another man. It sent him to the Western world, into a life of modest affluence and into the circles of authors who otherwise would have been beyond his reach. His family is of peasant origin.[29]

Then there follows what amounts to the spelling out of the life of this other man. Johnson says that in 1958 "an unidentified person" asked Johnson to "impersonate him." He gave Johnson a book called *The German Reich Railway,* a title which Johnson changed to *Speculations about Jacob.* It was this novel which the

---

[29] Johnson, "Dead Author's Identity in Doubt: Publishers Defiant," *Encounter 63* (Sept.-Oct. 1984): 74.

West German publisher Suhrkamp accepted "hesitantly," because of Johnson's bad record as an author. Johnson posed as an author for ten years and four more books. He went to boring parties and answered questions. As a student of literature he was fairly good at this. When he was commanded to live in Berlin, he went. He also was told to go to Rome and to the United States, ordered to wear a black leather jacket and never to be photographed without wearing glasses. He was even ordered to marry in the famous Roemer District in Frankfurt am Main. "In one case, he was forced to decline a drink." Then, in 1966, in New York, bored with his life, he began writing himself, attacking "the fiction that bore his name." He made "A Contribution to the Jargon of Upper Riverside Drive, with a Note on the Phonetic System." It was to receive a new manuscript called *96th and Broadway* that he went to Orly Airport in Paris. Johnson—wrote Johnson in his obituary—was "indignant" about this title, because he himself had lived near that corner and passed by it two or three times a day. Johnson dispatched the manuscript from Dublin to Cobh. Various publishers bid for it, including "Gian-Giacomo Feltrinelli, the wealthy Communist." The mythical obituary said that the *Times* had mentioned his death "in a report about the heavy casualty rate among passengers in the meandering hallways of Orly Airport, France."

Although I had no idea of the astonishing fiction or the astonishing facts when Schneider told me what he did, it was clear enough that Johnson's "nature" had driven him to the wall. I remember thinking then that Johnson had been ten when the war ended. I'd begun to notice that the pivot of remarkable lives often came during the ninth, tenth, or eleventh years. Shakespeare had been ten when his father lost his money and his position in Stratford. Hitler was the same age when his younger brother died and he turned from being a model student to being a rebel and a hater. The fault line that splits at that age is sometimes repaired with skills that last a lifetime. Hitler became a skillful liar and manipulator. As for Shakespeare, one can scarcely imagine the inventiveness his intelligence devised. I suppose the split in Johnson was objectified by the national split. His literary life—that other life—held him together. Would the "impersonation" have come to this congress? I remember Johnson at dinner with Hannah Arendt and Michael Polanyi. I remember him talking in class, being genial at parties. Obviously, the man who described himself impersonating that geniality would not have come to the PEN Congress.

Who did come, then?

[107]

Writers who were able to take a breather from a book or who did their morning or afternoon stint in their hotel rooms; writers who required a sense of solidarity they didn't otherwise enjoy. Perhaps part of the resentment of the American writers came from the fact that so many were comfortable in other ways. They didn't need and, in some cases, didn't want solidarity with other writers. Many had institutional connections. Some were a conspicuous, if minor ingredient of national well-being. National magazines and television programs interviewed them. That's why the invitation to George Shultz upset so many of them. Here was the very embodiment of national power cheek-by-jowl with one of the most celebrated national rebels. What was going on? It was clear that the rebellion was inauthentic. It looked as if the writers had been co-opted, as say Ernst Juenger and Gottfried Benn had been co-opted by the Nazis in the 1930s. The American writers were singng hymns to their country. Didn't they realize that the health in their country's cheek meant that it not only drained the strength of other countries—the latest was Nicaragua, but for a decade it had been Vietnam, Cambodia, and Laos—but the strength of a third of its own citizens? Grass had seen the South Bronx. He wondered if Bellow had. (He'd either not read or forgotten "Looking for Mr. Green" and *The Dean's December.*)

Many of the writers who were not here did not need the group support of a PEN. Some, who more and more enjoyed the fellowship of at least a few fellow writers, regretted not coming. ("We were schmucks not to come," Philip Roth told me Harold Pinter had told him.)

I went into the dining room and filled a plate with lamb, rice, shrimp, and other goodies. Back in the living room, I sat on a sofa under six feet of Rubens derivative next to a beautiful woman in a splendid dress which showed much of her splendid chest. She was, she said, just about to sign a contract to be a *Penthouse* centerfold. "If they want to pay fifty thousand to see my tits, who am I to deny them?" I didn't know. This was not her only gift, however. She'd just finished doing an interview with Mailer. She was, apparently, a good friend. An ex-alcoholic herself, she was trying to get him to come to AA meetings. He was a tormented fellow. "He needs all these parties to stop thinking about himself. He has no ego-strength." Mailer was everyman's topic. This view was as good as another. As for her, she said she was a "star-fucker." She listed some of the stars. I knew but one of them, a singer who, as it turned out, showed up on obituary pages a week later. Many of them had

[108]

used her body for more than erotic relief. She'd been punched, kicked, and gouged. It was waking up in a hospital that sent her to AA. She stretched and I looked over the shrimp to admire her legs. Caught in the stocking webs were butterflies and small jewels.

She went off to get what I was finishing, and I went down the hall past the beautiful Degas to a library where Mailer and Doctorow were having an argument. The onlookers were Bellow (who said Mailer had asked him to listen in) and, in a bit, Arthur Schlesinger, Susan Sontag, Robert Nozick, and two or three others. The principals were conscious of the spectators, but this only helped them make their points.

The dispute was the issue of the day, the invitation to Shultz and Doctorow's protest about it. Indeed, it was the publicity of the Doctorow protest which irked Mailer.

Doctorow looks like a spy from a 1930s film, bald, bearded, nervous. He has, though, more gestures and flutter than spies should have. The gestures were particularly galling to Mailer, whose big noble-Roman head (though snub-nosed like Nero's) seemed to be set on staying set. "Your fingers are in my face," he said, and after Doctorow fluttered some more, he repeated this with the barely subduable pugnacity so familiar to his friends and enemies. Doctorow said Mailer had had no right to invite Shultz without the board's consent. Mailer said Doctorow hadn't attended a meeting in a year. Doctorow said Mailer should have informed him anyway. Mailer said the minutes had been sent to him. Doctorow said they hadn't been. Mailer said Doctorow meant he hadn't received or maybe read them. It was heating up. But Mailer had had enough. He put his hands on Doctorow's face, but gently, said he believed him, they'd just have to agree to disagree and went off.

Bellow and I went off as well. We went for our coats. (I dodged a ten-year-old replica of our host who offered me a mint wrapped in gold paper. Never too early to instill appreciation for the sweet power of gold.) I wanted to walk back to the St. Moritz, but Harriet Wasserman pushed us into a taxi and only let us walk the long block between the Plaza and our hotel. She too was guarding what was precious to her.

[13]

SOME MEMBERS OF THE CONGRESS

1

In most groups, there's a sort of *commedia dell'arte* distribution of roles.

In families, factories, universities, corporations, people are known not only for their work, their looks, their social and economic status, but also for the characters they assume in the organization. So there are clowns and those who laugh at them, there are leaders and there are followers; some followers are worshipful, some resentful. Most people put on their organization-character as they put on their uniforms. It doesn't mean that the character isn't related to their temperament—they have, after all, chosen it as they have chosen what they wear—but it never represents all of what they are and often represents very little. It is a convenience, a way of smoothing the roughness of interaction.

At a congress of writers, things are somewhat different. At the PEN congress there were the clown-writers like, say, Salman Rushdie, the young Anglo-Indian novelist; there were dour, cynical observers from the periphery—I think of Sven Delblanc, the Swedish novelist; there were writers who'd pulled themselves out of Pleistocene social pockets which they'd barely survived and which they record: here I think of Kenji Nakagami, the Japanese novelist, screenwriter and critic.

Writers' work may come out of some internal fixity which was, is, and always will be what is most them. Then comes the writer reading—or hearing—critical reactions to his work. His response may be, "OK, they think I'm X. I'll show them Y." There is the pride of showing how much more there is to your talent: "I'll never repeat myself." As a matter of professional vitality, the writer tries to make his responses unique (even when, a true "believer," he is largely a vessel of his message). The heart of response is never— almost never?—ideology or ideas; it is always the powerful, eccentric expression which comes out of vitality, the sign that the writer is still with it.

At the Congress, you saw writers whose prepared talks were full of wit and playfulness picking up, in addition to applause, antipathetic reactions to which they responded by showing another part of themselves in their next talk. So Rushdie, dark, youthful, balding, charming an audience with standard literary anecdotes of vaunting self-deprecation—turning down an invitation to Downing Street because Indira Gandhi had disliked his book, then hearing that Mrs. Thatcher spoke to Mrs. Gandhi about "that fine young writer whom you met at lunch yesterday"—became, a few hours later, a Confronter, one heavy with other people's burdens; he challenged "the American Writer" to clarify the discrepancy between America The Beautiful and America the Terrible.[1]

2

The writer's job is to know himself and others, which usually means a moral leveling. Occasionally, writers at the congress spoke in this way and so fresh a note did it strike that they received extravagant applause. (On the second day, Amos Oz censured a panel of writers for assuming moral superiority. In addition to wild applause, he received a rhetorical right hook from Norman Mailer: "I didn't understand word one Oz said." The next time he spoke, Oz was as extreme in both opinion and rhetoric as any of the rest of us.)

The Congress was a trying event for many. For the pleasure of every rhetorical triumph, every jolt of sympathy and enlightenment, every dose of self-oblivious fusion with one's peers, there was the suspicion of such easy pleasures, suspicion too of one's hunger for singular attention. Even the pleasure of moral outrage carries its *basso rilievo* of self-suspicion. Maybe Victor Hugo, returned from exile to triumphant receptions in Paris, didn't worry about adulation, but few modern writers can be anything but skep-

---

[1] This was the question which provoked the response of Saul Bellow: "Writers don't have tasks. They have inspiration." Oddly, Rushdie's morning presentation was much like the first half of Bellow's: both writers played with the term "alienation," Bellow remembering when alienists were physicians to the mad, Rushdie saying that he came from an "alien nation." That is, his family was from Kashmir, Moslems in Hindu country, urban in an agrarian world, middle-class among the poverty-stricken. Now, in England, he still enjoyed "the useful condition" of alienation. Bellow reported an equally polylingual background. Born in French Canada, he spoke Russian and Yiddish with his parents, English in school, French in the streets, and the landlord was Sicilian. [1993. Rushdie's present "alienation," as the target of state-authorized murderers, remains one of the terrible circumstances in the history of the writer's relationship to the state.]

tical about it.[2]

At our Congress, many writers elevated themselves by representing causes, movements, or the geography, demography, isolation, or tyranny of their countries. The New Zealand writer
Michael Morrissey qualified all his comments as those of a writer
from "a small country." (John Updike said that Morrissey came
from that large nation called English.) Derek Walcott's obbligato
was that he came from a historyless part of the earth, the little
Windward Island of Santa Lucia. The Czech writer Jiri Grusa
unrolled a complicated parable about governments which concoct
divine certification for imperialistic fraudulence and malfeasance.
Updike descended for twenty-four hours from his rural literary factory with a lovely praise-song for the distant benevolent government which appeared in the blue mailboxes where he dispatched
manuscripts and which brought him back celebrity and money.
When Hans-Magnus Enzensberger remarked in his elegant, queru-
lous English that Updike had turned the United States into a tiny,
pastoral nation, Vasily Aksyonov, his five refugee American years
empowering his English, said that indeed the United States was a
pastoral country, filled with mountains, farms, tranquility, and
shepherds.

Hundreds of writers, hundreds of worlds, yet there were these
groupings, national and ex-national, sexual, ideological, even temporal. (The China of 1984, where *Death of a Salesman* broke
through an emotional dam, was—as Americans saw it—"living in"
1949.) For writers living under censorship, Franz Kafka was a
political contemporary: no work was more often cited at the congress than "In the Penal Colony"; for writers in countries which
suffered the *embarras* if not the *nausée* of choice, Kafka was a
psychological contemporary.

3

The Chief Confronter at PEN was Günter Grass. Burly, short,
with a thick, black, droopy Charlie Chan mustache, dressed in a
worker's Sunday suit, Grass looks like the local anarchist and athe-

---

[2] Cf. Leon Daudet's eyewitness account of a party for Hugo in *Fantômes et Vivantes:
Souvenirs des milieux littéraires, politiques, artistiques et médicaux de 1880 à 1905* (Paris,
1917), pp. 32-33. Has any modern composer written the equivalent of Saint-Saens's "Hymn à
Victor Hugo," which was played at the party? (A Chicago Lyric Opera tenor did sing "Happy
Birthday" at the party Mayor and Mrs. Richard Daley threw for Saul Bellow.)

ist: foreign accent, pipe, large gestures. His voice is *"baltisch tückisch stubenwarm"* (Baltic, wily, room-warm)[3], and this went for his English (where "Baltic" became "German").

Grass can look as sweet as Pinocchio's—Disney's—Gepetto, as comfortable as a pillow, but the Grass of the novels, poems, and drawings—*"aufgewachsen zwischen dem Heiligen Geist und Hitlers Bild"* (raised between the Holy Ghost and Hitler's picture)—is full of his favorite words: fury, rage, anger.

> We're always furious
> Already hoarse all over
> We're against everything; no use.
> So what can we do?
> What can we do with this rage?
> *Mach doch was. Mach doch was.*[4]

Do something. Do something. Take up the tin drum and beat it till the world changes. Reorganize the present and the past, campaign and keep your snail's notes, but above all, damn the authority, damn the confident, the well-fed, the easy.

Grass kept coming to the microphone to take on the big guns, those whose celebrity equaled and books excelled his own, or those whose sense or rhetoric drew from the audience more applause than he received himself. He charged Saul Bellow with portraying a generous, prosperous America which omitted what he, Grass, had seen in the South Bronx—a third-world America, purulating under America's haughty nose. He charged the princely Peruvian novelist, Vargas Llosa, with pillorying García Marquez as an ideological whore. In his lemon-striped blue shirt, the handsome Vargas Llosa looked down from the dais on the rumpled bristling Balt, the Onkel-Dagobert anarchist surrounded by a corolla of pretty girls and apple-cheeked forty-year-olds, and unfurled, in charmingly broken English, the eloquence of humane concern. It was confrontation destined more by anatomy than ideology, an icon of necessary collision.

---

[3] Günter Grass, "Kleckerburg," *Ausgefragt* (Berlin, 1967), p. 90.

[4] Grass, "Irgendwas machen," *Ausgefragt*, p. 62; my translation.

4

Though it was a Congressional sport to take American writers down a peg—American writers played it as well as anyone—writers from states in which writers had almost sacred positions were not attacked. Usually this was because they uttered the shibboleths of alienation even as they radiated the comfort of state support[5]. Often the dress of these writers proclaimed the schizophrenia: their clothes were aristocratically careless, as if to say, "I am bringing the way I am at home out for a walk. Aren't you lucky to get this peek at your betters?" Claude Simon, the sole representative of French prose—and the most recent *Nobeliste*—at the Congress, wore a leather, sheepskin-lined jacket over a tieless dress shirt. Here was the Hell's Angel as seen by French sartorial genius. Most of the West German writers were also tieless and wore sweaters or shirts with the top buttons undone. The views of Simon and the Germans were different, but in the Sartorial Common Market, they were *frères*. They did not criticize each other and had a common enemy. Simon spoke about those *"ordres du langage et de la forme"* which enabled him to distance himself from that *"culture de la masse " "crétinisée"* by *"les néfastes cinéastes d'Amérique."* Writers, he said, helped society imagine by making works like guns. As the sheepskin softened the aggressive leather of his jacket, so did the classic lilt of French prose soothe its violent content.

Short, handsome, with a square, wry face, William Gaddis sat beside Simon[6]. His suit was the most elegant at the Congress, a subtle assemblage of brown pleats, slits, and pockets. As for Gaddis' few minutes, they were the most revolutionary—and ignored—at the Congress, a furious, witty attack on the state's employment of the camouflage of sanctity to cover inherent—necessary—criminality.

He was followed by Wang Meng, a thoughtful, white-haired, gentlemen in Western dress. A real revolutionary, Wang Meng compared the state to a body of water, which "may either bear a boat or capsize it." He himself had been capsized, but was now, according to the American scholar Judith Shapiro, in congressional confrontation, a Capsizer (a member of the Politburo). In the "question period," she attacked both Wang and Lu Wenfu. How

---

5 These, though, are preferable to the allegiance of official writers in censorship states.

6 He told me later that Simon had asked him how long they were supposed to speak. "Five or ten minutes," he'd answered. "But the guy went on for twenty-seven. I timed him."

many people, she asked, had had to vet Lu's speech? And what did he have to say about Wang Meng's criticism of the depiction of sexuality in fiction? Mr. Lu said that he'd written the speech himself, but that he'd pass the other question on to Wang Meng. Mr. Wang rose and said that like people who only open a guest's present after the guest is gone so as not to show either greed or disappointment, he thought that sex too might be reserved for private time. Even filtered through translation, the response was that of a man of wit and maturity.[7]

5

Perhaps the toughest Confronter of all was the Nicaraguan Minister of State Omar Cabezas. He was on a panel chaired by one of the blond, soft West Germans, Hans Christoph Buch.[8]. Cabezas is short, muscular, black-mustached; his black hair rises violently from an assertive brow; his perfect teeth flash a seducer's smile. "I am," he said,

---

[7] Though the response was found unsatisfactory by most of the other writers there. A year later, Wang Meng, Minister of Culture, had the difficult job of acting as thermostat in the "anti-bourgeois" heat which saw the disappearance of the investigative writer Lu Binyan, a writer of whom, months earlier, Wang Meng could boast. In Beijing in February 1987, friends told me that Wang Meng six months earlier had said at a dinner that it was wonderful that Chinese writers—"even him," pointing at Lu Binyan—could write "whatever they wanted."

During that same winter of 1987, students at Fudan University and the Beijing University of Foreign Studies (spurred by an editorial in a recent Beijing Review [24 Nov. 1986]: 22-23) asked me why no Chinese had been awarded a Nobel Prize. "Was it politics?" I said the usual things about the capriciousness of prize-giving, but then said I thought the recent Chinese literature I'd read in translation showed a long retreat from the stories of Lu Xun and Yu Dafu in the 1920s and from the great writers of the Tang and Sung or the marvelous social and psychological analysts of Han and pre-Han times. Spend an hour reading Chuang Tzu, Mencius, or Han Fei Tzu—in Arthur Waley's *Three Ways of Thought in Ancient China* (London, 1939)—and you feel part of the contemporary world. Read the gifted, but laser-narrow, "problem-stories" of Zhang Jie, Shen Rong, Gu Hua, Ge Wujue, Wang Zengqi, or Jin Shui, and you know you are in a lively backwater. There is much doing, but you don't want to spend much time doing it. One reads for cultural insight, not for aesthetic transfiguration. In the comment periods, I contrasted Shen Rong's "At Middle Age" with Jane Austen's *Sense and Sensibility.* Most of the wonderful young men and women lit up and "saw" the difference. (Of course, I might have had a tougher time using Ann Beattie to wallop Ms. Rong, but the point still could have been made. "Modern" writers don't have to spell everything out.)

[8] Next to him sat the Hungarian poet and scenarist Sándoor Csoori. On Csoori's right was Kofi Awooner, the Ghanian writer and diplomat. To Buch's left was the Yugoslav novelist, Danilo Kis; the professiorial Sven Delblanc; and the American novelist Robert Stone.

thirty-five years old, the son of José María Cabezas and
Elietta Lacayo de Cabezas—she a housewife and he a genius
by profession. A genius because he had to come up with a
thousand ways of not starving...One day, when he was out of
work, he kicked a can as he was walking down a street in our
neighborhood and inside discovered instructions for making
soap. He went home, took one of mama's pots, and experi-
mented. It worked, and he repeated it in a bigger pot. It
worked again, and he went out, got a cauldron, and made
soap for the block, later for the neighborhood and the city,
and finally for the entire western part of the country. But in
1965, soap started coming from the big American companies,
and that finished him. When Somoza's National Guard killed
my father in 1979 for the crime of being my father, he was
living in utter poverty. First the ones from the land of opportunity killed my father's hope. Somoza only completed the
job by taking his life.

Disgust, hatred, hero-worship, and boredom formed Cabezas. In
the mountains, gnawed by solitude, broken by terrible marches,
half starved, he had turned into human steel. His account of the
transformation, *Fire from the Mountain: The Making of a
Sandinista*, had make him a Latin American hero, the poet of
Sandinism. No one at the Congress spoke as he did: he had *been*
there. If humanity is the persistence of being in the face of what
wants to destroy it, Cabezas was as human as anyone else in the
room. Yet there was excess in him. It came out as the sort of glow
you see in triumphant athletes. Cabezas's had to do with authority,
impatience, contempt and self-confidence. He had been hunted, he
had killed, he'd driven his body through torture, he'd been
betrayed, been punished, he'd punished and would punish. He was
also something else that distressed every writer in the room: he was
a censor. Cabezas defended himself:

> During American wars, there was censorship in the United
> States. We are at war. Yet it's not the way it is in Chile. Still,
> I want it to end, and it will end as soon as possible.

In his blue denim workshirt, Sándoor Csoori was heating up.
His face looked like a gun. He'd seen how dictatorships started;
he'd been in Cuba, he lived behind the Iron Curtain. Always there
were such defenses and sweet talk about future freedom.

[116]

We thought hope meant freedom. It didn't. In the name of freedom terrible things are done. I can never agree to a state of limitation, to censorship.

Cabezas took off his suit coat. Underneath was a grey sweater. Cigarette smoke shot from his nostrils. He said, "If totalitarianism comes back to Managua, I'll go back to the mountains."

Delblanc spoke with mordant self-mockery that was like a suit he put on in the morning. He had sat with friends in Eastern European rooms knowing the walls were tapped. The world had enough of tapped walls.

The flamboyant, curly-headed, French-speaking charmer Danilo Kis said that totalitarianism was an art of destruction, cruelty, and crime whose instruments were deception and *mensonge*.

At this point, a burly old baldie rose from the floor. "I am," he said, "Raditsa. Founder of PEN. Sixty years ago, we had a Congress in Dubrovnik. I heard all this then." From the back of the room there was growling: Who was this old trout? Who cared about what he'd heard sixty years ago? A shout: "Mr. Chairman, exercise your authority. Shut him up."

The shouter was the champion of liberty, Allen Ginsberg. At every session he shuffled to the podium bringing petitions and mellifluous objections. His shapeless, colorless pants hung off his thin rump, his fat beard and bald head seemed too heavy for his neck. Coat, pants, and tie looked carefully selected from piles in the salvage shop. Our Whitman.

Christoph Buch told Raditsa he had used up his time. The old fellow put on his beret and stomped out of the room.

Said Cabezas, "We only have *poco censura*. I'm uncomfortable with it, but it's necessary. If you're threatened by the most powerful country in the world, you have no option. Ten minutes after Reagan calls off his war, there will be no censorship. After the American Revolution, it took ten years for the country to have liberty of the press. Why question a nation that has existed only six or seven years?"

Or a Congress of Champions who squelched their own.

6

The Wednesday evening reception was sponsored by Fiat. Trust

[117]

an Italian corporation to pick a gorgeous setting: the Temple of Dendur in the Sackler Wing of the Metropolitan Museum of Art. This stubby glory is set on a dais surrounded by a shallow moat of black water. A bank of glass shields its massive blocks, fluted pillars and little pediment from the car and house lights of Fifth Avenue. My friend, the sculptress, Joan FitzGerald, and I arrived a little late. What a sight. Five or six hundred people in a silhouette frieze against the golden stone. In this little poem to the dead, the living buzzed and fluttered. Waiters passed trays of champagne, paté on *brioches*, caviar and potato skins, pineapple and cream cheese, sausages and little *crêpes*. A band played Cole Porter and Richard Rodgers.

Here was Danilo Kis, that Dead End Kid of letters,[9] encircling a beautiful brunette with his elegant French. Near him was another *beau-laid*, Jerzy Kozinski,[10] tanned, gorgeously suited on some Via Condotti or other, his black curls almost touching the raven hair of the poet-editor-wife of Nicaragua's General Ortega, aglitter in handsome necklace and gorgeous white dress. That afternoon she'd begged the writers of the world to stop the United States from committing genocide in her country. The word spread—I don't know by whom—that Señora Ortega had purchased $3,000 worth of sunglasses from Tiffany.

Here was the dear old granny of feminism, Betty Friedan, looking like a Bulgarian facsimile of herself. Joan told her how beautiful her Egyptian necklace was, and the dear old combatant blushed like a girl receiving her first valentine.

All around were familiar heads. Grass bounced around in cigarette smoke, surrounded as always by a membrane of young Germans; Vargas Llosa sported his striped shirt and white teeth; Arthur Schlesinger came in preceded by the fanfare of his famously tall wife. There was old Bogan Raditsa, looking very much like old and crabbed Edmund Wilson. I congratulated him for speaking out that morning. He took this as a cue to repeat what he'd said, and it was difficult to get away. Bob Coover was telling Jan Neugeboren—who looks young but not newborn—about his terrible struggles with his novel *The Public Burning*, while Neugeboren

---

[9] November 1989: I have not changed the phrase about the wonderful Yugoslavian writer who died a few months ago.

[10] 1992. The suicide of this remarkable man uncovered a life more bizarre than anything he'd written, a life of a hundred identities, a thousand hotel rooms and a passionate tragic devotion to the wife he asked at the end to understand and forgive him.

[118]

was countering with his own history of difficulty. Old pals from Chicago, Gene Goodhart and Bob Lucid,[11] showed up with white hair as if at an 18th century ball. Old publishers, agents, friends and acquaintances from every part of one's life walked around the temple and black moat, gossiping, joking, informing, complaining, deprecating, boasting. The band played

I'll Take Manhattan,
the Bronx and Staten
Island with you

While Joan went for her coat, I talked with a museum guard who asked what kind of a party it was. When I told him most of us were writers he said—in Italian, as a matter of fact—"If you write something about the party, my name is Luigi, and I'm from Syracusa in Sicilia." For sixteen years he'd been applying for a job as a hairdresser. No luck. He still liked America, but it was no bed of roses here. As for Americans, "Only trust them when they pay with a check. With cash,"—he pinched the air. "Watch out. They have glue on their palms."

7

The first and last confrontations of the conference were between Norman Mailer and some angry women. They were genuine confrontations, deeper than anything the Congress itself discussed.

From the beginning, literature has been enriched by feminine genius. Still, it is astonishing that there has been so little in literature of much that only women can know. So, until our time, there's next to no description of pregnancy and childbirth. There is a famous scene in Sigrid Undset's *Kristin Lavransdatter* and, from less privileged positions, parallel scenes in Tolstoy, Zola, and Hemingway. There is the oblique, transfigured or symbolic account in Mary Shelley's *Frankenstein*, but until our own time this is, I think, about it.[12] Many women writers never married; many who married had no children, and the few who did—Mrs. Gaskell, Colette—did not write about this physically and psychologically

---

[11] Mailer's literary executor.

[12] See Ellen Moers' chapter, "Female Gothic," in *Literary Women* (Garden City, N.Y., 19760, pp. 90-110. 1993.

complicated experience. (I myself have learned more about it from my observant, articulate daughter's account of her pregnancy than I have in a lifetime of reading.) Recently, the subject has come out of the closet. The poet Sharon Olds writes wonderfully about conception, pregnancy, and parturition; Shouri Daniels' *The Salt Doll* contains a horrific account of childbirth. Young women poets and prose writers have described, invented, and reinvented hundreds of subjects in the past two decades. If there is such a thing as a literary movement, I'd say that this is the most significant one of our time.[13]

That there were so few women writers present or speaking at the Congress became the charge leveled at Norman Mailer. "Out of one hundred and twenty panelists, only sixteen are women," said the petition some of the women drew up. Mailer listed the names of twenty-four women who had declined invitations to the Congress. (These included Doris Lessing, Mavis Gallant, Christa Wolf, Joan Didion, and, if I remember correctly, Simone de Beauvoir—who died a few weeks later.) As usual, Mailer fed the fire with oil. "There are not," he said, "that many women, like Susan Sontag, who are intellectuals first, poets and novelists second." This remark turned the roomful of PEN women into what a woman reporter called a "gigantic snake pit."[14]

During the conference on drama,[15] an emissary from the Women's Committee entered hot from the fray, took the floor microphone, and, trembling with fury, read the Women's Petition. (I didn't catch her name.) I felt for her, felt for her passion and the hatred her insistence aroused in much of the audience. In one of the celebrated manifestos of the new feminism, Hélène Cixous writes

---

[13] What counts in literature is the poem, the story, the novel. We read books, not movements. A movement is a way of dismissing literature (that is, a way of handling it). It is interesting to talk about movements because such talk elevates the talker and makes him feel he is taking a survey of many things. Literature, though, is the fusion of two minds—no, the fusion of one mind, the reader's, with the poem or story or novel. Anything else is conversation.

[14] Rhoda Koenig, "At Play in the Fields of the Word: Alienation, Imagination, Feminism, and Foolishness at PEN," *New York* (3 Feb. 1986): 47.

[15] Highlights of the conference on drama were Miller's economic survey of the parallel decline of the theatrical audience and mainstream drama and Judith Hertzberg's lament that Ronald Reagan had never acted in Chekhov and Pinter.

Listen to a woman speak at a public gathering (if she hasn't painfully lost her wind). She doesn't "speak," she throws her trembling body forward; she lets go of herself, she flies; all of her passes into her voice, and it's with her body that she vitally supports the "logic" of her speech. Her flesh speaks true. She lays herself bare. In fact, she physically materializes what she's thinking; she signifies it with her body. In a certain way she inscribes what she's saying, because she doesn't deny her drives the intractable and impassioned part they have in speaking. Her speech, even when "theoretical" or political, is never simple or linear or "objectified," generalized: she draws her story into history.

...Why this privileged relationship with the voice? Because no woman stockpiles as many defenses for countering the drives as does a man...There is always within her at least a little of that good mother's milk. She writes in white ink.[16]

For PENites who had been insulated from passionate rhetorical seizures of the sort that were seen and heard at the meetings, this marvelous account may explain more than mystify. To hear this speaker or, the next day, to see that peculiarly lyric but essentially down-to-earth writer Cynthia Ozick pour her terrible anguish about Israel into an attack on Bruno Kreisky, or to have heard Judith Shapiro drive her pain into the Chinese writers Wang Meng and Lu Wenfu was to be amazed, shocked, and—in my case—also annoyed.

8

Annoyed?

Confession time. The writer has to pay for the ease of moral superiority—alone at his typewriter, no one stops him—with some measure of frankness. Only he knows if the *culpa* he confesses is diversion from a greater one.[17] In any case, like the average white Southerner facing those blacks galvanized into bravery and confrontation by Martin Luther King, Jr., I was annoyed at this intrusion. My ease, my habitual expectation, was subverted; my precious time was taken up by an intruder. *Raucousness, rudeness,*

---

16 Hélène Cixous, "the Laugh of the Medusa," trans. Keith Cohen and Paula Cohen, *The "Signs" Reader: Women, Gender, and Scholarship*, ed. Elizabeth Abel and Emily K. Abel (Chicago, 1983), p. 285.

17 Were earlier writers as concerned with establishing their position, or is modern literary

stridency, assertiveness; this was the vocabulary of visceral out-rage. The enraged, trembling intruder was "mouthing simplicities" on these entrenched males and the female allies who took their stand. John Simon, rising from the self-churned foam of sexual swordsmanship, took the microphone—he also trembled—claiming that good writers were good writers, too bad so few of them were women, let them write better and earn their rewards. Luckily for the "intruder," Simon, a kind of marzipan Mailer, is incapable of marshaling anything but enmity. He was hissed more loudly than his glowering antagonist.

I'd had enough. My son Christopher and I took off for a cold walk on the avenues. Half an hour later, back on Central Park South, we ran into Miller, who, as a speaker, had been manacled to the platform.

"What happened, Arthur?"

"Things went from stupid to stupider. You missed nothing."

I let a bit of gallantry escape: "Fucking bitches."

Minutes later, Christopher told me that Miller, a statesman of the Republic of Letters, Ex-President of International PEN, "blushed." (I'd only remarked his laugh.)

I let this gallantry stay on the page because of an internal confi-dence that I don't have an ounce of chauvinist blood in me, at least, in my intellect. Yet, like a refined version—I think—of the Mailer of *The Prisoner of Sex* or the Napoleon who, long before Freud, said "Anatomy is destiny," I'm the creature of obsolete tradition. The earliest reader I know of *The Second Sex*, I lent my copy to the girls at Connecticut College whom I proselyted with it in 1954. After that, my female characters were creatures of liberated intelli-gence; theirs and mine. Still, the anger crawling around my chal-

---

self-consciousness part of the twentieth-century interest in the observer? Is anyone today as confident as George Bernard Shaw? "An...author may be as selfish as he like without reproach from the public if only his art is superb, and he cannot fulfil this condition without sufficient effort and sacrifice to make him feel noble and martyred" (Shaw, Preface to *The Doctor's Dilemma, Prefaces by Bernard Shaw* [London, 1934}, p. 246). Four decades later, W.H. Auden was more gnomic:

Time that with this strange excuse
Pardoned Kipling and his views,
And will pardon Paul Claudel,
Pardons him for writing well.

"In Memory of W.B. Yeats," *The English Auden: Poems, Essays and Dramatic Writings,* 1927-1939, ed. Edward Mendelson [London, 1977}, pp. 242-43.

lenged superiority was there. I left the meeting, I said what I said, and caused Miller to blush. (His self-recognition?)

9

The superiority of a writers' congress to most others is that sooner or later almost every position will be taken by one writer or another. And, since most writers are in the business of coming clean, there is as much confession as indictment, contrition as accusation.

Criticism, which is in the business of uncovering internal contradictions and, occasionally, their hypocritical facade, has a field day at such a congress. No wonder that so much periodical commentary focused on the discrepancy between the nobility of the writer's calling and the ignominy of his behavior or self-revelation. The commentary also fed on the rhetoric of discrepancy, the rhetorical color of the confrontations. The writer's solitary work is unchallenged except by those challenges his art imposes. Seduced from the solitude in which he takes all the sides and plays all the instruments, the writer often is stripped of caution as well as art. Instead of championing the complexity of positions, he becomes a Saint George of opinion and attacks creatures he diabolically magnifies.

Moral purity is rarer than literary genius, though most writers in public talk are, like most people, "holier than thou." (My guess is that writers *practice* cynicism, indifference and despair more than most people.)

10

Writers who become semi-public institutions have to keep removing the bronze and marble from their brains. Few have the nerve to be as nutty, angry or closed-minded as they were when their specialness was incubating its first stories, poems and plays.

Take Bellow, for instance. Left to himself, unpressured, or even half-dreaming out loud, in public, no one is better at letting you see the writer at work. In the film Henri Clouzot made of Picasso, the camera is under a sheet of glass on which Picasso painted. You can see the painter's brush hesitate, see it decide and make its stroke; above, you see the great black eyes signal annoyance, pleasure, decision, idea. Yet Picasso was not completely lost on his painter's

island. (He "destroyed" the four paintings which—who knows?—
might survive on this film longer than the hundreds which were not
painted *à la belle étoile* of cinematic futures.) When Bellow mixed
memories of childhood with responses to remarks which had just
been made around him, he was a Picasso on camera, a great impro-
viser, Charlie Parker at the Onyx Club, Bach at the Cöthen organ.
His fusion of modesty and creative security was unique at the
Congress.

Bellow swears by the truth of his sensuous memory. (It is extraordinary.) As for his opinions, though he defends them powerfully,
he knows that he runs into the dangers of "narrowness," "ideology," "special pleading," and "pedagogy." Old friends, we often
have to agree to limit talk about certain subjects. I trust he won't
mind if I offer one example. The summer before the PEN
Congress, within three weeks of his seventieth birthday, his two
brothers died. He was in a terrible state, and it made sense for me
to drive with him to his summer place in Vermont. En route, we
had a lot of laughs and a few disputes. The one I cite here began
with Henry James. Bellow had been rereading *The American
Scene*. "James thinks Italians are great in Italy, but not in New
York. He treats them like garbage." When, a few minutes later,
Bellow said something about another group, I triumphantly and
angrily stuck him with his attack on James. The trap of contradiction angered him. "All art is ethnocentric," he said in his own—but
not James'—defense. I think he meant that art springs from passions which arise from narrow encounters, local rage, adored
specifics. Bellow's art isn't ethnocentric. In it he is fair. What is
contradictory in the man isn't contradictory in the artist. The artist
uses the man's intensity. If it's roused by contradiction, the art
becomes dramatically more interesting. Out of art, the contradictions shiver in logical cold.[18]

At the Congress, Bellow's public, "ethnocentric, " "pedagogical" views followed hard upon his beautiful, dream-sharp reminiscence. These views were what was challenged by Günter Grass and
young Rushdie.[19]   Bellow is very good on his feet, and his
responses to them made headlines.[20]   What really counted, the

---

[18] 1993. Bellow said of this paragraph that people would think him a racist. If they think
this, they're wrong.

[19] Rushdie is the editor of the English edition of Grass's political and social commentary.

[20] Bellow said it was admirable of Grass to think of the South Bronx; he too thought of it.

dreamy reminiscence, was scarcely mentioned.

Then there's Updike. He has, as much as any well-known writer, insulated himself from the rare predicament of attack. He lives in small towns where he's the only writer of note, and he has published most of his work in a magazine which seldom prints letters of correction. In his few Congressional hours, you could see him sniffing out positions that would pacify his attackers. He was not throwing in the ideological towel; his "ideology" was not a political or social position but the beauty of expression. His talk was a lyric pledge of allegiance to the "tribe" in which he'd grown. Its totems were the stars and stripes, the eagle, and, especially, the postal system, represented by the blue mailbox in which he sent off his stories and the kind, uniformed postman who brought back the delighted responses and checks which supported him. Challenged by Enzensberger, Updike's counter was a gentle retraction: "The Nation-State might be on the way out...It's done a lot of harm." The retraction was not made less attractive by stammer and blush.

The boyishness of many gifted writers—especially writers who grow up in reasonably tranquil worlds—has much to do with the past they celebrate in their work. The greatest of such writers, Marcel Proust, always seems to be the same age. The writer and the boy are one: eager for experience and the words which fix it, yet almost simultaneously nostalgic for it. At seventy, Bellow has much of this quality, and, at fifty-four, Updike was acquiring more of it. As he opened himself more and more to his real past rather than the lyric gemmification which substituted for it in his earlier work—every grass-blade and gonadal croak heavy with lyric jewelry—his stories and essays have become finer and truer. (The beautiful account of his psoriasis which appeared in *The New Yorker* the spring before the congress is one of his most beautiful essays.)

11

There might have been another reason for Updike's blushes, one

Then he said, with what *Time*'s reporter, R.Z. Sheppard, called "patient grace":

"I was simply saying the philosophers of freedom of the 17th and 18th centuries provided a structure which created a society by and large free, by and large an example of prosperity. I did not say there are no pockets of poverty."

(R.Z. Sheppard, *Time* {27 Jan. 1986}: 77.) Bellow's private response—the next morning at breakfast—referred Grass, rather roughly, to *The Dean's December* (a novel, not a book of opinion).

which also explained the brevity and relative invisibility of his stay. For years now, he's been publishing criticism. Many Congress authors bore the welts of his attention. Of Kobo Abe's *Secret Rendezvous*, Updike wrote that it "is all plastic and aluminum, a shiny mess from its dust jacket in."[21] About Grass' *The Meeting at Telgte*, he said it was "a lead paperweight" (HTS, p. 475); about *The Flounder* that, instead of a plot, it had "a welter of programs," "what happens when a novelist performs every service for us but his intrinsic one of rendering events" (HTS, pp. 478, 480).[22]

Bellow, too, carried an Updikean welt (though Updike made it clear that Bellow is not just "a very good writer" but—this with some reluctance—a great one) (HTS, p. 263). Still, he clearly relished showing up "the hollowness" of *The Dean's December*. As for Susan Sontag, the Updike flick was our "glamorous camp follower of the French avant-garde" (HTS, p. 577).

In short, Updike was treading on glass (and Grass) he had broken and scattered over *The New Yorker* and collected in *Hugging the Shore*.

12

The writers who had been most described, photographed, and—usually—bought were composed of their critical welts as well as their creative wealth. Bellow had bashed—as well as been bashed by—Updike, Grass bashed Bellow, Bellow Grass. Many of us had reviewed each other's works in and out of print.

But writers had also praised each other, were indeed more than anyone else the promoters of each other's celebrity. Susan Sontag was the most lavish praiser. She distributed it like a Commissar.[23] She called her pal Nadine Gordimer "the greatest novelist in English" and her pal Elizabeth Hardwick "a great artist." Hardwick, herself a champion Commissar of Praise and Blame, a member of more lit-

---

[21] John Updike, *Hugging the Shore: Essays and Criticism* (New York, 1983), p. 741; hereafter abbreviated *HTS*. 1993. There's a new collection, *Odd Jobs*, equally brilliant and—often—beautiful.

[22] Updike can't get enough Grass-bashing. In Grass's *Headbirths*; or, *The Germans are Dying Out*, he saw "a novelist who has gone so public he can't be bothered to write a novel; he just sends dispatches to his readers from the front lines of his engagement" (*HTS*, PP. 482-83).

[23] Nadia Mandelstam describes Maxim Gorki's allocation of clothes to writers. Her husband, Osip, received a new shirt, but Gorki felt his poetry wasn't worth a new pair of pants. Cf. page 293 below.

erary award committees than any writer in America, had not been ungenerous to Sontag: "Susan Sontag . . . the name is a resonance of qualities, of quality itself . . . an extraordinarly beautiful, expansive, and unique talent."[24]

So the Congress was to a degree a meeting of statues sculpted and defaced by each other. Even those of us who felt outside the pantheon could be gratified and insulted.[25] Writers would say how much they loved this book or that, or, more generally—asking a writer directions to a john—one heard. "Aren't you X or Y?" or even "What a wonderful writer you are."[26] Off and on the platform, the writers were making and remaking each other. It was too intense, and that part of themselves which counted most—the place where alone they were dream-gods making up the worlds they wanted—sent warning signals to the public self: "Enough. Come home."

Thursday night there was a choice of four or five parties. One was given by Günter Grass's publishers to celebrate another edition of his book *The Flounder*. I didn't like the book, and though I rather liked Grass, he'd served himself up generously during the day; one didn't need him after hours. The Canadian ambassador was giving a party somewhere on the Avenue of the Americas, and *The New York Times*, which by now seemed the bank in which the Congress daily deposited itself, was giving a party at the New York Public Library. The party given by the National Arts Club in its headquarters on Gramercy Park sounded most appleaing.

I spoke to a Japanese in the lobby, a Mr. Sodie. He was going down there too. We went out in the cold night, walked down Fifth Avenue, then, failing to get a cab, over to Lexington. Mr. Sodie had written a best-seller, a biography of General MacArthur. On its strength, he'd been made a professor at one of Tokyo's two hun-

---

[24] Elizabeth Hardwick, Introduction to *A Susan Sontag Reader* (New York, 1982), p. ix. 1993. Sontag has been lavishly generous to my work, as well, at least in person.

[25] My old student, Bob Coover, had received a new novel of mine. "Still at it," he said, the only harsh note in an otherwise harmonious reunion, and, of course, the note I remember best.

[26] When I introduced myself to Doctorow, his eyes widened: "Richard Stern! You're famous." As peculiar a reaction as I've ever had, it came from the atmosphere of publicity we all breathed and all hated even as we participated in it. For so sensitive a man as Doctorow, the word probably just meant that someone he knew had read something of mine he liked; he, Doctorow, wanted to pass off a goody and get on with his errand.

[127]

dred universities. Now, at fifty-three, he planned to retire. Unfortunately, his next book, an account of Japanese-Americans who had returned to Japan—many to Hiroshima—before World War II, had not been a great success. "The bomb is a subject no Japanese wants to read about." In the cab we finally found, he told me his family name means "sleeve." "It comes from the mistress of a samurai from Hokkaido. Her shrine—our family shrine—is there."

The Arts Club is in one of the beautiful brownstones that surround Gramercy Park. It had belonged to Samuel Tilden, who's remembered for getting a larger popular vote than Rutherford B. Hayes in the election of 1876 and for leaving a fortune to what became the New York Public Library. His old house was aglow, servants circulated with trays of caviar and salmon, chicken and beef, champagne and glühwein. Coffee and tea were served from silver urns. I talked to the Spanish novelist Juan Benet, who looks like a tall Chester Conklin, the cross-eyed cop in the Keystone Comedies (except Benet isn't cross-eyed). He said he'd be glad to speak in French, German, Spanish, or English; we spoke in the only one in which I feel comfortable. A civil engineer, he'd begun writing during a period of intense boredom when he lived next to a dam whose construction he was supervising. He was now finishing a four-volume work. "What's it about?" I asked. That seemed to puzzle him. He said there wasn't much story.

"Who are the leading characters?"

Yes, he said, there were characters, but they weren't important.

No story and no characters. My face questioned the enterprise.

"It's about military engagements." The first engagement was based on a campaign of Stonewall Jackson, a general he much admired. Of couse, he'd transferred the locale to northern Spain.

"How so?"

"It's where my father's family comes from. My mother's Catalan."

"And you?"

"They met and married in Madrid. I was born there."

Who were the writers he liked?

Well, he didn't like Saul Bellow, who'd been on the panel with him the day before.

Ah, whom *did* he like? Well, he liked Thomas Bernhard, the Austrian writer, "the greatest German writer of our times." (Implied here, I thought, was criticism of Grass. Benet was not high on what surrounded him.) He also liked Beckett, and then he

[128]

liked one book by an American writer, Philip Roth. It was *Goodbye, Columbus.*

I couldn't make much literary sense out of this. I hadn't read much Bernhard,[27] but who was to say what canon makes sense for a writer? Now that I have looked at some of Benet's work, in particular the "novel" *Un Viaje de Invierno* (the title translates Schubert's *Die Winterreise*), I understand an alliance to the three advanced B's. Benet writes exhaustively about topography and minute variations in such small events as invitations to a party. The book covers next to no narrative ground of the sort my sort of writer traverses. What I read was not to my taste, although I did relish what seemed to my limited Spanish beautiful sentences and paragraphs. (Not much happens in Bernhard, but next to Benet he looks like John le Carré. In one of his stories, two men walk outside the theater: one hates the plays on which he has written a dissertation; the other loves them but won't go to a theater.)[28]

My old friend Betty Fussell appeared. I introduced her to Benet, who lit up, not, as it turned out, for Betty—though most men do light up for her—but for an extremely pretty, dark-haired woman. "This is my wife," he said warmly. (The popsicle had turned into a muffin.)

Across the room, surrounded by women, was the notorious critical assassin, John Simon. That afternoon at the drama session, he'd been roundly booed when he'd denounced the furious reader of the Women's Petition and prattled on about the aristocracy of art and the foolishness of sexual quotas. A rather charmingly terrible fellow, after a while you realize that he's worked up his fastidious fury to cover a lazy intelligence. In New York, though, well-phrased slander pays the rent and gets you girls. The only time we had met was with our then common agent, Lois Wallace, and my friend, the brilliant poet Eleanor Lerman. In the first minute, Simon flattered me by remembering that a page from a story of mine had been omitted from both the English and American versions of the book in which it had appeared; in the second, he was displaying excellent French to the waiter; in the fifth, he disparaged the body of the well-known dancer who was coming over to sleep with him that night. The disparagement was specific and colorful. Simon himself looks like an agreeable ship's steward and wears excellent

---

[27] I've read more now and do think he's one of the better Kafka-derivatives, a cousin of Peter Handke. 1993. Cf. below, p.249 ff.

[28] See Thomas Bernhard, "Zwei Erzieher," *Prosa* (Frankfurt, 1967), pp. 7-15.

suits which—a gossiper told me—were bought for him by a famous heiress. The same gossiper told me that his present companion was Alexandra Iles, the young woman who had been called back from Europe to testify against her former lover, Claus von Bülow. After our lunch in New York, I walked Eleanor back to her office. She said she didn't know if she could go to work, Simon had sickened her so, she felt she'd throw up. "I've never met a real woman-hater before."

13

One of the lines about the PEN Congress which was quoted sometimes straight, sometimes derisively, in quotation marks, was "the greatest collection of literary talent ever assembled."

There's no doubt that lots of talent gathered on Central Park South, but there was also a tremendous absence. In fact, absence became one of the Congress' unscheduled subjects. To a degree, of course, absence is always on PEN's agenda. One of the things it does best is call attention to mistreatment of writers, to their imprisonment and censure. At this meeting, the PEN Prison Committee announced that there were four hundred and fourteen writers in various jails around the world. (There was no higher certificate of their social importance than this.) The gentle and disheveled Heberto Padilla recited a list of his friends in Cuban jails, Adam Zagajewski a list of his colleagues in Polish jails. George Konrád, the Hungarian novelist, round, horn-rimmed, and professorial, said he'd just heard of a poet and actor who'd been jailed that week in Romania.

In a way, then, the writers in New York were the flesh extensions of imprisoned shadows. In my first New York hour, I waited for a St. Moritz elevator—funereally slow—with a man I first thought was Mario Vargas Llosa. This face, though, was more lined, the eyes recessive, less full of flash. In sleeveless sweater and tweed coat, the man resembled those lost-cause heroes Yves Montand plays in his political movies. He spoke Spanish in a quiet baritone to a young American who seemed to be his guide. Later, I saw his picture in a PEN newsletter. His name is Hiber Conteras. A university instructor, a Methodist minister, and a reporter, he'd been imprisoned in Uruguay from December 1976 to March 1985. Tortured, he managed in his prison years to write four novels and a collection of short stories. Five months after his release, his only

[130]

son, an agricultural laborer on a Nicaraguan cooperative, was killed by contras along with thirty-nine other volunteers. Conteras's presence was heavy with other people's absence.

There are different sorts of absence. In Africa, I'd met many writers and would-be writers. In Lomé, Kigali, Cotenu, and Freetown, they came up to me after talks. Some had copied their novels by hand in school notebooks; some had their papers searched by police; many had decided there was less point in writing than working for the government even if that made them censors of other writers. None of these writers was at the St. Moritz. (I'd guess our average age was fifty.) This meant that there were hundreds, even thousands of young writers, many of them first-rate, who were also absentees. If they were PEN members, they probably couldn't afford the dues and costs of a New York week.

Of course there were many established writers of the first rank who weren't there: Borges—dead in June 1986—and Beckett, Solzhenitsyn and Salinger, Pinter and Pynchon, Roth and Robbe-Grillet. There were very few French, Spanish, Italian, or Portuguese writers.

There were some McCarran-Walter absentees, writers who'd been refused entry to the United States in the past such as Graham Greene—who decided never to come again or—García Marquez who had been given a limited visa, which he rightly refused as degrading.[29] Eugène Ionesco, Tom Stoppard, and Wole Soyinka were male panelists who didn't show up. A panelist who came but stayed invisible was Jorge Amado, who arrived with a Brazilian bug that kept him in his St. Moritz room. (Perhaps that bug was the source of the Delegate Flu with which several of us left at the end of the week.)

As for the Soviet writers, Mr. Markov of the Writers' Union announced that they would have been contaminated by those "disseminators of hatred," the emigré writers who had fled the soft embrace of the east. (Apparently the Gorbachev thaw was up to melting missiles but not words.)

The American writer Toni Morrison spoke of still another sort of absentee. She said that she was here because "some black children got their brains shot out in the street all over this country" and had "the 'good fortune' to be televised."

---

[29] George Shultz had promised the writers that the United States would no longer use McCarran-Walter to bar anyone except "direct fomenters of subversion."

> I am a read writer (as opposed to an unread one) because of
> those children . . . Had I lived the life the State planned for me
> from the beginning . . . I would have lived and died in some-
> body else's kitchen, on somebody else's land, and never writ-
> ten a word.

The absent children were part of what earned Morrison the following salute in *Newsweek*:

> For sheer glibness, it was hard to beat the grandstanding
> gesture of black American writer Toni Morrison. Sporting an
> extravagantly wide-brimmed Caribbean sun hat, Morrison
> proclaimed that "at no moment of my life have I ever felt as
> though I were an American." The rhetorical excess prompted
> many to wonder whether some Western writers are perversely
> envious of the victims of true political repression.[30]

Sporting, extravagantly, proclaimed, rhetorical, excess, perversely.
Well, I don't know. Every speaker has his own form of rhetoric.
Was Mrs. Morrison lying? Wrong maybe, foolish perhaps, but for
me she was vivid and truthful. If she didn't feel *American*, who has
the right to question what it is to feel that one is American? Surely
writers who have suffered in the jails of other countries, who have
been censored, silenced, searched, pushed around, punched, and
starved, who have had wires wrapped around their gonads and
knives driven under their fingernails, have known what Mrs.
Morrison never knew; but she had knowledge, and her pains are as
authentic as theirs. South African writers can be told it's worse in
the Soviet Union, and perhaps Soviet writers in the Gulag can be
told that Auschwitz was worse. That isn't the point. Writers don't
deal in comparative misery. They write what they feel, and feelings
are not distributed along party lines. All right, dead is dead, and
publication and silence are very different. From there on, the writer,
in poems and stories, at any rate, can only tell what his imagination
tells him is powerful and right.

14

The lobbies of hotels in small American towns were places of
socializing and deal-making. What the exciting, dangerous streets

---

[30] David Lehman with Ray Sawhill, *Newsweek* (27 Jan. 1986): 60.

are to a kid from the projects, so the lobby is to the person Pascal condemned as a troublemaker, the one incapable of being alone in his own room. There were two main lobbies at the conference, or rather one lobby—at the St. Moritz—and a series of anterooms outside the Casino on the Park. These last rooms were used to distribute press releases, coffee, and water. After the sessions, panelists were interviewed there by reporters.

The St. Moritz lobby was small—a few square yards to the left of the entrance and a few more in a square around the bank of elevators between the information desk and the Café de la Paix. The smallness augmented the lobbiness. People *stood around* cheek to jowl with other people. Talk with strangers was a matter of friction; you were not being forward.

Grass was a constant lobbyist, surrounded by young Germans who either amplified or laughed at his remarks. Another was Joyce Carol Oates. She and her husband, Raymond Smith, were there in a space of their own. They talked to no one, no one talked to them. There was a vividness of abandonment about them. Oates herself is not vivid. If anything, she's the reverse. There are odd extrusions from her hunched thinness, a large Adam's apple, thick lips—darkened with lipstick when she appeared on a panel, but usually as colorless as the rest of her—immense, hyperthyroid dark eyes, usually screened by glasses, and a cap of light brown curls.[31] Despite the peculiarities, she seemed to aspire to invisibility.

Is this thrustlessness related to her extraordinary productivity? "Naturally, the woman's a rind," one tells oneself. "Every ounce of juice has gone into her work."

I'd never finished a novel of hers but was an admirer of many of her stories. I had read two-thirds of her novel *them*. It follows a group of people all of whom dream their way through life. The dreaming is punctuated by violence, shooting, robberies, assaults—none of which have consequences for the action. The murderers and robbers go undetected and spend very little time thinking about what they've done. You're immersed in the characters, but since they all think life's a dream and that nothing really exists or that what happens to them really counts, you begin to think this yourself. Why bother going on? You do go on though, half mesmerized, as the author seems to be, by the prosy rhythm of event-reporting. Now and then a real observation flashes through the paragraphs. Mostly

---

[31] [1993. Oates objected to the inaccuracy of this portrait. She's probably right, but these were my impressions and I leave them as they were.]

[133]

though, one drifts in the sullen—a favorite Oates word—experience of these submerged people.

A literary daughter of Theodore Dreiser, or better, James T. Farrell—who would not go to sleep till he'd written ten pages, the assemblage of which constitutes a cemetery of prose fiction—Oates writes as people eat and breathe. Perhaps that's why, standing in the lobby, she seemed so set apart, a creature from another medium. She gasped helplessly, away from the typewriter or dreaming space. It didn't appear as if she were observing anything or anyone, storing up notes for her current fiction; no, she was just there, a dutiful citizen of literature, perhaps waiting for a character to kidnap her, or for the ticket back home to the typewriter. We were all away from what counted most, but no one seemed further from there than Oates.

This is what I thought of Oates as I watched her. Then, back in Chicago, I read what she'd said to Claudia Dreyfuss about not signing the Women's Petition protesting the paucity of women at the Congress: "I really agree with you, but it's very complicated, and Norman's having such a difficult time that he's been in a difficult state all week. He worked very hard on this Congress, and I just can't sign."[32] A very decent refusal I thought, not at all the response of a martian or a human rind.

Then I read the last hundred pages of *them*, a section that begins with something that violated the Jamesian canon defined by Percy Lubbock.[33] The narrative is "interrupted" by letters to the author from the main character, whom the novel's preface has identified as one of Oates's ex-students. The letters to Oates are confessional, observant, resentful, and well written. They speak enviously of Ms. Oates's intelligence, wit, coolness, and love of books. The writer says she's seen Oates's husband drive her to school in a black Volkswagen. She envies this attentive love. For James/Lubbock, a novel was not supposed to lean on any reality but its own. The leaning destroys the aesthetic independence.

I usually feel as they do, but I admired the boldness of the device, especially when I saw what it did. It woke Oates, or at least the novel, up. Suddenly the book's fog is dispersed. In a few pages there's an intense and beautiful erotic scene. Nadine is twice brought to the edge of her erotic cell but left locked up there by Jules (through whom, oddly enough, we see the scene). The finale is

---

[32] Geoffrey Stokes, "When Words Collide: A Report from the PEN Congress," *Village Voice* (28 Jan. 1986): 54. Oates denies she said this.

[33] See Percy Lubbock, *The Craft of Fiction* (London and New York, 1921).

an eruption of violence, which unlike the deadened, meaningless, inconsequential violence of the book's first two-thirds, is consequential and powerful. Nadine shoots Jules—not quite to death—then shoots and wounds herself.

The next chapters are also vivid. Maureen falls in love with her English teacher. The affair is seen from his side as well as hers, and everything is clear and strong—as is the last key scene which follows the characters as they participate in or witness the 1967 Detroit riots. The novel is light years beyond the banality and dreamfog of its beginnings.

My view of Oates was turned around. The drained pallor of the woman in the lobby looked in retrospect like a sort of grandeur, the grandeur of literary and human knowledgeability. That she may be a sort of Simenon, a captive of graphomania, I don't know and don't care. Although I've read nothing else of hers that's come close to the last third of *them*, I've read enough (of *Marya, A Life*, and many fine stories and essays) to salute her artistry.

Usually one sees readers in lobbies, even in lobbies as small and poorly furnished with chairs and sofas as the St. Moritz's. In the Congressional week, I never saw a writer reading in the lobby. Indeed, I only remember one writer carrying a book. (It was the Flemish writer Paul Koecke. He carried a French translation of one of his novels.) I didn't even realize this peculiarity until I was checking out the last day. A new group was moving into the hotel: The Cracow Philharmonic Orchestra. While some members waited by elevators with cased horns and fiddles, others sat down and opened books. How fine to see that. (The Roman proverb about religion occurred to me: "Here we manufacture and distribute the faith which they believe elsewhere.")

15

Three moments with which to festoon the last Congressional morning (too unimportant to be events, too undramatic to be scenes). The first took place outside, the second within, and the third as a sort of adjunct to the Congress.

The first was close to a scene. It took place in Sutton's Café. A black waitress was slamming down plates, spilling coffee, responding harshly to customer's requests. A man complained to the boss who shouted at the waitress. Two other customers drummed orders at her, the jungle assault on weakened prey. She put down my coffee cup wearily, defeated.

On Central Park South, the Casino was full. A young woman
handed out a list of books the Israelis had censored (the first was on
Kuwaiti poetry). I found a seat in the front row beside the very tall
and lovely Alexandra Schlesinger. Up on the dais were three retired
statesmen, Pierre Trudeau, George McGovern and Bruno Kreisky.
In the center was the moderator, Arthur Schlesinger, to his right,
Frances FitzGerald. At one end was Kurt Vonnegut; at the other a
man not named in the program. Mrs. Schlesinger asked who it was;
I didn't know. Her husband came off the dais and she asked him; he
didn't know. Neither did Rose Styron, who said she'd find out.
Whatever looking harmless means, he looked it: an elderly white-
haired and mustached gentleman in a light brown sport coat and
bow tie.

Back on the platform, Schlesinger said the imagination of the
state was a Hegelian notion which Anglo-Saxons reject. Americans
varied in their views of the state. Thoreau called it "that semi-human
tiger . . . with the tip of its brain shot away"; Emerson was cozier:
"The state is our neighbor." Schlesinger quoted the famous sentence of Solzhenitsyn about the writer being a state within a state,
and another of John Kennedy. (Or had *he* quoted Robert Frost?)
"Poetry is a means of saving power from itself." I asked Mrs.
Schlesinger if her husband had written it for the President. She
didn't know.

Tanned and vigorous, Trudeau spoke briefly in French and
English. (It was hard to imagine him *en retraite.* Do leopards
retire?) He could not imagine why PEN imagined that the state, "a
legal abstraction, not an anthropomorphic creature," had an imagination. "Why do writers imagine they have no power? Paranoia?"
He quoted Czeslaw Milosz: "I don't believe in the necessary
estrangement of the writer from the state" and Kofi Awooner:
"Writers should seek to create a new state. If we turn away from this
task, we've failed." His last citation was from Plato's *Laws:* "The
price of not being involved in government is that we're governed by
those less worthy than ourselves."

Frances FitzGerald spoke next. I'd seen her only once before, an
occasion I remember clearly because an hour or so after we said
good night, Robert Kennedy was shot to death in a California hotel.
(She and Arthur Schlesinger had just been with him in California.)
I'd found her attractive and modeled a minor character in a novel on
her. Her remarks here were ragged and poorly delivered. They had
to do with the aesthetics of the state and were bolstered by allusions
to Bali—"where there's no word for 'art' because everything is

art"—and to Ryszard Kapucinski's remark that the fall of Haile Selassie was a form of art.

Then Schlesinger introduced George McGovern as the first historian since Guizot to play a major role in government. (Unlike Churchill, McGovern has a PhD!) McGovern cited dictionary definitions of imagination; he too didn't see that the state could have one. He cited Gordimer and Mailer.³⁴ McGovern praised the author of *The Naked and the Dead* and said he wished he'd been elected mayor of New York. Unfortunately, voters hadn't been imaginative enough. They rejected Mailer as they later rejected McGovern. Looking at Trudeau and Kreisky, he said Canadians and Austrians had been more imaginative. Studying Reagan, he longed for Nixon and Johnson. (I thought of Chekhov's "Old Age" in which two bitter enemies fall weeping into each other's arms at the grave of the woman who was one man's wife, the other's mistress.)

Schlesinger came down again to ask Rose Styron if the mystery man had been identified. Back on stage, he went over to confer with him. The man nodded, left the chair, and went into the audience.

It was Vargas Llosa's turn. In tattered, charming English, he said that the writer in totalitarian states is reduced to being either a courtesan or a dissident. In other societies, his problem was how *not* to become ambassador or minister of state. In countries which pay serious attention to writers, they're frequently arrested. In countries like the United States, writers feel they're simply entertainers. As for literature, it's made of contradictions and expresses what a community suppresses; this is its social function, and it's why, for a writer, obsessions are more important than ideas.³⁵

No one looked less obsessed than this handsome man, with his cream-and-coffee skin, healthy nose and ears, and smiling white teeth. In his blue and white striped shirt and blue and red striped tie, he seemed a sartorial version of the writer's Congressional self,

---

³⁴ The self-reference of the Congress was like instant nostalgia, the sort of thing television does as it bundles bits of time away to create the feeling of great emotional experience. It's what great art succeeds in doing.

³⁵ Writers who speak of "drives" and "obsessions" have probably lost their own. After a wonderful fifteen years—from the remarkable adolescent stories of *Los jefes* through *La ciudad y los perros* and *La casa verde* to the brilliant shiftiness of *Conversacíon en la cathedral*—Vargas Llosa seems to have settled for charm, wit, and technical intelligence. When he turned down the invitation to become President of Peru, the temptation was to borrow from Satie (on *La mer*): "He refused the invitation but his books accepted it." A second unresisted temptation (some words from Leopoldo Alas's beautiful story *Doña Berta*): "la llosa...a certain kind of corn-producing lowland." [1993. This is too harsh. I talked a bit with Vargas Llosa in Valencia (in 1987, shortly before he decided to run for the presidency of Peru, which, luckily for literature, he lost) and found him brilliant and delightful.]

the unsuppressed, visible expression of passionate health.

Beside him, balding, bearded, big-nosed, and eyeglassed, Kreisky looked like one of Walt Disney's dwarfs. He'd spent years in dictators' prisons, but since, had been in government twenty-six years. He began with "different ideas about the state, Plato's, Marx's," and went on to a history of "successful terrorists"—De Valera, Begin, Shamir, Kenyatta. Now and then, he addressed his fellow panelists: "Isn't that so? Don't we think this?" He wandered into American politics: he'd known all the presidents since Truman. The audience was stirring. Was the man senile? Or was this the insolence of powerful men who don't have to consider the feelings of their audience? Whatever, the talk undermined Kreisky's obvious intelligence and Viennese Gemütlichkeit. Length was a desire to dominate, and one suspected that it stood for decline, as the huge Austrian novels of Musil, Broch, and von Doderer seemed to compensate for the shrinkage of the Austro-Hungarian empire. In a way, this gentle, interesting, and useful man embodied the vanity which scarred the whole conference.[36]

Kreisky called across to Trudeau. "We've been invited because they need victims." My thought was, "Is this why he's making victims of us?" Even Coleridge's insistent mariner stopped only one of three. Kreisky had hundreds under his endless tongue. Finally, he ended: "Excuse the length of my speech, but I've come a long way."

Now it was Vonnegut's turn. His was one of the most familiar faces in the room, lined and gentle, despite its Mongolian mustache and bush of grey-black curls. Vonnegut said that he'd been an enlisted man, and like all enlisted men hated officers. The state was not a friend of enlisted men. Norman Mailer understood this too. So did Claude Simon who, like Vonnegut, had been a prisoner in Stalag 43.

> My section was a mini-state: 150 men. I was elected to divide up the loaves of bread and soup into a hundred equal portions. There were no scales. If I'd given bigger portions to my friend, that would have been "the imagination of the state" . . . I was allowed to report five sick men a day. If I decided that

---

[36] "In brief, we all were clerks and men of worth,
  great men of letters, scholars of renown;
  all by the one same crime defiled the earth."

Dante Alighieri, *Inferno* [trans. John Ciardi] 15. 106-8. In the *Inferno* the sin was homosexuality; here it was the desperate need for gifted men to be seen and heard.

my friends were sick, that would have been "the imagination
of the state."

It was witty, strong, but, like Vonnegut's charming and fanciful
books, it was a bit snarled in fancy.

Vonnegut wound things up officially, but the Congress's final
platform speaker turned out to be the unprogrammed mystery man.
He made his way from the audience and sat where he'd sat before,
at Trudeau's right. Schlesinger, who'd obviously made this arrangement with the man, now introduced him: "The distinguished
Italian novelist, Mario Soldati." Soldati began by explaining that
he'd been prevented from reading remarks he'd prepared for another session because of his wife's illness. He'd spent most of the last
four days by her side in a New York hospital. Luckily, she was well
enough now so that he could attend this session. We would not be
deprived of his remarks.

I had actually seen Soldati before. Perhaps if he'd looked as he'd
looked at the Congress on Translation held in Rome in 1982, I
would have recognized him. There too he'd sat up front, but not in
the elegant jacket and slacks he sported now, but in a red shirt, sus-
penders, and orange tie pulled down below the unbuttoned top button of the shirt. He'd both spoken and interjected loudly and comically, and when others spoke, he was still conspicuous, head
thrown back, snores filtering through his thick mustache. He'd left
that Congress early, off, he told us, to Spain to cover the World Cup
for *La Repubblica*.[37] Caught up in the games myself, I read some
of his articles. They were full of Soldati's classical and contemporary learning, his recollections of life in Spain, and, occasionally,
sharp and amusing observations about the games themselves.

That this "distinguished novelist," journalist, commentator, con-
ference-attender, learned and graceful speaker of three or four languages, and man of letters in the European tradition was generally
unrecognized in this congress of his peers may well have been the
fact that drove him to this unbilled takeover of the dais.

Recognition. Only the world's most flamboyant writers are recognized internationally, at least recognized in the American
Express Card sense of that work. Our Congress had dealt with
imagination in the larger meaning of the word, the one provided by

---

[37] 1987. See Soldati's *Ah! Il mundial: Storia dell'inaspettabile* (Milan, 1986), a packet of
reflections about these Spanish weeks, one of the tiny volumes this unclottable septuagenarian emits every other solstice or two. [1993. Soldati died a year or two ago.]

Coleridge and the German writers from whom he borrowed. Soldati came from the most *spectacular*, the most *visualizing*, the most image-dominated country in the world. Perhaps that sharpened his hunger for visual recognition. For astronomers, the stars are not primarily a visual phenomenon, but for the rest of us they are. To be a *star* would be a vulgarity for most of the people in this room, and yet vulgarity meant the appetite and response of the *crowd*, and that was important to many here. Literature had lost much of the appeal it had had in the nineteenth century to much of that crowd. It had lost it to new forms of "visual literature," to movies and television. The better-known writers here made brief appearances on television programs, occasionally in the news, more frequently in the three-and four-minute snippets of interview shows where they were quickly compounded into the tasteless cake of politics, sports and the day's sensations which people took in with their morning coffee.

It was fitting, then, that Soldati concluded the official business of the Congress. Unrecognized, unbilled, out of sequence, "Off-Program," skirting the border of tolerance and outrage, he treated us to his recollection of his first visit to New York forty or fifty years ago. It was charming, it was irrelevant, it was relevant. Kreisky had wearied the audience past endurance; Soldati mystified us, threw us off balance, charmed us. He'd now been seen and heard as well as read. He was up in the spotlight with his equals, and when he finished, the Congress was finished.

There was still, though, a little mopping up to be done, and that was done by the media. Between the dais and the first row where I sat was a cushion of photographers and people with microphones and tape recorders. They were slouching on the floor, from which they occasionally got up to take a picture. One, a tall, blond fellow in blue jeans and jacket, looked familiar to me. Once we even exchanged a nod. After Schlesinger gaveled the end of the Congress, he came up to me. "I'm Eike," he said. "Do you remember me?"

"Of course," I said, shaking hands with him. "But you've lost weight or something. How are you doing?"

Though I remember now from letters he'd written my wife that he wasn't doing all that well. He'd gone back to Germany, where he'd grown up, to be with his dying grandmother who'd raised him. She'd died and he'd come back to New York to find out he'd lost his job at Cooper Union where he'd taught journalism. In addition, the people to whom he'd rented his apartment wouldn't leave, and he was scared of making a fuss about it because the immigration people were giving him trouble with his green card. He was afraid he'd be deported and wouldn't be able to get back. He'd always suffered from migraine headaches, but they'd never been so frequent or prolonged.

One didn't have to look far to trace the source of those headaches. Eike Gebhart had been born in Berlin in 1945. His father was an officer in Rommel's African army. Captured, interned in Tripoli, and then escaped in a British officer's coat, he'd made his way back to his regiment and joined Rommel's army in western France. There, days before the end of the war, he'd been killed. In the ruins of Berlin, Eike's mother got the terrible word. She took the service revolver her husband had given her to protect herself and shot Eike's older, three-year-old brother to death, shot Eike in the head, and then killed herself. Hours later, her mother made her way up the stairs and found this horrible scene. Baby Eike was still breathing. She got him to the hospital and brought him home and raised him.

"What are you doing here?" I asked him.

"I'm sending back reports to German radio. It's enough to get by on. I have to rush off and make this last press conference. Can we meet later?"

"Sure," I said, and we shook hands without specifying a time or place.

Eike was a person of considerable intellect, widely read in several languages, and a fluent—sometimes too fluent—critic in three or four of them. He was part of that indispensable bridge between the high, often remote, sometimes chilling, sometimes absurd intelligence of the best writers and the many thousands, in fact millions, who didn't even guess how much they required them to reinvigorate, re-enchant, and reinterpret their lives, their world. From the ashes of the Great War on that intelligence, Eike had been almost miraculously rescued. He functioned now in the sensational world, but in a pocket where something other than life's small change jingled.

I think we will run into each other. He might well be at a Congress in Valencia to commemorate the one held there fifty years ago as Spain collapsed in the first act of the war which ended a few days after Eike was picked up by his grandmother from the bloody crib of the Berlin apartment house.

[141]

The correspondent for Spain's El País wrote that the PEN Congress ended "on the same political note on which it began and with the conviction that the imagination and the state are valores antagónicos" *(Jan. 20, 1986). I suppose that's as good a way to close the file as any. No boys fell burning out of the sky; there were no major triumphs or devastating humiliations. As for "political," though, El País hadn't seen anything. After the* Congreso Internacional de Intelectuales y Artistas *(held a year and a half later in Valencia), its correspondent asked "Why is it that it is only at a conference of intellectuals that one sees violent confrontations?" Yes, there in Valencia under the hot glass of the new* Palau de la Música i Congressos *(its concrete still bled), enraged students accused famous anti-Franco fighters of being "bourgeois toadies." Graybeards tore off their coats and squared off with young opponents; Octavio Paz, the Congress President, interposed and saved a few bloody noses. The next day I sat beside a student who'd taped an X across his face.*

A delightful, very different congress. Of the 200 participants, I think only Vargas Llosa, Hans Buch and I had been at PEN. (Expert congressmen, they are: I watched each work his way through a packed audiorium to a front row to be in position to make the statements they made after almost every session.) Eike wasn't there, but one met lots of other admirable people over the Hotel Jaime I's paella and the dinners given by Valencia's Generalität. I particularly enjoyed Kjartan Fløgstad, the Norwegian novelist, who, despite years in Lapland with his doctor wife, was up on all the political over- and undertones to which I was deaf; the charming Iraqi poet Saadi Yousif, author of How Did l'Akhar Ben Yousif Write His New Poem. *(The large many-nationed Arab contingent was exceptionally amiable and far more—politically—moderate than many of the North and South Americans and Europeans.) Others were Walter Janka, a Civil War hero of a book by Jorge Semprun (one of the challenged anti-Franco exiles); Rosa Chacel, a ninety-year-old Spanish novelist who had a volume or two to go on a tetralogy; Danny Cohn-Bendit, the famous Red Danny of the French barricades (of 1968), a hero of the students and a charmer in several languages; Agnes Heller, Ferenc Fehér and André Schiffrin from New York (via Budapest and Paris); Abraham Moles, the French polymath who explained fractals and chaos theory to me on table cloths; Stephen Spender and Octavio Paz; Jorge Edwards, the Chilean writer-diplomat whose portrait of Fidel is funnier than any I've read (though I can't find or remember the name of his memoir); and—but I must stop a list which testifies to the joy of the company, the fellowship and the hospitality of Valencia.*

[III]

THINKING ABOUT FICTION

[14]

INSIDE NARCISSUS

"Inside Narcissus" was written for a Princeton lecture in 1976 (I think). I remember rewriting it on that Toonerville train from Princeton Station, and revising as I spoke. Few noticed. (Few were there.) When I gave it next—at Johns Hopkins—I rewrote it again. In the two years between its acceptance (by Yale Review*) and its publication, much pertinent matter came my way.* Yale Review *used no footnotes, so the published text looked like a belly pregnant with sextuplets. In any event, the essay came out of and reflects exhaustion. (In 1976 I was worn down either by writing or suffering* Natural Shocks.*)*

The Narcissus portion of the essay is rooted in an old enchantment with Horace Gregory's superb translation of Ovid's Metamorphoses. *I'd read a bit of the original in 1951 when I exchanged Latin for English lessons with a graduate student at the University of Frankfurt. I wasn't doing too well, partly because of a cortical obtundity in the linguistic section of the brain, partly because I was simultaneously exchanging English for Italian lessons with a barber at the Frankfurt Military Exchange Post. The point of the Italian was not only to read Dante but to get a job in Rome. My tutor helped me write a long plea to the Personnel Officer in Rome. I delivered this telephonic monologue; it met with an incomprehensible response for which the only Italian I could manage was, "I can't hear you; the connection's poor." I did not call back. Which ended not only a Roman career but my Italian and Latin lessons. The Frankfurt assignment (teaching illiterate soldiers for Troop Information and Education) was over, and we sailed home.*

When I got my first full-time teaching job in 1954 (at Connecticut College in New London), I taught a bit of Ovid and translated lines 243-69 of Book 10 of the Metamorphoses *for the class. Since the passage (and the episode from which it's taken) embodies a theme of this book, I print it here:*

Pygmalion, who had watched whores thrive,
Shrank from such vice and would not wive,
Carved, instead, out of some snowy stone,
A woman free from all defect and stain.
His statue seems to breathe, seems to desire,
As if 'twere modesty alone restrained its fire.
So art hides art, and so Pygmalion loves
This semblance of life which almost lives.
Often his hand moves on his work to try
Whether its stuff be flesh or ivory,
Will not admit the last, but, with a kiss,
Kindles in stone, he thinks, responsive bliss.
He speaks to it, grasps it, seems to think
His fingers bruise where in the flesh they sink.
He courts it now with gifts and gallantries,
Smooth stones and speech, tears from the Heliades,
Shells, lilies, small birds, gems,
A necklace round its throat, silk on its limbs.
Adorned, it's beautiful, unadorned, the same.
He lays it on a couch on quilts of flame,
Rests its head on pillows soft as air,
He thinks it relishes the softness there.

INSIDE NARCISSUS

A modern life which is productive or peculiar is a kind of license to explain itself. Who isn't delighted by such explanation? Poets, politicians, muggers or musicians who won't supply their inside stories look as if they're trying to put something over on us. Magic is okay for kids, but the rest of us need truth; and not just the cover truths distributed to the naive, but the truths behind the truths.

Every fundamental particle appears to contain more fundamental ones, so every inside story has its story. In the Age of Openness, this story is what we require. For us, the hidden is sinister, perhaps criminal. (Real criminals serve up their careers along with all other self-sellers.)

The wonderful result is that we know more about thousands of remarkable people—many remarkable because they've been remarked—than people in epochs of discretion knew about their neighbors, their kings, and, in a way, themselves.

Knowledge of others promotes self-knowledge. It is a democratic and technological glory that millions of human beings are more

[148]

sensitive to their specialness than all but the pharaohs and poets of darker ages. Democracy and mass media require a sense of individuality in their participants. A collective "you" is broadcast, but in reception it is singular. (Individuals, not collectives, buy detergents.) Technology has democratized the apparatus of commemoration: Instamatics harvest billions of smiles, tape recorders as many babbles. These fill parochial annals. Official files are stuffed with equivalent information. Pollsters sample opinions, archives store the whorls of a billion pinkies.

So scrupulously observed, sifted, recorded, who could resist caring for himself? Who could help becoming a narcissist?[1]

The literature of narcissism climbs every molehill of the inner landscape. No quirk too quirky, no wound too foul, no encounter too repellent for exhibition.

Old portraits were indicted for omitting warts; contemporary portraits are often rashes of them beneath which one tries to discern features. Want your portrait painted? Your biography written? Better come up with a new and better wart. (The odor of glue rises from quite a lot of innocent flesh.)

Honesty, frankness, authenticity, nothing up the sleeve. With our history, who can fault such mottoes? Abandon cover, ye who enter modernity.

Until that emperor of concealment, Richard Nixon, signed a bill which helped depose him, even the government subsidized self-exhibition in the form of tax write-offs for donated diaries, notebooks, letters, early drafts, the pencils which wrote them, the sharpeners which sharpened them.

The materials of self-revelation have altered not only conceptions of creation but creations themselves. They also alter the lives of the creators.

More and more, makers and doers understand that part of their responsibility is to supply the "story of their story."[2] After all, better arrange your own show on a wide screen than discover peephole versions of it sold in porn shops. Better donate to libraries than have your garbage sifted, bugs put in your martini olives.

So makers and doers become their own specialists, their own voyeurs.

A few antique types believe art should conceal not only itself but the life behind it. Like James and Hardy, they burn papers; like

---

[1] I don't employ-or discount-the psychoanalytic specificity, libidinal egoism.

[2] This adapts Henry James's phrase.

Auden and Eliot, they forbid biographies; like Joyce, they warn wives to keep letters secret; like Shakespeare, they warn posterity off their bones. The results of such injunctions are well-known. No one is more observed, more hungered after than the reluctant self-exhibitor. These creators are concealed somewhere in the biblio-graphical continents named after them.

About 1975, I read an interview (in the *Chicago Daily News*) with one of these reluctant dodos, Philippe Petit, the funambulist who walked the air between the towers of the World Trade Center. He began the interview by remembering one given after that feat: "I was speechless when they asked me why I did it. Would you ask a kid why he climbed a tree?" No longer speechless—self-revelation is addictive—Petit went on to explain: "I did it because I like to climb. I like to feel fresh air and see the world from an unusual angle. I like to be alone and that's it." Even so decent a statement wasn't quite it. Petit came back to a position of security: "I think if we accepted more things without asking why, life would be a bit more interesting." Maybe, but even in Eden, half the human population didn't feel that way.

Petit is, however, on to something. Talking from the uneasy perch of the highwire performer, he sensed the peril of abusing his insider's privileged position. The performer or creator may contain the inside story, but can he publicize it? Can he know it himself? If Petit were to analyze his motivations and muscle tensions while walking the highwire, it would likely be his last analysis. His very advantage would be his problem. (According to Ovid, Narcissus said, "Since I am what I long for, then my riches are so great, they make me poor.")

There is one maker who is driven to narcissism by his occupation. This is the writer.

As athletes use their bodies, writers use their feelings, their insights, their fantasies, and, sometimes, the very events, the very shape and feel of their lives. Charged with revealing the world, the writer has learned that the world he reveals is conditioned by his way of observing it, and this by his feelings. (This last is not true of the physicist.) Many writers, therefore, have devoted themselves to self-examination and the exhibition of what Augustine called "the abysses of human consciousness."

Centuries before Augustine, Horace praised his satiric predecessor Lucilius for laying out his whole life "as if it were painted on a votive tablet." It was, though, not till the late sixteenth century that a writer claimed that he wrote because he knew nothing special but himself. Montaigne puzzled over his self-assignment. "Is it reasonable," he asked, "that I, so fond of privacy in actual life, should aspire to publicity in the knowledge of me?" He decided that this contradiction, like all others, was integral to his enterprise, which was revealing all of himself (*mon être universel*), or at least as much as decorum or caution allowed. "I speak the truth, not my fill of it, but as much as I dare speak."

"I want to know myself," Socrates told Phaedrus, a momentous conversion of the knower into the object of knowledge. "Knowlege cannot know the knower," goes an earlier text (from the Vedas), and many others describe obstacles to Socratic satisfaction. "I never can catch myself without a perception and can never observe anything but the perception," wrote Hume in his *Treatise on Human Nature*. Psychoanalysis describes hundreds of ways human beings hide from themselves.

How deal with such obstacles to observation of the interior? Physicists construct delicate enormities to register indirect effects; writers too have, over centuries, developed instruments of analysis and exhibition of the whirling interior. Varieties of lyric, hierarchies of illusion—plays within plays, tales within novels—soliloquies, letters, dramatic and interior monologues, fragmentation of narrative, passion-altered chronology, all are attempts to get hold of the flux.

Eighteenth-century fiction writers were almost as conscious of their instruments as twentieth-century ones of theirs. Richardson said of the letters in *Clarissa* that they "are written while the hearts of the writers must be supposed to be wholly engaged on their subject. . . so that they abound not only in critical situations, but with what may be called instantaneous descriptions and reflections." (This epistolary technique was adopted, altered, parodied, and dropped until picked up again with variations in such novels as *Wake Up, Stupid* and *Herzog*.)

Fine books survive the techniques of presentation in the amber of literary perspective, the literary equivalent of the "museum without walls."

Interior analysis has a similar trajectory. We enjoy Clarissa and Lovelace although we know that much of what they think would not be thought by anyone we know. Analysis alters as it records ever-odder reactions to ever more minute and eccentric sensations and events. This doesn't mean that novels, memoirs, or human beings are improving. It means only that good novelists don't repeat their predecessors and also that people take stock of more and more peculiar reaction. Lovelace is a complicated fellow, but much simpler than Julien Sorel; Julien is crystal clear next to Stavrogin, and Stavrogin is but part of what the narrators of Proust or *Dr. Faustus* or *Humboldt's Gift* eat for breakfast.

Each large advance into the interior abyss makes the old charts obsolete, and usually it bewilders even the best readers. So fine a one as Erich Auerbach said of the complex fiction of his own time—which he brilliantly described—that there was "often something confusing, something hazy" about it. The works "leave the reader with an impression of hopelessness." Auerbach attributed the "hopelessness" to authorial sentiment, but to those who today read *Ulysses* as a work of essentially serene comedy, the "hopelessness" belongs more to Auerbach's bewilderment at the new interior map than to the novel.

It is, I think, in part because the demand for analysis grew so much that fiction writers either bypassed it altogether or drew increasingly on their own experience. Despite the limits on self-knowledge, despite the dangers of self-exhibition, a writer at least felt confident about his feelings. If his memory were distorted, that wouldn't damage his fiction. If anything, it stood for strong feeling—which is what counts most. Narrative energy, working on memory, is likely to rouse more powerful feeling than when it works on less intimate material. In any event, it justifies an excavation which often has serious personal consequences for the excavator and those he digs up with his old self. It may be awareness of such consequences (as well as general disgust at any narcissistic display) which lies behind derogations of autobiographical writing. Montaigne complained about the complaints that he spoke too much about himself. Complaints today are more elaborate. Analytic literature—it's said—belongs to a class-ridden time of self-confidence in which bourgeois authors ignore their limitations and claim omniscience. These critics say modern fiction should be more modest, less direct. Like the sciences, it should reveal its apparatus with its findings.[3] Program notes should accompany, even substitute for the old-time main event.[4]

---

[3] Gide's *Les Faux-Monnayeurs* is a famous example of exhibiting the apparatus, a sort of playing peek-a-boo-with-your-mirror.

[4] Nathalie Sarraute's *Les fruits d'or* is an example of such substitution. It's made up of talk about a book.

Roland Barthes distinguishes between "writers," those who invent, and "those who write," that is, those who use the "prefabricated" material of their lives or the world. A case can be made that most literary matter is prefabricated—conventions of presentation, syntax, diction—but the Barthes distinction animates many a charge leveled at self-exhibition.

The anti-personal weapon which most affected my apprentice years was T.S. Eliot's famous injunction to be as disengaged from one's work as a chemical catalyst from the compound it catalyzed. Since young writers tend to go at the typewriter the way birds go at the air, making territorial claims of uniqueness with more or less tuneful bellyaching and brio, my writing pals and I were glad to turn ourselves into Sam Spades of the street, tailing our *données* to narrative connections, and dispatching them efficiently. Young Joyce didn't need more than a look at a priest's face—or a clock's—to take off; neither did we.[5]

The harshest critics of autobiographical fiction are often whose who've just finished writing it. It's not so much "Why did I do it?" as "Thank God, that's over. Never again. I've had it. What relief. From now on, I'll write about the first thing that comes into my head."

Many writers do follow autobiographical works with very different ones, satires, travel books, utopian fictions, or short stories full of distant matter. At least, most of the writers I know tell themselves—or me—that this is what they're going to write. And they—we—may cover lots of pages about, say, the deaf janitor and his pet wolf. Such pages seldom turn into books. They don't "sound right." The writer tries different "voices," different angles, different ways of telling the story. One day he hits on a way that seems to go. The book takes off and, a few years later, comes out. The writer gets the reviews and reads, "Here's another piece of Krumbacher's pretty carpet." Or, "Why doesn't old Krumbacher try something new?" It's like the Borges story of the artist who painted an immense landscape of brooks, mountains, and meadows which

---

5 Years after discarding the poet's chemical advice, it was still a bit of a shock to read that he hadn't been the literary dandy we'd thought. At least, of his most famous poem, he'd said that it was only "the relief of a personal and wholly insignificant grouse against life. . . . a piece of rhythmical grumbling." Would Einstein claim that relativity theory was a piece of mathematical distemper? Was the Declaration of Independence only Jefferson's grouse about taxes on Monticello?

turned out to be a self-portrait.

Many fine fiction writers would be wiped out if they were prevented from using their own experience for their books. Isaac Babel told an interviewer, "I can't make anything up. I have to know everything down to the last wrinkle or I can't even begin to write." One of the splendors in Bellow's work is the suggestion that there's an infinite amount to say about his characters. They're like the pictures of Van Eyck in which you at least believe that if you took a magnifying glass to a tiny figure in some background gathering, you'd be able to identify which king's head adorned the medallion on his coat. In Bellow's books there is the same sense of totality. The pages gleam with observations about the flesh, the voice, the eyelids, the odors, the gestures and expressions of the characters. Bellow told me that he needs real people in mind as a kind of sea from which to draw the endless detail which his narrative makes coherent.

A hundred years ago, Henry James reported to his brother William about Turgenev's dependence on actuality. Turgenev told him—said James—that "he had never invented anything or anyone. To his sense, all the interest, the beauty, the poetry, the strangeness etc. are there, in the people and things. . . in much larger measure than he can get them out and that (what strikes him himself as a limitation of his genius) touches that are too *raffiné,* words and phrases that are too striking, or too complete, inspire him with an instinctive *méfiance*; it seems to him that they can't be true—for to be true to a given individual type is the utmost he is able to strive for."

All right then, granted some fine writers claim they can't make anything up, that they have to draw every wrinkle from an actual face, that their creativity consists largely in the filtration of what strikes them as inconsistencies in actuality, still, why do some of these writers have to draw on their own intimate lives, on the people they know best, those whom they love? Why do they write about their own love affairs, children, divorces, the lives and deaths of their closest friends?

The fiction writer who wants his work to be a source of truth as well as diversion, beauty, merriment, whatever, may be unable to cut himself off from those situations which affected him deeply; and those situations may be impossible to detach from those who figured in them. It is sometimes next to impossible for a writer to shift even the locale of an event that gripped him. (Observe Henry

[154]

James, in his *Notebooks,* trying to get rid of Paris as the scene of Strether's advice to little Bilham.) The writer requires conviction before he can convince others. At least this is true of the writer who is not essentially a magician delighting in the tricks of his craft.

How then transfer a passion from the body which aroused it to a different one? How transform it from a love of person to, say, a love for money? It can be done, it has been and will often be done, but *sometimes* it is very difficult to do. The work is rooted in a pattern so compelling that to break it would be to break the back of the book. "I must know down to the last wrinkle." For some, that knowledge is bounded by what *has been*, what is.

Yet a Babel or a Turgenev must feel the joy of that work which has little to do with the xeroxing of events. Even if the source of the joy is absorption in the arrangement of a selected reality, it answers the fictional impulse to take off, to break out of quotidian schemes.

It's a truism that actuality is altered not only in memory but in the process of expressing it. What a Japanese tradition calls *muga,* "the removal of even a hair's breadth between the writer's will and his expression," is, I would guess, impossible. If a writer thinks he has written precisely what he wanted to write, my guess is that he is so pleased with what he reads that he thinks it's what he intended to say. Forster's famous remark that he couldn't know what he thought till he saw what he said is closer to the bull's-eye.

The "mere" verbal transformation of experience is usually insufficient for either the fiction writer or the libel lawyer retained by his supposed models.

Story itself is discerned and felt very differently by the lawyer, historian, reporter, and the fiction writer. The first three must get things right in such a way that their reports can be checked out along the world's time and space schemes. The fiction writer's story, even when it originates in actuality, comes to be dominated not by it as much as by the writer's feeling of coherence, amplitude, pace, his preferred ratio of scene to monologue, vertical—or sensuous—horizontal—or narrative—matter, his sense of comic or pathetic form, and what have you. Of course, every alteration made to suit such preferences, entails others. Reportorial omission deforms not just truth but the whole enterprise of reporting; fictional omission is intended to intensify and embellish; it is a requirement of most fiction.

All right, the fiction writer has gone down into the "rag-and-bone shop" of his heart for his story. There among the grievances, nutty ambitions, wild needs, fears, resentments, and manic plea-bargains he finds the rueful story of his wife's love affair with the mailman. He sets out to tell it, but, remembering when her hair seemed redder than it was, he makes her hair red, he fattens her lover and puts him in a different line of work, one which has always seemed a little sinister.

Shrink the tall, change the sex of the children, move them to Arizona, no, you've never been there and don't feel like taking a trip or making the place up out of old westerns; let's make it Wisconsin. The easiest thing to change is yourself. Make yourself better looking, no, uglier, and more naive, poorer; instead of your lisp, give yourself a bad leg and a profession rich in a technical vocabulary, which will suggest certain habits of mind or send you to places it'll excite you to work into the narrative. You know your own faults, let your character admit them, or better, save them for big scenes; let the wife, children, and the doctor friend lash him with them. (Didn't Dante do this beautifully in Canto 30 of *Purgatory*? Beatrice is so hard on the Dante character that the angels try to intervene.) There is a kind of purgation in such indirect confession, a special pleasure in this indirect honesty. Put in that time you stole Billy's pen, but, well, let the ex-mailman get punished for it. (Didn't Proust say that Dostoevsky split the crime and punishment in his own life between two characters?)

All right, now you're home free to tell this thing the way it rolled over you, knocked you for a loop, putting you where you are now.

So the book gets written, version succeeding version, ideas pouring in from actuality or from delighted invention. (*L'appetit vient en mangeant.*)

Three years later, it's published. Friends poke you in the ribs: "You sure showed Charley." Your ex-wife tells you to stay away from the children. A learned ex-friend quotes Lord Hervey: "He never remembered an obligation nor forgot an injury."

It's not a total loss. The book's done, you've got a little money, you buy a Mercedes, send the kids to the shore, give your ex-wife the New York edition of Henry James; you enjoy some praise, work up froth at thimble-brained reviewers, float for a while, busy yourself with this and that, then start feeling for the next book.

But the tank's empty. You're worn out. Maybe you should take off and see something. The Serengeti, Kabul, Washington. There isn't a decent novel about American politics. No, we're politicked to death. How about the multinational world? The key institution of the late twentieth century. What a terrific mesh of interests. You read up, see characters forming out of Harold Geneen, Henry Kravits, African strong men.

No go. It sounds like bad Waugh.

You hole up in the country with Japanese novels, French memoirs, Dostoevsky, case histories of the broken, the assailed. You've never done a story about the dregs. Get out on Skid Row. Advertise for a rapist. Maybe a female rapist. Daughter of a multinational executive. An Emma with the soul of Smerdyakov.

You give it a try; it doesn't go either. Nothing works. The trouble is your life. It's killing you. Lunch, dinner, the same talk. Everything veiled, evasion instead of drama. Granola instead of passion. You can't write *Karamazov* in a nine-to-five life. Get cracking. Take a chance. What about that girl who wrote you about your book?

The point is that the frequent messes, the complications in the lives of many writers are not unrelated to the business of making up stories. The contradiction between the feeling which generated the work and the necessary routine of the working life can, after working hours, lead to trouble. "Woe weeps out her division when she sings." If there's no woe, there may be no song. The writer knows that some of his finest passages have come after his heart has been rattled around and he's gone to a typewriter and put down more or less exactly what he's felt. He thinks he needs more rattling.

I write these lines shortly after I lay flat on a table while a camera swivelled over my chest and took centimetric pictures of one of my lungs. A jovial Hawaiian technician was hoping to find on the tomographs what had shown up indistinctly on cruder X-rays so he could go to lunch. He thought he'd found it, and, as his stomach bubbled, my heart sank. Yet, simultaneously, I was about the writer's business of noting his expression, the look of the machine, the coffin-size depression in the ceiling above it, and, above all, the shape of my own feelings, at least those I could separate from the writer's business. It was a diversion from the unpleasantness of ugly discovery. (Happily, the electronic Columbus didn't discover America.)

2

There is something ignoble about this process. Is one only a snooper? Is one's work so local an exercise? Will it be forgotten as soon as its little fibrillations of inside story and local color yield to the next wave of narcissistic snooping?

I think older artists often begin to think like this. The contradictions between life and work, between adherence to getting things exactly right and getting things said beautifully, between the desire for fidelity and the distortions of expression wear one down. Here is Conrad on the subject in the remarkable preface to a *A Personal Record:*

> I have always suspected in the effort to bring into play the extremities of emotions the debasing touch of insincerity. In order to move others deeply we must deliberately allow ourselves to be carried away beyond the bounds of our normal sensibility—innocently enough, perhaps, and of necessity, like an actor who raises his voice on the stage above the pitch of natural conversation—but still we have to do that. . . . the danger lies in the writer becoming the victim of his own exaggeration, losing the exact notion of sincerity, and in the end coming to despise truth itself as something too cold, too blunt for his purpose—as, in fact, not good enough for his insistent emotion.

Genuine as it may be, Conrad's doubt seems to me related to a discouragement with one's art which writers often experience in their last years. Rare is the writer who writes to his dying day with undiminished belief in his art. Perhaps the greatest of such authors, Proust, said a few days before his death that his work contained nothing but his "deep and authentic impressions" which flowed from "the natural progress of [his] thought." That is the rarest sort of declaration. (Even it is conditioned. Anyone who's seen Proust's manuscripts knows that "natural progress" was closer to the tumultous trial-and-error of natural selection than to, say, Niagara Falls.)

Narrative may be the deepest of humanizing patterns, one which begins in what René Spitz calls the "primal dialogue" between mother and child. All we know and feel is evaluated in terms of this deep story which is oneself. More than theory, it determines what we observe and how we feel about it. It shapes the way we love and even the way we die.

Yet narrative art is the least sensuous of the arts. Its material is essentially impalpable, invisible, silent and motionless. The codified scribbles (or unmusical phonemes) suggest all other senses, but only suggest them. Narrative compensates for this dryness with its fluency and suggestibility. These give it a hammerlock on memory. Its ability to slide up and down in time as well as in and out of the human interior makes it the art to which almost no one is totally deaf. But that dryness, that abstract matter, gives the older writer little support. Old painters muck about with paint, old musicians have keys to hit, sounds to keep them afloat. The writer isn't nourished by the physical stuff of his art, and this reinforces the contrast between the assurance and tranquility indispensable to creation and the turbulence which is so much of narrative subject matter. That immateriality of narrative, so perfectly suited to fluid retrospection, puts next to no physical barrier between the writer and his work. It is another invitation to narcissism; and like others we've described, it promotes Conradian bafflement. What counts most, the mysterious exaltation of what is ultimately self-transforming work, is, in time, ground down by these peculiar conditions. The contrast between the deeply-felt beauty of the art and the deeply troubling jaggedness of the life which generates it becomes insupportable. The writer may say to himself what a brother narcissist, Muhammed Ali, said near the end of his third fight with Joe Frazier: "What am I doing here? I don't need to be doing this."

Stratford beckons. "I'll bury my book." Or, as one of Shakespeare's favorite authors, the self-exhibiting Montaigne, put it: "Any man can play his part in the sideshow and represent a worthy man on the stage; but to be disciplined within, in his own bosom, where all is permitted, where all is concealed—that is the point. To be disciplined in our actions where we don't have to account to anyone, where nothing is studied or artful, that is the next step."

[159]

[15]

A POETIC EXCHANGE

On Running Into Old Friends in Somebody's Novel (viz.,
Richard G. Stern's *Europe, or Up and Down with Baggish
and Schreiber*. New York, 1961).

Inside the margins of a book
through the screen doors of ink
you find yourself among explained people,
whom you imagine from one clue, or two,
people you cannot bore or smell,
who will not love you or seduce your friend.
They have names out of telephone books—
Baggish and Schreiber—
but of couse they are not real.

How strange then
on a train in there
to meet someone you know;
one who remembers moonlight on two faces—
enough to read a face by
if old enough to read—
and hesitating near the shadow;
and that one's voice; that dog, that awful dog;
and him, the man without a neck,
whose grandfather invented
telephone insulators.
There they all are, characters, helpless now,
but looking round at the compartment door
when Baggish enters,
as if they could sense me,
invisible but behind his back,
a recognisable reader.

And then, how strange for them, now—

[160]

but maybe they're all dead—
to read these lines, to feel those days again:
Jocrisse, the burnt mountains,
the mysterious German gardener,
Caval-en-l'air, the dead snake in my bed,
the weeks of cherry-blossom-exclamation!

So afterwards, on your way to Austria,
for the cheap shoes,
you must have met this novelist on your train,
while I met Giuliana and the Sheriff.

Perhaps if you read this you'll write me
offering as you did before, a job-
teaching (a great-great-grandson, this time)
Latin and algebra.

Thank God I'm real only—
at least I can ignore a letter,
put a frame round it, hang it up
without answering; but you,
whenever I feel like looking,
remain there in that book,
rocking along in the train for me to stare at;
outside, the mountains of 1951.

Alistair Elliot

> On Reading Alistair Elliot's "On Running into Old Friends in
> Somebody's Novel (viz., Richard G. Stern's *Europe, or Up
> and Down with Baggish and Schreiber.* New York, 1961)"
> (in *New Poetry, An Anthology,* edited by Peter Porter and
> Charles Osborne. London, 1975)

Dear Mr. Elliot. Or—for these lines anyway—
Dear Alistair ("invisible, recognisable reader").
I wish I were as fictional as Baggish
And could answer with impalpable visibility,
but here I am, beside a Dutch canal,
two hundred clumsy pounds
and one American election older than you.
(I read the Contributor's Note.)
Your poem is on the bed beside my socks.

[161]

And you?

"From Liverpool."
The ugliest town "I've never seen."
Poet, Librarian,
good at titles (*Air in the Wrong Place*).

Is this as much of you
As Baggish is of your old friends?

Twenty-odd years ago,
Schreiber and old Baggish
showed up under these small hammers.
Harmless? Familiar?
Names in the air
in no directory.

Last night, rain fell on the Prinzengracht,
More beautiful in reflection there
till it muddled what reflected it.

Alistair, unrecognisable reader, for you
one doesn't have to spell this out.

> Richard Stern
> Amsterdam
> August 1975

[16]

COUNTRY FIDDLERS, CITY SLICKERS:
VITRUOSI AND REALISTS

Novels take off from any and everything, but novelists are mostly either virtuosi or realists. That is, they either aim at the remarkable, or organize what they feel about more or less imagined *familiar* experience until, because of their narrative gift, it seems remarkable to others. The virtuoso takes off from other writers' works. His virtuosity strikes the eye immediately: his language is different, the arrangement of it is different. We feel the eloquence, farce, fantasy, and technical mastery of his work. The realist focuses on what's *there* or could be. The realist wants his work to seem real.

Compare Cubists and Impressionists. The Cubists were virtuosi: they weren't interested in reordering the "real" and very little of it can be seen through their artistic glasses. (Though Picasso, to defend his earliest Cubist paintings, produced photographs of the rooftops of Horta, the town in which he'd painted them.) Their work, however, became part of the world, new actualities, like new varieties of melon. The Impressionist works are part of the world also, but they began as new prescription lenses: they altered—and still alter—ways of seeing trees, dancers, ponds, umbrellas, railroad stations.

There are also virtuosi-despite-themselves. These are often among the greatest artists and innovators. Schoenberg wrote that he did not consciously try to be different (that is, he did not set out to be a virtuoso); he said he'd been "thrown into a boiling sea" in which he had to make for shore without regard to the style of his stroke. Contrast this with my colleague Easley Blackwood and his work with new musical tunings. Like such literary experimenters as Robbe-Grillet and John Barth, Blackwood uses the word *exhaustion* to describe the condition of his art. He says the old musical material is exhausted: we've heard most of what can come of it; it's time for new musical matter out of which composers will create new music. The theoretical virtuoso—Blackwood, Robbe-Grillet—

works up his theory first. Sometimes it is in the form of a blueprint which he follows more or less mechanically. Barth told me—not totally for amusement—that the chief difficulty he had writing *Giles Goat-Boy*—once he'd worked up the scheme—was finding the right combination of stimulants to keep him awake at his type-writer.

Schoenberg's innovation came, I think, out of another process. Like the work of Kafka and Beckett, his innovations derived from expressive necessity. They themselves were not the necessity. Nor were they the expression of a need to be or appear original. I don't mean that powerful work can't come from a virtuoso's technical decisiveness, only that such work is rarely as fine as work which was blocked till the artist found new devices for realizing it.

Of course no *description* of an artist's process is very close to the process itself. Yet much literary process goes, I think, some-thing like this: one works awkwardly toward a work, that is, toward a whole composed of certain events, stories, themes, characters, developments, scenes; whatever engages the fictional energy. The assemblage is not easy. It has to make sense; it has to please the assembler. The result is sometimes strange. The more diverse the matter, the more striking the form of the ensemble (even when the whole seems real). One book revolves around imaginary letters, another around a confession, a third about a shattered and irrecov-erable history. In my experience (which includes that of writers to whom I've talked), the work gets written once the way of telling the story becomes inseparable from it.

Many realist writers have virtuoso impulses. They think of a method of doing a novel before they have any notion of its subject matter. Or they conceive of a way of doing a particular subject which itself doesn't interest them. ("I want to write a novel about gray," said Flaubert.) The chief interest is the method. I think that most such notions come to nothing. You put in many hours pursu-ing what fails to excite you enough to continue. It's very hard to transform what may be what we can call a basic narrative temper.

Similarly, virtuoso writers usually come a cropper in straighter modes. (The straighter fiction in Barth's *Lost in the Funhouse* is not his best work.) On the other hand, some writers with essential-ly mimetic gifts sometimes bury the gift to pursue what they believe is the proper theoretical course. (For me, Michel Butor's best work is the essentially realist *Degrés* and Robert Coover's is his "realist" first novel, *The Origin of the Brunists.*[1] Writers who evade their own gift often produce the most distended and tedious work. "The Unreadable Book" is a modern genre.)

I myself have wasted months on such ideas as: (1) a novel arranged alphabetically, characters being taken up in the order of the spelling of their names, the novel developing by thickening the connections of the apparently unconnected persons; (2) a narrative in the form of a computer conference in which conferees enter at any point of the basic discussion by appending their contribution to the appropriate, numbered section (the idea was to create an inter-locked narrative out of apparently heterogenous materials);[2] (3) a narrative in which different elements of narration relate the story over or through the author's head. So "Voice," "Plot," and "Subject" make their very peculiar narrative claims. Of the hundreds of pages and hours devoted to this enterprise only four pages—printed at the end of the volume *1968*—survive. The others are part of the Himalaya of wastage in my closet.

A geneticist friend, Robert Haselkorn, told me about something called a *nonsense mutant*. Professor Robert Edgar named this form of genetic material which contains segments that make no sense to the reduplicating molecules and thus marks the end of the line.

---

[1] 1985. I've changed my mind. I recently read his political farce, *The Public Burning,* and think it's wonderful. The realism, often a mass of historical fact, constitutes the powder which the farcical fury ignites. The brilliant stories of T.Coraghessan Boyle (cf. *Descent of Man and Other Stories,* 1979) are other marvelous, semi-realistic growths of the Joycean tree. Boyle writes variations on newsworthy themes. Tthe variations are extravagant, passionately literary—that is, the love of verbal pyrotechnics is at least as great as love for the exposure, revelation, treatment (demolition or apotheosis) of the event or type of event which is the story's ostensible subject—and usually musically beautiful. The Flann O'Brien of *At Swim Two Birds* is the closest post-Joycean to such work, though such Beckett work as *"Premier Amour"* is related to it. A fuller examination would contrast this work with some of Kafka's. A class reading of "The Country Doctor" will show the craziness within the apparent simplic-ity of the story. There is the usual Kafka dream-tempo, the leaps from place to place, subject to subject, but there is also the hardly conscious transformation of the doctor into the patient, the attack into the complaint, the lyric into the descriptive moan. Kafka would be a tough nut for this essay's thesis to crack. And all these writers would not serve those thinkers who claim that the contemporary, particularly "the contemporary American writer adds more and more images, more narrative, more 'characters,' more words—however, rundown—to cover up the emptiness at the foundations of his construction—an emptiness he fears." These fear-ridden Americans are contrasted with such French writers as the tedious Blanchot and—the Pope of Disguised Amourous Kitsch—Mm. Duras, who are comparted to sculptors "con-stantly [moving] around the material to be formed, never staying in one position very long, removing more and more material in order to create a shape . . . an extreme emptying out of images, narrative, character and words [you bet!] in order to reach their silent, but solidly sig-nificant core—an erotic core that [they] can then embrace" Alice Jardine, *Gynesis* (Ithaca: Cornell University Press, 1985), P. 235.

[2] 1993. This was twenty years before I'd read about hyper-narrative (in Robert Coover's lead piece in the Sunday *New York Times Book Review,* June 21, 1992.).

However, Professor Edgar then went on to discover suppressors of
the nonsense mutants, that is, certain proteins which made sense of
the nonsense and thus enabled genetic continuance. For me, most
virtuoso work can be compared to such nonsense mutants, interesting perhaps in themselves, but as sports, as more or less attractive
culs-de-sac. Now and then, though, such sports will be picked up
by very different sorts of writers who will be able to transform their
own work and thus continue the literary line. Joyce took—so he
said—the internal monologues of Dujardin's *Les lauriers sont
coupés* and employed them in the brilliant monologues of *Ulysses*;
and Flaubert, his own "suppressor," took the notion of "received
ideas" from his *Dictionary of Received Ideas* and employed it in
the narrative comedy of the druggist Homais and, later, in that of
the farcical entrepreneurs, Bouvard and Pécuchet.

I want to speculate about a different but related matter. It strikes
me that most of the leading contemporary American virtuosi are
Gentiles. The American-Jewish fiction of the post-World War II
years is basically realistic. This has not always been the case, and it
is not the case in other countries. Now, though, it seems that in this
country the best-known virtuosi of narrative fiction are non-Jews:
Barth, Barthelme, Coover, Gass, Harington, Hawkes, Purdy, and
Pynchon[3] (though he like Harington may be more of a realistic fantasist than a conscientious virtuoso). Why are such distinguished
Jewish writers as Bellow, Elkins, Harris, Mailer, Malamud, Roth,
and Salinger more or less straightforward writers?[4]

I can think of some explanations. Almost all the Jews are urban,
most of the non-Jews small-town or country boys. Perhaps the
urban writer is so bombarded by variety that, very early, he knows
his job is to make sense of it, while the country writer dreams or
fantasizes his way out of a familiar, comparatively static order. The
urban writer's problem is making sense out of heterogeneity; the

---

[3] 1993. One who should be better known is Austin Wright, author of *Camden's Eyes*
(Doubleday. 1969) and the recent, wonderful *Tony and Susan* (Baskerville Publishers).

[4] 1992. The situation has changed since this was written. Jewish assimilation has gone so
much further that there is a "danger" of an ethnic melt-down. Writers who are half or three
quarters or one-eighth Jewish mix with others who don't give six thoughts a year to their—or
their parents—"Jewishness." I think that Mark Leyner, author of *My Sister, My Gastro-
enterologist*, is Jewish. He is also a pure virtuoso. There are many others.

country writer's is the conjuration of something beyond familiar homogeneity.[5]

In art, virtuosity is linked with dream, with evasion, and with escape. From Chamisso (author of *Peter Schlemiel*), a French *évadé*, through Nabokov, refugees from revolution have taken to narrative fantasy. Of the leading post-World War II Jewish writers, only three, Singer, Wiesel, and Schwarz-Bart, are, I believe, refugees, and their work veers into fantasy. (Malamud, an occasional refugee of the spirit, was also—as in "The Jew-Bird"—an occasional fantasist.)

Psychic turbulence may precipitate the same sort of conspicuously ordered, virtuoistic structures as political turbulence. The disturbed writer reaches for every means of control, as sociopaths do in life. (Until they explode, they are usually the best of quiet citizens.)[6] So—to take essentially non-literary examples—the adventurous fantasies of an Ian Fleming, the sophisticated craft and dream play of a Strindberg, or the technical mastery of an Orson Welles may derive from—or relate to—serious, if not pathological, displacement.

Is there anything else in Jewish experience common to the twenty or thirty leading American Jewish writers which bends them toward realistic rather than virtuoso fictions?

My guess is that the realist feels a confidence born of the possibility of overcoming an eccentric social position. Virtuosity may derive from the despair of displaced insiders. (Indeed, this may be the trigger of most literary experience from Homer's on.) Given the temperamental extremes in writers—their individuality is nourished by articulating the specialness of their temperaments—they are nonetheless a class, a group with common characteristics. They are active people whose professional activity is physically restrictive. They use the most flexible, most easily dominated artistic medium, words, and encounter next to no physical restriction—no paint, marble, canvas, dancer's bodies, wood and catgut, actor's temperaments. They are thus artistically *spoiled*; they can indulge themselves with what pleases only them. If they are haters of the philistines who surround them, they can revenge themselves by

---

[5] Of his long periods of seclusion in the Esterhazy summer palace, Haydn told his biographer Griesinger: "I was cut off from the world—there was no one to confuse or torment me, and I was forced to become original."

[6] The very conservative politician is frequently a person whose need for public order helps control a disturbed interior.

writing works that are conspicuously impenetrable. (In a city, one is less likely to be immersed in ignorance and philistinism.)

Is it fair to say that all but the most-benighted Jewish families maintain respect for the *book*, for the learned *man*, the *writer*? Many burgher Jewish fathers don't want their children to be writers, but still usually respect books. In a community where every ounce of energy must be productive, this is not often the case.[7]

Years ago I got a letter from a writer, David Martin, whose first novel, *Tethered* (Holt, Rinehart and Winston, 1979), is about growing up in a small Illinois agricultural town. He said that he went back to his home town for Christmas, and one of his unamiable high school friends talked to him about the book. The fellow hadn't read or probably seen it, but he knew that a book authored by his old acquaintance existed. When Martin came by, the fellow was disembowelling a hog. His critical comment consisted of slicing out the hog's anus and tossing it to Martin. It would be hard to match this experience in New York or Chicago. (Nor are there that many Jewish farmers around—though prosperous Jewish authors may list themselves as farmers on tax forms.)[8]

Most of the Jewish writers I know come from families which were actively melting into the great American pot. The family direction was Americanization, that is, movement toward open-ended prosperity and full acceptance. Newcomers to games usually play by the rules. Is it too much to say that the novel-writing children of these new Americans tended to play by narrative rules? Their books—filled with an American experience which usually ended in either triumph or bittersweet loss—toe, often brilliantly, the realistic narrative line.

For a time, after World War II, Jewish and Gentile writers wrote the satiric, angrily farcical works that are called "black humor." Often their eye was on the war, a phenomenon whose maniacal orderliness, covering sometimes-total disorder, was a kind of public virtuosity. For the writers, what counted was the *object out*

---

[7] The case of country aristocrats who, for much of civilization, constitute the majority of writers, is another matter.

[8] One distinguished Jewish author became a chicken farmer after he found that literature couldn't support him: Henry Roth, author of the wonderful *Call It Sleep*. Incidentally, a contemporary of Roth's, Daniel Fuchs, recently (*Chicago Tribune Bookworld*, Nov. 3, 1985) wrote that as far back as 1935, critics were complaining about the excess of "Jewish novels." He cited John O'London's *Weekly*, Sept. 21, 1935: "They are becoming rather too many and too much alike.

there, not the method of presentation. So even such virtuoistic-looking books as *Catch 22* were essentially realistic. It would not be easy to distinguish such books by the social or religious backgrounds of their authors: the army is the truest melting pot.

BUSINESS CODA

In the palmy, postwar period of American publishing, federal and foundation funds subsidized library purchases, and publishers allowed new talent a couple of failed or marginal novels before they ran out its string. (I myself was indulged by publishers who lost money on my work.) The richness of post-World War II American writing, both realistic and virtuoistic, was as clearly related to such munificence as the Elizabethan drama was to the prosperity of audiences enriched, as well as excited, by the voyages of discovery. This palmy time is long gone. Conglomerate publishing has distended the modes of salesmanship: television advertising creates publishing expense which necessitates enormous sales; proportionately fewer good novels are published, so that the few which are will have the bookstore space needed to redeem the expense. What effect such constriction will have on the mental life of the nation remains to be seen. The menace is of a continued narrowing of taste and a shrinkage in the individuality which has for two hundred and fifty years been both invented and nurtured in fiction.[9]

---

[9] 1993. New methods of publishing and distribution are changing these conditions.

[17]

A WRITER'S STRAY THOUGHTS ABOUT TIME

At the beginning of a symposium of physicists on the problem of time, the cosmologist Thomas Gold defined the central question:

> We seem to derive the notion of a flow of time in the first place from introspection. We then use the introspective notion to classify observations in the physical world . . . Perhaps [the introspective notion] is only a deception of a biological sort which ought to have no place in physics. Is it really basic to the description of physical processes that time progresses? Or does the set of world lines of all the particles comprise a great pattern which represents the entire physical world without reference to passage of time or to any idea of flow? Must we think of the laws of physics as operating upon the present to produce the future? Or is it only through the details of the interrelations between events in space-time and the information within the brain, which are part of the great pattern, that biological mechanisms have devised a representation in terms of flowing time?[1]

Symposium participants discussed a variety of things: Gödel's conundrum that one can loop in time (that is, progress to the past); conditions in which time is immeasurable; and the temporal dependence on the distinction between observer and observed (which turned out to be that between an apparatus which is comparatively stable and an emission which is *declared* active).

For someone like me, who not only *feels* that time flow is one of the two or three deepest agents of experience but who, as a worker in a time art, regards the representation of time flow as one of his basic jobs, the symposium had certain shock value.

That truth is *not as we feel it* is one of the sources of literature; and the creation and delivery from illusion is one of its great pat-

---

[1] Thomas Gold, ed., *The Nature of Time* (Ithaca, N.Y.: Cornell University Press, 1967), p. 3.

terns. Still, talk of time as a biological "deception" poses at least an intellectual problem. One of the great masters of mental tricks writes: "There is nothing in the id that corresponds to the idea of time, and—a thing that is most remarkable and awaits consideration in philosophical thought —no alteration in its mental processes is produced by the passage of time."[2]

What, then, is time, and what does it mean for one's life, mind, and art?

Language philosophers supply a relatively easy out, namely the claim that different statements exist in different language systems. The feeling system is a subset of the biological—as that is of the physical[3]—and one cannot cash checks drawn on one system in the banks of another. For this nonphilosopher, this solution is the equivalent of getting out of a room by a small window instead of a door (though Kant gave this particular window beautiful stained glass).

For man and writer, what looms is the fact—or, if illusion, one that kills—that aging is the chief mode of ordinary human alteration. One is born weak, grows strong, ripens, coarsens, dies. This is built into everyone; every human system accounts for it. Daily life is a web of commemoration and anniversary, hellos and good-byes. Much that we know comes in season. Our behavior—if not our id—is dominated by time measurement. By change—which makes time for us.

My craft of letters involves a version of time which is not the scarcely felt (or unfelt) drift time of so many hours. The time arts intensify passage, so much indeed that one contemporary philosopher[4] sees them as the symbolic expression of the artist's knowledge of feeling.

Feeling is known only in passage. The greatest work of modern literary art, Proust's *In Quest of Lost Time,* represents and analytically destroys most major forms of human feeling by showing them dissolve in time.

An occasion is an attempt to impose intensity on drift. A baseball game (despite its theoretical endlessness), a church service, "a man on the moon by 1970," a lecture, these sieve time from the slag which year by year lowers us deeper into unfelt inanition.

---

[2] Sigmund Freud, "Dissection of the Personality," in *Works,* standard edition, XXII, P. 74.

[3] Professor Gold reverses the subordination.

[4] Susanne Langer, *Feeling and Form.* (New York: Scribners), 1953.

Even the space arts have a temporal dimension. Novelties of depth and color ignite the sense of where we are, the way in which we relate to other objects. They satisfy, I think, a deep need to hold fast against the time hurricane. We invest in land, in stuff, in the things of the world, to mark that we are here, here now. Against flow, against change, this is what we see, touch, relish. Time is the chief source of human fear, though perhaps now, on the verge of worlds where some of the time laws we know may be altered, we may reacquire the space fear which dominated men before Columbus.

Space fear is for men of action. Observers, witnesses, the untranquil if relatively passive, the unsaintly, the unheroic, *most of us*, are gnawed by time fear.

> Ruin hath taught me thus to ruminate,
> That time will come and take my love away.
> This thought is as a death, which cannot choose
> But weep to have that which it fears to lose.
>
> Shakespeare, Sonnet 4

Fear of loss and the traditions of craft generate much literary art. Most languages have special tenses for narrative, special beginnings ("Once upon a time" or such space-time metaphors as *Nel mezzo del cammin di nostra vita*, "In the middle of the road of our life"), special conventions of conclusion ("They lived happily ever after"). Story arts divide the time world.

Drama deals with a present jolted by appearance or remembrance in such a way that a single, inescapable future dominates the scene. Dance and music are sensuous varieties of this same drive toward the inescapable.

Narrative orders *what has been* into an illusion powerful enough to derange the reader out of his lamplit present tense, perhaps permanently altered by the force of his felt understanding of that re-created or imaginary past.

By imposition of an artful time order using the scarcely sensuous codes of language and literature, the narrator, the writer, may be the one who supplies what is not present in the id, not present in "the set of world lines," the sense of meaningful passage which makes of biological data a felt form.

Which is what we mostly mean by *time*.

[172]

[18]

THE PAST AND FUTURE OF LITERATURE:
A PLAY IN THREE SCENES

On December 3, 1979, the Supreme Court declined to hear the appeal of a novelist and a publisher who'd been successfully sued by a psychotherapist on the grounds that he'd been punitively maligned in a fictional portrait. The news resounded in literary space-time.

Scene 1.

Time: 1300. Place: Somewhere in Italy. Persons: Dante and Publisher

DANTE: Then Vergil will hand me over to Beatrice.
PUBLISHER: Beatrice Portinari?
DANTE: That's the one.
PUBLISHER: We might ride with Vergil. No living descendants. But the Portinari's o-u-t. There's a husband, kids, and her uncle's a lawyer.
DANTE: All right. I'll call her Arabella.
PUBLISHER: Call her Giuseppe, she's still out. Let Vergil turn you over to a schnauzer. You're very good with animals.
DANTE: I've got lots of animals in Parts One and Two.
PUBLISHER: Didn't I tell you they're out? Every other line's about someone walking around the streets. Or someone with grandsons walking around. The Ulysses stuff is O.K. But call him Filippo. Cavalcanti's brother's named Ulisse.
DANTE: I don't know, Paolo. This poem's got a lot of dead weight. I'm not sure it's worth the trouble. I hear Can Grande can use a Latin secretary. That might be the ticket.
PUBLISHER: Why not? Lie low till the heat's off, then try a few sestinas.

Scene II.

Time: 1600. Place: London. Persons: W. Shakespeare and Wise Friend

SHAKESPEARE: I see why the history plays have to go, but what's with Portia and Shylock?

WISE FRIEND: Not only do you have the Anti-Defamation League, you'll be hauled into court by Lopez. And the case'll be heard by Burleigh.

SHAKESPEARE: So?

WISE FRIEND: Burleigh's wife's called "the judge's judge." And what's your Portia? A fish peddler?

SHAKESPEARE: Wasn't much of a play anyway. But the Hamlet scheme's a good one.

WISE FRIEND: As idea, terrific. Just keep it to yourself.

SHAKESPEARE: The characters are Danes. Who can touch me in London?

WISE FRIEND: What a country kid you are, Willy. Did Lord Seale's widow marry his brother, or didn't she?

SHAKESPEARE: Claudius and Gertrude.

WISE FRIEND: You got it. You could make Claudius a friend of the family.

SHAKESPEARE: Not bad.

WISE FRIEND: And leave out that play within the play. The Seales love the theater.

SHAKESPEARE: Rosencrantz and his pal better go also. I'm sure the Seale kid went to college, may even have had a friend or two.

WISE FRIEND: Don't be such a wise guy. It doesn't become you. Polonius and the girl who goes off her rocker, that's also out.

SHAKESPEARE: Naturally. There must be twenty privy councillors with daughters in trouble. The thing to do is stick to sonnets.

WISE FRIEND: Only keep yours under the pillow. Every third nut in London's got a candidate for your *Schwarzerin*. One of them's bound to be right.

SHAKESPEARE: Little Annie bores the pants off me, but she's got a grand land operation going in Stratford. She could use someone with a head for figures.

WISE FRIEND: I'll sure miss you, sweet Willy.

[174]

Scene III.

Time: 2000. Place: United States of America. Persons: Professor and Student of Contemporary Literature.

PROFESSOR: Done the assignment?
STUDENT: Sure, Prof.
PROFESSOR: O.K. What's the book about?
STUDENT: It begins with this thing, and then something pours in
    these three cups of—what do you call that white stuff?
PROFESSOR: Flour.
STUDENT: Riiight. Flour. See, Flour's the main character . . .

Curtain

[19]

CHICAGO AS FICTION

There is an enormous, magisterial, and almost never read doctoral dissertation in the stacks of the University of Chicago's Regenstein Library. Its author is the late Lennox Grey, the title—not one of the century's catchiest—*Chicago and the "Great American Novel": A Critical Approach to the American Epic*. It is a survey, classification, and analysis of the approximately five hundred novels set in Chicago up to 1935 by two hundred different authors. The novels are classified by period and subject: Chicago as a Portage, a Fort, a Trading Post, a Boomtown, an Agricultural Metropolis before and after the Civil War and the Great Fire of 1871, Chicago the Industrial City, the White City, the Black, and the Modern City.

Nothing comparable has been written since, though Chicago is at least as complex a place as it was before 1935 and those who have set novels here are every bit as serious and able as their predecessors. Such brief surveys as Michael Anania's "A Commitment to Grit" (*Chicago*, Nov. 1983, 200-207) may be excellent in their way, but such a subject needs the leisurely immensity of a dissertation and the heroic patience of Lennox Grey.

Grey's thesis is that Chicago has been regarded as the most American of American cities and, therefore, the most appropriate setting for that literary unicorn, "the Great American Novel." Its geographic centrality, its rapid transformations, the exceptional individuals—especially transgressors and over-reachers—and the myths which local and national media excogitated from them, its tradition of being untraditional, its ethnic variety, its inventive, clamorous commerce and industry, its old status as junction and port, and, finally, its tradition of literary vaunting and self-explanation, make it the ideal "writer's town."

Whether or not it is more of a writer's town than New Orleans or Bordeaux, Worcester, Massachusetts, or Worcester, Worcestershire, is itself a complicated question. If, say, a group of Bronte-like sisters grew up in Worcester, Mass., it might become more a writer's town than, say, Moline, Illinois or even Kansas City, Missouri. Yet it is a fact that so many writers seem to have had something to do with Chicago that sixty-seven years ago H. L. Mencken was able to call it the "Literary Capital of the United States." Mencken's extravagance was widely circulated and probably stimulated what it described. "In Chicago," he wrote.

> there is a mysterious something that makes for individuality, personality, charm. . . . Find a writer who is indubitably American in every pulse beat . . . and in nine times out of ten you will find he has some sort of connection with the Gargantuan abattoir by Lake Michigan.

Such rhapsody, with its "mysterious something" and its "American in every pulse beat," is easy to grasp by unthinking and unliterary people, but on page after literary page, as Grey shows, it represents the note struck about this city: Chicago is the *real* America, the place where individuality—America's very juice—runs clearest.

Fourteen years before Mencken's hyperbole, William Dean Howells, writing in the *North American Review,* spelled out the Chicago connection to the Declaration of Independence.

> The republic of letters is elsewhere sufficiently republican, but in the metropolis of the Middle-West, it is so almost without thinking, almost without feeling; and the atmospheric democracy, the ambient equality, is something that runs like the prime effect in literature of what America has been doing and saying in life ever since she first formulated herself in the Declaration.

This is less hyperbolical, but who can get away with such personifications today? Howells's remarks make a Chicagoan suspicious. "Ambient equality"? "Atmospheric democracy"? Who's he kidding? What's he selling? America either says nothing or so much that you can't summarize it, especially in polysyllabic phrases.

Yet Chicago is as much a verbal as a stone and metal construction. Its verbal versions are as distinct, as salable, and as potent as the products it puts into boxes or electronic blips. Free-associate with "Chicago" and you get something very different than "Los Angeles." Los Angeles conjures up Disney miniatures, Hollywood illusions, Watts Tower's junk beauty, pretend castles, fake manor houses. It's Polynesia on wheels, a technicolor fragility menaced by earthquakes, fires, smog, the automobile freeway. [1993. Today the

[177]

menaces are internal, Balkan: racial-ethnic warfare, self-destruction, civic collapse.] With Chicago, the word "real" comes to mind. Farce amid grimness. Fires and fists, strikes, riots, clubs and cops, machine tools and machine politics, crooks and cardinals (sometimes fused, as in Andrew Greeley's fiction or in Nicholas V. Hoffman's recent novel, *Organized Crimes* [Harper and Row, 1985]).

Chicago belongs on the drama as well as the front page. The personae include the Boss, the Corrupt Alderman with heart and pockets of gold, the Deal-Maker, the Speechifying Smoothie, the Rhetorician, Municipal Sheep, The Syndicate, His Eminence—whose treasure is not exclusively celestial. America is entranced by Chicago characters. It expects, wants and needs this literary fix of fraud, con, toughness and slaughter. It's Disneyland—no, it's Oberammergau with real nails and real blood.

Since Chicago grew as popular journalism did, it was early legendary. The east needed explanations of this noisy child of the lake. Chicago's writers slaked this eastern appetite. In the columns of Ade, Dunne, Lardner, Hecht, Royko, Greene, Roger Simon, and twenty others, the Chicago comedy was the stuff of daily yuks. The column's heroes are the abused and the abusive, the poor slobs and the Paddies, Mikes, Vitos, Big Als, Fast Eddies, and Crazy Janes who run them into the ground.

The novelists, at least the ones who will be read next year as well as this, stand in back of the newspaper characters and conceptions. Even when their books are based on historical characters and events, it is the coherence of their imaginative world which survives. Dreiser's financial genius, Cowperwood, is based on the traction tycoon Yerkes, but he is more Dreiser than Yerkes. Dreiser's heroes come to Chicago in a trance. They turn the city into a field to be plowed, a pocket to be picked, a stage to be filled. They want everything. Money isn't enough, power isn't enough. What they ultimately want is explanation. "If he had not been a great financier," writes Dreiser of Cowperwood,

> and above all, a marvelous organizer, he might've become a highly individualistic philosopher. . . . His business, as he saw it, was with the material facts of life, or rather, with those third and fourth degree theorems and syllogisms which control material things and so represent wealth.

2

Material. Stuff. The real. The mass and variety of urban matter requires ever subtler shorthand to register and manipulate it.[1] The enchantment and the curse of matter have been the great Chicago theme.

> Chicago is an instance of a successful, contemptuous disregard of nature by man. . . . In. . . Chicago, man has decided to make for himself a city for his artificial necessities in defiance of every indifference displayed by nature. Along the level floor of sand and gravel cast up by the mighty lake, the city has swelled and pushed, like a pool of quicksilver, which, poured out on a flat plate, is ever undulating and alternating its borders as it eats its way further into the desert expanse. Railroad lines, like strands of a huge spider's web, run across the continent in all directions, wilfully, strenuously centering in this waste spot, the swampy corner of a great lake.[2]

The threat is quasi-Marxist: what's hauled in, the material of wealth, threatens to "become you."[3] In novels, Chicago is the emblem of mastered nature, and it pays for its mastery. Mrs. O'Leary's cow was the revenge of the prairie. Even in the Chicago sections of non-Chicago novels you hear the dirge of wealth. Scott Fitzgerald's most destructive characters come from Chicago. In *Tender Is The Night,* the Swiss psychiatrist in charge of Nicole, the broken Chicago heiress, tells Dick Diver he's often treated the victims of these Chicagoans. Nicole's father, the millionaire meat-packer, is, like Cowperwood, a transgressor, but the boundary he's crossed is kinship. Incest with Nicole has driven her mad. After years of treatment, the cured Nicole herself becomes a ruinous transgressor. Her beauty, intelligence, and wealth ruin the husband who saved her. But there are more remote victims.

> Nicole bought from a great list that ran two pages and bought the things in the window besides. Everything she liked that she couldn't possibly use herself, she bought as a present for a friend. She bought colored beads, folding beach cushions,

---

[1] The Chicago futures market would have excited medieval philosophers.

[2] Robert Herrick, *The Gospel of Freedom.*

[3] Edgar Lee Masters, *Children in the Marketplace.*

artificial flowers, honey, a guest bed, bags, scarves, love birds, miniatures for a doll's house and three yards of a new cloth the color of prawns. She bought a dozen bathing suits, a rubber alligator, a traveling chess set of gold and ivory, big linen handkerchiefs for Abe, two dozen leather jackets of kingfisher blue and burning bush from Hermès—bought all these things not a bit like a highclass courtesan buying underwear and jewels which were after all professional equipment and insurance—but with an entirely different point of view. Nicole was the product of much ingenuity and toil. For her sake trains began their run at Chicago and traversed the round belly of the continent to California; chicle factories burned and link belts grew link by link in factories; men mixed toothpaste in vats and drew mouth wash out of copper hogsheads; girls canned tomatoes quickly or worked rudely at the Five-and-Ten on Christmas Eve; half-breed Indians toiled on Brazilian coffee plantations and dreamers were muscled out of patent rights in new tractors—these were some of the people who gave a tithe to Nicole, and as the whole system surged and thundered onward, it lent a feverish bloom to such processes of hers as wholesale buying. . .

In our time, the extravagance of the rich (see the birthday party for the Great Dane in Bellow's *The Dean's December*) is comedy, not indictment.

In the thirties, forties and fifties, the Chicago writers James Farrell and Nelson Algren spent no time on the rich; they described the—usually defeated—poor. Farrell—one of the few Chicago writers actually born in the city—tracks the degradation of poor Irish Catholics. His description of their communities makes Joyce's exhausted Dublin look like Pericles' Athens. Farrell's Chicagoans are ignorant, bored, mindless and violent. Only now and then does a whiff of poetry stir one of them. A lake breeze, a kiss, a fight, raises them from their piggish life, but there's no hope they will change things. Only at the end, regret and nostalgia touch them with something more. But their poetry is shallow; the nostalgia is Verlaine's "garlic of low cuisine."

For Algren, Chicago is the beauty with the busted nose. It's Sancho Panza-Charlie Chaplin Chicago, that of tough little guys making music out of abuse and loss. The Algren characters just want small stakes, just want to make it through the day, but the day is controlled by the Big Shots and those who work for them. They leave the Algren loser nothing but booze, dope, and the bodies of other losers. Fine with him; he hates winners.

Ten or fifteen years before his death, Algren sensed that his Chicago poetry had run out. He more or less left the city to a writer who found poetry in its winners and its losers, in be-Sulkaed Loop finaglers and old Jews taking steam with smalltime hoods in Division Street bathhouses, even in professors and deans.[4] Bellow's heroes are also acquisitive border-crossers, but their borders are sensuous, intellectual, and spiritual. Bellow's books are education novels, and his heroes are educated by great men and great books as well as by the thugs, lawyers, businessmen, con men, and splendid ladies of the city. The Bellow hero is heavy with memory. The Chicago of the twenties presses on the Chicago sixties, seventies, and eighties. (There are geniuses of memory as well as geniuses of fact and theory.) No writer has written longer or better about this city than Bellow, and, of course, as he has changed, so have his versions of it. In early Bellow, people work in coalyards, haberdasheries, Loop departments stores, lake resorts. Wherever they work, they classify, analyze, transform fact into theory, theory into poetry. One hero delivers relief checks in the ghetto.

> He had four or five blocks to go, past open lots, old foundations, closed schools, black churches, mounds, and he reflected there must be many people alive who had once seen the neighborhood rebuilt and new. Now there was a second layer of ruins; centuries of history accomplished through human massing. Numbers had given the place forced growth; enormous numbers had also broken it down.... Rome, that was almost permanent, did not give rise to thoughts like these... But in Chicago, where the cycles were so fast and the familiar died out, and again rose, changed, and died again in thirty years, you saw the common agreement or covenant, and you were forced to think about appearances and realities.
>
> ("Looking for Mr. Green")

In the latest Bellow stories, meanings aren't conclusions. Memory creates an understanding which transcends meaning. It's as if material Chicago turns out to be its own explanation. Woody

---

[4] Like many Chicago writers of the last ninety years, Saul Bellow has been associated with the University of Chicago, but unlike many of those writers–Philip Roth, Austin Wright, Susan Sontag, George Steiner, Thomas Rogers, Robert Coover, James Purdy, Kurt Vonnegut, Douglas Unger, Janet Kauffman, and many others–he wasn't a transient for whom a few years of school-time were an icon of carnival or Paradise.

Selbst remembers when he worked at the 1933 Century of Progress World's Fair pulling a rickshaw,

> wearing a peaked straw hat and trotting with powerful thick legs, while the brawny, redfaced farmers—his boozing passengers—were laughing their heads off and pestered him for whores. He, although a freshman at the seminary, saw nothing wrong when girls asked him to steer a little business their way, in making dates, and accepting tips from both sides. He necked in Grant Park with a powerful girl who had to go home quickly to nurse her baby. Smelling of milk, she rode beside him on the streetcar to the West Side, squeezing his rickshaw puller's thigh and wetting her blouse. This was the Roosevelt Road car. Then, in the apartment, where she lived with her mother, he couldn't remember that there were any husbands around. What he did remember was the strong milk odor. Without inconsistency, next morning he did Old Testament Greek: the light shineth in the darkness—to fos en te skotia fainei[5]—and the darkness comprehendeth it not.
>
> ("A Silver Dish")

Bellow's Chicago is not the last, only—till now—the most vivid picture of the city, the equivalent of Dickens's London, Joyce's Dublin, the Paris of Stendhal, Balzac, Zola, and Proust.

3

In 1984, *TriQuarterly* published a Chicago issue. In it one finds fifteen or twenty new versions of the city. Leon Forrest, Cyrus Colter, Harry Mark Petrakis, Stuart Dybek, Eugene Wildman, and Larry Heinemann are a few of the authors whose transfigured memories or imaginative conjurings of streets, stones, ghettos, trains, of ethnic obtuseness, poetry and chauvinism, of street action and lacustrine musing create what readers will know as Chicago. James Hurt (writing in the best of the city's free newspapers, *The Reader*) said that the issue contains new "alternatives to the Hog Butcher Line" of Chicago writing. "There is a kind of compromised laughter, a survivor's cynicism" but also "sweetness and the awareness of human possibility" in these new Chicagos. He cites

---

[5] Actually New Testament Greek (John 1).

Dave Etter's "rejection" of Sandburg's "Chicago":

> City of bent shoulders, the bum ticker, the bad back. City of
> the called third strike, the blocked punt. City of the ever-
> deferred dream. City of the shattered windshield, the loose
> wheel, the empty gas tank. City of I remember when, of once
> upon a time. City not of "I will" but of "I wish I could."

From outsiders as well, the Chicago visions pour. So Nathan
Zuckerman returns to Chicago in Philip Roth's *The Anatomy
Lesson* and sees its "broken bands of illumination, starred, squared,
braided, climbing lights" as a paradisal constellation, while Denis
Johnson—in his marvelous first novel *Angels*—transcribes a
Chicago nightmare:

> Five billion weirdos walking this way and that, not looking at
> each other, and every third one had something for sale.
> Money-lickers; and black pimps dressed entirely in black,
> and a forest of red high heels. There were lots of lights—
> everyone had half a dozen shadows scurrying in different
> directions underneath them.

New tunes in the classic keys. The con, the sell, the paradise of
man's energy, Chicago, the setting for excess, rapidity, confusion,
gorgeousness, bitter triumph, overreaching, bitter collapse. Since
stories attract stories and fictions generate counter-fictions, this
most fictionalized of American cities grows ever thicker with its
selves, so much so that between the fictions and the actualities
there is hardly room for a shadow.

[20]

THE WRITER AND HIS OUTSIDE JOBS

The magazine *Arts and Society* devoted a number to one of the era's standard topics, "The Artist in the University." I contributed the following brief, Shylockian statement. Since then, I've given a talk on the subject, but it didn't work for this book. The talk dealt with the following topics:

1. Writers have almost always had outside professional lives.
2. In different eras, writers have clustered in certain professions: the stage (after the public theaters opened in the 1570's); the pulpit in the early seventeenth century; the book world (printing, translating, editing) in the eighteenth century; periodicals and coupon clipping in the nineteenth century; teaching in the twentieth century.
3. Professional life has some effect on the artist's work:

> . . . my nature is subdu'd
> To what it works in, like the dyer's hand.
> Shakespeare, Sonnet 111

4. The effect can show in the development of genres: the Elizabethan-Jacobean revenge play (because of the success of Kyd's *Spanish Tragedy*), the complex private poetry of the seventeenth century and then the length of the early novels. (Shenstone said Richardson's *Clarissa* was long because the author was a printer.) The self-confident contempt for the reading public of such nineteenth century rentiers or Bohemians as Flaubert and Rimbaud and the sentiment and form of the great popular novelists (Dickens through Wells and Bennett); the philosophizing intimacy and genre-testing of the twentieth-century teachers (Joyce of Berlitz, Pirandello of Bonn, Borges of Buenos Aires, Bellow of Chicago, and many others).
5. Unlike the earlier teacher-writers (Longfellow of Harvard, Herrick of Chicago, Moody of Wisconsin), the twentieth-century

[184]

writer-teacher (beginning with Frost at Amherst in 1917) was hired as a writer. Since the writer's work—like the advanced researcher's in any field—is dissociative and even anti-authoritarian, the writer's presence in the university may have augmented the restlessness of the late 1960's, which may soon make the university an impossible haven for writers (who, like all researchers, need time and quiet—that is, laboratory conditions).[1]

6. The doctor-writers—Empedocles, Rabelais, Schiller, Smollett, Keats, Jensen, Burton, Campion, Chekhov, Benn, Céline, W.C. Williams, Wang-Wei—and such doctors' sons as Flaubert, Proust, Sinclair Lewis, Auden, and Hemingway; the closeness of both professions to personal crisis, suffering, artful soothing, therapeutic consolation.

7. The relation of the immensely active public lives of Chaucer and Dante to their panoramic work.

8. The relationship of literature to the leisure of courtier, rentier, and more or less leisurely professional man; the change in professional standards (the effect on the professions) because of the writer-professionals.

9. The variety of writer's jobs: Vanbrugh, architect; Prior, Perse, Dante, Chaucer, Claudel, *et al.*, diplomats; du Gard, paleographer; Corneille, Maeterlinck, Fielding, Boswell, lawyers; Aeschylus, Vigny (and many others), soldiers; Goethe, Malraux, ministers of state; Musil, engineer; Borges, Wilson, Mao Tse-Tung, librarians.

STATEMENT

Perhaps the artist who works more or less happily in the university should prod his ease as Kafka prodded his quiescent neurosis: "The deeper one digs one's pit, the quieter it becomes." This furred burrow one inhabits, is it too remote from the green world of change? Is one sleeping through one's time?

Who could say "No" with perfect assurance? Novel-writing lion hunters? Statesmen in pasture? The parson-poets of the seventeenth century? The actor-playwrights of the sixteenth? Fleet Street editors, nineteenth-century rentiers, Renaissance employees of Pope and condottiere? Who couldn't "live" more by painting fewer walls, rhyming fewer lines?

Or is it that the college teacher's burrow is at a double remove, a

---

[1] 1993. There's been mostly peace and quiet in the decades since.

burrow within a burrow? After all, the university has its special precincts, carefully chosen personnel; its lawns are tended by polite retainers; its meeting places command good behavior. Plus which the university artist is lapped in the institutional radiance of tenure and pension. What can he know of street wars, cutthroat trade, the reluctance of field and bone?

Yet.

In a university one can be lonely; one can cheat, love, be loved; one can even be heroic, villainous. One breathes, eats, works, pays, engenders. What the writer writes about—alteration, doubt, illusion, gain, loss, forgiveness—are not these in the university as in every human nutshell? And for those who work with "the times," what other twentieth-century institution is at once pulpit, seedbed, laboratory, marketplace, the crossroads of what's been and what's to be?

If one's need for isolation and rent money can be met, the university will serve as Shakespeare's theater served him. There is no paradise for the artist; and he can make whatever hell is necessary for him wherever he is.

[21]

ON FEELING 'THIS IS THE WAY IT WAS'

Lately, I've begun to read books by authors whom I've dismissed without reading. Usually reliable critics have dismissed them for me; it simplifies one's reading life. So I'd never read Arnold Bennett because Virginia Woolf's essay "Mr. Bennett and Mrs. Brown" had convinced me he wasn't worth reading. A couple of summers ago, I read four Bennett novels Penguin had reissued, *The Old Wives' Tale,* and the trilogy *Clayhanger, Hilda Lessways* and *These Two.* I enjoyed them immensely. They lacked the brilliant narrative shortcuts Virginia Woolf and her peers invented, they stuck to appearance, confrontation and social and personal history, but everywhere there was intelligent analysis as well as a good story. More than that, the books radiated social truth.

That same summer I also read four volumes of stories by another heretofore despised writer, Somerset Maugham. (A favorite of such people as my parents, what could he mean to me?) His stories were old-fashioned—usually a Maugham-like "I" hears or overhears another person's story—but many of them had the sort of accuracy I'd felt in Bennett, as well as intrinsic narrative interest. One story, "The Force of Circumstance," struck me. After I finished it, I found myself thinking, "This is what being English means. This is as purely English a story as you can find." Now I wonder what I meant by that and why such conviction was itself a pleasure.

Like many of Maugham's best stories, "The Force of Circumstance" takes place in an outpost of Empire, here a small station upriver in the Malay Peninsula. Guy, the station chief, lives there with his new wife, Doris, in the bungalow she's been transforming from bachelor emptiness into a beautiful home. Guy is fattish and good-humored; Doris, plain, a former secretary to an M.P., had lived with her mother and never traveled. Married, she and Guy are blissfully happy. She studies Malay and works on the home; Guy deals with district business. Together, they dine, drink, play tennis, joke and read the London papers which are brought upriver from Singapore twice a month. One day, Doris sees Guy speak harshly to a Malay woman standing at their compound gate with a baby in tow. She inquires about it and is told that the woman is a troublemaker from the village. A few days later, the woman shows up again, this time accompanied by two little boys. Abdul, Guy's valet, yells at, then drives her off. Doris runs outside to stop him and later asks Guy to punish Abdul. He tells her that Abdul knows that the woman has been told to keep away. The woman shows up several more times, and Doris is increasingly disturbed by her. One afternoon Guy says he has a story to tell her; she mustn't interrupt until he's finished it. The story begins when he was assigned to this post as a very young man. The only other white people were the head of the station and his wife. When the head died, Guy, despite his youth, was picked to replace him. At first he was so busy that the lack of companionship did not disturb him, but as months went by, he found it very difficult to come home to solitude. One day, Abdul told him that there was a girl in the village who would like to stay with him. Guy met her, and, as things turned out, she stayed. She gave birth to a son, then another, and then, in the tenth year of their relationship, a daughter. The dark strangeness of the children had been a barrier to his caring for them. Of course, he saw to it that they had much more than they would have had as ordinary village children. When he and the girl had first met, he'd told her that one day he would bring back an English wife. She'd understood and agreed. The rest Doris knew. He'd gone to England on leave and had had the good fortune to meet and fall in love with her. He said he loved her more than ever, he was wonderfully happy, and his hope now was that she could understand the circumstances that had led him years ago to do what he had done. Doris' reaction to this recital is a mix of stupefaction, dismay, and anger. She runs to her room crying and when she sees him the next day, says that although she understands the situation he was in, it is so shocking to her that she believes it will be a least six months before they can live together again as man and wife. Upset by this, Guy says that he understands her reaction and, despite the difficulties, will wait in the belief that they will then resume their wonderful life together. At the end of the six months, Doris asks Guy to please let her go home. Although she understands what his situation was, something in her can't get over the fact that he spent ten years with another woman, had three children by and then abandoned her. In addition, he'd never said a word to her. Guy is devastated but soon understands that Doris cannot help herself. The force of circumstance is such that she cannot overcome her repugnance. She tells him that she thinks it best to depart with the river boat that will be coming by in a couple of days. She packs, leaving behind all the vases, dishes, and furniture which she'd bought to beautify their home. Guy cannot bear being in the house while she packs, but he returns to escort her to the ship. He gives her money and they walk together to the pier. Doris wishes to embrace Guy in farewell but can't manage it. They shake hands and say goodbye. Back at the house, Guy, in despair, orders the servants to pack up everything that could remind him of Doris. He sits drinking on the verandah till darkness falls. Then he hears a noise, opens his eyes and sees a Malay boy standing there. It is his oldest son. The boy says, "Mother wonders if you want her to come back?" Guy says "Yes." The boy asks "When?" Guy says "Tonight," and that is the last word of the story.

Within minutes of loosening myself from the grip of the story, I thought, "This is as English a story as I've ever read." I felt that I now understood—perhaps even *felt*—what being English was. The desperate quietness of the renunciation, the suppression of the gestures and words which most of us require in times of emotional intensity, the maintenance of good manners, these were the heart of the story, and it was an English heart.

From the outbreak of World War Two, many Americans began admiring English ways and manners which so many nineteenth century Americans had denounced as snobbish, artificial or hypocritical. The eloquence of quiet bravery became part of the American sense of what it took to engage in a great struggle. It was embodied in the easy jocularity which obtained between those two upper-crust gentlemen, Roosevelt and Churchill. Americans digested it even more readily in the person of the bi-national link, General Eisenhower, whose aw-shucks bravery was the American twist of English *sang-froid*. More recently, American feelings for English virtue focused on what had once been the despised world of privilege, the British upper middle-class, at home or abroad. Middle-class, middle-aged Americans relished the comforts of Edwardian houses with their numerous servants and the romantic intrigues in which honor played an important role. *The Forsythe Saga, Upstairs, Downstairs, A Passage to India* and *Brideshead Revisited* (with its Catholic turn of the screw) became the staples of American middle-class fantasizing. For bookish lovers of intellectual and sexual eccentricity, there was Bloomsbury and the inter-gender romps of Lytton Strachey, John Maynard Keynes, and

Leslie Steven's girls. In short, pre-war England became to post-war America what Greece had been to Augustan Rome, Imperial Spain to 17th-century France.

These are matters of cultural history, not of aesthetics. The question remains, "What is the conviction and the pleasure of social verisimilitude in works of art?"

The day after I read the story, my wife and I went to the British Museum to see an exhibit of Italian drawings on the third floor. Rising up the dark stairwell was an enormous black totem pole from Queen Charlotte Island in British Columbia. Its sculpted extension culminated in a raven-beaked head topped by a stovepipe hat. I remember thinking that this magnificent pole probably revealed the tribe which sculpted and—I thought—worshiped—it as the Maugham story revealed the English of its time. However, I had no other key to the mentality of the tribe. I could only admire its carved animals, smile and wonder at its top-hatted apex. My only critical thought was that it must have seemed to members of the tribe as enormous as the Sears Tower does to a walker in Chicago's Loop.

That afternoon, we fled the heat and funky filth of Tottenham Court Road for an air-conditioned movie, Robert Altman's film of the Sam Shepard play, *Fool for Love*. I don't believe my mind was set in the key of these reflections, but even so, as I watched it, I became aware that more and more the film struck me as deeply, uniquely and essentially *American*. As the picture opens, you see five motel cabins arranged in a rough circle, like covered wagons huddled for the night's bivouac. A neon sign blares to the surrounding desert that Breakfast, Lunch, Tubs and Showers can be had here at the El Royale Motel. Beyond the sign, beyond the desert, are purple mountains. The film's protagonist, Ed, is driving over them in a truck which is also hauling his horse. He's on his way to the motel, more particularly, to May, a beautiful young woman who, we learn, is not only his love but his half-sister. Their father, a boozy knockabout who plays the harmonica, runs the motel from his broken-down office-trailer which sits between a garbage dump and a car cemetery. A couple with a three-year-old girl drive to a cabin and lock the girl outside while they make love. The little girl stares at May, who is screaming at Ed for showing up when she doesn't want him to. May holds the little girl until the mother runs out and brings her back to the cabin, where we glimpse the man sitting dejectedly on the bed. May is expecting a boyfriend, who shows up while she and Ed are fighting and just in

[190]

time to see the Countess, an old girlfriend of Ed's, drive up, focus her headlights on May's cabin, and shoot at it, missing them, but shattering windows and splintering furniture. Then there's a flashback exposition as May and Ed explain their relationship to the boyfriend. You see them as high school sweethearts, then see the suicide of Ed's mother after she learns that Dad has another wife and child, and that the child is Ed's girl, May.

The intrigue hardly counts. What does count is the passionate, incestuous, bigamous intimacy which almost seems the natural consequence of the emptiness of these people lost under the great sky in the Western desert. The fools for love, Ed and May, shuttle between need and rejection of their indissoluble, intolerable pact. At the end, the Countess returns to set the place on fire. Ed, who's been lassooing garbage cans while May threatens him with a knife, rides off on the horse; May, too, takes to the road. After him? Who knows? Old Dad sits down in the ashes, and on his harmonica plays one of the mournful country songs we've heard throughout the film. The desolation, the neons, the casualness, the passion and carelessness of relationship—the melting pot aboil—the quick resort to violence, the flight to desert and mountain, the material extravagance in the middle of nowhere, and, finally, the dismal poetry of it all, cries out *America*, species, Western, sub-species, the neo-western film. Anywhere in the world where movies are shown, this film would be instantly *felt* as American.[2]

The relationship between a work and what literary scholars call its provenience dates back as a critical question at least two hundred and fifty years. The great Neapolitan, Giambattista Vico, wrote in his book, *The New Science* (1725) that Homer was the Greek people.

> He composed the Iliad when Greece was young and consequently burning with sublime passions such as pride, anger

---

[2] For Europeans—and others from small countries—America is often defined by—and *felt* in—its spaciousness. (Russia and China are as well. See discussions of Gogol and Tolstoy or the Napoleonic and Nazi invasions; for China, the texts date from before Prester John and Marco Polo. See Donald Lach's *Asia in the Making of Europe, passim.*) A currently chic French writer, Jean Baudrillard, writes about American space absorbing and being defined by movements in it, an absorption which enriches the viewer. (Cf. Wallace Stevens's lyric, "I placed a jar in Tennessee.") *"Le mouvement qui traverse l'espace par sa propre volonté se change en une absorption par l'espace lui-même. . . .Ainsi est atteint le point centrifuge, excentrique, où circuler produit le vide qui vous absorbe."* (*Amérique.* Grasset. 1986. pp. 27-28).

and vengeance—passions which cannot allow dissimulation and which consort with generosity: so that then she admired Achilles, the hero of force. . . Grown old, Homer composed the *Odyssey*, at a time when the passions of Greece were already somewhat cooled by reflection, which is the mother of prudence—so that now she admired Ulysses, the hero of wisdom.

In the next century, Herder wrote that poetry changed as the habits, manners, language and temperament of nations changed. Later in the century, the French writer, Hippolyte Taine, wrote that works of art sprang out of *time, race,* and *milieu.*

Literature as a sort of particularized sociology was born somewhere among the works of these thinkers. It is related to that generalizing tendency which simplifies—and sometimes menaces—our lives. Claude Lévi-Strauss's book *The Jealous Potter (La Potière Jalouse,* Plon, 1985) begins when an orchestra conductor tells the author his observations about instrumentalists and their instruments.[3] Oboists, he says, are invariably pinched and irritable types, trombonists expansive and jovial. Lévi-Strauss goes on to quote Sébellot, whose *Légendes et Curiosités des Métiers* inventories traits associated with different arts and crafts. So butchers are seen as robust and powerful, tailors, weavers and millers—people who transform basic materials—are accused of cheating, i.e., keeping back material.[4]

Many basic actions are inflected with nationalist, social or tribal values. In his book *Identity, Youth and Crisis* (Norton, 1968), Erik Erickson points out that when a child learns to walk he is praised in some societies for independence and boldness; in others, he is cautioned as "one who could go too far" and thus be a danger to communal life.

Centuries before Vico, Aristotle described the pleasure human beings get from seeing imitations of what they already know. It's as if by knowing something well enough to make an imitation of it, we were able to control it. Aristotle says that although we don't like to see a dead dog in the street, a painting of one may delight us. Art removes the aggravating, dangerous, disgusting and chancy

---

[3] Lévi-Strauss translates this as the "homology between the two systems of professional occupations and of temperaments."

[4] There is often rationality behind these generalizations. Lévi-Strauss mentions the English phrase "mad as a hatter", and says it may have something to do with the ill-effects of chemicals used in dyeing hats.

elements of life. The removal is effected by imitation and reduction. (So a child loves dolls, and most of us love miniatures.)

Generalizations are, in a sense, miniatures. To use a technical term, they are reductive. When such reductions, in the form of mean prejudice, deprive those reduced of their rights, most decent human beings discard them. (Many of us salve the loss of this comforting simplicity by making and welcoming jokes about it.)

In comedy, there is always reduction. So the jokes, and so the success of parodists and satirists who exploit their own prejudices as they triumph over them. My interest, though, is not with satire, parody or caricature, but in the pleasure which derives from that form of imitation which convinces a reader or spectator that he's understanding not just an individual but a type, and that this social verisimilitude, the sense that one is getting a true picture of social types, of the times, is itself pleasurable.

This is the way they were.

This phrase adapts the title of a novel by Anthony Trollope (*The Way We Live Now*) which I read a week or so after I read "The Force of Circumstance" and saw *Fool for Love*. The Trollope books deal with a large group of mostly upper-middle class mostly-Londoners in the 1870's. (The book was published in 1875.) The characters include a variety of wastrels of good family who spend much of their time drinking and gambling in their club, the Beargarden; their parents, who are under financial pressure to marry them and their sisters to wealthy people, though they prefer to draw the marital lines along familiar social routes; a group of outsiders—promoters, swindlers and semi-swindlers, Americans, Jews, and other would-be vaulters of social hurdles—who wish to marry themselves or their children into respectable society; the country cousins of the respectable and their village dependents; and the semi-literary journalistic world which reports, advertises and evaluates the others. The book is organized around the narrative seesaw of the Western novel, that is, the self-interest of passion versus the larger interest of family, society and nation as expressed by property, money, power and those commodities and activities which testify to them.

My description is abstract; the novel, of course, is not. It is explicit, individual, realistic. Again and again, Trollope's intelligence transforms obvious relations, actions and reactions in surprising, amusing and moving ways. Yet, unlike Dickens or the Brontës or the social satirist Thackeray, Trollope seldom works the behavioral extremities. He works along the lines of what *most of us*

[193]

think of as social norms. (In part, we think this because of his work.) Over a thousand pages, he justifies his title,[5] and makes readers think, "Yes, this is the way things really were in England in 1870. This is as much as we're going to know about these sorts of people. Now we know what they thought, what they feared, what they wanted."

Our pleasure in this knowledge is distinct from our pleasure in the story itself, that is in the depiction of events which satisfies our need to know *what happened then.* Not, of course, completely distinct. Sometimes it appears as the wake of the pleasure; after a while, it is another dimension of it, one which expands and deepens it.

Pure narrative pleasure is intense, unself-conscious and transient. Our pleasure in social verisimilitude is colder; it is an acquisition, a possession. "The Force of Circumstance," *Fool for Love* and *The Way We Live Now,* extend and solidify our knowledge of world-space and time. They vivify and certify our historical sense. They are the narrative equivalent of the pleasure Impressionist painters supply: not only do they give us beautiful masses of colored forms but also the houses, clothes, coiffures and life of *real* people in a real place and time. We art-lovers are gripped not only by beauty but by truth. The pleasures of such truth are smaller, tougher, more portable. They are augmented, not diminished, by passing from mind to mind. That we sometimes substitute them for esthetic pleasure—for "the real thing"—is an old indictment. Nonetheless, they too are *real.*

---

[5] Which is used by one of Trollope's honest characters to suggest that people are acting as they would have in the good old days. Of the contemporary reviewers of the novel, only the *Times'* anonymous reviewer thought the book "faithful. . .portraiture." Indeed that reviewer objected to the scrupulous, if not dutiful intrusion of balancing traits in such portraits as that of Melmotte, the swindler. For most of the reviewers, and for the author, the book was seen as satire, which meant exaggeration, if not "unfaithful" portraiture. Authors seldom appraise their work as their posterity does.

[22]

EVENTS, HAPPENINGS, CREDIBILITY, FICTIONS

Every now and then critics conclude that a species or genus of an art has been exhausted or superseded.[1] One object of this *genrecidal* criticism is prose fiction; here, from George Steiner, is a typical burial service:

> It is not only the traditional scope of fiction that is in doubt, but its entire relevance to the present, to the needs and idioms of our consciousness . . . As is now becoming generally understood, fiction has fallen well behind sociology and reportage.[2]

Such genrecidal conclusions as Steiner's are almost always worth careful study, for they usually testify to an artistic crisis. The crisis goes to the source of the art, the methods and conventions used to report or express the actualities at their source. The crisis occurs when new techniques take over some of the older genre's function. So, a hundred years ago, photography exerted enormous pressure on painting.

The fictional crisis described by Steiner is more complicated. The reason is that the verbal medium serves so many masters. Fiction is not even the only form of licensed lying. To study its crisis, then, we'll start with *credibility*.

Credibility problems are marked by such terms as "image," "propaganda," "cover story," "camouflage," "hypothesis," "legal fiction," "credit," "myth," "illusion," "dream," and "fantasy." They

---

[1] William Hazlitt's "On Modern Comedy" and Edmund Wilson's "Is Verse a Dying Technique?" are well-known elegies of this sort.

[2] *Book Week, Chicago Sun-Times,* 1967.

stand for ways of dealing with actuality. Because they operate within isolated systems, they are protected. When they leak from their systems into areas where their utility or fidelity becomes unclear, it usually means mischief or sickness. We then speak of such things as credibility gaps or hallucinations.

When an element from an open system—nature, actuality, the world—is introduced into a closed system, it also makes for trouble, or, sometimes, excitement. If a commencement speaker explodes a firecracker on the stage, the audience will express its awareness that an element from an open system has threatened the security of a closed one. Talleyrand, hearing that Napoleon was dead at last, said: "That is no longer an event. It is a piece of news." Dead, Napoleon belonged to print, to a closed and controlled system (where Talleyrand, whom Napoleon had called "shit in silk stockings," was safe from his barbs). Talleyrand's awareness of the distinction is like the artist's.

Artists employ the distinction all the time; from the beginning they have made it a subject of their work. In the eighth book of the *Odyssey*, the disguised hero listens to the blind bard Demodocus sing about the heroes of the Trojan War (it amounts to the *Iliad* [3]), but unlike the other listeners at King Alcinous's court, he weeps. What was a closed system, a fiction or an artful story for them was a heartrending, still existent experience for him.

Homeric anticipation of the modern subject of the story of the story, the play within the play, goes even further at the end of this section of the epic. To his unknown guest the king says: "Tell us why you wept so bitterly and secretly when you heard of the Argive Danaans and the fall of Ilion. That was wrought by the gods, *who measured the life thread of these men so that their fate might become a poem sung for unborn generations.*" This royal claim that reality exists for the sake of art marks the limit of artistic solipsism: the closed system embraces everything. Boasts of art's superiority to life are dwarfed by it.

The distinctions between art and actuality are part of a more general distinction, that between *being* and *having-knowing-picturing-remembering-loving-possessing-converting. Being,* and its alernate mode, *doing,* are unaware of existing or performing. A baby exists, unaware of existence. The beloved does not enjoy what the lover enjoys in her: she is; her lover knows, enjoys, possesses her. (When she herself enjoys, she is lover, knower, possessor; the

---

[3] Vergil and Cervantes are the two most famous imitators of the Homeric strategy of self-referral.

sweetness of love is this reciprocity.) The doer does, the observer sees, the witness and artist chronicle and convert.

An alteration in the equilibrium between art and actuality is the discovery on the part of many "do-ers" and "be-ers" that they are also characters; more, that they are or can be their own chroniclers, analysts, even poets. Max Scheler wrote that "feelings which everyone nowadays is aware of having in himself once took poets to wrest from the terrifying muteness of our inner life." Scheler remarked the effects of the novel of analysis and perhaps of psychoanalysis. These had given the silent lives of the world mirrors, but the tape recorder, the camera, the roving anthropologist, the reporter, the psychological caseworker, and the social surveyor have shown the "do-ers" and "be-ers" of daily life that they are not only specialized segments of opinion but proper subjects of biography, actors in potential newsreels, amateur sages, and semi-artistic performers in events, in happenings. It is in part this transformation of characters into self-conscious actors and then into storytellers which makes critics feel that professional inventors of stories are "irrelevant to the needs and idiom of our consciousness." When everybody bakes bread, who needs bakers?

The doer who tells his story, the reporter who puts it into a new context, the historian or sociologist who provides a more elaborate frame for it are artists, as the Greeks would have said bakers are artists. They assemble divers materials into useful, beautiful, and delightful objects. Susanne Langer calls them works of "practical" as opposed to "imaginative" art. We can get close to them by examining events like the firecracker-menaced speech; such events are called "happenings."

A happening is an artistic performance in the guise of an event. It incorporates uncontrolled, *actual* material into a closed system. Delight in a happening comes from the contrast between the special security of art and the potentially uncontrolled presence of (an intensified or rigged) actuality. A successful happening is unrepeatable. A happening's success depends on shock or surprise. Happenings have always existed, particularly in times of leisured opulence. Huizinga describes fifteenth-century Burgundian festivities which featured motet-singing bears, pies filled with orchestras, and forty-foot towers. He called them "applied literature."

Many happenings spring not from festive energy, Dadaistic wit, and opulent ennui but from social and artistic contempt, emotional rigidity, shallowness, cruelty, and perversion. Few national histories lack tyrants who convert human beings into "subject matter."

[197]

Such happenings are examined by historians, social psychologists, and anthropologists, but may be studied fruitfully by estheticians. (When art and nature are confounded, no specialist is privileged.)

Happenings are of interest to the arts because they stand for a desire to alter the relationship between art and actuality. Many, perhaps most, artists want to shake up an audience by violating its preconceptions about what belongs to art. The first-night performances or exhibitions of many such works resemble happenings. The premieres of *Hernani, Playboy of the Western World, Marat/Sade, Le Sacre du Printemps*, the first days of Fauves exhibit, even early reactions to *Les Fleurs du Mal* and *The Waste Land* exhibit the violent reactions characteristic of happenings. The violence springs from rage at the broken contract between actuality and art, the crossing over from an open to a closed system.

There is another artistic side of happenings. Art forms may be said to orginate in happenings. When an old religious ritual was altered by a figure stepping from the laymen's section of respondents, Greek drama began; and when someone altered a hunter's memorandum in a Cro-Magnon cave,[4] it was the beginning of mural painting. So Andy Warhol—following his master Duchamp—decided that the manufacturers of Campbell's Soup failed to realize that their product is as pleasing to the eye as it is to the stomach and signed his name as an artistic pledge of the observation. Result: a new type of sculpture.[5]

What takes place here is that an action or object which belongs to *being-doing* is appropriated for the world of *knowing-appreciating-loving*. The appropriation is usually bold, primitive, shocking. The shock is one of transition; the consumer or the worshiper has been converted into the spectator or appreciator. He has postponed the satisfactions of appetite for those of amusement, delight, emotional involvement in an abstract world. The shock itself, the happening element, can't be repeated. (If Warhol went on to sign a can Heinz Soup, he'd be called either an epigone or a bad promoter.)

Most artists make works which are not exhausted by initial performance, works which do not depend on shifts between art and actuality, which validate themselves in an artistic tradition and do not require validation by shock.

---

[4] Recent studies discuss the ritualistic, sexual implications of these old paintings. See Alexander Marshak's *The Roots of Civilization* (1972).

[5] See Hugh Kenner's brilliant discussion of this in *The Counterfeiters* (Bloomington: University of Indiana Press, 1968).

[198]

The claim that such works of literary art are no longer relevant "to the needs and idiom of our consciousness" ignores not only the crucial distinction between happenings and imaginative art but the one between these and such works of practical art as the reportage of Truman Capote and John Hersey, the wonderfully edited autobiographies assembled by Oscar Lewis and Danilo Dolci, such collections of heart-breaking letters as those found in the mailbags from Stalingrad, and hosts of fine memoirs, biographies, essays, and histories.

No matter how splendidly assembled, fascinating in detail or rich in linguistic, expressive, or speculative power, works of practical art are limited by having to conform—in sequence, place, number and character—to actuality. Delight in works of practical art is conditioned by conviction that they're true. Though the cameraman selects his focus, the reporter shades and dramatizes and the sociologist has a thesis, we nonetheless invest emotionally in their credibility. If we find that we've been taken in, our reaction is—properly—rage; and despite his skill we arrest the forger of Vermeers, throw away the text with beautiful but inaccurate blueprints, don't sleep on the handsome, backbreaking bed, and refuse to buy the fake reporter's story.

Works of practical art must be true; indeed, they usually begin with a statement of their credentials. Here are a few of them:

1. The tape recorder, used in taking down the life stories in this book, has made possible the beginning of a new kind of literature of social realism. With the aid of the tape recorder, unskilled, uneducated, and even illiterate persons can talk about themselves and relate their observations and experiences in an uninhibited, spontaneous, and natural manner . . . most of the recording was done in my office and home . . . Occasionally I recorded at [the home of the Sanchez family] in the Casa Grande . . .I used no secret technique, no drugs, no psycho-analytic couch. The most effective tools of the anthropologist are sympathy and compassion for the people he studies.

   Oscar Lewis, *Children of Sanchez*

2. The editor believes the thing to be a just history of fact; neither is there any appearance of fiction in it.

3. All the material in this book not derived from my own observation is either taken from official records or is the result of inter-

views with persons directly concerned, more often than not numerous interviews conducted over a considerable period of time.

Truman Capote, *In Cold Blood*

4. Throughout our work on [this book], I have been continuously impressed by demonstration of the extent to which that much abused term "total recall" can be literally true . . . I retraced with her, time and again, the threads of many of these episodes, always from a different vantage point. Each time they checked out even to the smaller touches of phrasing, style, figures of speech.

Carleton Lake collaborating on
Françoise Gilot's *Life with Picasso*

5. He left the custody of the following papers in my hands, with the liberty to dispose of them as I should think fit. I have carefully perused them three times: The style is very plain and simple; and the only fault I find is that the author . . . is a little too circumstantial . . . this volume would have been at least twice as large, if I had not made bold to strike out innumerable passages relating to the winds and tides, as well as the variations and bearings in the several voyages.

Five editor-authors delivering the real words of real people. Surely a praiseworthy activity, whatever the motive—entertainment or enlightenment. All deny that they are making anything up.

Now of these five claims two are manifestly false. The second is from the preface to *Robinson Crusoe*, the fifth some of the prefatory matter of *Gulliver's Travels*. How do these fictional claims differ from the truthful ones?

The two fictional claims are part of a different contract, an eighteenth-century convention of the art—revived now and then—which licenses departure from the real world while claiming to be a chunk of it. Readers of Gulliver will never be troubled as readers of Capote or Lewis may be—indeed, have been—by the question of the accuracy of their books. Capote and Lewis must justify their books in terms of the truth of their descriptions and renditions: the fiction writer justifies his book in a completely different way. Warhol would not be arrested if he sneaked into the art gallery one night, siphoned off the tomato soup from his six-dollar sculpture,

[200]

and substituted soapy water for it; but the maker of the original seventeen-cent can would be. The artist Warhol is not bound to the same standard of credibility as the practical artist, Campbell's designer.

Talking of public opinion half a century ago, Walter Lippmann wrote: "A work of fiction may have almost any degree of fidelity, and so long as the degree of fidelity can be taken into account, fiction is not misleading." The "credibility gap" causes rage in the actual world,[6] not the world of imaginative art.

Yet the degree of fidelity should be known to the imaginative artist. The imaginative artist "does the same as the child at play; he creates a world of fantasy, which he takes very seriously: that is, he invests it with a great deal of affect, while separating it sharply from reality" (Freud, "The Relation of the Poet to Day-dreaming"). The imaginative artist is—at least in his art—distinct from the lunatic and the lover, and in direct contrast to the practical artist, he works out techniques to separate his art from reality. Systematically, he alters actuality: places, ideas, characters, time schedules, meanings. His art derives in part from the dissociation of given materials. Even those artists who minutely reproduce their vision, who check their time schemes with almanacs (Fielding), their place names with city directories (Joyce), their memories of houses and clothes against personal or newspaper accounts (Proust) are only accumulating powder for fictional explosions. Far more than the tellers of romance, the cryptographic fabulists, the algebraic comedians, the heart-twitching parodists, these "realists" wish to assemble the world in order to control it. Whenever the remembered actuality will not suffer the explosive charge readied for it, it is thrown out. (Biographies which draw parallels between the artist's life and his fictional version of it reveal such changes. It's true even for artists who try to arrange their lives to provide material for their work.) This exempts the fiction writer from libel suits, and rightly so. Places, times, and details which first gripped the writer's imagination come to belong more and more to it—and

---

6 Washington (UPI)-Rep. Harley O. Staggers (D-W. Va.) announced Tuesday that his investigative subcommittee will study whether laws are needed to protect the public from 'factually false and misleading filming and editing practices' in the making of television news documentaries . . . NBC complied with its subpoena for a film copy and transcript of 'Say, Goodby,' a program dealing with the preservation of endangered species of wildlife. The program alleged to show a hunter killing a mother bear when in fact the bear was brought down with a tranquilizer gun. CBS was given ten days to reconsider the demand for unused documentary materials. The confrontation could lead to a contempt-of-Congress citation against the network and possibly a court suit . . . " *(Chicago Sun-Times, Wednesday, April 21, 1971).*

each other—less and less to the world from which they came. The result can be so overpowering that the artist may say with Alcinous that the life was lived for the art, or at least that only in art were the intensity and meaning of the life felt.

The art form helps provide this intensity and meaning, and the art form constantly alters. As fiction altered its modes of handling its special data, writers found that the modes and alterations themselves became an interesting subject. Since Flaubert and James, fiction—like music since the sons of Bach and painting since Cézanne—has been in no small part about itself. That is, it deals explicitly with its modes of representation. Perhaps it's in response to such incestuous concentration that the new works of practical art rose to put pressure on fiction, as if to say, "Back to nature, boys."

Fiction writers have often been men of unusual emotional, intellectual, and senuous energy, and so great works of fiction contain reports from the borders of human complexity and intensity. If we are to see practical forms expand to include such reports, all the better. Engineers follow in the wake of the most abstruse theorists; and theorists arise from great works of engineering.[7] From penny-dreadfuls to *Ulysses, Ulysses* through John Dos Passos to Hersey and Capote; and these to something further out.

It is not time for fiction's funeral but for weddings and births.

---

[7] Degas and Vuillard used photographs to define what they wished to paint.

[IV]

ON SOME NOVELS AND STORIES

NOVELS

Yes, novels...work in which the greatest powers of the mind are
displayed, in which the most thorough knowledge of human
nature, the happiest delineation of its varieties, the liveliest effu-
sions of wit and humour, are conveyed to the world in the best
chosen language.

Jane Austen
Northanger Abbey

   . . . but he
Must struggle out of his boyish gift and learn
How to be plain and awkward, how to be
One after whom none think it worth to turn.

For, to achieve his lightest wish, he must
Become the whole of boredom, subject to
Vulgar complaints like love, among the Just

Be just, among the Filthy filthy too,
And in his own weak person, if he can,
Must suffer dully all the wrongs of Man.

W. H. Auden
"The Novelist"
Collected Poems

But for something to read in normal circumstances?

Ezra Pound
Homage to Sextus Propertius

*The following pieces are products of a fiction writer's workshop. The
opinions—some of them harsh—are those of someone who believes
he knows what's going on. Others may regard them as infighting.*

There's undoubtedly some of that, but not as much as literary hard-hats would have you believe.

Unlike scientists, who can collaborate on all but the highest levels because they're working toward the mastery of what's really out there,[1] novelists work alone because their best work means dissociation from the familiar. (There'll never be a Darwin-Wallace coincidence in the arts.) Novelists count only as they are distinct from other novelists.[2] Everything that is different about them becomes their stock in trade.

Novelists need each other the way countries need boundary lines: "That's X's way or place." Essentially, there's no taking over another novelist's territory. It would mean taking over his mind. (There's a certain amount of theft, some of it for parodic— or other legitimate—purpose.)

Most novelists can and often do admire their colleagues' work; but convictions about the way novels should be written, the way life feels, the way it is, blind you to some good work. Criticism helps relieve feelings and, better, enables you to spell them out in terms of the art.

---

[1] I've read enough of James Watson, Stephen Gould and my old friend Dick Lewontin, and enough about the discussions between Bohr and Einstein, to question the felicity of scientific collaboration. (Most enlightening of all have been long talks with my brother-in-law, Arthur Karlin.) Nonetheless, the distinction between the work of artists and scientists still seems valid to me.

[2] I think this is true for all artists, including those who programmatically reject a form of individuality. ("Neo-Plasticism aims precisely at representing nothing that is individually determined." Determined by "nature" and "the senses," said Mondrian and van Doesburg. OK. But then they added determined by "sentiment." Does this mean Mondrian would paint only what had neither appeal nor interest for him? Ridiculous.) For architects the matter is, at least theoretically, different. Mies could well have meant that he'd like all buildings built in the same nonstyle style. (Of course, it was *his* "nonstyle.")

[23]

PICARESQUE EXTRA CUVÉE

The *Confessions of Felix Krull, Confidence Man (The Early Years)*[1]
derives from the picaresque as Dr. Faustus does from the biographical memoir: in both novels the ease and looseness of the traditional forms become components of quite formal works. "Formal" not
in the sense of the classic French novel (*The Princess of Cleves,
Adolphe, Madame Bovary, The Plague*), the novel which exhausts a
single situation by means of extensive motive analysis and crucial
scenes, but "formal" in the manner of the greatest moderns, that of
thematic control.

Felix Krull is another extension of that most accommodating
fictional form, a form which has served jest book, *Bildungsroman*,
travelogue, quest, and thriller. Mann makes use of most of its
traditional materials—nimble hero, complacent partners, ferocious
officials, sharpers, victims, rags to riches—as naturally in his
pedagogical format as did Smollett and Lesage in their adventurous ones. Indeed, the form seems made for a writer of Mann's
didactic inclinations; his return to these confessions three times in
his last forty years shows he knew it.

Mann had never taken to the French form, although he had taken
a great deal *from* it. (He reread *Renée Mauperin* three or four times
while working on *Buddenbrooks*.) His style, with its distance, its
internal, masochistic burlesque, its perpetual assertiveness, could
never "forget itself" in the restricted outlooks whose divergence
composes the novel of conduct. Mann's world is always at the far
end of his prose leash; readers are much less involved with Hans
Castorp than with Emma Bovary. Mann's narratives unroll almost
as conspicuously as Thackeray's and Fielding's. In his last two
full-scale novels, the style issues from a narrator, a broad but limited intelligence whose presence in the traditional form of the two

---

[1] Thomas Mann, *Confessions of Felix Krull: Confidence Man (The Early Years)*, translated
by Denver Lindley (New York: Alfred Knopf, 1956).

books constitutes their chief device and invention. In *Dr. Faustus* the expansive humanism of Serenus Zeitblom weighs every page with that ambivalence which is Mann's trademark; in *Felix Krull* the Germanic formalism of the "great man's autobiography" is compromised by the situation itself—a swindler recounting his truancies—and by the carefully heightened version of the *Dichtung-und-Wahrheit* style.

Of all Mann's heroes, Krull is the one who speculates most consciously, most in the manner of Mann's essays, about his experience; and he has by far the most experience. It is the manner in which this experience is selected from and narrated that distinguishes this version of picaresque. Compare a brief portion of it with one from a work whose general arrangement is similar to it, *Moll Flanders*. *Moll* and *Krull* are both first-person accounts of criminal careers written post facto from positions of safety, Krull in weary retirement at the age of forty, Moll in repentant security at seventy. Both narratives are organized chronologically and scattered with edifying reflections. Here are Moll and Felix at their initial thefts:

> . . . and the devil, who I said laid the snare, as readily prompted me as if he had spoke, for I remember, and shall never forget it, 'twas like a voice spoken to me over my shoulder, "Take the bundle; be quick; do it this moment." It was no sooner said but I stepped into the shop, and with my back to the wench, as if I had stood up for a cart that was going by, I put my hand behind me and took the bundle, and went off with it, the maid or the fellow not perceiving me, or any one else.
>
> It is impossible to express the horror of my soul all the while I did it. When I went away I had no heart to run, or scarce to mend my pace. I crossed the street indeed, and went down the first turning I came to, and I think it was a street that went through into Fenchurch Street.
>
> *Moll Flanders*, Modern Library, p. 181

> So great was the joy of beholding this bountiful spot completely at my disposal that I felt my limbs begin to jerk and twitch. It took great self-control not to burst into a cry of joy at so much newness and freedom. I spoke into the silence, saying: "Good day" in quite a loud voice; I can still remember how my strained, unnatural tones died away in the stillness. No one answered. And my mouth literally began to water like a spring. One quick, noiseless step and I was

[210]

beside one of the laden tables. I made one rapturous grab into the nearest glass urn, filled as it chanced with chocolate creams, slipped a fistful into my coat pocket, then reached the door, and in the next second was safely round the corner.

No doubt, I shall be accused of common theft. I will not deny the accusation, I will simply withdraw and refuse to contradict anyone who chooses to mouth this paltry word. But the word—the poor, cheap, shopworn word, which does violence to all the finer meanings of life—is one thing, and the primeval absolute deed forever shining with newness and originality is quite another.

Felix Krull, pp. 42-43

What Moll thinks is but a small part of what she does; the narrative moves into action. Moll says, "It is impossible to express the horror," and she doesn't try. Mann's narrative, however, moves toward commentary. Felix is around the corner in a second, and around that corner is an elaborate speculation, though one as important to the movement of Mann's book as Fenchurch Street is to Defoe's. In comparison, *Moll* (and, I think, all previous picaresques) seems a boundless, untreated flux.[2]

Every detail in *Krull* is part of a general notion; and it is these which organize the novel. One can relate the incidents of *Moll Flanders* and have an orderly action; if one tries this with Krull, the relation will make sense only if organized thematically. The digressions which Krull asks the reader to excuse are digressions only from the traditional order; the accounts of the circus performers, of a couple seen on a Frankfurt balcony, of shop windows, the speculations themselves, form the novel as the progression of incidents forms *Moll*.

Krull's themes are from the Mann warehouse. The dominant one is the nature of entertainers, artists, superior people, their relation to the world and, by virtue of a Mann lecture, to Being as well. In brief, these special people create themselves and their world: "Had I not instead the assurance...that my voice might quite easily have turned out common, my eyes dull, and my legs crooked, had my soul been less watchful?" Their talent for illusion—which is not so illusory—and for deception—which is craved—gives them entry to and power in the world, and leads to their overthrow. Their chief talent is for pleasure—"The Great Joy," Felix calls it.

---

[2] This is exaggeration for critical purposes; *Moll* is "treated" brilliantly, and *Krull*, though its events have an apposite, illustrative air, is a good deal more active than garrulous.

They gorge experience, and the novel supplies their feast. Their altar is the department store, which is also—for Felix—a university where he learns to discriminate clothes, jewelry, and women.

Krull celebrates a Dionysian bacchanalia. Words and their offspring, codes and laws, are the apparent villains. But words are what the weary Krull must now resort to in memoir. "Only at the two opposite poles of human contact, where there are no words or at least no more words, in the glance and in the embrace, is happiness to be found, for there alone are unconditional freedom, secrecy, and profound ruthlessness" (p. 83). These, final words from a writer, even one so notoriously ambiguous about the artist as Mann, are more than the "ironic German's" playful literary suicide. Smug literary security doesn't hide the uncertainty about power and culture which makes even the greatest works of modern German literature edgy, ambivalent, tremulously pompous, as if standing on tiptoe waiting to be turned into divine music.

Yet in Krull the questionable, unresolved feel of the action, the action which includes speculation, is what keeps the most didactic page fictional, eventful, controlled from outside, not, as in Fielding's inserted essays, from inside the novel itself. And though the style is, in a sense, the protagonist mocking the world it reveals, the style in this is Felix's, and Felix is not in control of the novel as an autobiographer is in control of his confession; the control of character and reminiscence in this book is incomparably greater than in that of the most aware autobiographer.

[24]

PROUST AND JOYCE UNDER WAY:
THE TRADITION OF AUTOBIOGRAPHY

Several years ago Mlle. Claude-Edmonde Magny protested against the publication of writers' discarded sketches, notes, and interim drafts. Of *Jean Santeuil*, the work which Bernard de Fallois assembled from the papers Proust left behind in an old *carton à vêtements*, Mlle. Magny wrote:

> Those critics who hope to learn by autopsy the mystery of creativity will find with satisfaction the themes of *Recherche* already prefigured—but minus that essential, the intricate architecture of the work, the transfiguration of reality by style, the transfiguration of time by selected experience . . . the reading of *Jean Santeuil* can scarcely bring us anything but anecdote. More seriously still, it "comes off on," fades into, our understanding of the *Recherche*: many an unpleasant trait which had to this point remained in the shadow, in the background of the author and the person, is roughly illuminated, and by a lurid daylight.

One does not rush to disagree with such critics as Mlle. Magny, but here, it seems to me, her objection excludes a work which I for one would prefer to reread, even at the expense of reading her excellent criticism of it. *Jean Santeuil*, and the remarkably similar early work of Joyce, *Stephen Hero*, are not distinguished by that "intricate architecture" which, since James' time, has been regarded as the source of our greatest literary pleasure. The pleasures they provide are possibly lesser ones, but there is no reason to throw them out; they won't damage the literary palate.

R.P. Blackmur writes in his introduction to the collected prefaces of James that "Proust...wrote always as loosely as possible and triumphed in spite of himself. Joyce made only such sacrifices as suited his private need—and triumphed by a series of *tours de force*." What are these triumphs which triumph in spite of the victor, and these "sacrifices" which suit the need—the "private

[213]

need"—of the sacrificer?

Proust scattered his views of form and composition all through his work. One appears in *The Captive* (*La Prisonnière*). The narrator is thinking about Wagner's operas:

> . . . I thought how markedly . . . these works participate in that quality of being—albeit marvellously—always incomplete, which is the peculiarity of all the great works of the nineteenth century, with which the greatest writers of that century have stamped their books, but, watching themselves at work as though they were at once author and critic, have derived from this self-contemplation a novel beauty, exterior and superior to the work itself, imposing upon it retrospectively a unity, a greatness which it does not possess. Without pausing to consider him who saw in his novels, after they had appeared, a *Human Comedy*, nor those who entitled heterogeneous poems or essays *The Legend of the Ages* or *The Bible of Humanity*, can we not say all the same of the last of these that he is so perfect an incarnation of the nineteenth century that the greatest beauties in Michelet are to be sought not so much in his work itself, as in the attitudes that he adopts when he is considering his work, not in his *History of France* nor in his *History of the Revolution*, but in his prefaces to his books? Prefaces, that is to say pages written after the books themselves, in which he considers the books, and with which we must include here and there certain phrases beginning as a rule with a "Shall I say?" which is not a scholar's precaution but a musician's cadence. The other musician, he who is delighting me at this moment, Wagner, retrieving some exquisite scrap from a drawer of his writing table to make it appear as a theme, retrospectively necessary, in a work of which he had not been thinking at the moment when he composed it, then having composed a first mythological opera, and a second, and afterwards, others still, and perceiving all of a sudden that he had written a tetralogy, must have felt something of the same exhilaration as Balzac, when casting over his works the eye at once of a stranger and of a father, find in one the purity of Raphael, in another the simplicity of the Gospel, he suddenly decided, as he shed a retrospective illumination upon them, that they would be better brought together in a cycle in which the same character would reappear, and added to his work, in this act of joining it together, a stroke of the brush, the last and the most sublime. A unity that was ulterior, not artificial, otherwise it would have crumbled into dust like all the other systematisations of mediocre writ-

[214]

ers who with the elaborate assistance of titles and sub-titles gave themselves the appearance of having pursued a single and transcendent design. Not fictitious, perhaps indeed all the more real for being ulterior, for being born of a moment of enthusiasm when it is discovered to exist among fragments which need only to be joined together. A unity that has been unaware of itself, therefore vital and not logical, that has not banned variety, chilled execution.

The Captive, Modern Library, I, pp. 211-13

There are a good many things to remark in this excerpt; but the chief interest here is the attitude that this master of "intricate architecture" takes toward this aspect of his craft, his illustration even, in the "he who is delighting me at this moment," of the brief phrases which may look awkward out of the narrative context, but which reveal the skeleton of the work. Without them, the work would appear formless. Form is *natural* to the work of artists, although it manifests itself only after the artist becomes his own critic, discovers the form of his work, sees the few touches needed to bring it out, and provides them.

Proust's notions are related to the better-known esthetic speculations of Joyce which appear in *Portrait of the Artist, Stephen Hero,* the notes which Gorman prints in his biography, and such byblows as the book reviews which he did for the *Daily Express* in 1902-1903.

Joyce's concern is also with the apprehension of that "vital form" which reveals itself to the artist with the sudden power he called epiphanic. Joyce does not write, as James does, of the methods of achieving form; in the early reviews he seems interested not in a novel's craftmanship but in its revelations of personality. His brother Stanislaus remarks in a note to Joyce's review of A.E.W. Mason's novels that he "was free from bigotry toward the literature of mere entertainment." The reason is that such literature can be as revealing as any other about the mind which conceived it. Joyce cites Leonardo's observation that the mind has a tendency "to impress its own likeness upon that which it creates," and he goes on to find motifs in Mason's novels which were there "without the author's consent." Joyce's favorite word of praise for fiction in the reviews is "epic," and that means, in his famous definition, the "form wherein...[the artist] presents his image in mediate relation to himself and others." Like Proust's, then, Joyce's notion of fictional excellence, fictional form, has to do with what for James belongs not to the work but to the author. For Proust and Joyce, fiction is a form of autobiography.

Just about the time that Proust and Joyce were writing the last pages of the works we know as *Jean Santeuil* and *Stephen Hero*, James was writing the preface to *The Ambassadors*, in which he described the perils of the "large ease of 'autobiography'" to which writers had better not yield unless they were prepared "not to make certain precious discriminations." James was actually considering the use of the first person, a post of observation he had eschewed in *The Ambassadors* and, as it were, made the almost farcical point of the novel which preceded it, *The Sacred Fount*. His technical warning, however, was directed at "the terrible fluidity" which threatens "self-revelation" of any sort. Since the eighteenth century, when such works as Wieland's *Agathon, The Sorrows of Young Werther, A Sentimental Journey*, and above all Rousseau's *Confessions* came to the fore, and the nineteenth, which saw even more varied mixtures of *Dichtung* and *Wahrheit* (*Adolphe, La Vie de Henri Brulard, The Prelude, Sylvie, David Copperfield, Pendennis, The Way of All Flesh*, and countless others), James's stricture would have served as a corrective; these revelations were usually corrupted by sentimentality or sensationalism, as their forms were by the uncertain position of the protagonist.

The reliance upon "autobiography" as a source of fiction is related, I think, to the changing conception of character which the novel of analysis helped to bring about. The conception that character is so fluid as to be in fact unknowable determines the construction of such novels as Dostoevsky's *The Devils*, where the planned unpredictability of Stavrogin is a result neither of the author's uncertainty nor of farce (a genre in which unpredictability is a major component). The fluidity of "characters" as different as Proust's Albertine and Joyce's HCE is also, it seems to me, a product of such a conception.[1] The notion of the unknowability of character helped to do away with that standard eighteenth- and nineteenth-century novel which depended on the clash of more or less fixed characters around central figures, who become at the end of the novel more or less like one of the fixed figures. When the new conception undermined this form of the novel, many serious writers turned to "autobiographical fiction." Not that writers could

---

[1] Strindberg's famous preface to *Miss Julie*, in which explains his "characterless" characters, and Pirandello's preface to *Six Characters in Search of an Author* indicate some of the influence the new conception had in drama.

know themselves better than they could know others, but at least they knew what they felt, remembered, and believed. This was material for a novel whose chief technical problem would be the position of the narrator-protagonist.

For Joyce, the problem was not as pressing as it was for Proust. His chief stock in trade was not the exploitation of his sensibility: he was not a lyric writer. His first published novel is a clever record of his own experience, experience which he assessed as "young" before he wrote. His later work deals more and more generally with the nature of writing about experience. In his first work he was concerned with guaranteeing the authenticity of Stephen's experience by indicating it had been his own. A note by Stanislaus Joyce to the shortest of Joyce's early reviews makes this clear:

> In condemning this novel cursorily, my brother condemns pseudonyms; however, when a year later his own first stories were published, he yielded to the suggestion (not mine) and used a pseudonym, "Stephen Daedalus," but then bitterly regretted the self-concealment. He did not feel that he had perpetrated bad literature of which he ought to be shamed. He had taken the name from the central figure in the novel "Stephen Hero," which he had already begun to write. Against that name I had protested in vain; but it was, perhaps, his use of the name as a pseudonym that decided him finally on its adoption. He wished to make up for a momentary weakness; in fact, in order further to identify himself with his hero, he announced his intention of appending to the end of the novel the signature "Stephanus Daedalus pinxit."[2]

For Proust, the fashioning of an "I" took nearly twenty years. It was crucial to his work because his concern was not only the meaning of his experience (the discovery of vocation) but recovery and extension of its extraordinary qualities: his sensibility was both subject and object.

In Jean Santeuil he is constantly wrestling the "I." The book begins:

> Should I call this book a novel? It is something less, perhaps, and yet much more, the very essence of my life, with nothing extraneous added, as it developed through a long period of

---

[2] The French translation of *Portrait—Dedalus: Portrait de l'artiste jeune par lui-même—* brings out the import of the definite article in the English title.

wretchedness. This book of mine has not been manufactured:
It has been garnered.

Then follows (according to de Fallois' arrangement) an introduction in which "I" meets the novelist "C" whose novel *Jean Santeuil* is supposed to be. Nothing more is heard of C, but "I" makes frequent appearances alongside C's hero, Jean Santeuil, and occasionally displaces him:

> It is a pleasure too—and a very great pleasure—to find ourselves confronted by a certain air of intellectual freedom, in such men who by a word can justify opinions which we ourselves should have liked to express, but have rejected because, in our constant effort to be sincere (I am talking now of natures like Jean's) we feel...(p. 352)

and

> We do not know whether we still love Madams S_____
> [Mme. S. is Jean Santeuil's mistress], but we...
> (p. 582)

There are many other awkward intrusions.

When Proust told Gide that the writer could tell all as long as he didn't attribute it to "I," he was talking about the necessity of keeping the observer's hands clean, or rather his eyes clear, so that the observations would not be suspect. If a novel's observer is suspect, this becomes one of the objects of the book; this is the case in *The Sacred Fount* and many other novels. The narrator of the *Recherche* is the one who discovers and who acts upon his discoveries; the writer behind the book's "I," Proust, is the object of discovery as well as the discoverer.

For the *Recherche* Proust fashioned a narrator who shared much of his experience and sensibility but who lacked his genius, perversion and tenacity. It is likely that Proust was helped to work out such a narrator by the critical examination of writers which he was making at this time for *Contre Sainte-Beuve*. What he says there of Dostoevsky's procedure is remarkably similar to what was to be his own.

> Mais il est probable qu'il divise en deux personnes ce qui a été en réalité d'une seule. Il y a certainement un crime dans sa vie et un châtiment (qui n'a peut-être pas de rapport avec

[218]

ce crime) mais il a préféré distribuer en deux, mettre les impressions du châtiment sur lui-même...(*Maison des Morts*) et le crime sur d'autres.

The fact that Proust's discoveries about his own work came (according to de Fallois's chronology) just after the revival of his critical powers in the writing of *Contre Sainte-Beuve* leads to another important difference between the work of Proust and Joyce and that of James and the earlier writers of the autobiographical tradition: this is the importance of criticism to *and* in their work. James reserved his criticism for his prefaces, and he called these "the story of the story." For Proust and Joyce, whose works are in a sense about themselves, the story of the story, the esthetics and criticism are part of the books. This exhibition of the writer criticizing his work as he forms it provides a logical conclusion to the tradition of "autobiography."[3]

---

[3] James himself was to discover the pleasures of "I" when he came to write his autobiographic volumes. Indeed, on the first page of *A Small Boy and Others* he sounds very much like Proust: "...to recover anything like the full treasure of scattered, wasted circumstances was at the same time to live over the spent experience itself...to see the world within begin to 'compose' with grace of its own round the primary figure...," and so on, as if he were foreseeing the Proust volume which he was to praise as worthy of Cervantes and Balzac (as Proust records in an article which he had Léon Daudet send to the editor of *L'Eclair* in 1919).

[25]

DOCTOR ZHIVAGO

For seventeen pages *Doctor Zhivago*[1] looks like an outline for a Tolstoy novel: three boys, different in character and circumstance, unknowingly interconnected, are treated with the sort of care that makes one anticipate a well-paced unfolding of their careers. End of Chapter One. Chapter Two takes place about two years later, and its first seventeen pages treat Lara Guishar, the book's heroine; her mother; her mother's lover, who seduces her; the cellist Tyshkevich; Olga Demina, an apprentice in Madame Guishar's dressmaking establishment; Faina Silantievna Fetisova, "Madame Guishar's assistant and senior cutter"; the lover's dog Jack; a strike on the Moscow-Kazan railroad; the railroad's divisional manager Fulflygin; the track overseer Antipov; Tiverzin, Khudoleiev, Yusupka, Gimazetdin; a demonstration march from the Tver Gate to the Kaluga Gate; the uncle of the hero, who "saw the fleeing demonstrators from his window"; the—but this will serve. These are but *some* of the characters and events on those seventeen pages. The "summary" is not less confusing than what it summarizes. Nor is the confusion ever dispersed, for the characters and scenes are scarcely developed and almost never exploited unless they are regarded as parts of a confused panorama. Even this explanation will not do, for many of these characters reappear in the novel, not so that one can distinguish them, but because even Pasternak knows that there is a limit to the number of ingredients which can be crammed into one dish. The effects of the first two hundred pages of *Doctor Zhivago* might be compared to a thousandfold expansion of the Hakagawa-Madame de Tornquist-Fräulein von Kulp section of "Gerontion."

---

[1] Boris Pasternak, *Doctor Zhivago*. Translated from the Russian by Max Hayward and Manya Harari with "The Poems of Yurii Zhivago," translaated by Bernard Guilbert Guerney (Pantheon, 1959). This review was published in 1959 while the Pasternak cheering section supplied the only literary noise one heard. Dwight Macdonald's blast at the book was published shortly after this one.

Dr. Zhivago

Edmund Wilson has called *Doctor Zhivago* a poem (among many other things, including an allegory and a folk tale), but although even narrative poems can slight narrative and get away with it, since they have other charms on which to rely, novels can't. Accretion is not narrative. Pasternak seems to learn this about a third of the way through the book and begins concentrating on his hero, the doctor-poet Yuri Zhivago.

Concentration, however, is a comparative term. Twenty-five pages of Tolstoy or Stendhal would give us the Zhivago of Pasternak's five hundred.

The weakness of Pasternak's work derives from serious errors in presentation, and these in turn depend in large part on the book's form, or rather the impulses to form, at which, since they are not fulfilled, one may only guess.

Pasternak seems to have had two major formal notions for the novel: the first was to write a large, Tolstoyan work, full of characters and scenes which would render the flavor of society; the second was to write a sort of *Red and Black*,[2] an historical chronicle focused on a hero's life. This twofold scheme proved impossible for him to execute. In the first place, a Tolstoy novel works not with characters and scenes but with situations which "pick up" character and scenes[3] as they are needed. Second, the Tolstoy situations exist in terms of each other as parallels, contrasts, or continuations. In *Zhivago* there are no real situations, no intrigues which are followed closely, developed suspensefully and in depth. The closest approach to a situation is the love of Zhivago and Lara, but this is so interspersed with other material and so larded with capricious coincidence that one never has the sense of effort a serious love story must have. No wonder Wilson and other critics have tended to think of *Zhivago* as an allegory; its narrative is too sparse to nourish a reader.

If this thin diet starves the Tolstoy impulse—unfortunately not to death, for we keep meeting characters till the very end—it is fatal to the Stendhalian one. The novel of careers lasts until the death or retirement of the hero; if you begin with the hero as a young boy, and at the same time do a kind of Tolstoy and have three boys, you set up an immensely long novel, even if all the

---

[2] Two of the five books Zhivago mentions in the Varykino chapter are *War and Peace* and the Stendhal novel.

[3] Cf. Tolstoy's midnight cry of despair that he had forgotten to put a yacht race into *Anna Karenina*.

careers end as early as Julien Sorel's. Even with one hero, Stendhal—unlike, say, the author of *Jean Christophe*—centered the career about two parallel situations, one provincial, one Parisian, and thus brought off his chronicle as well as his career novel. Stendhal's controlling idea—something like "What would become of a Napoleon in the antiheroic Restoration?"—looks like the ideal model for Pasternak, whose root idea would seem to be "What happens to a good man in the bad times of revolution and collectivism?" Ambition overlaid and ruined this central notion. Although I do not believe that Pasternak went so far as to attempt what Edmund Wilson suggests—"a phase-by-phase chronicle of Soviet policy, and a discussion of the development of Russian literature which touches on almost all its great figures from Pushkin to the school of modern poetry" or "a historical-political fable—see Larisa's relations with Zhivago, Komarovsky, and Pasha"[4] —I do believe that the ambition to present the career of a good man in bad times was fatally jostled by the attempt to simultaneously present the careers of a good many people drawn from many levels of society.

The scheme Pasternak employs to solve the problems of such a work consists in presenting the fictional matter in short, rapidly shifting scenes, or in Irving Howe's excellent description in "clipped vignettes...apparently meant to suggest a Tolstoyan breadth and luxuriousness of treatment." These scenes, or fragments, are "clipped" by a variety of narrative sins which succeed in blighting almost every breath of life in the book. Here are some of them.

1. Unwarranted, unsignaled transitions:

Nikolai Nikolaivich refused to believe him and dashed out but was back in a minute. He said bullets whistled down the street knocking chips of brick and plaster off the corners.

---

[4] I think it just as likely, indeed far more likely, that there are *roman-à-clef* elements in *Zhivago*. For Larisa Guishar I suggest the Soviet writer Larisa Reisner, at whose death in 1926 Pasternak wrote the poem "Pamyata Reisner" (*Stikhot voreniya y odnom tome*, Leningrad, 1933, pp. 289-90). In Reisner's book of sketches, *The Front* (1924), appear such Zhivagesque passages as

The revolution wears out its professional workers unconscionably. It is a harsh master with whom there is no use talking about a six-hour day, maternity benefits or higher pay. It takes everything – men's brains, wills, nerves and and lives – and, having sucked them dry, having wounded and exhausted them deposits them on the nearest scrap heap...

There was not a soul outside. All communications had stopped.

That week Sashenka caught a cold. (p. 190)

2. Displacement of dramatic narrative by curtailed observations:

For some time they sang the "Marseillaise," the "Varshavianka," and "Victims You Fell." Then a man who had been walking backwards at the head of the procession, singing and conducting with his cap, which he used as a baton, turned around, put his cap on his head, and listened to what the other leaders around him were saying. The singing broke off in disorder. Now you could hear the crunch of innumerable footsteps on the frozen pavement. (p. 35)

We see no more of the man walking backward; we don't know what "the other leaders around him were saying." This is the longest of the eight paragraphs which "present" the march from the Tver Gate to the Kaluga Gate.

3. Coincidence:

There is more coincidence in this novel than would be justified in a farce. The whole of Russia is like the lobby of a small-town hotel. People simply cannot get away from each other no matter how far they travel (nor is this the point). Coincidence is Pasternak's way of appearing to continue the Tolstoyan novel when he has really abandoned it for the novel of Zhivago's career.

4. Inability to relate an anecdote:

While they were waiting for Dudorov he told the story of Dudorov's marriage . . . The improbable gist of this story consisted in the following: Dudorov had been drafted into the army by mistake. While he was serving and his case was being investigated, he was constantly punished for absentmindedly forgetting to salute officers in the street. For a long time after his discharge he would raise his arm impulsively whenever an officer came in sight, and often he imagined epaulettes where there were none.

In this latter period his behavior was erratic in other ways as well. At one point—so the rumor went—while waiting for a steamer at a Volga port, he made the acquaintance of two young women, sisters, who were waiting for the same steamer. Confused by the presence of a large number of army men and the memories of his misadventures as soldier, he fell in love with the younger sister and proposed to her on the spot. "Amusing, isn't it?" Gordon said. But he had to interrupt his story when its hero was heard at the door. Dudorov entered the room. (p. 176)

Stories are frequently interrupted or broken off entirely (p. 71, 262). Or, as in this case, the stories are deprecated: the clause which follows "Dudorov's marriage" is "which he thought was comical." Such deprecation is allied to the next zhivagary.

5. Deprecation of the philosophical speeches:

After Zhivago has made a profound speech about life and death:

"What's come over me?" he thought. "I'm becoming a regular quack—muttering incantations, laying on the hands..." (p. 69)

Or a comic Tolstoy disciple after making one of the famous ideological speeches in the book:

"I haven't understood a word. You should write a book about it." (p. 42)

Or the speaker is said to be drunk (p. 182). The author's lack of self-confidence is contagious.[5]

6. Inadequate preparation (or proper sequence):

"And now since you've been so frank with me, I'll be frank with you. The Strelnikov you met is my husband, Pasha, Pavel Pavlovich Antipov, whom I went to look for at the front and in whose death I so rightly refused to believe." (pp. 298-99)

This revelation is sidestepped not only into but around. Zhivago responds to it in this way:

---

[5] After reading Mrs. Mandelstam's account of artistic hell (*Hope Against Hope*), I'm almost persuaded these

"What you say does not come as a surprise. I was prepared for something of the sort." (p. 299)

Or

Mademoiselle called up Kolia and told him to find Dr. Zhivago a good seat on the train, threatening him with exposure if he did not. (p. 155)

We never learn what can be exposed.

I end the list with a passage which displays one of the novel's stylistic faults which cannot, I think, be blamed on the translators.[6] This is the book's overinvestment in simile and metaphor.

> Narrow dead-end streets ran off the square, as deep in mud as country lanes and lined with crooked little houses. Fences of plaited willows stuck out of the mud like bow nets in a pond, or lobster pots. You could see the weak glint of open windows. In the small front gardens, sweaty red heads of corn with oily whiskers reached out toward the room, and single, pale thin hollyhocks looked out over the fences, like women in night clothes whom the heat had driven out of their stuffy houses for a breath of air.
>
> The moonlit night was extraordinary, like merciful love or the gift of clairvoyance...(p. 142)

Wilson complains that the translators sometimes lop off fine figures of speech. Though this is translator treason, Zhivago could use more of it.

I have gone through a partial list of the narrative flaws[7] in order to hint at the page-by-page difficulty of reading Zhivago, if you're reading it as a novel and not as an "historic utterance" (Howe) or as "one of the great events in man's literary and moral history" (Wilson).

What we have in *Doctor Zhivago* is a jumbled accretion ner-

---

[6] Wilson is the only critic I've read who seems to have read the original Russian text as well as the Italian and English versions. His demonstration of the inadequacy of the last is fairly convincing, although he praises, indeed overpraises, its naturalness ("it does not sound translated"), finds that it cuts through some stylistic defects of the original and is a good deal better that the English versions through which Tolstoy and Turgenev first made their reputations here.

[7] The original piece dealt with others. (See *Kenyon Review*, Winter 1959.)

vously strewn over a great many pages. Its occasional lovely descriptions and speeches float to the surface like the splintered witnesses of a shipwreck. For paragraphs here and there, the novel sounds like Tolstoy (p. 84) or Dostoevsky (p. 155); in fact, one might cut-and-paste from it an anthology of passages modeled on the great Russian fiction writers from Gogol through Chekhov. Here and there too are suggestions that apparently capricious events or isolated descriptions are truly related to each other, not in the artificial fashion of "The Rowan Tree" chapter, but in the subtle one which Stuart Hampshire claims exists between the natural scene and the narrative events. The trouble is that the formal collapse and botched rendering obscure desired connections and suggest undesired ones. The errors of conception and presentation corrode the novelistic ambition almost beyond guessing.

A melancholy event for a reader of fiction, a melancholy event for the citizen. For two years, readers have been waiting for this novel, their appetites sharpened by the early reports and its bizarre publication history.[8] That a great poet was treating one of the great themes of modern history, and from the lip of the grave itself, might well be a great event in "literary and moral history." It is understandable that when the novel did appear, many fine critics saw in this version of their own intellectual history a heroic and beautiful utterance.[9] For those less close to the ideological fire, this misshapen bequest from Soviet Russian literature testifies to what the book itself explicitly mourns, the dissolution of that sense of individual life which the great Western novel celebrates.

---

[8] This involved the Italian publisher Feltrinelli's smuggling the manuscript out of Russia. (In those days, Feltrinelli – whom I knew a bit – was not the revolutionary who, a decade or so later, blew himself himself up as he was setting up explosives on a railroad track.)

[9] Writing in *Dissent*, Lionel Abel confessed as much: "My liking for this book is a personal fact without significance for literary judgement; it is an accident of my own intellectual history; there is no reason why it should influence anybody else."

[26]

HENDERSON'S BELLOW

1

The first forty pages of *Henderson, the Rain King* are packed with enough material for two or three novels, odd, passionate relationships between husbands and wives, fathers and children, landlords and tenants, intricate, suspenseful, and disposed of with quick brilliance that is the first of this book's surprises. The next three hundred pages leap from this material into territory few novelists in the world are energetic enough to enter. Or rather to construct. Scanting his marvelous ability to reupholster the world's furniture, Bellow sends his hero into a country where almost nothing is familiar.

> The way grew more and more stony and this made me suspicious. If we were approaching a town we ought by now to have found a path. Instead there were these jumbled white stones that looked as if they had been combed out by an ignorant hand from the elements that make least sense. There must be stupid portions of heaven, too, and these had rolled straight down from it. I am no geologist but the word calcareous seemed to fit them. They were composed of lime and my guess was that they must have originated in a body of water. Now they were ultra-dry but filled with little caves from which cooler air was exhaled—ideal places for a siesta in the heat of noon, provided no snakes came. But the sun was in decline, trumpeting downward. The cave mouths were open and there was this coarse and clumsy gnarled white stone.

This country is neither conscientiously symbolic nor artificial; but seen through the eyes of Henderson, the regal, knowledgeable, keening slob who narrates the book, its topography has personality, one which seems to both objectify and spur the novel's bizarre notions.

Are there precedents for this sort of construction? In a way, there aren't.

Utopians, satirists and dream visionaries have been contriving countries for millennia, but to greater or lesser degree their contrivances are unlikely. Either the landscape is unearthly and the brute creation articulate, or the hero arrives by time machine or dream. In Bellow's Africa, custom and belief are strange, but all—including a semi-domesticated lion—seems real. Fantasy is reserved for speculation, where it can be accommodated as an early stage of knowledge.

There is a much more important difference in *Henderson*, and that is its hero. The Gullivers, Candides, and Connecticut Yankees may be scalpels, sensitometers, blank slates, mechanical pens, victims, physicians, PA systems, or even types, eccentric and amusing, but they are never characters whose fates mean more than their discoveries and situations. Eugene Henderson outlasts both what he learns and what happens to him, and constantly he pulls the book out of the perilous abstract. His American memories corkscrew through the African present tense with an ease which makes Ford and Conrad look elephantine; his rag-bag miseries and splendors—battered hulk, largesse, sweet ambitions, ever aching conscience—domesticate the unfamiliar. The book stays grounded in the real.

Henderson proceeds from the narrator's want. He's had the world and it isn't enough. It's what Bellow supplies for his want that makes the book a different sort of reading experience for faithful Bellovians.

2

An account of the difference might begin with a paragraph from Augie March:

> In his office Simon wore his hat like a Member of Parliament, and while he phoned his alligator-skin shoes knocked things off the desk. He was in on a deal to buy some macaroni in Brazil and sell it in Helsinki. Then he was interested in some mining machinery from Sudbury, Ontario, that was wanted by an Indo-Chinese company. The nephew of a cabinet minister came in with a proposition about waterproof material. And after him some sharp character interested Simon in distressed yard-goods from Muncie, Indiana. He bought it. Then he sold it as lining to a manufacturer of leather jackets. All this while he carried on over the phone and cursed and bullied, but

that was just style, not anger, for he laughed often.

There in a single paragraph out of Augie's thousand or so, the great know-how is at work, the skipping facts, the bunched variety more lively than life ever is, four or five different sorts of sentence, all held in and charged with Augie's tone. Places, things, people, pointed description, key movements—the alligator-skin shoes knocking things off the desk— and the characterizing summary, this is the way it goes, more brilliantly packed with the commodity and stuff of the world than anything in American literature since *Moby Dick*. "It was like giving birth to Gargantua," Bellow said of it, and that comparison may suggest why it stopped, for to the reader it looks as if it might go on as long as the world supplied Augie with objects to handle and people to watch.

Henderson starts where *Augie* leaves off. Augie was a knocker at doors, a Columbus of the "near at hand." Henderson is a Columbus of the absolute, fifty-five, not twenty, a man for whom doors have opened but who dislikes what's inside.

The problem for Henderson's writer is that the absolute is barely furnished, and what furniture it has consists of those Biedermeier hulks of fiction, ideas.

The strategy of idea-novels amounts to working out a form of concealment: the action is tied into the idea as illustration or contradiction. The organizing idea of a novel close to *Henderson*, Mann's *Felix Krull*, is something like the reality of fakery, and the book is cluttered with crooks, magicians, illusionists of all sorts, glorious-looking champagne bottles containing miserable champagne, actors seen first under lights and then backstage, a spectrum of fakery drawn from department store windows to interstellar space. The picaresque adventures are sunk into this detail, which is assembled to illustrate, or rather to compose, the themes. On the other hand, in such a book as *The Magic Mountain*, the characters do things which contradict the notions they expound. (A humanitarian pacifist challenges a Jesuit convert to a duel, and the latter kills himself.) *Henderson* takes neither one of these routes; its actions are discrete from the notions which make up much of the book—*Henderson*'s, those of the two beautiful obesities, the women of Bittahness, and those of the William James-reading, almost-MD totem king, Dahfu. *Henderson*'s notions glow like actions, its actions signify. (It is a truer expression of the Eliot-Pound thesis of sensuous ideas than most of what they wrote.) So toward the end of the novel King Dahfu is in the midst of a Reichian analysis of *Henderson*'s posture:

[229]

You appear cast in one piece. The midriff dominates. Can you move the different portions? Minus yourself of some of your heavy reluctance of attitude. Why so sad and so earthen? Now you are a lion. Mentally, conceive of the environment. The sky, the sun, and creatures of the bush. You are related to all. The very gnats are your cousins. The sky is your thoughts. The leaves are your insurance, and you need no other. There is no interruption all night to the speech of the stars. Are you with me? I say, Mr. Henderson, have you consumed much amounts of alcohol in your life? The face suggests you have, the nose especially. It is nothing personal. Much can be changed. By no means all, but very much. You can have new poise, which will be your own poise. It will resemble the voice of Caruso, which I have heard on records, never tired because the function is as natural as to the birds.

Dahfu tells Henderson to get down on his hands and knees and bellow. "Be the beast!"

And so I was the beast. I gave myself to it, and all my sorrow came out in the roaring. My lungs supplied the air but the note came from my soul. The roaring scalded my throat and hurt the corners of my mouth and presently I filled the den like a bass organ pipe. This is where my heart had sent me, with its clamor. Oh, Nebuchadnezzar! How well I understood that prophecy of Daniel. For I had claws, and hair, and some teeth, and I was bursting with hot noise. . .

Dahfu's speech is so wily a mixture of the lyric and admonitory, the descriptive and conceptual, that even if it were not couched in gorgeous Bellafrikanisch it would advance the narrative at least as well as more obvious action. Dahfu's assessment leads to Henderson's roar, the roar leads into further assessment. "I was the beast . . . [I roared]. . . the note came from my soul . . . This is where my heart had sent me. . . " The scenic extravagance, a large man on hands and knees bellowing like a maniac, is put into a context which makes it not only right but moving. Behind it is the sort of momentum Swift gave the scene in which Gulliver kisses his master's hoof farewell, one of the most beautiful in eighteenth-century fiction.

As for the ideas themselves, they exist in terms of Henderson's need and have as much relation to belief as Bellow's Africa to Tom Mboyo's. The major one—a version of the notion that we are in

[230]

large part the product of the images we absorb—can be found in such different places as the beginning of Plutarch's *Life of Timoleon, Felix Krull,* and the somatic psychology of Wilhelm Reich. What counts in the novel is that Henderson's reaction to them reveals and deepens his character; and for Bellow, as for Malamud and some of the other fine novelists of the time, character is back in the middle of the novel, not where their great predecessors—Mann, Joyce, and to a somewhat lesser extent the greater novelist Proust— put it, into a thematic scheme which trimmed every fictional element to size.

Henderson is a bridge between *Augie March, Seize the Day,* and those thematic novels. The difficulty is that the bridge must bear the weight of constant invention, invention which can hardly draw at all on the home detail in which the other novels luxuriate. An original like Bellow can't lean too much on the secondhand views of travelers and movies; he must be on alert for those special clichés which menace writing about the exotic. Consequently, much of Henderson's detail is landscape, physiognomy, and a few clothing props, and the investment there is great. Bellow readers, used to commodity markets, Mexican resorts, Evanston haberdasheries, Machiavellians, and con men, must go into another gear. They will be helped by the fact that Henderson is a stylistic masterpiece.

The *Henderson* prose had a wonderful tryout in a long story, "Leaving the Yellow House," which appeared a year earlier in *Esquire.*[1] The story's about a sort of female Henderson—but on her last legs—who drips out like hourglass sand in the Utah desert. Its clean sentences are now galvanized by the popping energy of *Augie,* and the result is such paragraphs as this:

> Itelo protruded his lips to show that I was expected to kiss her on the belly. To dry my mouth first, I swallowed. The fall I had taken while wrestling had split my underlip. Then I kissed, giving a shiver at the heat I encountered. The knot of the lion's skin was pushed aside by my face, which sank inward. I was aware of the old lady's navel and her internal organs as they made sounds of submergence. I felt as though I were riding in a balloon above the Spice Islands, soaring in hot clouds while exotic odors rose from below. My own whiskers pierced me inward, in the lip. When I drew back from this significant experience (having made contact with a

---

[1] Reprinted in *Mosby's Memoirs and Other Stories.* (New York: Viking, 1969).

[231]

certain power—unmistakable!—which emanated from the woman's middle), Mtalba also reached for my head, wishing to do the same, as indicated by her gentle gestures, but I pretended I didn't understand and said to Itelo, "How come when everybody else is in mourning, your aunts are both so gay?"

3

There are, I think, three very different sorts of literary experience: the writer's, the reader's, and the critic's, the last two being as distinct as the first from them. If we analogize the writer to an assassin, the reader is the corpse, the critic the coroner-detective. The feelings of the assassin and his victim are notably different, but at least for our purposes they can be called powerful ones. In the former's case, they are organized by purposiveness, in the latter's by force (scarcely conceived and rapidly terminated). The coroner-critic is the rationalist, the reconstructionist; he cannot alter the responses of the reader-victim, but he can, in a sense, alter those of future readers in such fashion that their reactions will be affected by his notions. An early Monet critic could instruct viewers to stand a certain distance from the canvas. (Indeed, the feelings of someone who knows he has been murdered—knows, because "murder" is defined—are surely different from those he'd have if he were run down by a truck.) I bring this up because my reactions first as reader and then as critic of *Henderson* are distinct.[2] As reader I respond more easily to the Bellow I am used to, the parts of Henderson which deal with his American experience—his pig farm, bad teeth, Sevcik violin exercises, his fights on Highway Seven, his high rides with the bear Smolak, his wives and children. As critic, however, that part of me which reading has not yet slain, I admire the boldness and brilliance of the whole, the "originality" and the style, and the other tributaries of great narrative. And I believe my feelings will in future readings catch up with my admiration.

_____

[2] As a matter of fact, I feel in small part with the assassin, perhaps as accessory after the fact. I read an earlier version off *Henderson* and some of my initial reactions to it turned out to be similar to Bellow's as he went over the book, so that changes were made which make me feel – proudly – implicated. (I reminded him that a scene in which Henderson killed some monkeys who turned out to be the lovers of some of the women was out of *Candide*. The scene of the dynamited frogs was substituted.) The point here is that I feel I know what effects were wanted at certain moments; I also feel "in" on such genetic factors as Bellow's interest in Reich. Such knowledge alters, and alters seriously, my responsiveness to the "magic" of the book.

[27]

PNIN'S DUST JACKET

It is not often that one has to hurdle the praise of writers one respects to come to an accurate appraisal of a book, but the dust jacket of Mr. Nabokov's *Pnin*[1] throws a lot of dazzling dust in one's eyes.

The most fantastic claim on the jacket is Edmund Wilson's:

> [Nabokov] turns out to be a master of English prose—the most extraordinary phenomenon of the time since Conrad . . . [He is] something like Proust, something like Franz Kafka, and, probably, something like Gogol . . . [but he] is as completely himself as any of these other writers . . .

Even with the bracketed additions and the dots, even knowing that Mr. Wilson doesn't think much of Kafka, even with the strangely timid "probably," the ambiguous phrases "completely himself" and "the most extraordinary phenomenon of the time since Conrad," there remains "turns out to be a master of English prose." Or could it be that the Nabokov supplied in the brackets was originally— who? Grace Zaring Stone? Just as likely. It must be that Mr. Nabokov has a house at Wellfleet[2] or helped Mr. Wilson learn Russian, because even the ear that discerned the death rattle of Western poetry in its finest poetic hour in a hundred years[3] could not, without some extraliterary prompting, acclaim such gimcrackery as

Some people—and I am one of them—hate happy ends. We

---

[1] Vladimir Nabokov, *Pnin* (Garden City, N.Y.: Doubleday, 1957). The Nabokov tide will, I think, subside, leaving the delightful *Lolita* and a few stories. [1993. My opinion of Nabokov is higher, not lower than it was in 1970, but I leave this review as it stands because its anger stands for what drove my work, and because I think what it says is accurate even if it doesn't say enough.]

[2] A pretty fair guess. Since then, the two old grumblers squabbled on literary pages.

[3] Edmund Wilson, "Is Verse a Dying Technique?" *The Triple Thinkers*.

feel cheated. Harm is the norm. Doom should not jam. (p. 25)
Or, if that is considered the burlesqued property of *Pnin's* ghostly
narrator, then this example will serve:

> The bells were musical in the silvery sun. Framed in the pic-
> ture window, the little town of Waindell—white paint, black
> pattern of twigs—was projected, as if by a child, in primitive
> perspective devoid of aerial depth, into the slate-gray hills;
> everything was prettily frosted with rime; the shiny parts of
> parked cars shone; Miss Dingwall's old Scotch terrier, a
> cylindrical boar of sorts, had started upon his rounds up
> Warren Street and down Spelman Avenue and back again; but
> no amount of neighborlinesss, landscaping, and change ring-
> ing could soften the season; in a fortnight, after a ruminant
> pause, the academic year would enter its most winterly phase,
> the Spring Term, and the Clementses felt dejected, apprehen-
> sive, and lonely in their nice old drafty house that now
> seemed to hang about them like the flabby skin and flapping
> clothes of some fool who had gone and lost a third of his
> weight. (pp. 29-30)

This pile of clause is neither comic nor rhythmically pleasing, the
imagery is either trite or wrong, there is useless fill ("of sorts"), and
the overall effect has a complex pointlessness ("projected . . .
hills") which would suggest some private joke if it were consistent.
Nabokov's style exhibits almost every stylistic vice from the
baroque vocabulary ("canthus," "calvity," "zygomatic") which
strays into neologistic ugliness ("reminiscential," "hostelic") to
mistakes in idiom ("arrived at last to," "twice bigger," "up the
country") which are pardonable, but not on the grounds that the
narrator is a Russian émigré, because the mistakes are not frequent
enough to be explicable, achieve no effects but awkwardness, and
should have been taken care of along with a number of annoying
mechanical blemishes ("Are they only mechanical?"). The allitera-
tion ("proceeded to impress upon Pnin the following points") is so
annoying that again one wonders "Is it planned? Is it funny?"
There is a similar mania for parentheses[4]— "so as to have the one
he wanted among the rest (thus thwarting mischance by mathematical necessity)"—funny names (Dr. Rosetta Stone), and a Conradian
excess of qualifiers. There is, occasionally, a good paragraph (see

---

[4] The reader of this book may notice that Nabokov isn't the only devotee of the parenthesis.
[1993. Incidentally, I now like the paragraph a good deal more that I did thirty-six years ago.
Something has softened.]

last half of page 120).

Style, however, is a question of manner. What are we to say to Mark Schorer, whose rapture centers more about basic issues?

> How to describe it or its effects? I'll settle for profoundly delightful, because under the wonderful and hilarious comedy, which any academic person at least will recognize at once and delight in, there is a deep pathos that takes us out of all academies into the befuddled sufferings of humanity at large ... I honestly haven't enjoyed a novel so much in a long time.

Mr. Schorer is a novelist and a critic of the novel, and though he considers imagery patterns of novels more important than I do,[5] he knows the shapes of fiction, long and short. *Pnin* is no novel, and mere publisher's thirst for the commodity should not conceal the fact. *Pnin* contains material for a novel, notes for a novel, but even the strange final chapter in which the narrator at last appears more conspicuously than in an aside— "the kind Russian lady (a relative of mine)"—and tries to organize some of the events of the book cannot conceal the indirection, the waste of character and incident, the false soliciting of expectation which come from jamming these casual sketches into the "novel" category. Notes for a novel, because there is a moving situation, a clumsy, comic, sentimental, good-hearted Russian émigré isolated in a country whose ease and mechanism he adores but who is victimized by them and almost all the people who surround him. Such summary does too much honor to these one hundred and ninety pages. The book's only continuous lines are Pnin and the setting. They sit around waiting for anecdotal movement. The end of the book uncovers the narrator— the popular lecturer who is to take Pnin's job—listening to the anecdotes.

The reader who says about this device, "Look, you've just pointed to the clever, original form of the book," will be guilty of Nabokov's own makeshift notion of form. As *New Yorker* sketches, the Pnin stuff had some charm. Not as a novel. The academic wisecracks trip over each other; the notation of American detail ("a copy of Gertrude Käsebier's photographic masterpiece 'Mother and Child'"), Pnin's crying spells, the pedagogical parentheses—"He picked up his portfel' (briefcase)"—the Pninisms—" 'Unwrap,' said Pnin"—get heavier and heavier, until the last hope that they are going to function in a moving work is lost and one waits out the end.

---

[5] Mark Schorer, "Technique as Discovery," *Hudson Review*, 1 (Spring 1948), 67-87.

[28]

THE COUNTERLIFE[1]

The Counterlife will probably not be the last of the Zuckerman books. One could not have said the same thing after the publication of *Zuckerman Bound* (or for that matter *The Anatomy Lesson*). Then it looked as if the series of books about an American Jewish writer—from his excited, contemplative but nervous, even chilled youth—*The Ghost Writer*—to the burnt-and-copped-out acher of *The Anatomy Lesson* and the stunned literary voyeur of the Epilogue to *Zuckerman Bound*—had traced his career from promise to silence. What happened then is one of those semi-miracles which can occur when a gifted person applies himself intensely to his art (craft, trade, or profession, for that matter). Roth opened up another notch, let himself go and then, seeing what came out of the typewriter, made wonderful sense of it. What came out came out directly from the material of the other books, not from a theoretical decision or critical logic. What came out was a technical innovation, one true to the premise of the work. In *The Counterlife*, the writer writing is exhibited in front of the reader's eyes, yet this is not the center of the story as it is in ten thousand works of this genre since *Ulysses*. As always, Roth is not just attached to the fathers, mothers, brothers, girl-friends, freaks and wise men who fill the pages; he is committed to them. Roth's material, Jews and writing about them, writing, pain, lust, affection, family, no-family, solitude and glory, these are all here in *The Counterlife*, but the technical innovation, the author's delighted discovery of his freedom to do what he wants as long as it interests him, enables him to do even better and more brilliantly what some of his critics don't credit him with doing before, which is to give a hearing not only to his protagonist, Nathan Zuckerman, but to almost every character in the book. The characters in *The*

---

[1] *The Counterlife*, Philip Roth. Farrar Straus Giroux. 1986: 324 pp.

Counterlife are seen more than ever from their own positions, often in dialogue and letter. In one section of the book, though, Zuckerman is "dead," and his brother—who had "died" in an earlier episode—takes the floor and rules the narrative roost.

If this account is confusing, the novel is not, once the reader has accepted its premise. Then there is the delight of liberation (related, I'd guess, to the feelings the author himself had when he decided to *let her rip*). The claustrophobia which oppresses so many self-reflexive novels isn't here because Roth's worldly intelligence, satiric power, gift for portraiture, milieu, scene and action, are too strong to be mesmerized by technical discovery. If the writer has a measure of Tolstoyan worldliness in him, he will not have to pay the price of being caged by the techniques of exhibition. The Bellow of *Herzog* was not mangled by the epistolary device, nor was Proust brought to his knees by commitment to an autobiographical form.

There is another consequence of Roth's signing up with the armies of self-reflection: his gift for dramatic argument has more room then ever to work. It's similar to what happened to Updike in his most successful novel,[2] *The Coup*: the narrative voice, that of a deposed African leader, was both remote and intelligent enough to allow Updike to use his own brilliance. He could go all out, whereas in most of the other novels, the intelligence is either cramped by more or less ordinary characters or is released in lyric asides and lectures à la Father Mapple's Sermon (cf. the pages on Bach's cello music in *The Witches of Eastwick*). So in the Judea section of *The Counterlife* a brilliant discussion of Israel is dramatized, *embodied* in different characters including Zuckerman, who hears and sometimes responds to the others. The discussion of anti-semitism might be detached as a brilliant debate, yet it never feels detached from the narrative. In some of Roth's books, characters are stranded in a marvelous burlesque fixative. Here, even the most ludicrous character, Jimmy Lustig, of the West Orange Lustigs, author of the *Five Books of Jimmy* and the petition Forget Remembering, is given a shot at making a reasonable case. That Jimmy's fate is both exciting and uproarious is a measure of how solid the book is, everywhere fiction, not argument.

Everywhere but the last five pages where the brilliant argument Zuckerman offers the pregnant wife who left him is also the theoretical foundation for the book and for Zuckerman's life. It is still

---

[2] 1992. Before the wonderful *Rabbit at Rest*.

fiction, but may show a bit of the strain the author feels in the liberty he's given himself (and which this book's earned for him). This is one reason I think this won't be the last Zuckerman.[3]

To think of Roth in the line of those great non-Tolstoyan authors Proust, Beckett, and James is to realize again their credo: that the only thing which makes ultimate sense is what they're doing: writing a book. The author himself is either "the man of a thousand masks" (James) or what Roth at the end of this book calls "the performer":

> If there even is a natural being, an irreducible self, it is rather small, I think, and may even be the root of all impersonation—the natural being may be the skill itself, the innate capacity to impersonate. I'm talking about recognizing that one is acutely a performer, rather than swallowing whole the guise of naturalness and pretending that it isn't a performance but you.

This, in a letter from Zuckerman to his flown Maria, is, however, not philosophy but fiction, Zuckerman's stab at ultimate self-justification; it is also the farewell love song which is a subliminal theme of this book and which helps make it such a fine one.

---

[3] I've proposed a sequel and told the author I might write it myself under the title *Zuckerman's Pal*. It would involve Zuckerman taking on the much-vaunted author of the Old Testament.

[238]

[29]

AFTER-HEMINGWAY HEMINGWAY

If I were a publisher and the manuscript of this book[1] arrived on my desk signed by a name I didn't know, I'd say, "This is a fine book, a little old-fashioned and derivative of Hemingway, but it's too good to lose. Let's publish it."

Hemingway didn't submit this book to his publisher. Although he wrote all—or nearly all—the words in it, there were a lot of other words that went with them. Apparently Hemingway couldn't control the material, couldn't decide what to include. The book itself is about David Bourne, a writer full of self-doubt. Bourne's self-doubt is resolved; Hemingway's wasn't. *The Garden of Eden* exists because a quarter of a century after Hemingway killed himself a skillful editor named Tom Jenks did what Hemingway couldn't do, pruned, condensed, cut and shaped a novel. Jenks saved Hemingway from himself.[2] Carlos Baker, the Hemingway biographer, called the long version of this book "an experimental compound of past and present, filled with astonishing ineptitudes and based in part upon memories of his marriages" to Hadley Richardson and Pauline Pfeiffer. Jenks was far more deferential to Hemingway. He told the *New York Times* (Dec. 17, 1985) that "a complete major work" existed "within the unfinished manuscript." His cutting consisted of the removal of a sub plot which wasn't "integrated into the main body of the novel."

As is, *The Garden of Eden* is Hemingway's most literary work of fiction. It is about a successful young writer and the stories he writes while his beautiful wife undoes their new marriage and tries

---

[1] Ernest Hemingway. *The Garden of Eden*. New York: Charles Scribner's Sons. 1986. pp. 258. $18.85

[2] Barbara Probst Solomon believes Jenks' work betrayed Hemingway's success and failure both. She regards the book as an abortion ("Where's Papa?" B.P. Solomon. *New Republic* 196. March 9, 1987).

to undo him. It is Hemingway's bow to the genre of books about themselves. Happily, it is also about the joys and deceits of love. Finally, it's about the excitement, beauty and waste of hunting. There are two hunt sections in the book: one is the story Bourne writes about his father; it is a literary response to Faulkner's "Bear" as that was a southern, terrestrial response to *Moby Dick*. For the Hemingway who worked on this novel from 1946 till his death fifteen years later, the hunt is not only fascinating in itself, but its excitement and finality are an equivalent of writing and finishing a book. "Finishing," says Bourne, "is what you have to do . . . If you don't finish, nothing is worth a damn."

Finishing is what Hemingway found hard to do. The one good book he finished in the last decade and a half of his life was a novella about the pursuit of a great fish (which, when caught, is devoured by sharks).

Much of Hemingway's fiction centers about wounds. In *The Sun Also Rises*, the wound causes Jake Barnes's impotence. The wound of much of the late fiction is literary impotence. This is inflicted not by shells but rich women. In "The Snows of Kilimanjaro" and *A Moveable Feast*, rich women seduce the writer away from a supportive wife. In *A Moveable Feast* the theme is doubled by Hemingway's version of the ruination of Scott by Zelda Fitzgerald.

In *The Garden of Eden*, Catherine (the name of the beautiful, compliant dream girl of *A Farewell to Arms*) is as much like Zelda as she is like any of Hemingway's wives or like Agnes von Kurowsky, the nurse who—Hemingway felt—deserted him for an Italian officer. Catherine Bourne envies her husband's work and ends by destroying it. The novel doesn't match the facts of Hemingway's life, but his feelings about those facts. The feelings arise from nostalgia for paradise and resentment of it, from the confused intoxication of love and the "sudden deadly clarity that had always come after intercourse," from hatred of the women who tempted, and thus—in his view—dominated him, and from joy in the clarity which enabled him to escape from the paradise they offered to the accomplishment they resented.

The book begins in the late spring of 1927 in le Grau le Roi where David and Catherine spend the first weeks of their honeymoon. Catherine adores David but hates his literary success. Unable to write or paint, and usually too lazy to read and learn, she finds an outlet in destruction. She begins with fun and games. The main game is to become a boy. She cuts her hair short, tans her body, and does "boy things" to David in bed. (This isn't spelled out, only pussy-footed around and called "perversity" and "devilry.") Catherine persuades David to cut his hair like hers, she calls him Catherine and herself Peter. She goes though the Prado and looks at pictures "like a boy." One day she brings home a girl who's asked where they got their haircuts. The girl, Marita (a version of the dream girl-heroine Maria in *For Whom the Bell Tolls*) falls in—and soon makes—love with both Catherine and David. Gender confusion turned erotic confusion becomes confusion about self and purpose. Catherine is the worst off. Spun out of control, she burns the stories David has written partly to control the excitement of simultaneously loving two beautiful women.

As for the stories, they are about a young David's freeing himself from his father's affectionate and destructive authority. With the father's Kikuyu guide, Juma, father and son hunt an old bull elephant Juma had wounded. After days of trekking, David comes upon the elephant standing by the immense skull of its friend, a bull Juma had killed. Juma and his father kill the great elephant, and David hates himself for betraying it, hates hunting and hates the father who hunts and kills.

After Catherine burns this story, she comes halfway back to her senses. Gripped by remorse, she sets off for Paris so her banker can assess the story's monetary value and she can pay David double it. The mad pathos of this gesture helps David break from her with more pity than fury. His consolation is rich, beautiful, adoring Marita. The last chapter sees him rewriting the burnt stories; they are better than ever.

This blissful ending obviously didn't suit the self-doubting, sometimes paranoid man who shot out his brains in the Idaho hunting lodge. (Thirty-three years earlier, Dr. Ed Hemingway—another woman-ruined man as his son saw it—had shot himself to death.) He didn't, perhaps couldn't, finish the book.

If *The Garden of Eden* is God's plenty for aficionados of the Hemingway legend, what about its intrinsic worth?

It's large. Hemingway supplies the look and feel of places, the puzzled excitement of complex relationships, the slow precision of a hunt or a breakfast, the tension of sexual intrigue. Everything is clear. Minor characters are sketched with marvelous rapidity, dialogue is subtle, unexpected and full of underplayed fierceness and passion. Exciting stuff, only rarely too lyric and unspecific for

[241]

modern taste. The famous style with its conjunctive agglutination (and . . . and . . . and) has been killed by its own fame but here and there Hemingway discovers new rhythms, complicating the syntax derived from Gertrude Stein's "Melanctha." (A faithful Hemingway reader will double back and reread some of these new sentences.) In short, the book's a feast, even though there's a fast-food wrap-up and an occasional ingredient the old master would have subtracted here (or added there).

The last good book, then, we're to have from this pioneer of modern pleasure. How many industries have spun off Hemingway's epicurean discoveries? How many millions have been formed by his credo and routines? Now once again Hemingway doesn't just stand for these life brochures. He's more or less the author of a book which shows what hasn't been shown before, a story especially touching because he didn't know how to finish it, didn't know how to break through the decorum of his time to spell out what had happened to—and inside—him.

[30]

BARRY HANNAH'S RAY

Ray looks at first like such a wee pile of novel fragments, I thought my pal Barry must have swept them together to keep up his morale and make himself remember he was a writer. Two years ago, he'd read its most inconsequential fragment to a Chicago group. He'd come up here in his green leather jacket, dark goggles, and the brown suit his wife had made him pack instead of the revolver he thought he'd need in these mean streets. To the audience, he played a borrowed trumpet to show he was only a fair musician, but a hell of a writer.

Which he is.

Airships was the best new book of short stories I'd read in years, and his two early novels, *Nightwatchmen* and *Geronimo* Rex, are also grand, lyric, surprising, and both big-hearted and mean. Pure Hannah.

As is *Ray*, this—if each word is wringing wet—*novella*. Twenty thousand words, which, oddly enough, give you the weight of a novel, everything you'll ever know about Doc Ray, his second wife Westy, his kids, her kids, his girl—Sister—her parents, the soap factory foreman and poet, Hooch, and his wife Agnes who "watches Home Box Office Movies, which cause her untold anguish for not being slim, twenty-three, in a black dress and pearls, with a sub-machine gun in her hands, in an old fort on the Mediterranean." Summarize the novel's events and you'll think it's a full-size affair. Which is part of the point.

Since the novel began, a few novelists have taken out its stuffing to purvey miniature, rapid or burlesque versions of it. *Tristram Shandy* (1759) and Machado de Assis's *Epitaph of a Small Winner* (1880) are no twenty-thousand-word weaklings but full-grown with that sportive nonchalance which tells the reader, "You get the idea, I don't need to spell out all this old stuff." These novels spin

around central characters who are as eccentrically selective as
charm permits. Part of the pleasure is seeing how much they skip.
If, here and there, a reader feels cheated (of the promised novel),
the compensation is the lyric whirl of observation, the vigorous
uproar of language.

> The land is full of crashing jets, carbon monoxide, violent
> wives, and murderous men. There is a great deal of metal
> and hardness.
> (*Ray*)

The heroes of these books often dream several lives at once.

> First, I took the form of a Chinese barber . . . soon after I
> became . . . St. Thomas' *Summa Theologica* . . .
> *(Epitaph of a Small Winner)*

When Ray is not shooting up "gook jets" in Vietnam, he's commanding Confederate cavalry in Maryland. "Oh, help me! I am
losing myself in two centuries and two wars." A doctor, he's getting cured, probably in a loony bin. It hardly matters. (The
writer, inventing, is half there himself.) What matters is that he
lays out his lust, his scruples, his needs: to "duke a big guy," to
drop "the big one" on the States (especially Ohio), to ravish—i.e.,
describe?—

> a tall girl, twenty-six, and her legs are an amazing long event.
> Beyond that, she's just a straight honest slut.

Despite provocation, temptation,

> I never had her. It is a perversity. . . . I hired her just to tempt
> myself and resist . . .

The prose, magical, tricky, lyric, comes out of that Mississippi of
great prose, post-World War II American fiction. There must be a
hundred writers[1] who can write magic.

He saw spacious skies and amber waves of grain. Most of all

---

[1] 1993. I'd up this number to "a thousand." Here, from one of the twenty magazines
("zines") I've looked at these past weeks (*Denver Quarterly*. Vol. 27. 2. Fall 1992) are sentences from just some of the fine writers printed—and reviewed—there:

he saw the alligator hummocks of Florida and, in his mind's eye, a stately bat tower standing in an endless saw-grass savannah over which passed the constant shadows of tropical cloudscapes; merry bats singled out stinging bugs at mealtime; Payne confronted a wall of Seminole gratitude.

(Thomas McGuane, *The Bush-Whacked Piano*)

Or, from a lesser-known writer, Paul Spike:

Tall as a Watusi, she seems. Dark brown hair flowing long, a rich mane crossing the small elegant bust. A face which is deadpan and wealth and front page.

(Bad News)

I think the source of this river may be Céline's *Voyage au bout de la nuit*, published in France in 1932 but retranslated for New Directions in 1960 amidst the *vendange* of black humor:

After a moment of friendliness, I slithered up against her body. It was fine with the lantern on the ground, because you could catch at the same time the shifting reliefs of the light on her legs. Ah! Nothing must be missed of moments like that! One's cock-eyed with excitement. It's worth it every time. What a fillip, what sudden good humor overtakes you!

Even in translation, Céline's voice sounds real, that is, what a reader of Barry Hannah can recognize as being part of the day's world.

You may ask, "Are you citing these comparisons to make

In Payment one winter, the county budget exhausted, the roads went unplowed, packed down instead so that by late March the snowmobilers could reach up and touch the blinking yellow light that hangs in the middle of town.

Jack Driscoll, "Payment"

She smokes a Salem precisely, discursively, posing the problem of limits with her naked hand.

Jan Ramjerdi, "The Boat Was in Constant Peril"

A fact: my father was forty-eight years old when I was born. A result: he has always carried for me the fragility and gravity of the shined shoe, the snap-brim hat, the black droop of a silk sock against an ankle thin and dry as a white lath stake.

Mark Costello, "Young Republican," *Middle Murphy*
(a fine book of a writer I've admired for almost twenty years)

There's excellent writing in this single periodical—an exceptionally good issue—from four or five other writers.

Hannah seem superfluous?"

Absolutely not.

You had a good dinner last night, but you want another tonight, *n'est-ce pas*? Music, flowers, your girl's mouth? These aren't once in a lifetime events, I hope. That Hannah has cousins, parents, and will soon have sons and nephews doesn't mean he's not unique. He is, and even so tiny a scoopful of him as *Ray* is precious, unxeroxable, an intense and rereadable joy.[2]

---

[2] 1993. Barry, dried out, remarried, back in Mississippi, is writing like the title of his new book, *Bats Out of Hell.*

[31]

BLACK BOX[1]

Seven silent years after she has been divorced by Alex Gideon
for her numerous and enthusiastic infidelities, Ilana Sommo
writes to him in Chicago where he is a professor at "Midwest
University". She tells him that Boaz, the son whom he has
wrongly disclaimed, is running wild. At thirteen, he left the kib-
butz and now three years later, he's run away from agricultural
school after a quarrel in which he's smashed the night watch-
man's head. He needs help. She and her second husband,
Michael Sommo, have neither money nor influence while he,
Alex, has both. She knows that shortly after Alex had come back
to fight in the war of '73 (it is now Feb., 1976), and Boaz had a
kidney infection, he'd secretly offered him one of his kidneys. If
he'll help once more, she'll do anything. "I'll even sleep with
you if you want." It will turn out that this is one thing that Ilana
wants: she is sexually, emotionally and intellectually obsessed by
Alex even though she is sexually, emotionally, and intellectually
happy with Michael as well. Alex writes her back a "Dear
Madam" letter informing her that his lawyer will convey two
thousand dollars to her husband's account on the condition that
he's not bothered by either of them again. "Over the remaining
contents of your letter, including...the simple, garden or common
grossness, I shall pass in silence."

But there'll be no silence. Letters fly back and forth between
passionate, lyric Ilana, chilly, skeptical Alex, and between both of
them and Alex's flamboyant lawyer, Zakheim, wild, semi-literate,
handsome Boaz, and humane, candid, candidly manipulative,
self-deprecating, boastful Michael. There are a few other corre-

---

[1] *Black Box* by Amos Oz. Harcourt Brace Jovanovich: San Diego. Translated from the
Hebrew by Nicholas De Lange and the author. 243 pp. $21.95.

[247]

spondents and some other characters, including the lustful, Poppa Karamazov-like father of Alex, but most of the book excavates, analyzes, reanalyzes and then transforms the five chief correspondents. By the time that, eight months later, Alex has come back to Israel to die in the desert farmhouse which Boaz and his friends are renovating, the reader has been given a coherent, fascinating world.

So much contemporary fiction advertises its own virtuosity (while covering up disbelief in the knowability of the world) that it's a relief to read a good book which doesn't even make a pass in this direction. In fact, the author of *Black Box* risks telling it in one of the creakiest narrative forms, letters. They're handled expertly. No one will mistake the writer of "Hello Michel. Look, I'll come strait to the point with you. I need a lone." (Boaz) for the writer of "I happened to catch a sight of your old jalopy [Ilana] in Ben-Yehuda street. It looks as though the gentleman is keeping her well-serviced; she looks pretty good for her mileage, especially bearing in mind how many times she's changed hands" (Zakheim). Unlike the Mark Harris of *Wake Up, Stupid* or the John Barth of *Letters*, Oz isn't interested in playing with epistolary form. In fact, to avoid its inherent monotony—the letter-writer is always safe enough to report what happened—he includes telegrams, a private detective's reports and some of Alex's notebook reflections. Unnecessary, but welcome.

Most of us have read hundreds, if not thousands of non-fictional pages about Israel. How is it then that I at least feel that Oz's novel enables me to feel what it's like to support the Jewish settlements—as Michael does—and then, a few pages later, to feel the wrongness of that position—as Boaz and Alex do. I think it has to do with the fact that shadows every piece of non-fiction, no matter how "exhaustive." This is that no experience or event can ever be totally recorded, whereas fictional events are always complete, always self-definitive. You'll never get more than the book—or series of books—has given you. The reader cooperates in this illusion and consequently feels the authenticity and finality of the views passed through the characters. Readers hungry not only for a fascinating novel but the felt knowledge of a fascinating country won't do much better than reading Oz's novel.

[32]

ON BERNHARD'S "LOSER"[1]

"We say a word and destroy a person..." The word that destroys the wealthy Viennese piano student Wertheimer is "loser." The one who utters it casually, playfully, accurately, is the great Canadian pianist Glenn Gould (at least this novel's version of him). The one who overhears and reports it is another pianist, the narrator. The three meet in Salzburg, that "disgusting town...antagonistic to everything of value in a human being," where they take lessons at the Mozarteum from Horowitz, the only great teacher they've encountered. At the end of the session, Gould has become greater than Horowitz. After listening to him play Bach's *Goldberg Variations*, the narrator gives away his Steinway to a 9 year old girl (who ruins it), and Wertheimer disposes of his Bösendorfer, his ambition and eventually his life. He actually surrenders the last 28 years later, a year after Gould dies slumped over the piano on which he'd been playing the *Variations*. (The 'real' Gould died in his sleep.) Wertheimer gives a house party for people he despises, then plays them out of the house by thumping on a "miserable untuned instrument," goes to the house of the sister he's tried to dominate—"I misused her as a *page-turner*"—and hangs himself.

The story is told retrospectively and repeatedly—with Goldbergian variations—by the narrator who has for years lived in Madrid working on a book called *About Glenn*. As he goes over and over the story, details and interpretations accrue, thickening the texture, altering the pattern. So the encounter of second-raters and genius—the Salieri/Mozart theme—is chipped at: "Every person is a unique and autonomous person and actually, considered independently, the greatest artwork of all time..." But Wertheimer, not content to be an "artist of life...although precisely this concept provides

---

[1] *The Loser*. Thomas Bernhard. Tr. by Jack Dawson. Knopf. 188 pp. $19.00.

everything we need to be happy," sinks into the failure he comes to love, the "awful existence machine" which spews him out, "a mangled pulp."

For Gould, the burdensome thing is to be a middleman, something between score and sound. He wants to *be* his Steinway. (He gives up that other interference, the concert audience.) This reinforces the import of Wertheimer and the narrator's surrender of their pianos and sharpens the final scene, Wertheimer's thumping on "the miserable untuned instrument" he'd specifically ordered from Vienna.

The narrator reflects later that it isn't Gould but the *Goldberg Variations* themselves which "murder" the hapless Wertheimer. Composed "to delight the soul" and to "help an insomniac put up with his insomnia," they reach across time to show the narrator his uselessness.

The *Variations* may also account for the book's narrative quality. The reiterated phrases, place names, scenes and events, the awkward iteration of the narrator's "I thought," bulk large in the thin story. An ex-violinist, Bernhard apparently wanted the power of baroque music in his work. "The main thing is it must sound good," he told an interviewer. But music has charms narrative doesn't. Narrative repetions need richer matter than Bernhard offers.

Not that *The Loser* is a loss. One reads a book, not an oeuvre, but this book is a clear segment of the most famous oeuvre in recent German-language fiction. It is steeped in its rage, pessimism, despair and ascetic wilfulness. The domineering, paragraphless monologue somehow sets and even counters the gloom, obsessions, spent fury and hopelessness of Bernhard's death-centered, but lively novels.

Many of them—in English—are reissued by the Phoenix Fiction Series of the University of Chicago Press, and new readers might be better off starting with the graceful, amusing memoir *Wittgenstein's Nephew*[2] or *Concrete*, *The Lime Works* or *Correction*. Like them, *The Loser* is another model of this line of "desperation machines" which Bernhard turned out to handle his own suicidal despair, rage and disgust (spelled out in the autobiographical essays in *Gathered Evidence*).

Like the beloved grandfather, who helped raise him, Bernhard was "of the Montaigne School." His novels are closer to the shift-

---

[2] Bernhard's version of Diderot's *Le Neveu de Rameau*.

ing meditations of those wonderful *Essays* than they are to the fictions of Musil, Pavese and Henry James which he read and against which he struggled. They deal not with the events of a story but their ashes, the reflections and interpretations of the retrospective narrator. That so static an *oeuvre* should have been rewarded with every national prize is as ironic as the author's death (in February, 1989) being announced as the world's most powerful literary critic, the Ayatollah Khomeini, was issuing his murderous edict against the author of *The Satanic Verses* and Austria's own Kurt Waldheim was denouncing Bernhard's last play as "an insult to the nation."

[33]

ON RUSHDIE

Jack Miles, the book editor of the Los Angeles Times, asked me to write a piece about the Ayatollah Khomeini's call for the assassination of Salman Rushdie. This Mafian directive from a head of state was a new turn in current events, and the media responded massively to it. I worked on a tight deadline, unusual for me. I scanned the book in an hour, then dictated these hasty thoughts to a verbal, but otherwise unreactive, machine on the other end of a phone. (An experience new to this dictator.) It turned out that the Op-Ed editor—who had priority—needed the piece for his page. I reprint it as an example of the instant reaction which fixes the news-hungry public's taste for instant opinion.

Friday, Feb. 17, 1989. Another day on this extraordinary planet. That planetary comedian, the daily paper, reports that the terrorist bomb which brought down the Pan Am jet over Scotland was hidden in a radio-cassette recorder.

President Bush, informed that he's the No. 1 resident of the world's murder capital, says he hopes that the press will do something about it. (Not report the murders?)

In Iran, India and Pakistan, streets are filled with shouting marchers, some burning effigies of a book they haven't read, calling for the death of its author—of whom they know next to nothing. The head of the Iranian state has sentenced both the author and his publishers to death; supporters have offered millions of dollars to his murderers. In the calmer prudential tradition of France, the French publisher has withdrawn the translation from his list; and the leading American book chain has withdrawn it from its shelves.

Books.

Every once in a while a reminder comes from the precincts of craziness that books have power. It's not only that "in the beginning was the Word" but that "in the end, everything comes down" to it (Mallarmé).

Most of the civilized world consists of children of the book—societies shaped by more or less sacred text, scriptures, constitutions, declarations, sayings, even works of economic and political analysis *(Das Kapital, Mein Kampf)*. In some traditions these texts guarantee the right to search for truth; in others the text itself is the truth, and anything that doesn't conform to it is blasphemous. When the great library of Alexandria was burned, the defense was that it wasn't needed: its books either repeated the sacred text and were redundant or contradicted it and were evil.

The Western tradition, stained and deformed as it has been from time to time, is one that welcomes new as well as old and renewed truths. It takes the chance that awful books come into the world so that good ones will as well; but this tradition is also rich in censorship and banning, in indices of prohibited books, even in book burnings. Many of the world's most beautiful and moving books have been indicted in law courts, censored, forbidden, burned. Scarcely a day goes by without some announcement of outrage at a book or play. (In Friday's paper there's an obituary of the Austrian novelist and playwright Thomas Bernhard, whose novel *Woodcutters* was banned and whose play *Hero Square* was denounced as "an insult to the Austrian people" by that reborn democrat, Austrian president Kurt Waldheim.)

Books are feared by those who can barely read or understand them. Politicians use this fear for their own purposes. They play on a few words that constitute, say, a pledge of allegiance or, as in the case of Salman Rushdie's *The Satanic Verses*, a whole book.

What is this book that outrages so many millions of non-readers? First of all, it is a work of fiction, a work that deliberately, artistically, separates itself from the world of factual report and factual history. The idea of fiction is to create a world insulated from the ordinary pain and pleasure of the actual world so that a special kind of intense pleasure may be derived from its playful inventiveness, deeper penetration, loftier speculation, elaborate and beautiful symmetry. Like a church or theater, it constitutes a kind of sacred precinct where human beings act and think in special, even especially holy, ways.

The Satanic Verses is huge and difficult. It begins like the newspaper, with a terrorist bombing of a plane over the British Isles.

[253]

The bombs are concealed not in a cassette player but in the baby-like bundle that a woman passenger is carrying. Two men survive the explosion. One is Gibreel Farishta, a Bombay film star who has made as many as 11 films at once, playing all sorts of roles, human and divine. The other is Saladin Chamcha, a British-educated radio star whose remarkable voice has impersonated as many as 44 characters in one drama.

These artists of appearance and metamorphosis now change again—one along angelic, the other along satanic lines. The book is made up of their adventures, affairs, fantasies, dreams; of the people they know, the people who have given birth to them, the people they confront. The texture is composed of the gold and dross of East and West, present and past, rock lyrics, commercial jingles, great poems, sacred texts. Its mock-epic style is free-wheeling, elusive, playful. Readers of Rabelais, *Tristram Shandy, Ulysses, The Recognitions, Gravity's Rainbow, USA, One Hundred Years of Solitude, Hopscotch*, and many other books will recognize it.

Many Westerners will miss the Eastern allusions. The book is full of the devices of the *Arabian Nights* and the *Panchatantra*; references to sacred texts abound. Particularly important are references to the text dictated to the remarkable prophet who in meditation on Mount Hira in the month of Ramadan in the Christian year 610 heard the voice that told him to "Recite [*qara'a*—hence, *Qur'an, Koran*] thou in the name of the Lord who created man out of clots of blood." At one point Gibreel, about to lose his mind, dreams that he's the archangel Gabriel who preaches to a business-man-turned-prophet named Mahound (pejorative Christian name for Mohammed). Mahound's gospel is "one one one," and it's preached to the people of a city built on sand. He also preaches about three pagan goddesses, whom he later repudiates. The repudiation of these satanic verses is praised by his water carrier Khalid. "You've brought us the Devil himself, so we can witness the workings of the Evil One and his overthrow by the Right. You have enriched our faith." Mahound thinks, "Bringing you the Devil. Yes, that sounds like me." Gibreel also dreams that a scribe named Salman takes down the Revelation from the prophet's lips but then purposely, half-playfully, half-daringly alters it. When he reads the altered message back to the prophet, the prophet nods and thanks him politely.

This is some of what has aroused the arousable. Rushdie plays with sacred text as he plays with many of the shibboleths and givens of East and West.

Is the author of such fiction a heretic, a "mercenary of colonialism" who should be hunted down like a rabid dog and done to death? Radio Iran announces that suicide squads have embarked on a hunt for him.

The history of imaginative art has seen collision after collision between the real and the imaginary worlds. Perhaps the reason is that the same words are used for the worlds of fact and fiction, and this confuses simple people. And, too, for we shall not be ingenuous, the people who write novels are also people who read the newspapers, who are enraged and enchanted by the world, who go to their typewriters and processors with ideas, images and feelings generated in no small part by what they have seen and felt about the actual world. Rushdie is himself an ambitious man of strong political beliefs. At a P.E.N. conference two years ago he challenged American writers to take on the task of discriminating "America the beautiful from America the terrible." For this he was rebuked by Saul Bellow: "The writer doesn't have tasks. He has inspiration."

Salman Rushdie's book is better than his political self. It seems to me a work of genuine inspiration. It is fiery, playful, beautiful and—as I read it now—excessive and confused. No matter. Without it and works like it, human beings will be reduced to bestiality—reduced, that is, to the state of mind that removes such books from the shelves, sends men shouting and burning into the street—or sentences them to death for writing in the first place.

[255]

SHORT STORIES

The short story, as a product, perhaps even a formative condition, of human society, is, I'd guess, the oldest of narrative art forms. Buried by the novel in the nineteenth and very early twentieth centuries, it came back strong in the twenties, and now, in the last decades of this century, is once again one of the most sophisticated art forms of the West. It's not just that people can satisfy their hunger for narrative quickly, it's that increasing sophistication breeds aesthetic hunger for compression, ellipsis, obliquity, and rapidity. A sophisticated culture needs fewer preparations and signals, less supporting data and conclusive demonstration. Post-Mondrian—Minimalist—painting, post-Brancusi sculpture, post-Webern music, these arts rise from the same mind-set as the laser and silicon chip. The short stories of Raymond Carver, Mary Robison, Tobias Wolff, Amy Hempel, Bette Pesetsky, Ann Beattie,[1] and twenty or twenty-five other brilliant masters of surface realism are the most recent American exempla of this understated, bare, deceptive, and rather chilly art. They are not poetic parodists like Donald Barthelme or Jorge Luis Borges; they are not tragic, philosophic farceurs like Beckett; they're not experimentalists like Sarraute, Barth, and Robbe-Grillet. They are American realists in the line of Sherwood Anderson and his treacherous disciple, Hemingway. Although I adore many of their stories, my own preference—and practice—is for fuller, more richly

---

[1] In a review of Beattie's novel, *Love Always*, John Updike compared her procedure with Hemingway's: "It was she who first found the tone for the post-Vietnam, post engagé mood, much as Hemingway found the tone for his own generation's disenchantment with all brands of officially promoted importance. Both authors made reality out of short, concrete sentences and certifiable, if small, sensations; in the absence of any greater good, the chronic appearance of food on the table becomes an event worth celebrating." I don't think Beattie is the first New Minimalist—quite a few roasted the leaner meat of the fifties and sixties before the Beatties and Carvers worked up the soybean, meatoid versions of the seventies and eighties—but Updike, himself one of the fine chefs of the oldtime roasts and gammons, is, I think, right about their recipes and ancestry.

detailed ones. Bellow is the greatest recent story writer in this line, and it may be that his art is more conspicuous in the long story than in the novel, simply because he's had to find ways to control his desire to comment about everything. Newer masters, though, are the Barry Hannah of Airships, *Padgett Powell, Denis Johnson, and the Bobbie Ann Mason of* Shiloh. *John Cheever, Peter Taylor, J. F. Powers, Philip Roth, John Updike, Bernard Malamud and Flannery O'Connor are other post-World War II masters of the full story. It's foolish, though, to cite a few names. Almost every fine modern writer has written wonderful short stories. In this section, I comment on three of them.*

[34]

HESSE'S STORIES

Thomas Mann told a young American writer[1] that when he and his brother began writing in the 1890s, "we had to do it all ourselves." He meant that German fiction had had no Balzac, Gogol, or Fielding. It had not taken a grip on society but had shuttled between the dream tales of Novalis and the little-burgher rusticity of Gottfried Keller. Helped by—of all things—Wagner's treatment of three generations in his Ring operas, Mann performed the Balzac/Flaubert/Zola graft on German literature in one operation, *Buddenbrooks* (1901).

Two years younger than Mann, Herman Hesse began writing under his almost lifelong deference to Mann's superior power. (Mann graciously accepted the "fraternal" deference and graciously reciprocated with praise of Hesse. The *Hesse/Mann Letters* are full of reciprocal compliments.) Male artists often function as twin stars: Picasso/Braque, Stravinsky/Schoenberg, Wordsworth/Coleridge, Eliot/Pound, Sartre/Camus. These pairs remain conscious of each other's work, attempt what the artistic twin hasn't, answer questions raised by their twin's accomplishment. With Mann's playful, sensuous, ironic power twirling beside him in literary space, Hesse followed that un-Mannian part of his nature which, every twenty or thirty years, has turned him into the Pied Piper of the reading young.[2] In 1974, Hesse's publishers issued a selection of his stories under a Mannian title.[3]

Like Byron or Solzhenitsyn, Hesse is more remarkable as a human being who writes than as a sheer writer. His work is a series

---

[1] Me.

[2] In 1974, eighty percent of my sophomore and junior students said they'd read some of his work. Eleven years later, it was down to fifty percent, but as the literary market goes, that's not bad.

[3] *Stories of Five Decades.* New York: Farrar, Straus & Giroux. (Mann's are collected as *Stories of Three Decades.* The amiable rivals tussle beyond the grave.)

of trails into self-discovery and self-transcendence. The trails are journeys east, up and in; to India and Indian thought (with *Siddhartha* as the great trek); to Swiss mountains, where, behind No Visitor plaques, Hesse read, translated, edited, and invented tales about the world's sages; and then inwards, for, in a manner hearts calloused by fact can neither comprehend nor enjoy, Hesse suffered and expressed crises of doubt about himself, his country, and about ways of knowing anything. Psychoanalyzed by a Jungian, divorced, exiled, he moved further and further away from Europe's civil life, a learned, spirited, gentle cultivator of gardens and instincts, a seeker after ecstasy and revelation, a writer who wanted to be a seer but remained a professional man of letters who—like most others of worth—often doubted his literary powers.

The twenty-three stories in the collection (all but three new to English readers) were written between 1899 and 1948 (the year after he won the literary Good Housekeeping seal, the Nobel Prize). In them, one can trace a career more absorbing than any single literary version of it.

Not that there aren't good stories here. There is, for instance, a three-page account of the creation, growth, decay, and forest-burial of "The City," as beautiful and much richer than Marcel Marceau's sixty-second mimicry of the ages of man; there's a story of a merchant's return to the mean Swabian town where he delicately courts a slandered widow; there's another about an English missionary whose desire for a bare-breasted Indian girl alters his mission.

Many stories are charged with that leaden servitude to suppressed sensuality which is the forerunner of so much mysticism and mischief. The finest stories are the barest and most direct, or so it seems to a modern reader who wants stories which say, "You know I'm true because I'm hiding nothing."

To younger truth-seekers, Hesse's line is the shortcut to Ecstasy. Yet, looked at closely, his trips aren't easy. In the tiny story "Edmund," a student of Indian tantras meditates on the text.

> If you find yourself in a situation where your soul falls sick and forgets what it needs for life . . . then make your heart empty . . . perceive the center of your head as an empty cave . . . and concentrate on the contemplation of it. Then the cave will . . . show you an image of what your soul needs in order to go on living.

Edmund follows the prescription, sees where his salvation lies and,

[259]

"with joyful certainty," strangles his professor.

"Ethereal as a dream, exact as a logarithm." This is how Hesse described Kafka in 1925. Kafka was that fusion of Mann and Novalis, storyteller and seer, which Hesse wanted to—and knew he couldn't—be.

> Only at long last . . . he realised that he must content himself with being a true poet, a dreamer, a seer, only in his soul, and that his handiwork must remain that of a simple man of letters.
>
> "Dream Journeys"

No mean thing, though it didn't satisfy Hesse. Still, for young questers, there is a Hessian blue in the world which would not exist if Herman Hesse had not been for fifty years a working man of letters.

[35]

MARY ROBISON'S DAYS

Dick trims his nails and sniffles about one of his ex-wives who lives in the Oldsmobile his parents gave them. His mother reads and listens to a tape of *Porgy and Bess*. Dick's brother, Spencer, sunbathes in a nylon lounge chair while his father hoses the drive-way (spraying Spencer). A young woman, seven months pregnant, passes out a flyer about a school bond issue. Spencer tells her the economy's collapsing: "There'll be a global depression by 1990." Summoned into the house, he sticks the blue flyer on his chest. His mother tells him he looks fit, tells Dick he's very attractive, tells them both their father is the pregnant woman's OB. Upstairs, Spencer puts a cordovan loafer on Dick's foot and buffs it with a yellow cloth. They hear their parents laughing.

> "What are they laughing about?" Spencer said.
> "I wouldn't know," said Dick. "Probably not about us."

End of story. Four pages. Twenty-three hundred words, title "Doctor's Sons."

The modern short story, brief, oblique, epiphanic, was invented, or better, tripped into, by the young medical student Anton Chekhov in the early 1890s. Its complex telegraphy—*micrography*?—is one of the premier art forms of the century.

Since the art is that of exclusion, the pressure is to keep exclud-ing, the menace that of stripping down to the skeletal, the anecdo-tal, or even to a void signed in the philosophic bravado of Duchamp or Johns. The reader has a right to ask, "If you've told the story in seven hundred words, what do the other sixteen hun-dred do?"

Fair enough. The "other words" of "Doctor's Sons" give us the "linen placemat decorated with Coast Guard flags" on which Dick's hands rest, the navel orange he bumps on the window to call his brother, and the pointed-pointless talk of the three Sorensons.

That is, the words sustain a world of oranges, hoses, brothers, and loafers long enough so that we can ride the ups and downs of their uneasy comfort and feckless tension. "Doctor's Sons." The world of the doctor—of provisions, earning, Oldsmobiles, lawns, lounge chairs, loafers—and that of the sons, who loaf, lounge, tan their bodies, trim their nails, sweep, predict collapse, and know they bring no laughter to their parents. The four pages are the surface of an unwritten three hundred. (The unwritten chapters deal with Dick's wives, Spencer's world, a—perhaps—intrigue with the pregnant girl, the disintegration of what is momentarily suspended in the story.) The art and the joy are in our ability to pick up the signs of this sour world.

Narrative spareness concentrates the mind as a microscope does. And ordinary language increases a reader's desire to press meaning out of the bareness. So the words "lounger" and "loafer" stir small currents which would be beside the point in longer, "richer" stories. Generations of fine writers and alert readers lie behind such understanding. There are a few longer, richer, and more complicated stories in *Days*, but all twenty are made for lovers of obliquity and compression.

Social scientists could read this book for their purposes as well. There is much to learn about this 1970s America of comfortless comforts, one-parent children, ulcerous fifteen-year-olds, unhappy nuns, sudden punches or needs to punch. An oil painter's paints are clotted, he makes kites to fly as a hurricane blows up; ex-wives and husbands pester each other; a pretty girl provokes a fight amid the wreckage of a beach hotel; a woman rereads and abandons a sentence which begins, "I saw the Earth cower . . ." The stories unroll in Beverly Hills, Indianapolis, Cleveland, Philadelphia, Erie, Chicago. This ubiquity is itself social theory.

[36]

KUNDERA

En route to a two-week vacation in Czechoslovakia's Tatra Mountains, a young man stops for gas. His shy girlfriend goes off to pee in the woods. Then she pretends to be a hitchhiker and flags down his car. The game intrigues him; he pretends she's a pickup. The pretense excites them. The shy girl strips with seductive confidence. The young man treats her like a whore. They lie in the dark. "I'm me," she says. "I'm me."

Milan Kundera's stories can't be read in Czech.[1] This non-literary fact is somehow embedded in these stories and, in fact, in almost any writing that comes out of Eastern Europe. The Czech writer Vaculík writes about the "indulgent forbearance" with which he feels even sophisticated Western readers listen to the "eternal babbling about one thing" which comes out of Eastern writing. The counter to this is the tyrant's knowledge that good writing endangers the Penitentiary State. Even when stories deal with private lives, the setting becomes a large part of the story. In "The Hitchhiking Game," the setting tells us that the lovers' usual lives are boring. That is, The State is boring. The reader of such stories knows that the unexpected is dangerous, that pleasure has to be reserved well in advance, and that a life is supposed to be exemplary rather than personal.

American literature swept the world not just as poems and stories but as a promise of possibility and variety. The stories of Eastern Europe smell of the ingenuities which human beings use to extract pleasure from the stinginess of a nagging state. "Today," writes Vaculík, "Ugly deeds are not characteristic of the prisons but rather of the tranquil civic existence of those who are not in prison."

They're part of literature as well, and not just the literature of

---

[1] 1993. They can now, although I'm told there were—are?—tensions between the Czech writers who stayed in Prague and Kundera, who became a world figure in Paris.

hypocrisy, recantation, and betrayal. The very texture and form of Kundera's stories—the philosophic riddles like "Symposium," the cold farces like "Edward and God"—are triumphs of evasion as well as invention.

It is easier to run away for short periods. Novels are for the rare long-distance runner. (Solzhenitsyn's *The First Circle* is one of the few Eastern novels of sustained force.) Kundera's novel, *Life is Elsewhere*, has some brilliant descriptions of a young poet's discovery of the odd powers of poetry and a good portrait of a woman's affair with an artist who uses her body as his canvas and her head as his classroom, but political anger breaks the book— becomes the book—and the stories dribble out. Kundera attempts to sustain them by making the poet all poets, but the snippets from Lermontov, Keats, Baudelaire, and Shelley water the book down.

Kundera is best drawing out the farcical complexity of anecdote and situations. He's at his easiest in sexual comedy (*The Farewell Party*), his worst in highfalutin lucubration (*The Unbearable Lightness of Being*). He doesn't have the tenacity—or is it the will?—to organize a long haul into a single situation or group of situations. But why punish him because he isn't Tolstoy or Graham Greene or his friend Philip Roth?

[V]

A BIT ABOUT POETRY

[37]

SCANNING AMERICAN POETRY: 1947-1987

*Most of my own few poems are controlled by the formal patterns of
the 1940's and 1950's; I neither elaborated nor broke with them. I
observe poetry a bit better than I write it.*

   *Sculpture and painting are said to shuttle between the "realis-
tic" and the "Byzantine"; so does poetry. Metrical formality is the
usual Western sign of "Byzantinism." When poetry moves toward
some form of "prosaic realism," it departs from it in other, "poetic" ways—diction, syntax, sound schemes—or in quicker and
longer jumps from notion to notion, scene to scene, than any but
surreal or farcical prose tolerates. So the Eliot-Pound* Waste
Land—Cantos departure from Edwardian formalism has as much
to do with elusive, shorthand intelligence as with broken meters
and syntax. The Wordsworth-Coleridge departure from Collins-
Gray formality went by way of meter-loosening, "prose" subject
matter and "prosaic" diction; its poetic triumph is in such innovation as the speeded, elusive narratives of the Lucy poems.*

   *"Scanning American Poetry: 1947-1987" was conceived and
delivered as an introductory lecture to students at Fudan University
in Shanghai, which accounts for the Chinese references and, perhaps, for didactic simplification.*

Human beings have always been troubled by the ease with which
they can be fooled. We see something, then realize it wasn't there;
we'd been fooled by a shadow or some other trick of light. Then
there's the question of distance: How far away should we be from
what we observe? You make out some things from an airplane,
very different things from the ground. Which are correct? Both;
neither.

   Asked by my Chinese host to survey American poetry of the last
thirty or forty years in a single lecture, I found myself in this obser-
vational predicament. In some ways, I'm too close and see only

things that have interested me; in other ways, I'm too far away, knowing little or nothing about too many poets and poems. Some poems and poets have formed my rhythmic appreciation of the world, others my sense of modernity.

Anthologies and critical histories help fill in the landscape, but each is itself a special view, and by its nature a scheme of preference. They often exclude works that break through the present borders of accomplishment to reconstitute the landscape of expressive possibility.

The actor Walter Matthau was once asked to play the part of an old man. He was then in his mid-forties. He decided he didn't want to settle for the usual stooped, weak-kneed snuffler with rheumy eyes and trembling hands. He decided to consult his eighty-year-old father-in-law, Frank, an intelligent, alert, erect man who walked rapidly and talked clearly. "Frank," said Matthau. "How would you play the part of an old man?" Frank thought a minute, then stood up, crooked his back, snuffled, held out trembling hands, wiped his eyes, and spoke in a thin voice. "This is how I'd do it."

So there's the danger: speaking from a privileged position of observation and knowledge, you can still adopt standard notions. To some extent, they are accurate, and Frank, the old father-in-law, was correct. At eighty, he was, in a way, not old. Perhaps at ninety or a hundred, he would be stooped, weak-kneed, rheumy, a snuffler and trembler. So there's the other danger: fleeing clichés, you can miss basic truths.

In 1947, an anthology of Chinese poetry from the earliest times to the present was published in an inexpensive pocket edition by the New American Library. Thousands of Americans bought and read the book and enjoyed hundreds of poems translated by Chinese scholars and put into readable, simple English by the remarkable graphomaniac, Robert Payne, who knew Chinese and ten or fifteen other languages. I want to quote some remarks from Payne's fascinating introduction in order to appraise the way many Americans of my generation found their way to Chinese poetry.[1]

> The Chinese until recently did not share our passions. Their
> greatest passion was for decorum and for some kind of under-

---

[1] Some, of course, had been introduced to it by the versions of Ezra Pound, others by those of Arthur Waley, still others by translations associated with Amy Lowell.

standing with heaven. Though they sang love songs, they did
not exalt romantic love; and though they hated wars, they
seemed to have seen war in a spirit of fatal expectancy, as
though they knew it would always recur. They were people
with the strength and virtue of moderation; they delighted in
the smallest things in life, and took pains to remember the
details of which life is made . . . They were never affected
with too great a sadness. Though there is sorrow continually
in their poems, it is not the final sorrow of the Vergilian
West, which looked forward to the end of the world in some
catastrophe or a resurrection outside time.

The contrast between the sorrow of the Virgilian, catastrophic
West and the moderate, ubiquitous sorrow of the Chinese is particularly striking. I wonder, though, how Chinese students of poetry
regard it and Payne's other generalizations. There is no doubt that
groups of human beings, influenced by differences in climate,
upbringing, systems of government, parental training, and so on,
differ from other human beings; but of all the arts and sciences,
poetry best enables human beings to express what makes an individual differ from his fellows. I'd like to guess that not a few
Chinese poems and Chinese poets resemble American poems and
American poets more than they resemble one another. After all, as
Payne says in his introduction, "In the T'ang Dynasty, at least
twenty-two hundred poets wrote 48,900 poems" which have been
preserved. How draw a useful profile of so many individual poets?

Here is another Payne generalization: "Until the T'ang Dynasty,
there was little complexity in poetry: emotions were as clear-cut as
the simple colors that adorn the *Book of Songs*. . . We," continues
Payne, speaking for fellow Westerners, "have nearly always aimed
high in our poetry; the Chinese deliberately aimed at the earth,
away from the angelic hosts, and made something that is universal
because it is common to all men."

Now I will be quoting some American poems of the last thirty-
odd years, and I think it'll be clear that some of these poems also
"aim at the earth." Perhaps the earth they aim at was altered by the
poets' having read Payne's anthology, but I think one could more
easily trace the earthiness of these poems back through Robert
Frost, William Wordsworth and Geoffrey Chaucer to the conventions of Greek and Roman classical poets. There are differences,
yes, but intelligence flies around the world more easily than air-
planes, and it may be that the invention of an unknown poet located
on some island in the Red Sea sped—two thousand years ago—

[271]

eastward to China and westward to Greece and is the source of the poetic earthiness Payne remarks. Or what is more likely, poets in Greece and the old empires of China saw and described the world in similar ways.

In 1957, I decided to collect some good poems by poets who were my contemporaries. The result is, I think, the first anthology[2] made of such poems. The list of poets includes such now well-known American poets as James Wright, William Stafford, Adrienne Rich, W.S. Merwin, James Merrill, Edgar Bowers, Donald Justice, and W.D. Snodgrass. Here is a poem from the anthology, Justice's "The Stray Dog by the Summerhouse."

This morning, down
by the summerhouse,
I saw a stray,
A stray dog dead.
All white and brown
The dead friend lay,
All brown with a white
Mark on his head.

His eyes were bright
and open wide,
Bright open eyes
With worms inside,
And the tongue hung loose
To the butterflies,
The butterflies
And the flying ants.

And because of the tongue
He seemed like one
Who has run too long,
And stops, and pants.
In the August sun.
I smelt the scent,
And it was strong;
It came and went

---

2 "American Poetry of the Fifties," *Western Review* (Spring 1957).

As if somewhere near
A round, ripe pear,
So ripe, so round,
Had dropped to the ground
And with the heat
Was turning black.
And the scent came back,
And it was sweet.

What exhilarates me about this poem is the contrast between its elaborate lyric form and the ugliness of the subject. Its poetic ancestor is Baudelaire's "*Une Charogne*," a poem that Cézanne memorized and which Rilke believed was an important source of modern objectivity.[3]

Another poem from that 1957 anthology is a section from "Heart's Needle," the title poem of the book that won W. D. Snodgrass a Pulitzer Prize. In it, the poet goes into a Natural History museum and looks at the display of animals in cases.

> Here in the first glass cage
> the little bobcats arch themselves,
> still practicing their snarl
> of constant rage.

The poet describes the bobcats, then "two great Olympian elk," their "horns...fixed in their lasting hate." They remind him of his own family. He and his wife have separated; the elk, locked in hatred, remind him of their fighting. He sees aborted fetuses preserved in jars of alcohol, and wonders what will happen to his daughter. He sees

> the branching, doubled throat
> of a two-headed foal;

---

[3] Here are two stanzas of "*Une Charogne*" ("A Carcass") in the translation by Roy Campbell which Justice read.

The sky, as on the opening of a flower,
on this superb obscenity smiled bright.
the stench drove us with such fearsome power
you thought you'd swoon outright.

Flies trumpeted upon the rotten belly
Whence larvae poured in legions far and wide,
and flowed, like molten and liquescent jelly,
down living rags of hide..

I see the hydrocephalic goat....
here is the curled and swollen head,
there, the burst skull;

     skin, of a limbless calf;
a horse's foetus, mummified;
     mounted and joined forever,
the Siamese twin dogs that ride
belly to belly, half and half,
that none shall sever.

     I walk among the growths,
by gangrenous tissue, goitres, cysts,
     by fistulas and cancers,
where the malignancy man loathes
is held suspended and persists.

     And I don't know the answers.
     The window's turning white.
The world moves like a diseased heart
     packed with ice and snow.
Three months now we have been apart
less than a mile. I cannot fight
     or let you go.

    Again a poet of the 1950s is writing about horrible material in a musically complex stanza. Horrible subject, beautiful sounds. It's as if the poet could only handle this burning material with an elaborate handle. So English poets of World War I—Owen, Sassoon, Graves, Isaac Rosenberg—wrote war poems in the elaborate stanza forms invented hundreds of years earlier in French and Italian courts.

    Snodgrass was to prove very influential. He and Justice—I too, for that matter—were graduate students at the State University of Iowa in the 1950s. One of our teachers was a poet ten or twelve years older who'd become well-known in the forties with a book called *Lord Weary's Castle*. This teacher, Robert Lowell, was much taken by Snodgrass's poems. He admired Snodgrass for writing about intimate, painful situations so directly and skillfully.

    A few years later, Lowell, suffering one of his recurrent mental breakdowns, was advised by his psychotherapist, himself a minor poet, to write an autobiography. He wrote one brilliant section in prose, then, perhaps remembering Snodgrass, wrote the rest of the book, *Life Studies*, in verse. Up till then, most of Lowell's poetry had been written in couplets, blank verse or sonnets. Now, though, he broke from the Snodgrass-Justice pattern and decided to write without the constraints of fixed meters or stanzas. If, now and then, rhymes came or even if a poem fell, more or less, into formal patterns, he wouldn't avoid them, but he wanted the direct, unfettered speech in which he'd written the prose chapter. So in "Sailing Home from Rapallo" he writes about his mother, who has just died there:

> In the grandiloquent lettering on Mother's coffin,
> *Lowell* had been misspelled LOVEL.
> The corpse
> was wrapped like *panetone* in Italian tinfoil.

These lines have the ring of Lowell's speech, though they are largely controlled by iambic accents. In the sonnet "To Speak of Woe that is in Marriage," the reader peers through the keyhole of Lowell's bedroom. The language is idiomatic, charged with words like *screwball, tick,* and *hopped up.* It differs from "Sailing Home from Rapallo" and from Snodgrass in that the poet is not speaking in his own voice, but through what American poets, following Pound, call a persona, a mask. (Pound used the word for his versions of the dramatic monologues worked out in the nineteenth century by Browning and Tennyson.) The material in this marital poem is intimate, but the poet is looking at himself through the eyes of the only other person privy to the scene, his wife. So one voice combines intimacy and distance, freedom and form.

> The hot night makes us keep our bedroom window open.
> Our magnolia blossoms. Life begins to happen.
> My hopped-up husband drops his home disputes,
> and hits the streets to cruise for prostitutes,
> free-lancing out along the razor's edge.
> This screwball might kill his wife, then take the pledge.
> Oh, the monotonous meanness of his lust....
> It's the injustice...he is so unjust—
> whiskey-blind, swaggering home at five.
> My only thought is how to keep alive,
> What makes him tick? Each night now I tie
> ten dollars and his car key to my thigh....
> Gored by the climacteric of his want,
> he stalls above me like an elephant.

The Lowell of *Life Studies* had moved from Iowa back to the East Coast where he'd been born. There in Boston and Cambridge he gave classes to students, some of whom became famous by writing poems of a confessional intimacy that made Snodgrass' and Lowell's seem oblique and distant. The two most famous were Sylvia Plath and Anne Sexton. They opened the doors to hundreds of poetic confessions, many of them made by women. (I believe this played a much larger role in what became known as the Women's Liberation Movement than has been realized. Plath is one of its idols.)

Here is Plath's short poem "The Hanging Man."

> By the roots of my hair some god got hold of me.
> I sizzled in his blue bolts like a desert prophet.
> The night snapped out of his sight like a lizard's eyelid:
> A world of bald white days in a shadeless socket.
>
> A vulturous boredom pinned me in this tree.
> If he were I, he would do as I did.

The poem's verbs and similes are violent, the poetic feeling that of almost supernatural rage, bitterness, and terror. The few lines deal with electrocution, exposure to fierce sun, and "vulturous boredom." On the surface a successful, charming, attractive girl, Sylvia Plath was tormented, enraged. She was able to use these feelings to drive herself toward bizarre, original verbal expression. She could write as perhaps she might not have been able to in any other time and place, and that beautiful expression of rage helped form her time. She joins the sisterhood of such great poets as Sappho, Louise Labé, Sor Juana de la Cruz, and Emily Dickinson.

There are probably a hundred or more wonderful women poets of the last twenty years who have written with the freedom and sometimes the violent power of Sylvia Plath. I open a volume that's just come into the house and turn more or less haphazardly to a poem. The author is Christine Zawadiwsky, the poem is "The Hand on the Head of Lazarus." A stanza picked at random from the poem reads:

> No other name can make itself as useful,
> can be as much a part of me
> as my kiss and my tongue,
> no other flame burns down a path of shining gold
> on which there has traveled an alphabet of girls
> sweet and only partially unclothed—
> oh lotus in a blue vase,
> oh lover, oh true neighbor,
> no other voice is exactly like yours.

[276]

Zawadiwsky writes quietly and naturally about a subject that even thirty years earlier would have been treated obliquely, if at all—lesbian love (which of course Sappho treated with equal naturalness, though—as far as the surviving fragments attest—with more physiological restraint).

Three other fine new women poets are Sharon Olds, Eleanor Lerman, and Alane Rollings. Olds has written some of the first really good poems about pregnancy and childbearing. Lerman writes fantastic poems in idiomatic yet mysterious speech, poems difficult to understand in the usual way.

We teacher-readers are used to taking a difficult poem, T.S. Eliot's "The Waste Land," say, and showing how its lines, sections, allusions, jumps, and connections belong to each other and make a coherence that can be explained in prose. It's like having been in an accident. After the shock, you pull yourself together, see where you've been injured, who else is, how seriously, what to do about it, how it happened.

In the case of Lerman's poems, the accident occurs, but you've been thrown so far from it, you're not even sure what happened. You're hurt, but you can't locate your injuries. If there's a policeman to whom you can describe the accident, it turns out he doesn't understand your language. Here is part of Lerman's "Ecclesiology." It's full of sky, starships, evil planets, necromancy, a church in Oklahoma, space travel, and gods.

> germicide baths are prepared in the schoolyards:
>
> from one to three the female children are cleansed
> by virgin hands, from three to five the males
> at dusk the others are sent into the briar
> with a horn canteen and strong soap
>
> No one mentions the star ships
> (I have saved you a piece of lichen a crevice in the earth)

There is some sort of progress in the poem, "Attempts are made to shoot down the star ships," and there is a sort of solution:

> a church in Oklahoma is overgrown with yellow weeds
> Inside, the priest walks with a stick
> and has come to his grace with an infinitely tiny, rolling god
> (I have saved you a wheel, a mobile heart)

[277]

There is the sense of a defeated universe, a bit of it saved for the "you" of the poems, but this poem can be reduced to clear prose far less easily than traditional poems can. (Of course, no poem is a sum of prose explanations, but almost all good poems are related to such summaries.) In Lerman's poem, one has to be—and I am—content with the vaguely religious language situation that has been put though a subtly beautiful verbal machine.

Alane Rollings's poems leap from the earthly and familiar to the extraordinary and learned. At their center is a remarkable temperament, full of wild comedy and dreamy power. Her poem "Life Expectancies" is full of the imagery of physics:

> Life was good, the best thing that happened,
> theories fell from you in dazzling strokes,
> the nature of sound, the speed of light, unimagined spectacles
> far beyond the double dawns and sunsets of Alpha Centauri.
> You played the radio beautifully, and every morning
> you got the paper to see what you were worth.

What counts here—and in the best of the newer poets—is the revelation of a remarkable, yet down-to-earth poetic personality, not only unafraid to tell you everything, but desperate, often comically desperate, to do so.

A Chinese girl studying in the United States recently told me she was struck by one difference between young Americans and young Chinese. Young Americans, she said, were as absorbed by sex as young Chinese were by politics.

What strikes me when reading through a few hundred American poems and stories is not so much their sexual intimacy as their persistent, almost innocent and unaware, narcissism. Sometimes it is confessional, sometimes exploratory, but the confessions are seldom shameful and the explorations are usually self-referential, eccentric, and inflected by the poet's sense of his or her uniqueness. Most of the Chinese love poems translated in Payne's anthology, *The White Pony*, in Ezra Pound's collection *Cathay*, or in A.C. Graham's *Poems of the Late T'ang* are often beautifully personal and intimate as well, but poet after poet seems to take a different route from that of the American poets. The route is an oblique one; the obliquity and indirectness are almost as important as the revelation; and this is as true for the complex metaphorical poetry of Li

Shang-yin as for that of Tu Fu or Li Po. It's as if the Chinese poets want to preserve their secret from all but the subtlest reader. The reader who penetrates the poetic mystery earns the privilege of intimacy.

The American poets are more lavish with secrets and friendship. Some recent poets, though, seem to be fed up with this self-packaging and delivery; they know there must be something more to poems than eccentric observation and intimate confession. These poets become quasi-reporters or sociologists, what John Dos Passos called "camera eyes." They at least pretend to be impartial observers. Even when they're as botanically accurate as Theodore Roethke, and as zoologically precise as Elizabeth Bishop, it often turns out that their observations are basically comic, so that the reader knows the poet is burlesquing, say, botany or journalism, sociology or case histories. Here's a mock case history taken from Richard Shelton's 1978 volume, *The Bus to Veracruz*.

> 1956: She is the girl with the biggest
> breasts in Sloan, Iowa. She will take
> a backseat to no one. He is young
> and handsome. All summer he fondles
> her breasts in the front seat. Sometimes
> she rests her fingers on the round knob
>
> of the gearshift. 1957: After the wedding
> they live in a white house. She suspects
> he is colorless. One day, while she
> is shopping, he paints the house green.
> She says it is garish. 1960: She decides
> he lacks polish. For his birthday she
> gives him sandpaper. He uses it, hoping
> to please her. When his face bleeds,
> she says he lacks character. He drinks
> to ease the pain. She says he is going
> to the dogs. To avoid it, he drinks alone.
>
> 1963: His face has healed but is scarred.
> She says he is hideous; he should take
> care of himself. She suggests a diet,
> exercise, vitamins. He prefers alcohol,
> loneliness, pain. 1965: She tells him
> he neglects her. She threatens to take
> a lover. The next day he brings home
> a friend. She and the friend become lovers.

After three months the friend kills her
and goes to the mountains of Peru.
The husband is convicted of murder and goes
to prison, where he is almost happy.

1975: But the mountains of Peru are very
high. The friend has a heart attack
and dies. Before he dies, he confesses
to the murder. The husband is released

from prison. 1976: His hair is beginning
to gray, but in spite of his scars he is
still handsome. He takes a job
driving a truck and meets a waitress
in a truck stop. She is a grass widow
with the biggest breasts in Enid, Oklahoma.
She will take a backseat to no one.

This poem is far from the musical poems of the 1950s. Though it's largely written in four-beat lines, the lines are prosaic, even telegraphic. It sounds *bored*.

Again and again in recent American poetry, one senses the boredom of the poet with the variety and richness which surround him. It is *fin-de-siècle* boredom, urban boredom, a version of what Baudelaire and Stendhal invented in France at the beginning of the nineteenth century. Dizzied by the enormous possibilities of the average bourgeois and even laborer's life in post-World War II America, many poets and prose writers turned away from them by listing in mock-Whitmanian catalogues, items, products, or scenes, ridiculing them with invented comic names, diminishing them by concentrating on the repetitive nature of the life the products supposedly enriched. Shelton's poem treats the ordinary and the extraordinary, the familiar and the violent, with the same offhand speed. The suggestion is that all things recur, and that it doesn't matter.

If American life is a grab bag of present and past, the violent and the ordinary, it is also conspicuously the poetry of people who have traveled. Here is Carolyn Forché's "Photograph of My Room."

         the china cups are from Serbia,
the curtains are those
           that hung in a kitchen in Prague,
              the bundle of letters were sent
           from Southeast Asia,
  and

> the lies told to myself were told
> because of Paris, the stories I
>
> believe
>
> in Salvador and Grenada.

Many American poems glitter with worldliness. Many ordinary Americans travel as only the wealthy traveled before World War II. Some, like the untraveled Wallace Stevens, are what Blake called "mental travelers," who see the world through books and television. In either case, American poets not only exhibit the earth's exotic places, they travel in time through world literature. Inexpensive books, free libraries, and public television programs give them the patina of Sir Francis Drake or of scholarly encyclopedists. In Norman Dubie's volume *The City of the Olesha Fruit* (1979), there are poems to, about, or in the manner of Kafka, Edgar Allan Poe, Kierkegaard, Thomas Hardy, Chekhov, and Yuri Olesha. In the book's last poem, "The Great Wall of China," the poet speaks as a 53-year-old Chinese sentry stationed at the Great Wall.

> near the Black Desert, but
> East of it, beside the mariposa-tiers
> of the green Husi Gorge.

He eavesdrops on lovers, plucks seeds from an apple, dreams. The poet enters into his being with the same confidence with which he enters the minds of Kafka, Kierkegaard, and Chekhov. It's as if the assured American poet believes nothing can hold him back from understanding or being anybody.

A word in this ragged, rapid survey for poets who follow the Mark Twain tradition of turning American idiom into revelations of character, such poets as Don Lee, Nikki Giovanni, Lucille Clifton, and Sonia Sanchez. Here's Sanchez's "summer words of a sistuh addict."

> the first day i shot dope
> was on a sunday.
> i had just come
> home from church
> got mad at my mother
> cuz she got mad at me. U dig?
> went out, shot up
> behind a feeling against her.
> it felt good
> gooder than doin it—yeah.

Without the Cummingsian devices, the poem would have little

power. With them, it brings the sly pleasure of the offhand, a casual, quotidian jazz that says, "This is authentic. This is the way it is. This is all the poetry you're going to get."

Between the artful reproduction of ghetto speech and the syntactic surrealism of a John Ashbery are more than a few miles. You have the interpolar scope of American poetry.

Like such brilliant burlesque prose writers as Donald Barthelme, Ashbery uses complex syntax to organize what otherwise is unorganized. The content of an Ashbery poem may turn on itself, but its broken syntax remains snootily confident—disdaining the ordinary—its rhetorical music superb. Here is Ashbery's "The Chateau Hardware," the title an Ashbery joke. (Nothing is further from a chateau than an American hardware store.)

> It was always November there. The farms
> were a kind of precinct; a certain control
> had been exercised. The little birds
> used to collect along the fence,
> it was the great "as though," the how the day went.
> The excursions of the police
> as I pursued my bodily functions, wanting
> neither fire nor water.
> vibrating to the distant pinch
> and turning out the way I am, turning
> 　　　out to greet you.

The poem has a setting, a time, some actions—"as I pursued my bodily functions"—and a conclusion, "turning out to greet you," but we don't know anything about the you and little about the I. It's as if the poem were assembling the elements of a traditional poem in a new order, the way stained glass windows bombed during World War II were reassembled into abstract patterns of brilliant fragments. The colors were still glorious, but there was no realistic depiction left.

Almost all the great ethical and religious figures of the world have urged people to either shed their heavy selves or to behave in such a way that the selves would be exalted beyond desire and pain. Glory, earthly or eternal, means self-transcendence. Art, too, is a sort of glory, a self-transcender (even when it's a self-revealer).

Recent American poetry is largely an art of self-expression: hundreds of poets, hundreds of more or less remarkable individuals exhibiting their uniqueness in lyric poems. The uniqueness is offered to, if not created for us. The result is that each good reader takes in and, to a degree, becomes more like the poet behind the poem.

Thousands of feelings work away in all of us. Every culture teaches us to praise some feelings, to censor, ignore or exorcize others. American culture emphasizes individuality. Derived from such Greek slogans as Pindar's "Become yourself" and the Delphic "Know thyself," American credos center around self-achievement and self-improvement. The country's most popular books are self-help books. Get stronger, bigger, wiser, have whiter teeth, cleaner houses; become a better cook, a shrewder investor, a richer and happier person. Every man a king, a saint, a star.

Older traditions spell out the dangers of individuality. There are the Judeo-Christian tradition of sin and the Confucian and Greek traditions of restraint and social contract. The self can only develop in society; society is endangered by excess individuality. The relationship of self to society was formulated in an Enlightenment enriched by newly translated Chinese classics, particularly the Confucian texts. The makers of the 200-year-old American constitution—the social document that stands beside our great text of individuality, the Declaration of Independence—were influenced by French, English, and Scottish thinkers of the Enlightenment.

The debate between the limits of individuality and the requirements of society continues in every country (even totalitarian ones). Recent American poetry has, on the whole, celebrated individual development and expression. It has moved away from masters of modernity as Pound and Eliot, who, in very different ways, praised submission to political, ethical, and religious systems.

This threadbare survey has mentioned scarcely a thousandth of the names behind the 50,000 American poems that could have been discussed. The point here is that twentieth-century American poetry may be as rich a repository as the T'ang poetry of seventh-century China.

[38]

READING AND REMEMBERING DONALD JUSTICE'S POEMS[1]

Although I know that the poems in Donald Justice's *Selected Poems* are among the loveliest written in this century, I cannot write an objective review of them. I know the poems' worth as surely as I know that the Art Institute is on Michigan Avenue and that "Sunday Afternoon on the Grande Jatte" is a work of supreme mastery, know about them with the same assurance that I know about other things in the range of love, strawberry shortcake to family and friends; and that is part of the problem I have with an objective review. Justice's poems are a part of my life, and have been since before any of the poems that appear in this collection were written.

Thirty-five years ago this last October, I was sitting in the library of the University of North Carolina in Chapel Hill. I was sixteen, a freshman, and I'd just, an hour before, come upon a wonderful book, the enormous double anthology of *Modern British and American Poetry* edited by Louis Untermeyer. I'd become a poetry reader four years earlier, when Pocket Books issued its first volume, the *Pocket Book of Verse* edited by M.E. Speare (shorn of the magical "Shake," but sacred, nonetheless, to me). Here in the amazing snugness was this zoo of marvels. I read, reread, memorized without trying; the poems of that volume became my mind's currency.

As for the special pleasure of verse itself, that must have come to me (as it comes to most children) through the voice of someone I loved. My grandmother, born in New York of German parents, and dead there in 1933 when I was five, had recited German, English and French rhymes to me. Though I knew these "by heart," I was not conscious of them as poems.

The next memory of poetry is bookish: I can feel, almost relive the delight of holding *A Child's Garden of Verses* which I read during one of the many illnesses I either had or faked to stay home

---

[1] *Selected Poems.* NY: Atheneum. 1989 Cloth: $10.95. Paper: $6.95.

from school.[2] The Speare book was not part of that child's book life; it came into the hands of a conscious twelve year old who was not just starved for print but anxious to assert himself through it. In the exotic verbal islands of Keats and Marlowe, that boy took his pleasure.

In high school, poetry was beaten down by a poor teacher, but I continued to read it outside class. I read *The Ring and the Book* on the Independent Subway and associate it—as I associate Berkeley's *Dialogues of Hylas and Philonous* —with screams of rage. Nose in the terrific book, I didn't notice when I swung my bookbag with its loose brass strut against the silk-stockinged legs of fellow passengers. In those wartime days, stockings were rationed. "You little son-of-a-bitch, I'll kill you."

All right. In the library at Chapel Hill, I felt someone looking over my shoulder at the Untermeyer. "Good stuff." A soft voice, hardly Southern. A long-faced, eyeglassed fellow, tall, thin. "Like it?" Surprise and pleasure inflected with the slightest patronage. He was nineteen and worldly. From Miami and on his way to New York. Sometimes he stopped at Chapel Hill, where he occasionally took courses. In Miami, he studied composing with Carl Ruggles.

We saw each other now and then, and when we didn't there were letters—his were wonderful. Many enclosed poems. We were sharp but generous critics of each other's work. In 1946, Don was a graduate student at Chapel Hill, where, in a Renaissance class, he sat beside Jean Ross, who became his wife the next summer. (See his first book, *The Summer Anniversaries*.)

Don and I always had ups-and-downs. There'd be some dumb slight or imputation which would rupture relations for a week or a month. Once we decided to write a play together. We laid it out, scene by scene, and began writing. There was only one comfortable chair in the house. He had it one day, I the next. One day, we argued about whose turn it was; that finished our collaborative life.

The play—I finished it—was called *The Gamesman's Island.* Gamesmanship was crucial to poetry and life. We were frenetic gamesmen, constant, usually amiable competitors. Every Christmas, the Justices came up from Iowa City to our Chicago house. Christmas created a new world for our competition: the kids' new

---

[2] I'd learned the effectiveness of putting the thermometer on the light bulb. Only when I miscalculated, and my 107° temperature brought my father home from the office in a taxi to see his son reclining easily in bed with a book and a glass of lemonade, did I abandon this device.

toys. One year, we raced jack-in-the-boxes; another we played tid-dleywinks for twelve hours.[3] The kids didn't get a look-in, though when they were older—say, five—Don competed with them. Our competition died with Pounce, a game of double patience. (Patience!) Don played this game with maniacal speed and frenzy. I retreated and retired, saving myself an ulcer as big as the Ritz.

It was always an event to get a Justice poem in a letter. I knew many by heart, even taught the children some. I think some discarded stanzas survive only in our memories.

Even the best reader of poetry takes it from outside; that is, the reader is subject to the whims of sequence. The whims, and they are often the delights, can be contradictions as well as reinforcements, shocks as well as fulfillments. As for the poet, he too knows the pleasure of surprise—if his inventive power didn't surprise him, there'd be no point in writing—but his surprises exist in another universe, one whose gods are Adjustment and Transformation. Between the inside and outside of poetry, then, there's a large gap. If I did not become a good poet in the years of my exchange with Justice, I did at least cross the gap.

For me, his *Selected Poems* is a journal of an almost-lifelong friendship. The poems have the familiarity and value of old friends. (The latest, "uncollected," poems are new to me.) I have old favorites, and will have new ones. Poems built so finely shift in the mind from reading to reading. In that way, they're like complicated friends, always there, but different as one's mood is different. They are the products, if not the barometer, of an extraordinary temperament coupled with enormous verbal and rhythmic skill. Some tell of bleakness, some regret, some passion, others affection. There are family poems, love poems, poems about moods, about the words that create moods, about empty rooms, about the minds of the insane, about music, about the old Muse of an old poet. The poems are themselves the form and the occasion of moods, ones that may be only distantly related to the poet's. After all, the working poet, trying out, say, fifty versions of a line, does not sustain the original feelings of the first version. No poem here, though, could have been written by anyone but Donald Justice. This is his world, faintly tropic, faintly melancholy, musical, affectionate, a fixity of evanescence. Beautiful as little else. How lucky to have had its creation be what its existence now is, a part of one's own life.

---

[3] Norman Maclean always came by with a Christmas bottle of wine (a wonderful New York State *Grav es*) and laughed his head off at the two of us on the floor snapping chips or winding handles like demons.

[39]

THE POETRY OF EDGAR BOWERS[1]

Edgar Bowers' poems[2] are those of someone who doesn't resort to meter at every robin's appearance. The poems sound like ones the poet seems obliged to write. They are controlled in a way which transforms personal feeling into commentary, rage into a kind of civic anger, tenderness into analysis of tenderness. The poems deal with important, common topics—love, death, reflections on great men, landscapes, dedications. They are rarely idiosyncratic; the aroused feelings are manifestly controlled; reference is explicitly made to them and to their magnitude.

Bowers is master of a complex syntax and a small, fairly common vocabulary composed to an unusual degree of abstract nouns and such words as "bone," "flesh," "light," "shade," and "dark." There are few bizarre qualifiers, no interchanged parts of speech, no "*Erhebungs*," "concupiscent curds," or "dithering in the drift of cordial seas." Standard meters are employed in a way which seems the inflexible expressions of the feelings' small flexibility. In a century whose favorite poetry has so often been violent, allusive, antisyntactical, and theatrically idiosyncratic in subject and style, Bowers' work looks more conspicuous than it would in an eighteenth-century collection.

Bowers' distinguished teacher, Yvor Winters, wrote that a poem

> is good in so far as it makes a defensible rational statement about a given human experience (the experience need not be real but must in some sense be possible) and at the same time

---

[1] 1992. Edgar Bowers is one of my oldest friends. He came to Chapel Hill in 1946 after years at war. He's written few but fine poems. This deals only with his first book of poems; later ones (*The Astronomers*, for instance) would require the kind of close analysis of which I am no longer capable. I do though want to mention a wonderful recent poem, "For Louis Pasteur."

[2] Edgar Bowers, *The Form of Loss* (Denver: Alan Swallow, 1956).

> communicates the emotion which ought to be motivated by that
> rational understanding of that experience.[3]

This clumsy statement[4] will serve to distinguish the temper of
Bowers and the more usual modern poet who, like Miss Compton-
Burnett's Lesbia Firebrace, announces on the steps of the house
she's come to visit that she has come to offer herself "because I
have nothing else to offer. When people say that, they are content
with their offering, and expect other people to be."

Bowers' poems are reasoned meditations usually centered about
a single experience, a city view, a conversation with his grandmother, an elegy, reflections on a maxim. The poetic pressure
comes from an insistent, complicating analysis. There is almost no
narrative movement, even in poems whose events seem to beg for
narrative treatment,[5] none of the emotional progress characteristic
of Keats' odes, seldom movement which leads to emotional climaxes or turnabouts. The poems revolve about and close in on the
experience until its import is transformed. They expose not so
much breadth of perception as the serious, complex mind which is
stirred into poetry by the original perception. This holds true for
the few dramatic poems in the book as well; Bowers's William
Tyndale and Joseph Haydn seem like each other and like the person
who declares in the prefatory "To the Reader"

> These poems are too much tangled with the error
> And waste they would complete. My soul repays me,
> Who fix it by a rhythm, with reason's terror
> Of hearing the swift motion that betrays me.

"These poems" brood over loss, over the malice of both reason
and unreason, and they are nostalgic for the old religion which softened loss and malice by placing them in a larger scheme. (See
"The Virgin Considered as a Picture" and "Epigram on the Passing
of Christmas.") Other poems deal with the aftermath of World War
II seen from the side of the defeated (Bowers was an intelligence
noncom in occupied Bavaria), the stones of Venice "in which great

---

[3] *In Defense of Reason* (New York: William Morrow, 1947), p. 568.

[4] Consider the uselessness of "defensible" next to "rational," of "given," and of the parenthet-
ical expression, the lack of antecedent for "that rational understanding" (stemming from a
confusion of the two occurrences of "rational" in the sentence), and the bizarre "motivated."

[5] Though Bowers is one of the best storytellers I know.

works decay," the loss of love, friends, relatives, surety, and innocence. Loss is the book's temper, but its richness comes from the
analytic tenacity whose chief instrument is the most elaborate syntax in recent American poetry. The syntax is built not with phrase
clusters, parallel constructions or novel clauses but on such things
as brief prepositional phrases which suddenly extend and modify
the direction of the poetic sentence:

> Now at the last he lies back, still unspent,
> In passion and in time, relinquishing
> All that he gathered from them to their use,
> Clasps in the dark will he could not refuse
> Ingenuous patience eager with assent.
> "Oedipus at Coloneus"

The stanza consists of rapid modifications of the original view of
the ripened, "unspent" king, and its strength is in the syntactic
economy of "from them to their use" and the qualifier "Ingenuous."

I should like to look at one of Bowers's poems in order to exhibit some of its virtues and then point to a defect which is related to
them. The poem is called "Dark Earth and Summer."

> Earth is dark where you rest
> Though a little winter grass
> Glistens in icy furrows.
> There, cautious, as I pass,
>
> Squirrels run, leaving stains
> Of their nervous, minute feet
> Over the tombs; and near them
> Birds gray and gravely sweet.
>
> I have come, warm of breath,
> To sustain unbodied cold,
> Removed from life and seeking
> Darkness where flesh is old,
>
> Flesh old and summer waxing,
> Quick eye in the sunny lime,
> Sweet apricots in silence
> Falling—precious in time,

> All radiant as a voice, deep
> As their oblivion. Only as I may,
> I come, remember, wait,
> Ignorant in grief, yet stay.
>
> What you are will outlast
> The warm variety of risk,
> Caught in the wide, implacable,
> Clear gaze of the basilisk.

The elegiac meditation is an address by the mourner to the one mourned. The tone is quiet but varied; the variations are embodied in a subtle metric which mostly departs from an anapestic dimeter base. A moving, quietly complicated statement leads to resolution in the last stanza.

Bowers balances great weights on tiny pivots, which is fine when the pivots are steady: so the use of "may" for the more likely "can" in the fifth stanza at first seemed a mistake, as did the "yet" in the same stanza; when the connection between the two is understood, an ordinary statement about mourning becomes a refined account of helplessness. If such pivots wobble, however, the poem is damaged more seriously than a poem built from more conspicuous blocks. Thus the confusion which rises from the questionable antecedents of "Removed from life," "All radiant as a voice," and "Caught in the wide...basilisk." The punctuation after "time" and the use of "old" to describe the flesh of the dead (if it described the speaker's, it would be an intolerable diversion) leave debates which can't be resolved with the surety which resolved the uncertainty about "may" and "yet." Consider

> All radiant as a voice, deep
> As their oblivion.

Does "All" refer to the apricots? So it would seem, but then why so heavy an investment in this detail, and why further complicate the dubious simile of the "voice" to which they are similar in radiance? Or is it "time" which is radiant? The punctuation would indicate that, but "their" makes this impossible, unless "their" refers to the apricots. Or "All" could refer to all the scene's components; but the difficulties attendant here are insurmountable. The point is that the "clear statement" is sometimes unclear, and the cause isn't intellectual difficulty but mechanical complications of expression derived from the poet's practice of never letting a simple statement stand. The practice accounts for much of Bowers' success, but out of the firm control it constantly requires, it mars lovely poems.

There are also, I think, two "mistakes" in diction which twist the poem away from the straightforward, if complex, situation toward false complication of the speaker's character (he becomes "literary"): "basilisk" and "precious in time," miscalculations of the strain that traditional diction exerts on poems. Such mistakes seem to me the sort which Bowers' difficult procedure invites and makes conspicuous, but the procedure is responsible for some of the most beautiful poems in recent American poetry.

[40]

THE MANDELSTAMS

The plague which spread over the Soviet Union was the extinction of personality; its cause, the rupture of old relationships. "We saw it come about in front of our very eyes," writes Nadia Mandelstam. "All intermediate social links, the family, one's circle of friends, class, society itself—each abruptly disappeared, leaving every one of us to stand alone before the mysterious force embodied in the State."

Thirty years earlier, the Flesh-eating Machine had devoured one of its greatest personalities, the poet Osip Mandelstam. For his widow, "there was no longer life or sense of life." If she was "saved," it was by "the thought of a 'you.' Instead of sense, my life had a concrete purpose: not to allow 'them' to stamp out all traces of the man I thought of as 'you,' to save his poetry."

In a way no Westerner I know can imagine, poetry—the unquantifiable registration of what is most original in personality—was the secret breath which sustained millions in their underwater Soviet existence. The great poets of the language had all been either killed, terrorized into suicide, imprisoned, exiled, *silenced*: Gumilev, Tsvetaeva, Yesenin, Mandelstam, Mayakovski, Blok, Akhmatova, Pasternak. Yet somehow, poetry broke through the stone of Soviet life. Decades after her work was officially obliterated, Akhmatova read in Moscow to cheering thousands. Stalin—the terrible essence of stone itself—inquired about the organization behind such a welcome.

Surviving.

"I survived only by a miracle or an oversight, which is the same thing." Mrs. Mandelstam was a *stopiatnitsa*—a "hundred-and-fiver," forbidden to live within 105 kilometers of large cities—she taught English linguistics, or, fired for sitting on a window sill instead of a chair and talking about Grimm's Law (of consonant change), lived off the charity of such friends as Akhmatova. The two women preserved in memory and talk the verse and personality of Mandelstam.

Every remarkable book writes itself (the author feels its true force, meaning and rhythm in the writing) and many supply their own theory. Following—as always—her husband's notions, Nadia Mandelstam explains her unique books.[1] Tragedy doesn't exist on the Russian stage, but it lives in Russian narrative prose. As for prose, it is the "disjunctive expression" of life's continuum. So this book is as disjunctive as Montaigne's essays. Its tragic power is scattered in anecdotes, character studies, comic scenes, social observations, diatribes, textual and philosophical analysis. Mrs. Mandelstam is not the original Montaigne is; decades of survival life do not promote that idiomatic grace and inventiveness which mark what we call literary genius. Her book, though, is unique, and it offers the world another model of humanity, a brilliant, comprehensive devotion fixed by a tenacity of mourning which, oddly, is as much a source of joy as melancholy.

"In our age, everything has become so serious that any view not rooted in values sets the teeth on edge as a knife drawn over glass."

The story of the Mandelstams begins one May day in 1919 when the tiny, spirited, artistic twenty-year-old Kiev girl meets the twenty-eight-year-old Petersburg poet. It is a month before Lenin has launched the first terror (after the attempt on his life and the assassination of Uritsky). The theory of terror has been readied. In *Gulag Archipelago I*, Solzhenitsyn quotes a 1918 Lenin essay on "the common, united purpose of a 'purge of the Russian earth of all harmful insects.'" In September 1919 Lenin is telling Gorki "not to spend his time whimpering over" that species of insect he calls "rotten intellectuals."[2]

Yet it's still early, the golden time of revolution. The Mandelstams have hope and even a small place in the new world. Poets can serve, there is some traveling and a reporting job.[3] Gorki

---

[1] *Hope against Hope* (New York: Atheneum, 1970) and *Hope Abandoned* (New York, Atheneum, 1974).

[2] May 1981. I now think Solzhenitsyn's view of Lenin oversimplified to the point of viciousness. It's partly the result of reading his lifeless *Lenin in Zurich*, partly reading about a more human, if still grim Lenin in Justin Kaplan's biography of Lincoln Steffens.

[3] A brilliant 1923 interview with Ho Chi Minh (then known as Nguyen Ai Quoc) isn't mentioned in Mrs. Mandelstam's book.

[293]

himself allows Mandelstam a sweater, though—disliking
Mandelstam's poetry—Gorki crosses out his request for trousers:
"He'll manage without."

Mandelstam lacks that quantifying talent which makes equations
of pants and poems so easy for Gorki. He is the real thing, one of
fifty million who can express depth of being in the same words the
other forty-nine million-plus use to order hamburgers and court
their sweethearts. In these early days, such men sometimes had the
protection of important officials. Bukharin was Mandelstam's
"transmission belt," not only for special rations and trips to
Armenia, but for saving some of the insects the state purged with
such expertise.

In the thirties the system flowered into its perfect expression, the
Georgian (or Ossetian) genius of human cynicism and meat-eating,
Joseph Stalin. The collision between poet and dictator was as natural to human physics as the gravitational force between earth and
a bit of dust. Every single personality of worth in the Soviet Union
fell—one way or another—to that gross planet. The immediate
cause of Mandelstam's fall doesn't matter; it was either his slap-
ping Alexei Tolstoy (for being rude to Nadia) or writing a short
poem about the great man:

> Words final as lead weights fall from his lips
> His cockroach whiskers leer
> His boottops gleam . . . And every killing is a treat
> For the broad-chested Ossete.

They carried Mandelstam off in 1934. But the "transmission
belt" still functioned, and the Great Destroyer was informed about
the protests. A former divinity student, he understood the miracles
of grace and remission. One night he made the famous telephone
call to Pasternak which assured him that Mandelstam would be all
right.

More or less. For four years, Osip and Nadia moved from place
to place, "frightened by dogs barking," begging "alms from shadows." Then, nineteen years to the day after they'd met, it was over.
Mandelstam was carried off into the oblivion of the death camps.

For twenty years Nadia drifted over Russia in a semi-stupor.
Then, during the Khruschev "thaw," she got a room of her own and
began writing the furious, funny, heartrending memorial of her life
with Osip, its jokes, battles, tyrannies, profundities. Its last page is
a letter written in 1938:

Osip, my beloved, faraway sweetheart, I have no words, my darling, to write this letter that you may never read. . . . I am writing it into empty space. . . . I bless every day and every hour of our bitter life together, my sweetheart, my companion, my blind guide in life. . . . I speak only to you, only to you. You are with me always, and I who was such a wild and angry one and never learned to weep—now I weep and weep and weep. It's me, Nadia. Where are you? Farewell.

[VI]

BIOGRAPHY, AUTOBIOGRAPHY, LETTERS

[41]

RACEHOSS

"Voices, voices—Listen hard,
as saints listen."
Rilke, *Duino Elegies*

Like petroleum, some human genius is formed under great pressure exerted over time. It may be why there is so much prison literature, why certain penalized groups burst into song and story. The literary genius of black people has been emerging in this country for about a century. Forty years ago, one of its monuments, Richard Wright's autobiography, *Black Boy*, was published. Recently, a small Texas press published a book as remarkable as Wright's, Albert Race Sample's *Racehoss*.[1] *Racehoss* describes some of the same pressures Wright's book did—the meanness, tyranny and violence within certain poor black families—but it is a very different description. *Black Boy* was formed by literature; Wright was *saved* by the printed word. *Racehoss* is the work of a man whose literary training came late. Race Sample's mind was formed by voices telling stories, so he is able to go back to each segment of his life and recall what he heard and saw as if it were present now. There is scarcely a Proustian shadow in his work.

Those who heard Race's own voice on Studs Terkel's radio broadcast knew they'd heard something remarkable. The voice was not just reporting bizarre and terrible events, it was registering and expressing them in a way no actor can imitate. The mild tenor told its story in precise, colorful, slightly ungrammatical language with a purity and force that brought Studs more audience reaction than any broadcast he's made in thirty years. When Race sang along with the recorded prison songs or broke down as he told

---

[1] *Racehoss: Big Emma's Boy.* By Albert Race Sample. Eakin Press, P.O. Box 23066. Austin, Texas, 78735. 320pp. $14.95.

about what happened to him a dozen years ago in the blackness of solitary confinement, listeners felt an extraordinary power.

What we might not have expected was that Race's book would be as moving as Race's voice. The further surprise is that it is very different.

Race had told us of the cruelty and brutality of the plantation prison at Retrieve, Texas (where he spent seventeen years). Voice trembling, he talked of Boss Band, the field boss, threatening him and his fellows with death if they so much as looked askance at him. He spoke of serving under Boss Band for seven years, then watching him fall off his horse and die. "I saw him draw his last breath." He spoke of the tyranny of Big Devil, the Warden, who stripped two homosexual prisoners, married them publicly, then assigned them to different tanks. There was much too about his remarkable mother, Big Emma, and how he learned to forgive her. Finally, he told about the voice which came to him in his despair and told him he wasn't an animal but a man, that he wasn't alone, that he was loved.

What he did not and—FCC regulations being what they are— could not tell were the violent, obscene and farcical stories which fill the book. Brilliantly set down in street talk, these stories exhibit not only Race and Emma's lives but those of the prisoners, four hundred of whose names are put at the end of this book like a Hallelujah Chorus. The prisoner's love stories alone are marvelous. There is Filet Mignon and his stolen ham: "Oh, Bessie May, you sweet thang . . . tell me how it's good to you"; Flea Brain and Pork Chop, the married cons, and Flea Brain's defense of his love to the psychologist, Dr. Gates: "Most uv us can't git to dem cows, mules, an horses . . . whut we spose ta do?" One con who did git is called Cowfucker, a bit unfair since it makes the man's love generic: Cowfucker, like Faulkner's Ike Snopes, loves a particular cow. Then there's Ol' Bull, whose unwilling punk cuts off Bull's enormous penis while he's asleep; and Rat Wine, whose rebellious 'gal' decapitated him as he sat smoking in the mess hall. (Big Devil keeps a picture of the headless torso in his office.)

Then there are rehabilitation stories. One day, it's announced that glass eyes will be supplied to the one-eyed and dentures to the toothless. Three prisoners, one with a large, one with a small and one with a medium-sized mouth are recruited to bite into "them false teeth molds." When Mama Better Drawers' "mouf" is one of three chosen, his ol' man, Ape, announces, "Evuh onea you muthafuckas whut gits a pair of my baby's teefs is gon' gimme a sack o'

[300]

dust [chewing tobacco] evuh week or I'm gon do sump'n to his ass!" As for the glass eyes, they turn out to be blue. Nonetheless, they serve as collateral in card games. "When Squat Low won Blood Eye's eye, he put it in his pocket. Blood Eye didn't like it: "Say man, take my eye outta yo pocket?" Squat Low responds, "It ain' non e a yo eye no mo." Blood Eye asks him to at least put the eye in his locker. Squat Low refuses. "Nigguh, I don' wont that thang lookin at me evah time I go in dere to git sumpin." Says Blood Eye, "Ain' nuthin in yo locker my eye wonts to see no how."

The stories are not a haphazard jokebook. They create the people who filled Race's life and dominate his memory. When he describes the inter-plantation cotton-picking championship which made him "a legend in the bottoms" or the annual baseball game with the Ramsey Hardhitters, the walls of the prison break open and you see that the cells of this American gulag connect.

The best and longest stories have to do with the people who formed Race's life and turned it around. The most important is Big Emma. The book begins with her, age four, riding to church with her sisters and nine-months-gone mother. A wheel breaks off the cart. The enraged father seizes a singletree, clubs his nagging wife in the back and kills her. The children, including the delivered baby, are sent to live with the devilish tyrant Grandma Louduskie. One day, fifteen-year-old Emma threatens the tyrant with that weapon of domestic liberation, a butcher knife, and runs off. Beautiful, she sells what is most desired by whites and blacks. A white cotton broker fathers Race and gives him his first name and his "peckerwood" hide. (Race's complexion makes him a minority within a minority.) Emma becomes a skilled gambler, bootlegger, madam, cook and manager. Race becomes her servant, her confidant, her victim. She leaves him, returns to him, threatens him, betrays him, and one day, age twelve, he runs off. He rides the rails around the country, works for a carny, steals, bootlegs, assaults, goes in and out of jails and is told by a judge to either join the army or go to prison. He enlists and makes money gambling and bootlegging but is too restless to stay in one place. After a return home to see Emma—a visit which ends when she threatens him with the butcher knife and he knocks her down—he goes AWOL, is arrested, discharged, and finally, after another robbery and assault, is given heavy time, two concurrent thirty year sentences at Retrieve, the plantation for the Incorrigibles (who call the place "Hell").

In this house of the dead, Racehoss is baptized by Boss Band (whose own name derives from the day he killed the "whole band

[301]

of nigguhs" working under him). Band tells Race's Number One
Hoe Squad:

> If airy one uv ya tries to run off, I'm gon' kill ya. If you lay
> th' hammer [the hoe] down under me, I'm gon' kill ya. An if
> I jes takes a notion to, I'm gon kill ya . . . That last boss ya'll
> had didn' git a Gotdam thang outta ya'll, 'pared to whut I'm
> gon' git. I bet no see airy nigguh comin' thru 'at backgate wit
> his shirt not astickin to his ass. Ain' gon' be no dry nigguhs
> in my squad. DO YOU HEAH ME NIGGUHS?

To which they give the response Boss Band demands, "OH
LAWD." For seven years, Racehoss slaves under Boss Band. It is
hell on earth. (One convict gets his hand chopped off to escape it.)
Yet, writes Racehoss, the tension of living under this murderous
tyrant "compelled me to recognise, to look, to become aware of
where I was and what was going on all about me. I had become
confident . . . and I opened my eyes."

One day, some years after Boss Band drops dead on the job,
Racehoss is put into solitary confinement. Alone in the dark, he is
at the end of his tether. Mauling himself, clawing the concrete ceiling, he begs God to kill him. Suddenly he sees a ray of light in his
hand and a voice—the one despair has projected into sublimity
since the days of Moses and Job—tells him he is all right now.
("Who, if I cried, would hear me?" is the beginning of the *Duino
Elegies*.)

The last pages of *Racehoss* describe his release from Retrieve,
then from a less terrible prison. He is free just in time to say goodbye to Emma. From her deathbed, she says,

> "Mama knowed you wuz comin. I wuzn' bout to
> go nowhere til you got here . . . Is me an you
> still buddies?"

> "The best kind, Mama."

Racehoss is appointed to the Governor's staff and begins the
work rehabilitating ex-prisoners which has made him a Texas
celebrity. Now he's married, a father, and the author of this book.

The book ends the way it's written, with a story, a Chekovian
one. One day, after visiting one of his ex-prisoner clients,
Racehoss finds himself driving back home on the wrong road. He
notices he's only a few miles from where Big Devil, now retired,

lives. He turns off the road and drives to the ex-Warden's home. Big Devil is delighted to see him, delighted to hear how well he's done. They sit on the porch swing talking about Flea Brain and Pork Chops and the old life. Big Devil tells his wife to "brang us two glasses uv 'at lemonade," and when they have the frosty glasses in hand, he says, "Ol' Racehoss, I'm glad I had sump'n to do wit hepin git yore heart right."

"That's where you're wrong Warden," says Racehoss calmly. "You didn't have shit to do with it."

[42]

LIQUEUR FLANNER

In 1940, Janet Flanner, age 48, came back to America from war-time Europe. Since 1925, she'd been writing for the *New Yorker* the famous *Paris Letters* which appeared under the pen name its editor, Harold Ross, had given her "without asking me first," Genêt. Genêt embodied and purveyed that humane, chic, contemporary awareness which was the *New Yorker's* sophistication. She knew and wrote about painters, dancers, writers, politicians, designers, criminals, chefs, and actors. Her sentences were famous for declarative purity, her Letters and Profiles for their accuracy, factuality, balanced cool, and high wit. She wrote brilliantly about Picasso and Pétain, Thomas Mann and Anna Magnani, Bette Davis and Adolph Hitler. Her description of Brigitte Bardot's strange feet or the machinations of a village mayor transfigured both into delectable prose. Week after week, year after year, she reported scenes, people, opinions, events. Most of what she wrote remains as clear, useful and enjoyable as when it first appeared. (I just reread her 1936 profile of Hitler [in *Janet Flanner's World*, 1979]. Its deadpan, intimate ferocity supplants a thousand baroque, death-mask versions of the monster.)

Back in New York the summer of 1940, Flanner met Natalia Danesi Murray, an Italian woman ten years her junior. Mrs. Murray was separated from her husband, living with her son and her remarkable feminist mother, self-exiled from Mussolini's Italy. She and Janet fell immediately in love. Thirty-five years later, a few months before her death, Flanner remembered "how we burned and so publicly. I could report on each motion of our bodies." In the same remarkable letter she remembered how she herself had tried marriage and was "so at sea in my disappointment in not being in love as I had been with women that I had no sense of recording veracity of any sort, my emotional push toward my lesbic approach to all of life being so dominant that if I did not have it so vibrant a permanent problem in my daily life, I had nothing at all to replace it."

Darlinghissima—"most darling one"—is a selection of letters written by Flanner to Murray pieced out with the 83 year old survivor's account of where they were and why they were there.[1] For most of the 35 years, the lovers lived apart, Flanner usually in Paris, Murray either in New York or Rome where she worked for the Italian publishers Mondadori and Rizzoli. The letters are a monument to their relationship. Too much so. What is necessary for lovers, the expression of their love, can satiate if not annoy readers. Still, there is plenty here to be enjoyed, especially for Flanner devotees. Indeed, the very excess of expressed adoration—marked by the book's title—makes concrete for them the passionate underside of a writer distinguished for her ability to plunge feverish upheaval and overheated genius into cool prose. The prose of these letters is often neither cool nor commanding. If it were all we knew of Janet Flanner, we wouldn't know it or her.

One of three artistic daughters of an intelligent and sympathetic Indianapolis Quaker couple, Flanner knew early that she was not like the geniuses she described although at five she had wanted to be one of them. When she was seventeen, in Europe with her parents for the first time, she also knew where she wanted to live. In 1912, in Chicago, as another gifted Midwestern woman was founding *Poetry Magazine*, and still another, Margaret Anderson, was starting the magazine which first published Joyce's *Ulysses*, Janet Flanner came to the University of Chicago to study writing with Robert Morse Lovett. That was a success, but two years later she was "requested to leave Green Hall Dormitory as a 'rebellious influence'." She wrote a novel, *The Cubicle City*. It convinced her that she was only one of the "little artists," a "high-class artisan," a person "with intimations of and appreciation of great talent and yet not having it...somewhat talented but essentially lazy, ignorant and poorly-read because lacking that true spark of superb energy which marks the genial high fire..." For such "petty creators" there is— she told Natalia—"a loneliness that is terrible."

Recording the deeds of others is a way of latching onto their glory. Janet Flanner is one of the premier recorders, one of the premier journalists of the century. She shuttled between shame and pride in the designation. Finally she accepted the plaudits and rewards which prized her journalism as literature. Reporting and recording were so deeply a part of her that even the intimate letter about her erotic nature uses the verb "report" to express this way of

---

[1] *Darlinghissima...Letters To a Friend* by Janet Flanner. Edited and with a commentary by Natalia Danesi Murray. Random House.

dealing with the world.

I suppose that these letters are more Murray's record than Flanner's. There's no indication that Flanner thought they would be published. She published only what she worked on and worked on hard. One of the best letters here describes the sort of work she did for a profile: the observations, interviews and assemblages of fact which could be scattered "like croutons in a broth". All would condense into the "liqueur" of the personality.

The Liqueur Flanner is not in *Darlinghissima*. That Flanner is the Genêt who preserved the Liqueurs Pétain, Picasso, de Gaulle and Alice Toklas, the plays on the boulevards, the crimes in the countryside, the intrigues of politics, love, and literature, the beauty of Parisian skies and provincial gardens, the liqueur of Europe itself with which so many Americans were intoxicated for the fifty years of her remarkable career. Still, now we know that without this beautiful, passionate, and sustained love, that career would not have existed.

[43]

ISAK DINESEN

More than fifty years ago, Karen Blixen, a middle-aged Danish woman, packed up twenty-five crates of "such things as I have been unable to get rid of" and prepared to leave the Africa she had loved for the past seventeen years. Six months before the outbreak of World War I, she'd come to run a coffee farm in the hills outside the growing town of Nairobi. The day she landed in Mombasa, she married her second cousin, the young Swedish baron, Bror Blixen, the twin of the brother she'd really loved. For a while, they were happy in the beautiful country, but the work of running a complex coffee farm was not for him; nor, apparently, was his complex wife. That he infected her with syphilis—she returned to Denmark for a cure—was only part of what led her family to urge her to divorce him. She resisted them; she did not want to fail the central relationship of her life, nor did she want the farm to fail, not so much for herself, but for her family, which backed and owned it, and for those who worked with her on it, the people she grew to love more than anything in the world, "my black brothers."

The farm did fail. The family dismissed Bror and put her in charge, and then the marriage failed. Sickness, loneliness, endless worry about rainfall and coffee prices, the responsibility of being judge, doctor, veterinarian, manager and chief correspondent, made Karen Blixen despair. She wrote to her brother Tommy

> I often felt that I myself had had ability and a great capacity for work but for some reason or other or in some way or other had not brought these to fruition. I, who felt that I had been ready to stake everything, and in some ways had been beaten as black and blue as someone who has staked everything, had never been *in gear*, had ended up by giving my life to *making both ends meet* on a remote coffee farm whose future continues to be dubious.

It was not the whole story. Even at the end, she could write her remarkable mother, Ingeborg Dinesen,

> You must not think that I feel, in spite of it having ended in such defeat, that my 'life has been wasted' here, or that I would exchange it with that of anyone I know.

Although, of

> all the idiots I have met in my life...I have been the biggest...a certain love of greatness, which could not be quelled, has kept a hold on me, has been 'my daimon'...I hold to the belief that I am one of Africa's favorite children. A great world of poetry has revealed itself to me and taken me to itself here...I have looked into the eyes of lions and slept under the Southern Cross, I have seen the grass of the great plains ablaze and covered with delicate green after the rains, I have been the friend of Somali, Kikuyu, and Masai, I have flown over the Ngong Hills...my house here has been a kind of refuge for wayfarers and the sick, and to the black people has stood as the center of a friendly spirit.

One wayfarer was Denys Finch-Hatton, a brilliant exile from the world's vulgarity, who taught her Greek and music, and was loved and entertained by her for thirteen years. Denys would not be fixed into a role, and, Karen learned, neither would she. She wouldn't be defined as a lover, mother or child. Nor did she want a child of her own.

> I have always felt that to resort to "living in one's children" after having oneself *"failed in life "*—and thus to have no faith or substance to give the children—was one of the most pitiable things one could fall back on . . . and to me it seems both morally despicable and logically utter nonsense.

When the family closed down Karen Coffee Company Ltd., she left what she loved. Like a funereal exclamation mark, Denys was killed in his Gypsy Moth as he was flying back to say goodbye to her. She thought about ending her life, not in despair, but because "it would seem the most *natural* thing to disappear with my world here." Yet in the same letter, she wondered "whether I could learn to cook in Paris or a hotel." There was a third possibility: "I have started writing a book...in English, because I thought it would be more profitable."

Back in the upper middle-class Danish world, the middle-aged Baroness (she said it was worth getting syphilis to be called that) worked for two years on a book of stories similar to those that, back on the farm, had enchanted Denys, Farah and Juma. The book was sent out, rejected and sent out again. Dorothy Canfield recommended it to her publisher Robert Haas who first rejected, then accepted it, so a few days before the author's forty-ninth birthday, *Seven Gothic Tales* was published in New York under her maiden name, Dinesen, and the *non de plume* Isak, "the one who laughs," the one saved from the sacrificial knife at the last minute. The book was a success. Karen translated it into Danish and became the country's leading writer.

Three years later, it was followed by the beautiful memoir, *Out of Africa*. Here, the material which shows up raw in her letters takes on the form of purified recollection. It remains one of the finest books ever written about Africa.

Karen Blixen is one of the few white people honored in today's Kenya. Her old farm is now the suburb Karen, and the grandchildren of those she loved honor her memory there and elsewhere.

In the last few years, with the publication of their diaries, memoirs and letters, a few remarkable women have proved to be even more remarkable. Flannery O'Connor's *The Habit of Being* revealed not only an unsparing farceuse but a great Catholic thinker; the diaries, letters and memoirs of Virginia Woolf and Nadhezda Mandelstam revealed them as brilliant social observers as well as the sufferers and recollectors of extraordinary private lives. Karen Blixen's *Letters From Africa*[1] are the legacy of a profoundly brave, decent, entrancing person whose analyses of sexuality, feminism, colonial and African characters are as fascinating as the scenes and portraits which run side by side with them. If these are not as brilliant as those in her great memoir, there is at least the material for one portrait greater than all the others, that of the human being behind them all.

---

[1] Isak Dinesen. *Letters From Africa 1914-1931*. Edited by Frans Lasson. Translated by Anne Born. The University of Chicago Press. 1981. 474 pages. 1993. Since their publication, Judith Thurman published her wonderful biography, the basis of the Sydney Pollak film which featured Meryl Streep's extraordinary performance as Karen and Robert Redford's strong but banal enactment of Denys. The lovely old books now in the bookshelves at Karen's home were left there by the film-makers (or so I was recently told by the devoted curator).

[44]

MERWIN'S MODESTY[1]

The "upland" is the *causse*, the limestone plateau of southwestern France, where the great *Bordeaux* wines are nurtured and merchandised. And "lost"? Not the upland itself, but the life above it, the life of respect for grain and grape, the sensuous, esthetic and moral life which follows from millenial cultivation.

The book's subtitle was *Stories about the Dordogne*. Was it discarded because "stories" suggested more fiction than the author wanted to suggest? Or was it that the three sections of the book are focused less on individual fates than on the transformation, the disappearance, of traditional rural life in the *causse*? Merwin is neither sociologist nor historian, although his observations are often sociological and his learning historical; he is one of the *petits maîtres* of contemporary letters. At its best, his book exhibits an accuracy, concision, humor and beauty of observation and expression which will advance his reputation.

Two of its three sections center about individuals. The first— which appeared in the *New Yorker*—describes Pierre, le Comte d'Allers, known as "Fatty," an impoverished aristocrat, snob and scrounger who cannot bear the vulgarity and ugliness which, stone by stone, chair by chair, replace the elegance and strength of ancient craftsmanship. Pierre travels the countryside, stripping abandoned palaces and churches of their musty beauties which he sells to keep himself in *foie gras* and to provide his mother, Madame la Générale, with an audience for her salacious comic stories. (Her final ones are about the rectal cancer which kills her.) Pierre has run through all the gas stations and grocery stores which have given him credit, and dies when a favorite storekeeper turns on him, taking the filched cans of *foie gras* from his pocket, and forcing him to a rare disgorgement of actual money. He is sur-

---

[1] W. S. Merwin. *The Lost Upland*. Alfred A. Knopf. pp 307. $22.00.

rounded by those of his children who haven't yet escaped, and by the shopkeepers, bankers and inferior noblemen he denounces as *arrivistes* and despoilers. He shuts out modernity— "What is the *Tour de France?*"—and dies as he lives, a "character." (When the windshield wiper of his broken down car is frozen, he climbs on the hood, unzips and services it personally.) He is an icon of the humor and grotesquery of preservation, as well as of its sadness.

His counterpart—in the book's third section—is a truer, finer embodiment of the beauty of old ways. This is the wine merchant and hotel keeper M. Blackbird. (The use of his English name amidst all the French ones is strange; perhaps the author thought "M. Merle" less amusing or reminiscent of Madame Merle in James's *Portrait of a Lady*.) Blackbird is getting on, but doesn't want to leave his marvelous trade and first-rate wine to his milk-drinking son-in-law, or to his daughter, a hater of the old ways. He thinks of the priest whose eczema he has cured in a freezing spring, then of an Irish painter who adores wine, and of several other wise, local sensualists. Finally he resigns himself to leaving it to his nephew, a reasonable man and decent beer merchant.

Like Fatty, Blackbird travels the countryside, but to service, not to strip and con it. Like Fatty's, too, his story is set among many others. Merwin has a gift for brief characterization and paragraph-long stories, though too many are too slight even for so lacy a texture. In both sections, the interest is diverted from the fate of the characters to the panorama, the scenic. Rousseau censures writers who "make up for the sterility of their ideas by multiplying their characters and adventures . . . incessantly introducing amazing events and new faces, which pass like the figures in a magic lantern." A bit too harsh for *The Lost Upland*, but à propos.

The middle section, "Shepherds"—which appeared in the *Paris Review*—contains both the strongest and weakest writing in the book. There are six or seven marvelous pages on the transformation of the old agriculture by modern methods and commerce which are like a miniature Zola novel. (I also thought of Douglas Unger's beautiful novel *Leaving the Land*.) There is as well too much dull, poorly controlled lyric description of flora and fauna. Sentences are overextended, and fine observations cancel each other out:

> After the house roof had been repaired, he got into the habit
> of taking the bread and cheese, and a small pitcher of wine, up
> into the kitchen and putting the bread and cheese on a plate,

on the table, but there, too, he usually ate standing up, looking out through the open door onto the stone terrace, the iron railing, the traceries and translucent pale leaves of the *Chasslas* vine climbing a trellis of chicken wire attached to the eaves.

The translucent leaves and trellised chicken wire wipe out the bread and wine.

Perhaps the mixture of strength and weakness has something to do with the structure of this section. There is an "I" here, the foreign writer who keeps a garden and is accepted by the natives as one of themselves. He's seen very briefly as a boy in Pennsylvania, going to shop with a mother who turns up her nose at the "foreign" vegetables, sausages and cheeses, the very things which fascinate him. At night, he listens to foreign radio stations. This is surely the boy who grows up to be W. S. Merwin (initials courtesy of the great poet of his learning years, T. S. Eliot?), who has lived most of his life abroad, in Spain, France, Portugal and now Maui (no longer officially "abroad"). Merwin has made a living, and has been justly celebrated, as a translator, mostly from the Romance languages. The fine translator's precise diction, scholarly deference and personal reticence emerge in this book as defects. Merwin is reluctanct to use the "I" where it would be natural: "Every day after that, as long as they went on falling, they were picked up from the grass." It is "I," and "I" alone, who picks up the blue plums. The writing is puffed up to cover this unrevealed, overly modest self.

Still, this is an excellent book which springs from the same kind of passionate attachment and humorously observant detachment which created Isak Dinesen's *Out of Africa*. That book, though, has as its center the author, "Karen," revealed as clearly and beautifully as any one or thing in it. Merwin's modesty is personally admirable, but it keeps a fine book from being a much finer one.

[45]

MALRAUX AND DE GAULLE

> Ah, what a dreadful sound they make in the waning light,
> The oaks being felled for Hercules' pyre!
>> Victor Hugo

December 11, 1969, a Thursday. The snow falls on the isolated park behind Charles de Gaulle's house in the low Merovingian hills where–perhaps–Vercingetorix lost the crucial Gallic battle to Julius Caesar. De Gaulle's old minister, companion, and intellectual conscience, André Malraux, drives out from Paris, and the two men spend the day talking. The conversation and the scene were reconstructed by Malraux for their place in the second volume of his *Anti-memoirs*, but, after de Gaulle's death, correcting proof, he saw that they made an independent book. "My reasons for publishing now these fragments...will be clear to anyone who reads them."

Clearer, perhaps, than Malraux thought. *Felled Oaks[1]* (*Les chênes qu'on abat*) is a remarkable, disagreeable, profound, un- and re-settling book. Out of it comes a de Gaulle simple, grand, accurate, modest, assured, puzzled, *human*, and as deeply serene as any well-recorded man of history I know or can recall. Beside him, interrupting, flattering, provoking, interpreting and misinterpreting him, is the self-proclaimed "great artist," who either bravely (or defiantly) allows us to see him as a buzzing intellectual pollen-gatherer or believes that his self-portrait is that of the reflector-creator of his truly loved friend and leader.

"Free man is not envious; he willingly accepts what is great and rejoices it can exist," Malraux quotes from Hegel, and, surely, he believed that he published this fragment to recall France to the greatness de Gaulle wrenched out of *her*.

What is talked about here is mostly remarkable, sometimes repetitive, sometimes the irrepressible intrusion of Malraux's memory-fragments cohering about the insecure ego of a brilliant man

---

[1] *Conservations with De Gaulle.* Translated by Irene Cléphane, revised by Linda Asher. Holt, Rinehart and Winston. 1971.

[313]

who was seldom able to make moving sense or beauty out of them. Finally, there is what will last here, the iron simplicity, wisdom, and decency of a man who before had seemed almost insanely pompous.

The talk is about history, historical action, the ideas and models people draw from clouds, cats, butterflies and great works, about France, despotism, civilization, women, Napoleon, the end of Europe, the use and uselessness of endeavor. De Gaulle's' remarks are in italics, Malraux's talk and speculation in ordinary print. This is graphic propriety. Again and again, de Gaulle brings intelligence out of Malraux clouds:

> MALRAUX: And if our civilization is certainly not the
> first to deny the immortality of the soul, it is the
> first in which the soul has no importance....
> *DE GAULLE: Why do you speak as if you were a believ-*
> *er, since you are not?*
> MALRAUX: Renan was not a fool....
> *DE GAULLE: That depends on the day.*

And:

> MALRAUX: Athens was crushed by Sparta with no great
> effect on its art.... But it would all have ended with
> Alexander anyhow....
> *DE GAULLE: Yes. And at dawn, the wolf ate Monsieur*
> *Séguin's goat, which had fought it off all night.*

The difference between a great artist and a great man of action, even when the medium for both is words, is that the great artist makes what counts for him on his own schedule, while the man of action has to respond immediately to what's given, or, at least, has to create an occasion at the right time. Even if Malraux were a great artist—which he has never been, even in *La condition humaine*[2]—he would probably suffer in an unrevised exchange. (Though Malraux "reconstructed" this "non-interview," I think he was true to de Gaulle, and didn't escape—or felt he needed to alter—his *idea of himself.*)

De Gaulle is aware of the difference between writing and talk: "How odd it is that a man has to drive himself so hard, to tear out of himself what he wants to write! Yet it is almost easy to draw out what one wants to say in speech." Malraux intersperses the

---

[2] 1993. *Antimémoires*, 1967, is, however, a great book. I suppose I meant that Malraux wasn't a great novelist.

December talk with great lines from de Gaulle speech "occasions": "These realists who know nothing of reality... Vichy, which holds France by the wrists while the enemy cuts her throat...Those who claimed to govern our country open their mouths only to order her to roll in the mud."

There is another surprise in *Felled Oaks*. It turns out that de Gaulle is more a man of words than Malraux, Malraux more a poet-in-action than a creator of beautiful works. (I'd guess de Gaulle admired Malraux's famous courage more than his famous intellect.)

Malraux was on the move for fifty years, all over the world, hunting artistic, personal and political excitement, and responding to it with fearlessness, ingenuity, and his sense of heroism. He is the polyperformer for whom vast learning and many books are but the ash of heroic activity. Yet these are what he leaves behind.[3] (The Paris monuments, cleaned when he was de Gaulle's minister of culture, blacken each day.)

De Gaulle too will pass away, at least on the time scale of oaks and butterflies (or even Aeschylus) of which they talk so often. But Malraux, a nonbeliever, hungered for historic permanence. His book on de Gaulle, the finest record available of the great man, was his way of hitching to a more fixed star than any in his life with the exception of Mao Tse-tung (whose portrait is the gem of the *Anti-mémoires*).

What one carries away of de Gaulle is the man who at times thinks of himself as Tintin (the dear innocent of the French comic books), at others as Don Quixote, or the old man in Hemingway's book who drags home a skeleton fish.

De Gaulle, playing with his cat, twitted by his slyly charming wife—another surprise—remembering his beloved, feeble-minded daughter, recalling Stalin's fierce grip on his leg every time a German was killed in the film they watched, speculating on Jackie Kennedy's future ("I thought she'd marry Sartre or you"), this immense old fellow with a Cyrano nose (he liked Cyrano) personally, uniquely, revived the greatness of a country. He elevated the politics of almost every man he met (although Lyndon Johnson "never seemed to take the trouble to think") and left behind in this important if unbeautiful book, a print of himself which offers human beings a new, surprising model of personal grandeur.

---

[3] Malraux said he wanted to be remembered as a writer "and not a writer, *hélas*, but a writer without the *hélas* and without the exclamation point." See *Lazarus* (New York: Holt, Rinehart and Winston, 1977).

[46]

NIXON ON NIXON

> Delightful was a codeword we used to connote trouble. We did not have a codeword for disaster.
>
> from the diary of Tricia Nixon Cox

August 6, 1974. The Presidency is falling around his ears, there are no forces left to rally. Even George Wallace won't help; he doesn't hear too well on the phone, besides he doesn't think it's his place to persuade Representative Flowers to vote against impeachment. The family listens to the "smoking gun" tape, is shaken but rallies round. Julie rushes over to the White House and leaves a passionate note of support on Daddy's pillow: Don't decide for a week, I love you.

Passionate, yes, sincere, yes, but also, dated (August 6), for, after all, even in passionate haste, a Nixon cannot forget that every scrap of paper is historic.

History, in full regalia, bedevils our recent presidents. The shallower the historical imagination, the more historical trinkets are assembled. Johnson had squads of photographers recording every presidential belch. And Nixon, that lover of privacy, installed the recording machines. No reader of the *Memoirs* will imagine this President destroying those tapes.[1] Wipe out the footprints on the sands of time that lives of great men leave behind them? (Grandma Milhous had written the Longfellow lines under Richard's thirteenth birthday present, a picture of Lincoln. It is never too early to instill historic ambition.) Even when some footprints lead to smoking guns, History will exonerate the well-meaning. This book charts the good intentions of its author.

>   if any here,
> By false intelligence, or wrong surmise,
> Hold me a foe;
> If I unwittingly, or in my rage,
> Have aught committed that is hardly borne

---

[1] *The Memoirs of Richard Nixon* (New York: Grosset and Dunlap, 1978).

By any in this presence, I desire
To reconcile me to his friendly peace.

This is not the King Richard for whom our Richard was named—that was Richard Lion-Heart, Richard "Yea and Nay"—but Shakespeare's hypocritical charmer, Richard Crouchback. His lines *do* describe one function of these memoirs; but only one. This book is composed, not merely assembled, and I think the composition is meant to reflect a deeper kind of tragedy than that of *Richard III*.

In the last days, Nixon's son-in-law, Edward Cox, warns him that resignation will not end his troubles, the legal jackals are getting ready to pick his bones.

> I said to him [Cox] that this was just like a Greek tragedy: you could not end it in the middle of the second act, or the crowd would throw chairs at the stage. In other words, the tragedy had to be seen through until the end as fate would have it.

The story has at least the ingredients of tragic narrative: idyllic beginnings among orange blossoms, mountains, ocean, a haunted house ("viewed with awe, approached with caution"); devoted, hard-working, God-worshipping parents (bad-tempered Dad,[2] saintly mom); early hard work, music lessons, dreams of far places (his favorite magazine the *National Geographic*); early encounters with death and separation (mother off to nurse one of the two brothers who died); school triumphs (debating, acting, student politics) and disappointment (losing the class presidency, the dream of going to school in the East frustrated by the medical expenses of the dying brother); doing well at Whittier; becoming a Tolstoyan (intoxicated by his pacifism and spirituality); winning a scholarship to Duke Law School; doing well but failing—again in the East—to get a job in New York or with the FBI; joining the oldest law firm in Whittier; marrying the pretty teacher met at the tryout of the local drama club; then the war, the OPA and —despite Quaker and Tolstoyan pacifism—the Navy; the invitation to run for Congress and the long public career ending in the unique resignation in the face of impeachment. If not exactly a "mirror for magistrates," why isn't the story a historical tragedy?

---

[2] Nixon traces his "aversion to personal confrontations" to that temper.

Two reasons, I think. One is a profound confusion of historical glitter and reality, and the second, which accounts for the first, is the disproportion between experience and character. That first modern confessor, Rousseau, wrote that unless a man had certain key experiences, he would never discover his own nature. There is, I think, a corollary of this which applies not only to Nixon but to many public men whose experience is so various, complex, and intense. It is that the experience exceeds the capacity of the man to absorb it into his nature. Forced to appear as if he understands and cares deeply about everything, the man manufactures an air of concern which floats over a spreading hollowness. The public characters of Johnson and Nixon testify to the strains of the condition. The Nixon Zigzag—in which he must show that his choice has always bypassed the easy, popular options—shows up not only in public decision (approving the Huston anti-terrorist plan) but private ones (the difficult decision to put his mother in a nursing home). We all have difficult decisions, few of us are strong enough to dismiss public opinion (à la Tawney's description of the Puritan "spiritual athlete" dismissing "concern with the social order as the prop of weaklings and the Capua of the soul"), but Nixon not only constantly thinks of the gallery but wants to make it think he is the solitary soul driving on no fuel but his principles and beliefs. This discrepancy partly accounts for the length of his book.

Length, though, contributes something important here. As it wears on, hundred pages after hundred pages, Nixon wearies of fàçade, and the book erodes into a kind of honesty. It's as if the "ordeal" (Nixon's word) of writing the book had peeled off the make-up. Virtue is often just exhausted vice. (A tormentor may surrender to his victim.) The length of this book then serves a historic, if not a literary purpose. Nixon shows more of himself than he probably intended to show. Indeed, this book makes the other presidential memoirs—Van Buren's, Grant's, Truman's, Eisenhower's, and LBJ's are the ones I know—seem prudish, if not devious.

It is in part the pressure of this Age of Openness. So much has already come out that anything less than what Mr. Honest-man (*Ehrlich-man*) called a "modified limited hang-out" would seem like fraud. It is also because Nixon has some skill with words. He does not have a profound intellect or imagination, his observations are usually puerile—unless he is estimating the deceptiveness of enemies (in negotiations or poker)—his style is unenchanting, his humor febrile, but he is a trained debater, a lawyer, a skilled interpreter and planter of verbal signals, and he belongs to a Quaker tradition of self-accountability. So this book brings us diary entries which show him wrestling with himself (not championship matches but matches nonetheless) as well as descriptions of meetings with Mao and Brezhnev which have intrinsic historic interest. There is a fine long account of the negotiations with the North Vietnamese in which Nixon's tenacity and boldness appear to count for more than Kissinger's mastery of detail, persistence, and subtlety. (Nixon's generous treatment of his professorial *Wunderkind* is one of many generous tributes in a book which also features the "other Nixon," vengeful, suspicious, and mean-spirited, never failing to kick his enemy's other cheek).

Indeed the book has a great deal for every Nixonian (haters and sympathizers, students and decoders). Read closely, it reveals much. There are many themes more or less dropped into the pile: the shuttling between East and West; the contempt for the American establishment; the awe of exotic gurus (Adenauer, Rhee, Whittaker Chambers); the desire to love one's enemies (see the references to John Dean). An essay could be written about the role of food: from the Nixon family market and mother's angel-food cake to the final day in the White House when he treats himself at last to an orgy of corned beef and poached eggs (instead of the loathed wheatgerm). Food stands for pleasure self-denied. His first inkling that he might be President came at a Republican dinner when Tom Dewey told him it was in the cards if he didn't get fat. The book's rare lyricism pours over food, over Connally's country sausage and Ike's homemade watermelon preserves—although this has more to do with Ike's grudging acceptance of him than sensual pleasure. That the Pentagon codewords for another secret indulgence, the bombing of Cambodia, were operations Menu, Breakfast, and Lunch, will make the essay black comedy.

There is a secret affair with something more important than food: tourism. Would he ever have eaten Peking Duck with Chou En-lai if it hadn't been for his desire to have the world rapidly delivered in pretty packages? Thank God for the *National Geographic* and for Hollywood's old sound-stage glamorizing of exotic places.

Foreign Policy. Nixon's *spécialité*. To debate—through moderators, no confrontations—to confer at summits, this is the Nixonian passion. And to ground this passion in concepts of world order as spelled out by an exotically accented professor, a philosophic authenticator of cultural depth, this is the life.

Back home though, the slovenly, selfish, disorderly politicians spewed up by those professional distorters, The Media, threaten to pick up the pieces of his triumph. He has to guard his flanks; the key is information, and he uses the same instruments of government his predecessors got away with using to get it.

Fatal convergence of foreign negotiation and domestic fly-swatting: and Nixon's presidency comes apart. The book ends with a "scene" "like a frame of film forever frozen": not the haunted house near Yorba Linda, but that other haunted house, "viewed with awe and approached with caution," before which the crowd stands: the "elegant curve of the South Portico: balcony above balcony" and "someone waving a white handkerchief from the window of the Lincoln Bedroom." A "final salute" and into the helicopter, Pat saying "It's so sad. It's so sad," and it's off for Andrews "where *Air Force One* was waiting for the flight home to California."

Is *The Memoirs of Richard Nixon* a good book?

Does the earth have a good moon?

It's the only one we have. And, as one of Nixon's diary entries puts it, "you can see in the moon whatever you want to see."

[47]

KISSINGER ON KISSINGER[1]

> Señor Mio, it would be a good thing if we were to go a little
> farther, for I am sure we should be able to find someplace
> where we might quench this terrible thirst that is consuming
> us.
>
> Cervantes, Don Quixote

October 8, 1972. A cool October Sunday in a country house which the painter Léger bequeathed to the Communist Party. In a "large quiet room, hung with abstract paintings," Henry Kissinger experiences the greatest moment of his career. The "droning voice" of the "elderly revolutionary" Le Duc Tho delivers the peace terms for which Kissinger has worked so long. That night he walks the Paris streets, surrounded by the history which "inspires but...does not overwhelm." Half a week later, he flies home "in blissful ignorance of the future," that Watergated future which will nullify the meaning of his deepest moment.

Over and over again, this enormous book tolls the catastrophic bell. In Peking, the tottering "colossus," Chairman Mao, tells Nixon no, his writings have not changed the world, only "a few places in Peking." Every public accomplishment is sabotaged by foolishness or chance, by "the limits of human foresight" or by "the wickedness of objects" (which "always" rolls coins under beds and bureaus). The book's last page sees its second-greatest figure, the courageous, absurd, victorious hermit, Richard Nixon, "on a pinnacle, that was soon to turn into a precipice."

After another diplomatic triumph, a lyric Kissinger returns to the Kremlin "while the first rays of sunlight" fall "on its golden domes, ochre walls, and red brick battlement." He is "seized by one of those rare moments of hope that makes the endless struggle with the contingent endurable for statesmen." The gloomy, bold,

---

[1] Henry Kissinger, *The White House Years* (Boston: Little, Brown, 1979).

Byzantine Nixon is the incarnation of that struggle, the icon of a human perversity which despises its own triumph even more than it does those who thwart it.

A book is like a crisis. While chronicling commotion, its author works in an intense, exhilarating, and exhausting solitude to strip the essential from the inessential. When a serious and gifted man like Henry Kissinger labors on a book, it becomes—even more than a crisis he's resolved—the signature which will survive him. Such a book may be intended only as "an historical record" (Kissinger's words), but the manner in which it heaves itself into literary orbit against the mass and gravity of its fact reveals and then recreates its author.

This book is—to use the blurb word which is a favorite of its author—monumental, and like many such solid commemorations, its form is not beautiful. It is repetitive, needlessly detailed, and sometimes clumsily ornamented. More effort has gone into assembling than composing it. Nonetheless, it is much closer to being a great memoir than just the memoir of a great man. Its author has opened himself up. In this Age of Openness, he finds a thousand ways of bursting through reticence and policy.

The book is laced with portraiture, with lyric jets, with thumbnail essays on bureaucracy, national styles, crisis management, the rhythms of diplomacy. And it is lit by that comic spirit which far more than hope converts the Hegelian *endless struggle* into a great life game. (A game that now and then is a death game. See the scene in which Nixon, infuriated by his own—wise—restraint towards North Korea, eases himself by ordering extra bombing raids. On Vietnam!) The comedy of Kissinger is seldom lethal, and it is as indispensable to the health of his book as it was to the author.

There is a great variety of comedy: scenes, such as the one in which Nixon and Brezhnev, lost in the technicalities of weaponry, begin arguing for each other's positions; farcical portraits like those of the charming political cutthroat, Melvin Laird, the brilliant fantasist general, Vernon Walter, and that decent barbarian dullard, H. R. Haldeman, whose cretinous myrmidons of publicity work out the traffic jams in Rome and Belgrade which enable their image-mad President to take advantage of "photo opportunities." Above all, there are the two seriocomic portraits which dominate the unmonumental portions of the book.

Most literary portraits fall into already-created types. So, in *White House Years*, we have another version of Don Quixote and

[322]

Sancho Panza: the foolish, courageous, intuitive, confused, half-mad, self-made presidential knight and the paunchy, shrewd factotum who both sees through and helps create his master's dream. It will be a surprise to many that the Henry Kissinger who lives in this book is not a profound thinker, not the "great man" of history. He is, he knows, too healthy-minded, too worldly to be one of those "obsessive monomaniacs" (to use two of the words which, with *Byzantine, geopolitical, folklore, unsentimental* and, *nuance* compose the book's ground base) who become the world's presidents, premiers, revolutionaries, and colossi. Kissinger understands the great thirst of these men, and, like Sancho, helps his master "in an age of Iron, try to revive what is known as the Golden Age." But though he rages, weeps, and laughs en route, it is the laughter of the thinker which dominates. And it is comedy, not tragedy, of which his literary style is capable.

Has our Sancho written a great book?

No, for it is the world's Cervanteses who do that. He has, however, written a splendid one, formed—and deformed—by manifold obligations, but redeemed by an honesty and intelligence which reveal even more that he may have intended.[2]

---

[2] A somewhat harsher view of the book, its edematous self-justification and "soggy, Proustian tea-bags" is in "Missingeria," *Georgia Review*, Spring 1980. The comedy of the book might have looked more like hangman's humor a few years earlier. (I was writing pieces comparing the Nixon world to the Oprichniki spies and terrorists of Ivan the Terrible.)

[48]

ON THE JOHNSON LIBRARY

> Licht wird alles, was ich fasse,
> Kohle Alles, was ich lasse..,
> Nietzsche, *"Ecce Homo"*

In a dispatch from the Washington Post, Don Oberdorfer reports (December 8, 1968) that Lyndon Johnson's presidency will be the most scrupulously or at least most completely recorded of all presidential administrations. There are enough personal official papers to fill two thousand four-drawer filing cabinets, histories of every federal department and major agency, a collection of photographs of the President at work and play which in the administration's first seven weeks included more than eleven thousand shots (the eight-year total for Eisenhower's administration was ninety-five hundred), and newsreel coverage of the President and his family which resulted in a monthly documentary prepared by a special naval detachment of twenty men. All of this plus the President's "countless memoranda," Mrs. Johnson's diary, and whatever comes afterward will be[1] stored in the Lyndon B. Johnson Presidential Library on the campus of the University of Texas. Oberdorfer quotes an official saying that "nothing like this has ever been done before...the value to history is likely to be priceless."

For years historians have bewailed the dearth of documentation in the time of the telephone and jet plane. Oral history projects compensate for the historical vacuum supposedly left by the resistance of modern political figures to pen and paper. It is surely true that fewer political arrangements are made by letter in our time than was the case in the eighteenth and nineteenth centuries. Nor has there been a President who matches, say, John Quincy Adams for interrogating his conscience and putting the results on paper.[2]

---

[1] 1992: is.

[2] 1992: Although we know that most presidents keep diaries. Since the recent subpoenas of pages from the Reagan and Bush diaries, it may be that even these no longer "protected" pages will cease to be written.

It was the history-soaked Harry Truman who revived the presidential memoir (which had accounted for such first-rate works as the autobiographies of Grant and Van Buren as well as the splendid papers of the early Presidents now being edited in Cambridge and Princeton, Chicago and Virginia). Truman's volumes were followed by Eisenhower's, and surely the history-minded (dominated?) Kennedy would have added his own version to those which he suggested people as varied as Paul Fay and Arthur Schlesinger should write.

When, though, did the gigantesque element creep into the Respect for History? When did presidential action include the simultaneous recording of that action? Those who watched the political conventions in July and August 1968 saw in October that the nominees had allowed the filming of their reactions to nomination. As they experienced victory, so they experienced the recording of their experience. In July we watched Romney congratulate the Republican nominee from the convention floor but refuse to say what the nominee told him; by October we saw the nominee thanking Mr. Romney for his call. In August we saw Mrs. Humphrey smile in her convention box; in October CBS showed Mr. Humphrey kissing the image of his wife on the glass screen.

The Adams family seems to have acted in private as in public. Their dignity was generally of a piece. They would probably not have been ashamed of being observed at almost any time, but it is most unlikely that they would have tolerated it. Their self-confidence was intimately connected with a sense of privacy.

Naturally, one cannot expect the "communications media" to starve for presidential news. Modern Presidents have learned to regard "the media" as important conditions of their administration. Crises rise and—in the case of Khrushchev's key dispatch in October 1963—settle with their aid; elections are won and lost "through" them.

The pressure of events and the hunger of men to know about them quickly is not something new. Wordsworth, a contemporary of John Quincy Adams, discussed it in the preface to his poems of 1800:

> ...a multitude of causes, unknown to former times, are now acting with a combined force to blunt the discriminating powers of the mind...The most effective of these causes are the great national events which are daily taking place, and the increasing accumulation of men in cities, where the

uniformity of their occupations produces a craving for extra-ordinary incident, which the rapid communication of intelligence hourly gratifies.

It is not, therefore, only tribalized electronic society which hungers for that being-in-the-know which "news" gratifies; but the ubiquity of news-recorders creates the special conditions of these times.[3] (Still the news today is what it always was, the wrapping of a package which may not be opened for weeks or years.)

The quantity of "historic" recording permitted by presidents reflects thirst for both glory and justification. The materials constitute an externalized (thus false) conscience. Few public men will let themselves be photographed doing something wrong. A huge mass of material, therefore, declares that there was no opportunity for the President to act badly. It is not only an externalized conscience but evidence of a clear one.

How deformed are decisions conditioned by the presence of History? Are the coat and tie on the neck of the decision as well as on that of the decider?

I suggest that the deeper the historical culture of the man recorded, the less he needs and the more he will reject the presence of the Historical Justifier at his elbow. The mountain of physical evidence to be scaled by future historians may be the sign of the historical flatness of the actor.

The contrast between the petty secretiveness of President Johnson and the mountainous frankness of his record is less paradoxical than may at first appear. Both spring from that mixture of egoism and uncertainty which is common to the powerful weak.

---

[3] When asked by reporters what he was thinking as he ran toward the goal line, the San Francisco receiver Gene Washington said: "I was thinking what I was going to say to you about the way I felt."

[49]

FARMING THE TUNDRA

The rapid, cigar-chewing little radio man Chicagoans call "Studs" has drawn seventy "non-celebrated" fellow citizens into the sort of self-revelation that until very recently could only be heard from the mouths of poets. For most of history, the ordinary man's interior was a tundra of silence. In the eighteenth century autobiographers and novelists began making the maps by which the mute Jean Jacqueses discovered themselves and their voices. First individual discovery, then social revolution.

In our century, popular analysis enables every man to see himself as a complex, fluent character. Who knows if this isn't the noblest expression of modern opulence or the second noblest — for in the past few years, something else has happened: self-awareness has become self-revelation. Sympathetic men with tape recorders have revealed the extraordinary ordinary man as sage and poet. And the poetry and wisdom of the tundra are systematically farmed and then gathered into marvelous collections like *Division Street: America*[1]

Reviewing Oscar Lewis's *La Vida for The Nation* (January 2, 1967), Elmer Bendiner wrote:

> Is it possible to know a person by listening to a tape-recording of his autobiography...? I doubt it. The art of knowing a person demands an ability to pierce the self-pretense which uses language to disguise rather than to reveal... Those with a taste for people and for life may wish that a novelist—without a tape recorder—would take up where Oscar Lewis left off.

This is intelligent stuff, but it seems to me off the mark. My view is that we do "know" the people in Terkel's, Dolci's, and Lewis' books as we do those in novels, in histories, or in our lives, through appropriate and differing conventions of knowledge. The conventions of tape-recorded autobiography include such props to the guided monologues as "self-pretense" and "disguises," as well as

---

[1] Studs Terkel, ed., *Division Street*: America (New York: Pantheon), 1967.

the monologist's sense of his own typicality and how far the occasion and the interviewer allow him to depart from it. So in *Division Street* none of Studs's people, no matter how violent or asocial, comes within miles of saying what Joyce has the mild Bloom say to himself, let alone what Dostoevsky has a Verhovensky say to a Stavrogin. None of the remarkable Chicagoans approaches the enchanted complex of even a good minor character in a good novel. A meal in Lapérouse is one thing, a roadside apple is another; both delight, and "those with a taste for people and for life" will find immense pleasure in *Division Street* and in much of Lewis.

Is *Division Street* more than a pile of good human apples? Is it, in other words, a real book? Once again, this is too large-holed a net for the fish. A book like this has little to do with build-up, careful collision, *scénes-à-faire*, brilliant climaxes, a coherence whose every line reveals a single mind. It is, though, a carefully arranged collection of selected and well-edited materials. The old, the middle-aged, the young, rich, poor, black, Mexican, Wasp, the broken and those who break them, city strays, John Birch cabbies, brilliant black businessmen, gentle Irish police and their brute colleagues, teachers who save and teachers who ruin, all pour out their witness to the workings of the city, the death of neighborhoods, the threat and promise of machinery, the war, the mayor, God, buying and selling, delivering, conning, dropping out, rescuing. Without forcing opinion into coherence, Studs exhibits a great spectrum of distinctions. If no Chaucer, he is at least the good host Harry Bailey.

The book is not dominated by its topics or its facts. It's a treasury, not a ledger. The treasury is of articulate energy engaged with concrete experience. No matter where Studs's people stand on the scale of usefulness, narcissism, triumph, defeat or despair, if they have expressive power, they triumph here. The heroes are those who construct their lives or opinions with power.[2] A miserable, self-serving lout outlasts a useful, self-denying bore. It is the masters of the concrete who survive in what the Indian, Benny Bearskin, calls here "the abstraction of the city."

Studs, a good man, is on the side of those who love outside their own skin, but he is an honorable host and lets his guests have equal say. "Each of the subjects," he writes

---

[2] The book is dedicated to three Chicagoans who made beautiful, useful constructions out of contemporary, local materials: Ring Lardner, Louis Sullivan, and Jane Addams.

[328]

is, I feel, uniquely himself. Whether he is an archetypal American figure, reflecting thought and condition over and beyond himself, is for the reader to judge, calling upon his own experience, observations, and an occasional look in the mirror.

(Wrote Saint Augustine about only one archetype: "Do I then measure, O my God, and know not what I measure?")

Here are some of Stud's "subjects":

Kid Pharaoh, 37, who's found in front of the hot-dog stand he owns:

> A guy goes to school, what does he want to be? A doctor? A lawyer? These are the biggest thieves in our society. One steals legitimate, the other kills legitimate... Guys like me they want to put in jail. Because I'm dedicated to one principle: taking money away from unqualified dilettantes who earn it through nepotism. I work at this and I'm good at my trade. I don't labor. Outside of being a prize-fighter, I took an oath to God I would never again labor. But there's a million people on the street that want to be taken and should be taken, and they're gonna be taken.

Sister Evelyn, 26, a Glenmary nun who works with Appalachians on the near North Side:

> We are not married. Is this simply an attempt to avoid the pain and ambiguity of a sustained human relationship? If so, this is a travesty of what it means to be a Christian. a Christian must be involved in sustained human relationships, because there is where Christ is found.

Lucy Jefferson, 52, who isn't going to raise her children "on aid" because she "just don't like doles":

> They call you by the first name, the students, everybody. You see, this was the policy to keep the Negro in his place. But I happened to be the kind of Negro that became controversial, because I read such things as The American Dilemma and walk around with the book in my hand, see? I defied them in so many ways. I almost terrified 'em... Let's face it. What counts is knowledge. And feeling. You see, there's such a thing as a feeling tone. One is friendly and one is hostile. And if you don't have this, baby, you've had it. You're dead.

[329]

Phil Eagle, 55, who built up a large business with his wife, then after eighteen good years got sick and was told by her to get out and sell newspapers:

> When she suggested I be eliminated, it gave me incentive. The medical profession credits my hundred percent recovery to my will power. I latched onto an idea. The idea is contained in the book, *Folk Medicine*. The book is almost a hundred percent concerned with apple cider and vinegar and honey and water and eating fish. And using Lugol. L-U-G-O-L. A solution which can be bought for pennies, enough to last for a year... Which everybody should have a drop or two drops a week. Following this book and changing my diet, eliminating sugar from my life and pop and orange juice, I recovered my health. That's one of the things that helped break up my home... The only thing between her and all this wealth is my heartbeat.

Charles Landesfahr, 34, a copy chief:

> It takes a great deal of con to sound honest in this world.

An American Nazi in jail for defaming a Negro celebrity:

> To me, one of the most beautiful things in the world is an Oriental rug or a flower. They're the epitome of whatever they are, the peak. I don't mean something should be perfect. I wouldn't want anything to be perfect. I like that one little flaw... It's the opposite of the order I was looking for. It's the human touch.

Again and again, the life heart is shown by such indirection; again and again, one's expectations are cracked by such unexpected feeling and intelligence.

The Cubists found new eyes in African sculpture and children's art; two French physicists, Abele and Malvaux, constructed the theorem of summary velocity out of Piaget's insights into children's notions of duration and speed.[3] So, I think, new forms of history and fiction will spring from such collection of "naive" narrative as

---

[3] *Vitesse et Univers relativiste* (Paris: Edition Sedes, cited in Jean Piaget, *Six Etudes de Psychologie* (Geneva: Editions Gonthier, 1964), pp. 97-100.

Terkel's.[4] Their variety and energy derive from a confidence which before was seldom shown or, if shown, shown only in trial reports, *penitentes* or rogues' confessions. The new democracy of art, in which camera owners think that they are doing Leonardo's work, hi-fi possessors that they are fusions of Beethoven and Edison, "candid camera" characters that they are brilliant performers, the subjects of interviewers that they are dispensers of wisdom (and this while they step from the shattered store window, television sets in arm), this is the source of that confidence which is pouring as much new material into the hopper of modern narrative art as urban realism poured into that of the nineteenth century.

---

[4] 1993. This has happened. I've just read Richard Price's terrific novel *Clockers*. I have no idea if Price has read Studs' books, but he has read hundreds of reporters, essayists and novelists whose prose has been affected by them and/or their ancestors, peers or descendants.

[331]

[50]

THAT DEVILISH, THINNING ART

The fourth volume of Leon Edel's biography[1] of Henry James ended with James's new face. For the new century, he had shaved off his beard. Fifty-seven, he felt forty. He'd worked through his failure in the theater, written a series of novels about abused children which—Edel's view—released him from the soft shackles of the James family and from an old fear of erotic love, and he had come as close to it as he ever would. Now, in the fifth volume, the massive little man, ensconced with five servants and a secretary-typist in his Rye home, respectful colleagues (Conrad, Wells, Crane, Hueffer/Ford) within easy—sometimes too easy—reach, keeps fit with bicycle rides and prepares to write the three dense novels of the discovery, renunciation, and acceptance of love. In 1904, after twenty-one years away, he returns to America, lectures on "the lesson of Balzac" to amazed audiences from Philadelphia to Los Angeles, and writes his brilliant analytic evocation of *The American Scene*; he works out his literary monument, the Balzacian New York edition, suffers its financial failure, and then, just after becoming an English citizen, dies in the middle of that "horrible, unspeakable, iniquitous" war which undid the society he had rendered and subtilized. On his death bed, mind peeling, James dedicated two coherent letters about the splendor of his plans, one of which he'd signed "Napoleone," the other with his own name. In Edel's view, he had long shared the Corsican's glory-hunger. (Oddly enough, the physical resemblance—at least in the death masks—is remarkable.)

For the twenty-one years he devoted to this biography, Edel worked against James's detestation of the "devilish" and "thinning" art of biography which "simplifies even while seeking to enrich."

---

[1] Leon Edel, *Henry James: The Master (1901-1916)* (New York: Lippincott, 1972). All five volumes have been condensed and touched up for the edition which Edel wants preserved. A sprightly, large-minded gentleman, Edel acknowledged (at least in person) his gratitude to such severe criticism as this. I have not checked the new edition for alterations.

Hoping to control his biographic future, James burned a mountain of papers. What counted for the higher consciousness did not exist as a man, only as "the monster and magician of a thousand masks...so generalized, so consummate and typical, so frankly amused with himself, that is with his art, with his power, with his theme, that it is as if he came to meet us more than his usual halfway." Such an illusion-dispensing monster cannot fool a biographer. An Edel will dig up another monster, the James whose flirtatiousness may have led Constance Fenimore Woolson to kill herself; who, annoyed at a rutting cat, killed it with a stick; who fell in love with Hugh Walpole, and who (according to Maugham in volume 4 and Spender in volume 5) turned down his gallant offer with "I can't. I can't."[2]

The romantic artist has been famously hungry for attention and famously jealous of his privacy. The romantic biographer is professionally inured to his subject's desires and equipped with the documents to foil them. I heard Edel recall a dream in which James reproached him for claiming that he—James—owned a certain piece of furniture. "You're wrong," refuted the dreaming biographer, triumphantly producing the receipt.

Edel needs more than receipts. James's warning about the biographic menace to an artist's work forces his biographer to include a self-defense. "James was prepared to accept the art of biography if it became a 'quest of imaginative experience.'" An artist's "imaginative experience" exists in his work. The biographer's quest means the definition of characteristics, figures in his subject's carpet. The danger is that he shreds the carpet to the figure. What James attempted in his own biographies was an artistic re-creation: a portrait. Well aware of that, Edel invites critics (in the preface to this last volume) to consider *his* artistry: it is only "proper for artists to write about artists."

A perilous invitation. But serious, and worth a look.

Here is the artist Edel introducing a chapter on James's most famous typist: "When Theodora Bosanquet went that summer's day in 1907 to Miss Petherbridge's secretarial office, an employment agency, she had no notion that this would be one of the most eventful days of her life. She felt somewhat slack and headachey. She was disinclined to brave the noise of the tube, and took a bus to Conduit Street."

---

[2] 1993. I understand that in Fred Kaplan's new study of James, this anecdote is consigned to the myth-bin.

This is not quite "The summer evening had begun to fold the world in its mysterious embrace," but close enough to make one sniff unintended burlesque. (If "that summer's day," "disinclined," and "headachey" are Miss Bosanquet's words, let's have the quotation marks.) Miss Bosanquet's "diary of that August gives us a distinct picture": James's "grimy gardener" takes her luggage, she settles in, takes dictation, keeps her journal, and becomes "increasingly worshipful of the Master, yet it was not blind worship. She retained a strong sense of her own identity." Edel summarizes the identity: "She was a true hand-maiden of the Master."

When James urges his brother to let his son stay in Paris, Edel's contribution is, "Henry James was thinking of his own art-starved condition in Cambridge forty years earlier."

In a long work, so much of which must be tied to documentation, insipidity of this sort may signal the biographer's relief at a moment of freedom. Unfortunately, there's too much of it in these volumes.

Then there is the coy allusiveness (Edith Wharton discovering "new realities within the house of mirth") and poesy ("the latter in a letter"; "The pompously-embanked river") of Edel's prose.

Yet, yet. Not a work of high art, but, somehow, a moving biography. The long volumes give a sense of James's days and evenings, of the years as James slows down, shuffles off his social armour, deepens, strengthens. Like many remarkable men, James evoked responsive intelligence from those who talked to or about him. Conrad, Wells, Shaw and Edith Wharton spar with or describe him brilliantly. Edel, too, occasionally rises to a spare analysis of a situation or novel.

The initial question in his biography was, "Did nothing happen to Henry James except the writing of an extremely long shelf of books?" In my view, James lived a good deal more intensely than most of us burgher adventurers; that is, if living be depth of feeling, comprehension, sympathy, and range of expression. James was a wonderful friend who elicited strength, vivacity, hope and a sense of beauty from nearly all who knew him. At an age when most turn into self-indulgent curmudgeons, he learned, worked, and felt at the top of his powers.

No Boswell, Edel discovered and assembled most of James's remains. In a way, he is James's ideal biographer: his assiduity is reined by an honest banality which preserves what James wanted to preserve, the irreducibility of his work.

[51]

ORTEGA Y GASSET

On the dust jacket of Rockwell Gray's book[1] on Ortega is a wonderful photograph taken in 1949 by his daughter Soledad. It shows a dapper sexagenarian in a beautiful fedora. He's holding a cigarette holder next to his laughing mouth; his other hand crosses his body with the amiability of someone embracing a friend. The eyes are alert to sight or speaker, smiling and brilliant with intelligence. This is a man of the world and of himself.

Photographs may be posed by clever models and photographers; prose is more difficult to counterfeit.

Among the thousand objects of Ortega's intelligence was Spanish prose.

> The predominant manner of speaking in our books has customarily been of an aberrant complication: a paragraph was more difficult to build than a triumphal arch and, like the latter, was born of purely ornamental inspiration. . . . Like bishops' robes woven with metallic threads, literary forms cloaked the miserable little body of a timid and puerile psychology...In all the other ethnic functions we have also suffered from this characteristic ornamental infirmity...When strangers speak of us they always mention the "grandeur" of the Spaniard. But it turns out that...is not the grandeur of the Spaniard, his magnanimity, splendor, or nobility, but rather the grandeur of the Spanish gesture.[2]

For one hundred and fifty years, "Spain as a problem" has been at the center of Spanish mental life. Ortega was the heir of such intel-

---

[1] *The Imperative of Modernity. An Intellectual Biography of José Ortega y Gasset.* Rockwell Gray. Berkeley: University of California Press. 1989 xiii plus 424 pp.

[2] Ortega, *Obras* 9: 480-481.

lectual reconstructors of "this spiritual promontory of Europe"[3] as Sanz del Rio and the Spanish Montessori, Francisco Giner. Ortega brought in the new strengths of modern Europe, particularly those of the France of Renan and the Germany of the Marburg philosophers, Herman Cohen and Edmund Husserl.

> At twenty I was totally immersed in the liquid element of French culture, and I went down so deep that I felt my feet touch bottom. I also felt that for the time being Spain could no longer derive nourishment from France. This made me turn to Germany, about which there was only the slightest knowledge in my country. The older generation had spent its life talking about "German mistiness." What was pure mist was their information about Germany.[4]

> In spite of appearance, the Germans have a virtue we lack: respect and love for the past. They have conservative, philological souls, and precisely from their philology and their grounding in what has gone before they derive the strength for daring in scientific or artistic thought.[5]

This ethnic and nationalistic way of thinking and writing went up in smoke in 20th century ovens[6] and only its ashes can be found in the Spain of today, a Spain run by the thirty- and forty-year-old grandchildren of Ortega. Unlike his sometime colleague, Heidegger, Ortega was never stained by collaboration with the dark regimes of the Thirties.

What also makes Ortega a less occult modernist is a lifelong commitment to the "mass" whose menace he chronicled in *La rebelión de las masas*. A "cocky little fellow from Madrid who has been through Kant," Ortega saw his job as the formation of an audience for advanced thought. He wrote for newspapers, *El Imparcial* (founded by his father, Ortega Munilla) and *El Sol* (the

---

[3] Ortega, *Meditacion del Quijote*. cited Gray, 93.

[4] From the 1934 prologue to Ortega's *El tema de nuestro tiempo*. Gray, 76.

[5] *Obras* 1: 425. Gray. *ibid.*

[6] Although Primo Levi writes—in the last of his great books, *I Sommersi e i salvati* (Einaudi: Torino, 1986)—"I don't think I would deny that there exists a spirit of each people (otherwise it would not be a people) a *Deutschtum*, an *italianitá*, an *hispanidad*: They are the sums of traditions, customs, history, language, and culture." (P. 183 of Raymond Rosenthal's beautiful translation, *The Drowned and the Saved*. Vintage International: New York. 1989).

liberal daily he helped found); he developed the publishing house Calpe (later Espassa-Calpe) which published pocketbook editions of fine literature; he founded and directed the monthly, *Revista de Occidente*; he lectured all over both as a university professor and as Spain's most distinguished man of letters. He was a combination of T.S. Eliot, H.L. Mencken and Bertrand Russell, or someone like his idol Renan.

A year after collaborating with Heidegger in a Darmstadt colloquium on technology and architecture, he wrote about the differences between their work:

> Heidegger is profound, whether he speaks on *bauen* or anything else...I need to add that not only is he profound but that, furthermore, he wishes to be so, and this no longer seems to me so good. Heidegger...suffers from the mania of profundity. Because philosophy is not only a voyage to the profound. It is a return trip and is, thus, bringing the profound to the surface and making it clear, patent common knowledge.[7]

This Spanish-caped version of the Socratic mission was Ortega's.

---

[7] Obras 9.

[52]

KAFKA'S LIFE[1]

A lawyer who worked for The Workers' Accident Insurance Institute of Bohemia, one of two Jews in the company, he was admired by fellow employees, management and even the injured workers whose claims he reviewed. (When he felt they received too little, he gave them money of his own.) He enjoyed country walks, swimming (nude, if no one was around), rowing on the river, beer, billiards, tennis, gardening, the theater. He read in several languages and wrote wonderful letters, particularly to women whom he loved and who loved him. Most of his life he lived at home with his parents (who survived him), or later with or near one of his three sisters. Only in his last two years, ill with tuberculosis, did he live with a woman he loved.

He also wrote: stories, sketches, fables, meditations, novels—none finished—but in his lifetime he published only one book. It was enough to convince such writers as Mann and Hesse that he was a remarkable writer.

He died in June, 1924, a month before his forty-first birthday, after what seems—on the surface I've described—a successful, happy life.

In a way, of course, it was. Yet Kafka is the subject of this enormous biography (and many others) not because of success, but because he is the century's exemplary poet of failure. His name stands for the monstrosity and mystery of worldly and otherworldly injustice, frustration, anxiety and defeat.

What lay beneath the pleasant surface?

Drawing on thousands of letters, his diary, and the memoirs of those who admired, loved and even adored him, biographers like Karl have supplied the facts.

First, foremost, there was his father, Hermann. Burly, raucous, crude and aggressive, where his son was passive, dreamy, weak (six unmuscular feet, he weighed 130 pounds), Hermann rebuked

---

[1] Frederick Karl. *Franz Kafka. Representative Man.* Ticknor & Fields 1991. 810 pp. xix. $40.00.

the "parasitical" son with accounts of his own rise from a one room country shack to Prague success, owner of a fine-goods store (parasols, canes, clothing). Second was Julie, Kafka's mother, by whom he felt abandoned to cooks and maids as she worked in the store and otherwise served her husband. Said Franz, her oldest child, she was a "beater" for his hunting father. Kafka couldn't endure his parents' life, their evening card-playing and conspicuous domesticity. He hated their noises, especially the erotic noise from their bedroom next to his. Noise in general was a torment to him; and every rustle was a noise. Only late at night, his parents and Prague asleep, could he sit by the window dreaming and writing. Yet he stayed at home until he was thirty-one.

Kafka also hated his work, yet he stayed in the same office for fourteen years, receiving increases, promotions, praise.

Food, and its digestion, disgusted him. A vegetarian, he disgusted others by "fletcherizing," chewing each bite till it almost liquified. (His father hid behind his newspaper to avoid this charming sight.) Attracted to many women, he thought the sex act filthy and "made love" only with prostitutes and, perhaps, with two or three other women met briefly on vacations.

He was estranged from his own language: German was Goethe's language, not his. The word *Mutter*—he said—could not mean "Mother" to him.

The assimilated, German-speaking Jews who surrounded him in Prague seemed rootless to him; he loved the Yiddish theater of the unassimilated Eastern Jews, one of whom, Dora Dymant, became his final companion.

Kafka's women are now as well-known as Goethe's, Zeus's or the Beatles'. First, there was his merry, saintly sister Ottilie ("Ottala") who, like his two other sisters, and many of his friends, died in a concentration camp. Then there's his longtime fiancée Felicia Bauer, to whom he sometimes wrote three times a day, often trying to show her how poor a husband he'd be. There was Felicia's friend, Grete Bloch, who made the unlikely claim that she'd borne Kafka's son. There was his most intelligent and sympathetic correspondent, Milena Jesenká, a young Czech aristocrat who defied a brutal father by marrying a Jewish philanderer named Ernst Polak; she translated Kafka's stories.

Within the net of such connections, obligations, affections and torments, Kafka wrote his farcical, tragic fables of entrapment, self-indictment and guilt. (When he read them to his friends, they burst into laughter with him.) Miserable when he couldn't write,

[339]

usually miserable after he'd written, this tormented perfectionist transformed disgust and torment into supple, spare, beautiful German prose.

Karl's biography supplies all this—and much more. It interprets his work, often in fascinating ways; it places him too in the center of "modernism," the elliptic narcissism of twentieth century creativity.

It is a useful, interesting book, although a third longer than it should be. A specialist in modernism, Karl dumps its familiar debris on his subject's head. After twenty comparisons with composers, painters, architects, philosophers and writers, one comes with joyful relief to Kafka facts and Kafka sentences. Yet Karl gets understandably impatient with his subject's articulate, prolix misery; when this happens, his book slows and dulls.

In the end, though, Karl seems to think about Kafka as Max Brod did about his beloved friend:

> The category of sacredness (and not really that of literature) is the only right category under which Kafka's life and work can be viewed. . . . If angels make jokes in heaven, it would have to be in Kafka's language.

[340]

[53]

FAULKNER IN GENOA

In the fall of 1962 I was Fulbright professor at the University of Venice (then called Istituto Universitario di Venezia because the University of Padua wanted no full-fledged university competing with it, and the Minister of Education was a Paduan). A splendid life for me. We lived in a little palazzo called the Gioconda next to a Palladio church, the Zitelle, on the Giudecca, an island across from the main Venetian island. The place included a uniformed butler, a pleasant young red-haired fellow who did the cleaning, assembled the tubing (which failed to dent the chill in this coldest of Venetian winters) and spent much of the day with a telescope watching his boyfriend, a cameriere *in a palazzo across the canal. My wife cooked lunch for Ennio except when he wished to show us how to prepare one of his special pasta dishes. After all, he was a* cameriere, *not a cook. He did "serve us" in the little be-muralled slot of dining room.*

"Us" was my middle son, Andy, home from kindergarten in his white smock (grembiule), *my wife, and I. The baby, Nick, was fed by signora Lydia, who wheeled him up and down the* fondamenta *and took him with her when she played* tombola *with her neighbor, signora Olga. The two older children (Kate, eleven, and Chris, twelve) were in the Salesian Sisters' School. Every morning they went across the canal in their black smocks and returned at four. Kate was quite happy, got religion, and loved her Sister, suora Emmanuele. (Ten years later, she walked into Sister Emmanuele's class, which rose in unison to call "Ahh, Kati.") Chris dropped out after Sister Emmanuele explained that Lincoln was axed to death by a southern planter. When the facts were delivered by her two American students, she said that after all, the idea was the same. The older wisdom.*

One of the duties of a Fulbright visitor was lecturing in other Italian towns. I was invited to lecture at the American Cultural Center in Genoa. Faulkner had died in July. I'd reread him for the first time since college and talked about him. Spiced with Italian

[341]

reference (see below), the talk was considered a success, and the professor of English at the University of Genoa, who'd refused to invite previous Fulbright lecturers, asked the Fulbright Office to have me speak to his students. He wanted a survey of American literature since 1945. Clearly a talk one couldn't prepare. Anyway, I'd understood it was to be a seminar for a few graduate students. We could just "fire on the breeze" as one of my Venetian students put it. In Genoa, there were posters with my name and the subject plastered on public announcement boards. I was driven to an enormous lecture room and found six hundred faces waiting to be stuffed. I'd been a professional teacher for thirteen years, but was no good at public speeches. Not, at any rate, impromptu ones. Terror leans on syntax. Sentences mazier than Henry James's clunked out in the great aula. The audience, once so bright and open, closed, clouded. (The professor was delighted: another American failure.)

The talk was given November 22, 1962, one year to the day before President Kennedy's assassination. I couple the events because I think Kennedy belongs more to the group of great charmers who died during his administration, Hemingway, Faulkner, Marilyn Monroe, than to the victims of 1968. All these deaths made for a kind of dusk of individuality.

It's no accident that Hemingway's name appears—misspelled— in the diaries of the assassins Lee Harvey Oswald and Arthur Bremer, the dark side of the Inidviduality moon. The enchanting loner, the heroic skeptic, who made his own system of restraints, imposed itself on almost every schoolboy of the Forties and Fifties: to have experience and to record it finely, to contrive a natural, yet exciting, public personality, this meant almost everything.

Faulkner's impassioned public shyness became a glamorous public fact. When the Kennedys invited him to the White House, everyone in the country knew that he said it was pretty far to travel for a hamburger.

The next phalanx of literary celebrities look like old carbons: Salinger, the Hermit-Saint, and Mailer, the Performer. Deeply serious and gifted, in "the dark glass of the media," they look like neurotic caricatures of Faulkner and Hemingway.

Faulkner is a name known to all literate people in Italy. Indeed, Faulkner was written about here almost as early as he was written about in his own country: Cesare Pavese's famous review of *Sanctuary* was published in *La Cultura* in April 1934. Although

Pavese's opinion of Faulkner altered for the better, one can still read this early account of Faulkner's relationship to Sherwood Anderson and be pleased by how much Pavese noticed, even if one feels—as he later must have—that he did not notice enough.

When Faulkner died, Italian newspapers and magazines recorded the death with as much solemnity as anyone. (I discount the necessitous rapacity of these hounds of print for stories.) In *L'Espresso*, Paolo Milano recalled that Faulkner sported a Van Dyke beard and dressed like a dandy in the Hollywood of the thirties, detaching himself from the depression garb of most writers, the worker's tieless shirt and dark suit. That Faulkner should have been as conscious about clothes as, say, Baudelaire, may surprise Americans more than Italians. Many American students who know Faulkner through his work and through the literary underworld which brought accounts of his "cracker" habit of carrying a gallon jug of corn whiskey suspended by an index finger over his shoulder, his Garbo-shyness of interviewers, literary people, and the press, must have thought him a neanderthal man, a literary accident, better reflected in the monstrosity of his unclassical English than in the emotional brilliance which that monstrosity expressed. Indeed, Pavese was of this school: *"Un angelo senza cura d'anime,"* he called Faulkner in 1934; and also: a man with magic narrative gifts but wild and morally neutral, a writer who registered actions without caring about them.

Now, of course, almost all critics, Italian, English, Japanese, know that Faulkner was a most conscious artist, a man who, if fired by immense passions, nonetheless developed literary equipment to deal with them, who was much more conscious and self-conscious than those of us who criticize him because so much of consciousness had to be—and was—reduced to narrative expression. The great passion which Faulkner's work suggests is not the passion which the inorganic tumult of a volcano might represent, but the passion which long concentration on loved and hated objects will yield. I suppose the best natural symbol for such passion is the incessant power of the sea. Such passion was sensed by Pavese long ago and described in such phrases as *"la lenta realtà "* and *"il tono transognato"'* and it was that despite what Pavese called *"i piatti e faticosi monologhi interiori"* of *As I Lay Dying.* This passion was capable of making *"scoppiare una voce, un dialogo in un alto silenzio, in una tensione quasi di prodigio."*

Faulkner's passion is one which slows up reality, though the slowness is not that of ennui, but of tension, of continuous and

[343]

growing clarification as more and more is brought to bear on, say, a simple encounter, the past of a character rising around him mixed with his sense of the objects which now surround him. I remember being amazed at the tension of the early scene in *Light in August* in which one wonders simply whether Mrs. Armstid, that "gray woman, not plump and not thin, manhard, workhard, in a serviceable gray garment worn savage and brusque, her hands on her hips her face like those of generals who have been defeated in battle" will consent to give the pregnant Lena breakfast. It takes almost as much time in the reading as it would in life, and in one sense you might say that it is not part of the *real story* of the novel. Yet just as the word *brusque* was never before used to describe the way a garment is worn and is still revealing, compelling, *right*, even as it outrages—or at least twits—one's sense of classical English rightness, so the long moment in which Mrs. Armstid decides to cook for Lena is right for the *real story*, that of acceptance and birth.

"*Lenta realtà.*" So much of our own life is passed in a fuzzy, undefined feeling-state that an encounter with the form of that fuzziness—the rise and fall of our feelings as they relate to the rest of our life and the lives of others, the collective lives of families and societies—is shocking, thrilling, beautiful. A month ago, in the Scrovegni Chapel in Padua, I was struck by the length, the space, the "*lenta realtà*" of the woman who is spinning while Saint Anne is on her knees receiving from the angel the news that she is to be Mary's mother. That right arm, stretched out along the invisible yarn the spool of which dangles from the hand, took as much time to paint as anything in the picture, especially as it is pictorially broken by a porch pillar. Is it part of the *real story* of the annunciation to Saint Anne? Of course. The "story" is that of the presence of the marvelous in the familiar, and the great, permanent gesture of weaving—itself a form of creation—is the human sign of participation in the miraculous.

Here in Italy, even in this most active Italian city, where every day that powerful "symbol" of continuity and passion brings novelty to your door, and whence, every day, you dispatch upon it what will bring renovation and discovery to others, even here, you are surrounded, as we in America are not so conspicuously surrounded, by the artifacts of patience and of genius, most of them assembled in times during which what Wordsworth called "the rapid communication of intelligence" did not break hourly upon artisans and artists, despoiling them of the concentration that works of considered passion demand.

[344]

Like Giotto, shut up for months in the small chapel which was his alone to fill, Faulkner, as much as he could, stayed away from the buzz of production and publicity which make a Calvary for a serious artist. He stayed close to home. Home was, of course, a place designed for the retreat which a man needs, especially after he has had—as Faulkner had—a period of time between his mastery of the familiar and his return to isolate himself from the unfamiliar. Faulkner in the South, in Oxford, Mississippi, was not so unlike Joyce in Trieste, Zurich, and Paris, shut up in a study, remembering and finding words for what was remembered, getting refreshed now and then by visitors from Dublin or letters from his aunts and friends; not so different from Giotto, in Padua, far from Tuscany, remembering perhaps a cousin's face as she spun yarn; or Dante in Padua or Verona or Ravenna, as, say, he remembered the "Bicci, *vocato* Forese" with whom he had exchanged joking *tenzone*, putting him into Purgatorio when he needed someone there for gluttony (perhaps in a vein of jovial nostalgia). Faulkner, exiled by the need for solitude, fuels his conception from the memory of the place which was not, as much as it was, the same place in which he wrote.

There are twenty-five books on Faulkner's roll, and perhaps half of them are great additions to all literate lives: *The Sound and the Fury, As I Lay Dying, The Hamlet, Light in August, The Town, Go Down Moses, Collected Stories, Sanctuary, The Wild Palms*, a few more. All these books have strong, almost classical narratives, though all—more or less like every work of the new fiction which Henry James and Conrad and Ford Madox Ford developed in the nineties and the early part of the twentieth century, and which Joyce and Proust brought to its greatest height in the teens and twenties of the century—have broken the conventional time scheme of narrative and fitted the temporal pieces together in accord with a more realistic style of recollection, a recollection shaped by passion under the pressure of narrative. Not content with this apparent destruction of the "natural happenings," Faulkner, like the other artists, particularly Proust and Joyce, rearranged his narrative in other "unnatural" ways: a story is told though four different minds, each allowed a series of interrupted sessions; or through a mind which is suddenly and frequently taken over, as it were, by another mind. So the natural world of fuzz-flow is carefully, consciously shaped, misshaped for the purpose of alienating, and then clarifying, outraging, and then thrilling familiar perception.

[345]

From the beginning of a Faulkner novel we are in the midst of a situation, and it may be pages before we can find out where. Sometimes the confusion is increased by the disorderliness of the report; it may take quite a time before we acknowledge the truth of a title and decide that the opening monologue of *The Sound and the Fury* is being "told by an idiot," though it does not signify "nothing." Listen to the opening paragraph of this great book

> Through the fence, between the curling flower spaces, I could see them hitting. They were coming toward where the flag was and I went along the fence. Luster was hunting in the grass by the flower tree. They took the flag out, and they were hitting. Then they put the flag back and they went to the table, and he hit and the other hit. Then they went on, and I went along the fence. Luster came away from the flower tree and we went along the fence and they stopped and we stopped and I looked through the fence while Luster was hunting in the grass. "Here, caddie." He hit.

It will be some time before we know that it is Benjy, a thirty-three-year old castrated idiot confusing the talk of the golfers asking the caddie for golf clubs and his own beloved sister Caddie. One asks why Faulkner needs to confuse the"real story" with such a narrator, and the answer is of course that the real story depends on Benjy's purity: the idiot is incapable of reporting things incorrectly even if he does not know that the flag is the marker of a golf hole and that the men on the course are not talking about his sister. In this whirligig of impression, we need a stable set of judgments. If these judgements are an idiot's, this is not without significance.

Faulkner's great stories transmit the delight of new ways of thinking and feeling associated with a special place and filled with special, now familiar, characters: wild, thick-necked farmers, maddened by poverty; shrewd, omnipresent, almost omniscient sewing-machine salesmen; displaced romantics as sensitive as air, incapable of ordering their feelings about people or places; inexorable half-acre tycoons moving to the ownership of towns; demented cow-lovers; earth mothers, so lushly sexual that the most fanatical career can be disarranged by them; acid-hearted haters, maniacal and fatal; great women, enduring every hurt and injustice, triumphant no matter what their end. These and many more, all given names, homes, clothes, given stories, all as immediately identifiable as Hamlet or Francesca of Rimini, Madame Verdurin, Bloom, il Gattopardo or any of the thousand men and women whom we

[346]

know better than we know ourselves or our fathers: Ratliff, Jason Compson, Flem Snopes, Eula Varner, Henry Armstid, Dilsey.

I must not let a foreign audience forget that Faulkner must be thought of as one of the world's great comic writers, great in the sense that his comedy is not finished off with joke, anecdote, or peculiarity, but by pathos and tragedy. There are comic scenes in Faulkner which, written from a slightly different point of view, would not stir a breath of laughter, and there are, as well, immensely moving scenes which could become occasions for roars. Much of Faulkner is borderline, and can be read one way one time, one way another.

To refresh fatigued responses, to make much of little, little of much: it is an artistic mission. So, when Faulkner died in July, even many who had never read a line of his mourned that special mourning for the departure of unique makers. Perhaps it is not too much to say in a public address by a foreigner that the international reciprocity of which we think so much in political terms is achieved most naturally by such a man, who, even while turning his eye on his own narrow preserve of locale/time/self, releases the reverberant power of that "*lenta realtà*" which Pavese, thirty years ago, recognized as a magnificent export.

[347]

[54]

AN EXEMPLARY LIFE[1]

In January, 1905, a thirty year old Alsatian preacher asked the Director of the Paris Mission Society for an assignment in the Congo, something he'd dreamed about since "my childhood when I donated pennies for the little African children." Single, independent, "in good health and a teetotaler," he'd earned 700 francs from a book about Bach, which "will pay for my trip so that the Mission Society, which already has so many expenses, may have a few less."

It was eight years before he got the assignment. Meanwhile, he'd preached, published, played organ recitals, built organs, studied medicine ("so that I can be as useful as possible") and married a nurse, Helene Bresslau, who was to help him build the hospital at Lambarene before her health broke and she had to return to Europe. "I feel I've done the right thing in coming here," Albert Schweitzer wrote his sister, "For the misery is greater than anyone can describe." He lists the illnesses and injuries he treats: leprosy, sleeping sickness, elephantiasis, "terrible abscesses. . . many heart cases. . . The people are suffocating." Every night he goes to bed dead-tired, "profoundly happy that I am serving at the outpost of the Kingdom of God!"

Fifty years later, he writes a friend

> Every morning life confronts me with realities that I have to cope with: making broken pumps work, improving roads, replacing walls. . . conquering the weeds. . . and keeping the hospital properly afloat. My heart has to make sure it doesn't succumb to old age. . . Seldom has a human being been so fortunate. I am able to work day after day: in the hospital, on the construction site, in the plantation, with my mind, and with my pen. . . I have twenty dear coworkers, and the common goal of our work is: helping to fight pain, saving lives.

---

[1] Albert Schweitzer. **Letters. 1905-1965.** Ed. Hans Walter Bähr. Trans. by Joachim Neugroschel. Macmillan. 456 and xii. $35.00.

> Sometimes I'm embarrassed at being able to do such beautiful
> work and having such a beautiful old age.

The hospital lay on the equator. Every day the sun disappeared
at 6 o'clock. If there were no surgery under petrol light,
Schweitzer would roll out his special organ-pedalled piano and
play Bach for an hour. He wrote to those who donated equipment,
supplies and money to the hospital, worked on his philosophical,
theological, musical and, later, autobiographical texts. He wrote to
all, the simple and the great, with courtesy, modesty, humor and a
work-grounded spirituality.

In 1917, he and his wife were interned as German citizens.
After, he returned to Europe to raise money in recitals and lectures.
He gave advice about building organs and churches and about playing Bach. He learned surgical techniques, bought new medicines,
responded to all who sought him out, thought through and wrote
down his views of life and the world.

Back in 1915, canoeing in the Ogowe River, the famous keynote
phrase of his life came to him: the *Ehrfurcht vor dem Leben*, the
Awe or Reverence for Life. It "comprises everything that can be
called love, devotion, compassion, shared joy and cooperation." It
was an ethics of activity, a realistic love, not the passive compassion of India which Schopenhauer tried to introduce into European
thought. This reverence was neither sentimental nor fanciful:
Schweitzer killed mosquitos, not—he said—because they were
annoying, but because they were sickness-carriers; he nurtured four
injured pelicans by feeding them fish—and tried to think out the
balance of those lives and deaths. Constantly acting and constantly
weighing his actions, he did nothing lightly, even lightness (though
he was humorous and jovial.)

Schweitzer was part of the great world; he was crushed by its
disasters as well as those of those around him. His wife—the
daughter of Jews—had fled with their daughter to Switzerland;
friends died in death camps. He spent hundreds of hours studying
and corresponding about the arms race, atomic energy and the cold
war. He wrote and was written to by Einstein, Russell,
Hammerskjöld, and Nehru, and exchanged joyous letters with John
Kennedy after the arms pact of 1963.

Famous now, he won prizes—the Nobel, the Goethe, the
Hebbel—his name was on streets, schools, hospitals, a KLM plane.
He refused some awards (he didn't want other names dropped for
his), but accepted the rest with graciousness and intelligent mod-

[349]

esty. More and more, though, he stayed in Africa where he felt "essential," "necessary." He had the "luck" of working to the end, at ninety.

Since his death in 1965 there have been the usual attempts to trash the beauty and grandeur of his life with stories about his authoritarianism. His recipe for criticism was silence; it will be mine as well.

In a world which sinks deeper into junk and noise, whose intellectual degradation is so great that it boasts about it, Schweitzer's letters come from a cloud of grace. Readers will feel impulses of nobility rising to counter the lassitude, cowardice, arrogance, vanity and pride which pour from us. If this sexagenarian reader feels that the book gives him hope he can improve at least a bit, what will it do for a young person?

In the aristocracy of humanity, the same names show up again and again. They show up in Schweitzer's letters: Gandhi, Einstein, St. Francis. For Schweitzer, there were two greater names, Jesus Christ, the transcendent Exemplar, and Johann Sebastian Bach. Those of us with too much lead and mud in our souls to aspire towards the first might be able to absorb enough of the second's magnificent art to give us a sense of what Albert Schweitzer must have felt for so many days of his exemplary life.

JOYCE, POUND, ELIOT

These three "non-English" writers did more than any other English-language artists to make literature once again the form of mentality which made sense and beauty of more thought, behavior, scene, and feeling than any other. Their prime subject was the relationship of what people did, felt, and said they did and felt to what the traditions of—largely—Western culture said people have felt, done and should do. Joyce's Bloom, a wastebasket of the culture, is en route to something else; he is the extraordinary-ordinary man whose emotional life takes over the center of contemporary English and American literature. In Joyce, the character is a controlled part of a great, formal scheme.

The artistic "schemes" of the post-midcentury writers have been—on the whole—closer to the emotional trajectory of their stories and characters. This has meant closer views of the inner life and of the world distorted by it. I'd guess that those of us writing now, whether conscious of it or not (it's mostly not*), pour these inner lives over one traditional assumption after another. Whether we begin with a lust for novelty or just a desire to write about a person or situation as deeply as possible, the best results should reorder consciousness along now-hidden lines. New energy, new scarcity, new gain, new misery will be registered and worked out in the new forms. The results, not the job, will be new.*

Eliot, Pound, Joyce, and Proust took up a lot of my apprentice time. Eliot's poems, notes, and essays gave me my reading lists; Proust and Joyce were graphs of literary possibility; Pound, through an accidental meeting in Venice, made me feel the life behind the textbooks. (My one meeting with Eliot was a small-joke scene. He "misheard" my name, and said, "Ah, Stearns. You're from Watertown, Mass." I said, "I'm afraid you're a hundred miles, two letters, and a few other things wide of the mark, Mr. Eliot." "Ah well," he said. "Families wander in a generation.") Since then the old masters sometimes seem much closer at hand,

[351]

sometimes impossibly remote. (Friends are too close for useful per-spective.)

These small pieces were done for little magazines or Chicago newspapers. Perhaps they're more devotional than practical, but that may be the right tone for an apprentice.

[55]

JOYCE'S VANISHING ACT

For half a century Joyce scrutinized his own life. The results were remarkable books and a remarkable personality. Richard Ellmann has written an account of this autobiographical career[1] that not only extricates it from Joyce's versions of himself but explains the need for his versions. Explains, that is, what is explainable, for after eight hundred pages stoked with discoveries and insights Ellmann permits Joyce to remain mysterious.

The mystery begins about halfway through Joyce's adult life, as he leaves Trieste for Zurich and begins the large-scale construction of *Ulysses*. Up to this point, Ellmann dominates his subject, judging with intimate severity the sponging egoism of the early years. In this ugly cocoon, one of the subtlest imaginations of history has been forming, one that resists the classifications of biographer, wife, brother, or itself. Ellmann keeps describing Joyce, but he makes clear that we are seeing less and less of what counts. (Even photographs of Joyce in these years capture little more than blank features.) The most nomadic of European writers inhabits himself. Almost everyone who meets him—Busoni, the composer, Jung, the psychologist, intellectuals from all over the world—senses the rare interior power. One of them, Archibald MacLeish, after decades spent with men famous in politics and art, described (to Ellmann) his reaction in 1954:

> I don't know what "greatness" in a man is though I think I know what it is in a man's work. But a great man! I've been close to some accounted so but it was always the deeds or the work I felt—not a greatness in the man himself. But in Joyce you felt a hard, strong actuality that, if not greatness, was at least something you were always conscious of.

---

[1] Richard Ellmann, *James Joyce* (New York: Oxford University Press, 1959).

Eliot said that a work of art "is not the expression of personality" but an escape from it. This famous claim will not hold up in Joyce's case. Ellmann's book shows that Joyce's work involved so thorough an exploitation of his personality that in a way there was nothing "accidental" in his life. Joyce seems never to have had a useless experience. His ability to transform earthly detail into literature lies behind his superstitiousness and behind the ease of seeing in a Dublin advertising canvasser Ulysses, Christ, Shakespeare.

It is because Joyce's life and work together form a track to what are still formal, linguistic, moral, and emotional frontiers that Ellmann's biography is also a work of criticism. Its strength, as well as its length, derives from this double load. That it is also a wonderfully amusing and very touching, even heart-rending book is a tribute Ellmann must share with his subject. The account of Joyce's efforts on behalf of the tenor John Sullivan would make a comic novel (the climax Joyce's cry in the Paris Opera House that he has miraculously recovered his sight). A very different novel would contain the scene in which Joyce stands quietly at the railroad station while his insane daughter screams bloody hell at him. Ellmann subdues the scenes so that the biography is never anecdotal but cumulative and telling. When, on the last page, Joyce is buried, his wife stretching out her arm to the coffin while a deaf man across the way shouts "Who is it? Who is it?", this reader for one felt like answering "The greatest man around."

[56]

POUND VS. JOYCE

In 1912 Ezra Pound, thrashing hints of modernity out of the London bush, turned out a quatrain of invocation:

> Sweet Christ from hell spew up some Rabelais,
> To belch and fart and to define today
> In fitting fashion, and her monument
> Heap up to her in fadeless excrement.

A year later the spew arrived in the manuscripts of a thirty-two-year-old Berlitz teacher living in Trieste. By the time Pound's enthusiasm and impresario energy had run their course, the new monument maker had himself become a monument. As for the heaped-up matter, the supply turned out to be greater than the invoker could manage.

"I am perhaps a little more phallic and less interested in the excrement and feces of men and beasts," he wrote the Rabelaisian supplier, and his editorial shears tried clipping a few Joyce bits from Bloom's relaxed session in the garden privy. No great harm done, but it was a sign of growing distance between discoverer and discovery.

This finely edited book[1] tells a great deal about the relationship. From it, and from the wonderfully edited letters of Joyce (the work of Stuart Gilbert and Richard Ellmann), one can see much and guess more. One of the guesses is that neither Pound nor Eliot would have bitten off half as much without the discoveries of Joyce; another is that the receptive atmosphere Pound created enabled Joyce to attempt far more than he otherwise would have. So here's documentation for a great shift in human expression. Short of finding a transcript of Jonson's talks with Shakespeare, we're not likely to do better.

---

[1] Forrest Read, ed., *Pound/Joyce*. The letters of Ezra Pound to James Joyce, with Pound's critical essays and articles about Joyce (New Directions, 1967).

The Read book contains notes for at least one extraordinary story. Within the bawdy jockeying, complaints, and sensitometer reports, one sees the brilliant American revolutionary coming up against the first man whose genius and tenacity are clearly greater than his own. He yields pride of place, assists him, advances him, and then discovers that the demands of his own work and ego force him to reconstruct both; the reconstruction makes him devalue the other man and ignore his development. "Nothing so far as I make out," he wrote Joyce after trying the early passages of *Finnegans Wake*, "Nothing short of divine wisdom or a new cure for the clap can possibly be worth all the circumambient peripherization."

Receiving this, Joyce "despaired," then resisted his own never forgotten sense of deep obligation to contend with Pound in the later sections of *Finnegans Wake*. "If I can't upset this pound of pressed ollaves [bards; olives] I can sit up zounds of sounds upon him." (The sound man, Joyce, assailing the imagist, Pound.)

The contention was serious, but the contenders remembered each other's splendor. Joyce's last letter advised his brother to call on Pound for help, and four years later, thirty-three years after his quatrain, Pound invoked the liveliness of his dead companion:

> and Jim the comedian singin'
> 'Blarney Castle me darlin'
> You're nothing now but a stOWne'

[57]

STUMBLING INTO MODERNITY[1]

In October 1921, Thomas Eliot, a thirty-three-year-old American living in London, realized that he was on the verge of a nervous breakdown. A few years before he'd given up an academic career, although he'd finished a doctoral dissertation (on the philosopher F. H. Bradley). Against his family's wishes, he left the United States and settled in England. He got a job in Lloyd's Bank, specializing in their foreign department; after hours he wrote reviews and articles for technical magazines and literary pages and gave evening lectures to working people on a great variety of subjects. In 1915 he'd married an English girl whose neurotic instability reinforced what he later discovered to be his own lifelong "aboulie and emotional derangement." Aboulia, "loss of will power," was an undercurrent of a few remarkable poems he'd written and published in literary magazines. The poems brought him to the attention of an ebullient and energetic American a few years older than himself, Ezra Pound, already a well-known figure in London literary life. Pound, a discoverer, had found his America. He got Eliot's poems published (borrowing money for the printing costs); he got an American lawyer named Quinn to help Eliot negotiate with reluctant American publishers; and he observed, with growing anxiety, that Eliot would soon be lost to poetry under the burdens of his wife's invalidism and the fierce schedule required to pay her doctors. In October 1921, under the additional strain of a visit from his mother, brother and sister, Eliot was told by a specialist that he would have to get off by himself for three months. The bank— where he was now a valued employee specializing in debts and claims complicated by the various peace treaties— gave him paid leave, and he went off, first to Margate, then to Lausanne. For two

---

[1] T. S. Eliot, *The Waste Land*. A facsimile and transcript of the original drafts, including the annotations of Erza Pound; edited by Valerie Eliot (New York: Harcourt Brace Jovanovich, 1971).

years he had thought about writing a long poem; his convalescence gave him the opportunity to write it, indeed consisted in his being free to write it. In January, 1922, he came back to London with the poem. But not quite the poem with which he had left Lausanne. That poem was a much longer, clumsier affair. En route to London, he had stopped off in Paris, where Pound then lived. Together they went over the batch of manuscript-typescript and eliminated whole sections and great parts of other sections of the poem. The end result was one of the triumphs of literature, a poem generally regarded as the chief poetic expression of twentieth-century modernity.

The story has been known for a long time, but the details of the Parisian operation on the clumsy creature which became the *The Waste Land* have been hidden, because the batch of manuscript was lost. In gratitude for John Quinn's help, Eliot gave him the manuscript drafts and revisions. At Quinn's death, the uninventoried treasure was put in a storage box. where it wasn't discovered until the 1950's. Quinn's niece sold it for eighteen thousand dollars to the Berg[2] Collection of the New York Public Library, whose curator finally informed the second Mrs. Eliot of the acquisition in 1968. Mrs. Eliot has now edited this facsimile edition with a transcript, an introduction, and notes. In this important labor of love she had the assistance of Pound, whose short preface calls this "mystery of the missing manuscript pure Henry James."

One mark of modernity is its passion for the inside story. Given a choice between a New Testament and the inside story of the Old, it would opt for the latter. Process fascinates the modern, products only briefly enchant him. When process involves so important a transformation as the one this book exhibits, the modernist reader feels like a participant in creation.

A good account of the making of the *The Waste Land* will be a long endeavor, but here are some rough speculations.

A man of enormous energy, intellectual experience, and ambition has been driven into an emotional corner. While this has been happening to him, the stupidest war in centuries is going on. His and everyone else's "individual lives are so swallowed up" "that one almost ceases to have personal experiences or emotions . . ." With the war's end, there is an enormous release of energy and the

---

[2] 1993. The doctors Henry and Albert Berg were older cousins of my father, who writes about Albert, a great diagnostician, in the beautiful little memoir my late sister, Ruth Leviton, edited, entitled, and had privately printed, *Reminiscences of a Gentle Man. Henry George Stern. 1887-1979.*

creation of enormous problems of adjusting to it. This affects him personally to the point of breakdown. A poet, he is not a first-person celebrator or complainer. He adopts a strategy he has used in early poems, dramatic monologues, and dialogues, and he writes a series of poetic scenes and lyrics in other voices. He has an organizational principle picked out of a scholar's book on the degeneration of a religious ritual— that of an impotent king and his sterile land— into poetic romance. The theme of sterility touches the poet in many ways; and the book supplies much of the imagery and symbolism of his poem as well as its eventual title. The original title, "He Do the Police in Different Voices," is taken from a bit of *Our Mutual Friend*, a scene which deals with a half-witted foundling named Sloppy who is said to be "a beautiful reader of a newspaper. He do the Police in different voices." The poet, with that familiar aristocratic mix of inverse snobbery and true affection for working-class life, will write a good deal of this poem in the different voices of men and women of different classes. The ugliness which has driven him to the corner is everywhere—palaces, pubs, past, present, inside Western culture and inside his life. The poem exhibits as many social and cultural scenes as he can manage, each written in a metric which comments on it (one of the many tricks picked up from Joyce).

This procession of long, varied poems was what Eliot brought to Pound. What he took away a few days later was a poem which, though still made up of discrete parts, was also of a piece. A footnote proclaiming Tiresias the poem's center was as yet unwritten and probably unconceived, but this new poem had a center: the judgment of a sensibility made clear in every allusion and meter. From the lush, "Shakespeherian" blank verse describing the society boudoir to the fresh, irregular lyrics of the fourth and fifth sections, not only is that sensibility felt but its convalescence is charted. The end of the poem is a collection of fragments, a microcosm of the Pounded poem, that rapid, jagged, elliptic juxtaposition of brilliant scenes and cultural shards which became the flag of modernity. Under Pound's guidance, Eliot had stumbled into it.

Years later a confident, prosperous, public-minded Eliot said of *The Waste Land:*

> Various critics have done me the honour to interpret the
> poem in terms of criticism of the contemporary world,
> have considered it, indeed, as an important bit of social

criticism. To me it was only the relief of a personal and wholly insignificant grouse against life; it is just a piece of rhythmical grumbling.

If every artist who felt or said such things about his early work could cause its oblivion, there would be very few beautiful poems or pictures left in the world. Eliot wrote nothing greater than his "grouse."

[VII]

GETTING AT ONESELF

[58]

THE INVENTION OF THE REAL

> "Real" is not a normal word at all. . . but highly exceptional;
> exceptional in this respect that, unlike "yellow" or "horse" or
> "walk," it does not have one single, specifiable, always-the-
> same meaning."
>
> J. L. Austin, Sense and Sensibilia

> "Margaret," said Marianne, with great warmth, "you know
> that all this is an invention of your own, and that there is no
> such person in existence."
> "Well, then, he is likely dead, Marianne, for I am sure there
> was such a man once, and his name begins with an F."
>
> Jane Austen, Sense and Sensibility

Imagine that you wake up the first day of your conscious life on
some planet's moon. A space ship has somehow nourished and now
abandons you. You have consciousness, a dozen years or so, a
body. Nothing else but food and bright lunar emptiness. There are
no words in your world, no other beings at whom to grunt in wonder, terror, hunger.

Now imagine the stages of discrimination, but not with the
sophisticated naïveté of René Descartes. He was equipped with
whole vocabularies of discrimination. But you, alone on that moon,
are not even a complete "I"—for to be fully "I" there must be a
sense of "you," of "it." Nor is the fuzz of glare and black, the flash-
and-chill-charged kinesthesia exactly thinking. You are; you feel,
see, puzzle, but can you make the assertion that you think, therefore you are? (Working out "therefore" would require a combination of Einstein and Shakespeare.) Can you in fact make any assertion? Maybe, one day, shivering with chill as you approach the dark
side of your moon, the noise of shivering on your lips becomes, as
it were, the word for "cold," and a light bursts inside. Then you
can begin assigning other varieties of moan and groan to walking,
waking, swallowing, to bright, to dark, perhaps even to their orderly succession.

[365]

Would you ever attain to something that could be called an explanation of yourself? Your existence on this stone crust? Would you, that is, have what human beings need almost as much as they need air and water, the story of themselves: What am I? Who am I? (Of course on a one-person planet, "who" would be superfluous. So would many crucial human questions: What are others? Are they for me? Against me? Though a genius might conjure up: What is knowing and what can I know? How do I connect with this, separate from that? Am I the same awake as I was asleep? Awake today the same who awoke yesterday? And: What is it all about? What is the meaning of these waking-sleepings, eating-emptyings, these easings, these distresses?)

Very early, surely, in the process of the humanization of humanoid creatures, story must have come in. Not just that separation of inner and outer which is perception and which naming transforms into cognition, but a coherent serialization of events which fuses process and personality. Is there anything else more humanizing? Is it even possible to say that this "storification" is itself the means of humanization?

I'm neither philosopher, psychologist, historian nor anthropologist. I sneak into a great university through a cellar window reserved for a class of falsifiers permitted that entrée as jesters were given privilege by old kings, for diversion, sometimes bitter, sometimes sweet. The fiction maker is even freer than the jester. His stories need never be checked against the time-and-space coordinates of those other reality-stories which order and dominate human life. He does have complicated social functions, but that isn't the business of this essay. This business has to do with the process itself—with invention. Not precisely with the invention of those special stories called fictions, but with a small portion of the story-making process as it occurred in me about a year ago.

I'd better qualify this. To some degree I want to describe a kind of essay or lecture-making process: that is, I will try to reproduce some of what I noticed last year from the story maker's viewpoint, a viewpoint that was conditioned by the title of this talk, one which I'd given in answer to a request a few days before I left on the trip. The conclusions, then, are reflections on the theme sounded when—under pressure to come up with a title—I uttered the five words which I discovered on bulletin boards when I returned.

Its first dateline is one of the greatest of all story towns, Venice; the second is a small town visited on impulse; and the third is another

[366]

of the four or five greatest of all story towns, Paris, where I report two conversations, one with a gentlemanly hoodlum, the second with another—rather more distinguished—story writer.

So: To Venice.

1. Early September. This room is five feet above a canal. Moon and lamplight stipple the water. Two A.M., quiet as a deaf man's skull. The *fondamenta*—a street on a canal—is banked by three- and four-story houses, none eminent or especially handsome, but spookily beautiful now. Two bridges staple the gold-touched water. The room is filled with drawings, watercolors, pieces of sculpture. One of these, fixed to the wall, is a crucifix made by extending the outer tines of a fork. Joan—my hostess—says it was made by Ibrahim, a half-Jewish, half-Shiite Iraqi who shuttles between Paris and the Middle East, selling his work, looking for his children, and perhaps for an old dream of greatness which his shuttling life has dissipated.

I often wake to the warning cries of boatmen who steer garbage sacks or lovers around the bend of this canal. Then upstairs for coffee and rolls in Joan's workroom. She's carving a horse's head in black wax. It and her feisty dog, Sammy, make up the breakfast foursome. Two of us exchange juicy items from the local newspaper, the *Gazzetino*, which this morning reports that a woman in Lima, Peru, had her gold fillings stolen as she was riding a bus. "The thief," she explains to the police, "took advantage of me while I was yawning." The phone rings. A woman says (in Oxbridge English): "Hello. This is the Queen of——" and names a country that has for thirty-odd years been ruled by a well-known dictator. I repress the impulse to say, "And how is King ——[the name of the dictator]?" because I know that this lady is no crank, but was, once upon a time, the official queen of that country, and that her father, king of a neighboring country, died of his pet monkey's bite five months before her birth. I know too that she is now known in Venice for swiping rolls of toilet paper from the bathrooms of hotels which used to allow her to stay free of charge. Thirty-odd years ago, she was married to her little king—like herself, one of the numerous great-grandchildren of Queen Victoria—after a bitter political fight with her husband's mother. Once upon that time, she was a slender princess, raised for the strange life of royalty.[1] Now she's a twisted

---

[1] This is described in a heart-rending and bathetic autobiography which, though ghost-written, is a self-exposure almost beyond decency. I've written about the queen in the title piece of *Shares and Other Fictions* (Delphinium Books. 1992). Her country is breaking up as I write.

bit of regal superfluity (a kind of Ibrahim's fork), yet an element of some of the bloodiest episodes of twentieth-century history. The Queen announces she'll be by for lunch, that we shouldn't bother with champagne, she will content herself with fresh vegetables-preferably *fagiolini*-boiled and served *senza burro, senz'olio.*

I get in a *traghetto* and walk to Campo San Barnaba, where I buy a cappuchino and write in a notebook. Construction workers take an espresso-and-grappa break at a stand-up bar, but otherwise it's quiet in the little *campo.* Two of the other five people at the café are engaged on business similar to mine; a bald man, thirtyish, Austrian or German, writes fiercely in a school notebook; a young woman with glitter-rimmed eyeglasses sketches the church which gives the campo its name. At the store where I used to buy books when I taught here in 1962-63, there is a sale, and I've picked up a volume of poems by one Alfonso Gatto, born in 1909. I read a four-liner called "Giotto":

> Nulla che non sia dolce e buono
> e l'uomo e la montagna uguali
> e la casa come la mano
> posato per questa sera

Not bad, I think, just the thing for my lecture. I write a translation in my notebook:

> Nothing which isn't good and gentle
> the man and the mountain equal
> and the house, like the hand,
> posed for the evening

The girl sketching, Joan and Ibrahim will understand this. In the artist's heirarchy, mountain, man, house, and hand lose their worldly priority and are—in the evening painted by Giotto—just different-colored shapes.

Back at Joan's. The doorbell rings. It's not our sad queen, but a scrawny ancient, magnificently dressed in a striped, rust-colored turban and matching ankle-length dress. "I yam," she says in a Russian-phonemed English, "Ovairrcome." It is Madame—I will call her—Incognita who dressed the world's rich and famous in the thirties and forties. Her husband fell in love with Greta Garbo, and, rumor goes, so did Incognita. Today, decades later, she and Garbo, though they live in the same New York apartment house, do not speak to each other. Now Incognita is distraught. Her "vairry bast friend," Count (I'll call him) Sigismundo, died yesterday afternoon at the "vairry moment when I am buying pitches in the campo." She is, she says, "feenished with Eetaly, feenished with Vainice." Sigismundo, she says, was the last representative of "high style" in the city. "Canal Grande feenish. All is feelth and chipness." She offers her historical analysis: "Eet begeens with feelthy jins"—blue jeans—"than comes knifes." That is, the terrorists of Italy's Red Brigade are the inevitable consequence of wearing blue jeans. After that comes "Ravolushon wheech I saw, nine years olt, weeth mine own eyes in Sebastopol."

The Count's funeral will be Friday. "The thirteenth?" asks Joan. Incognita's still beautiful eyes grow huge in blue fright. "Friday ze four-teens! Ze sirteens I do not leaf my rrooom. Ze sirteens I *stay hum.*"

Two days later, we go to the funeral service in the nuttily baroque church of San Moise.[2] The church is usually empty, the priest is a famous bore, but today it is full of Venetian cream which the preacher, delirious with rapture at the crowd, churns into great curds of tedium. Finally, rhetoric subsides, the hat is passed, and we move into the campo to watch the mourners. The Countess, who has a face as sharp as the teeth on a gondola's prow, goes from group to group extending her wicked face for kisses. From the family Vendramin, she is usually called Contessa Benzadrine. She was an enthusiastic Fascist. In 1945 the partisans shaved her bald, stripped her naked, and ran her through the streets from the Stazione to the Piazza San Marco. Now she steps into the black funeral gondola which will take her husband's coffin to San Michele, the cemetery island.

I've touched here on a fraction of the people I saw in Venice last year, but you can see how even these flakes of the reality-cake make promising story matter. Stories flow from any town—or from a hermit's cave—but story machinery has been pumping so long in Venice, that people feel licensed to act in provocative ways. And of course, the peculiarities of a carless, trainless, water city create such odd versions of human situations that there is theater on every street and campo. Then too, strangeness attracts the strange. So ex-queens come here, along with the idle, the decadent, the beautiful, the famous and would-be-famous, most with time to make mischief, trouble, and stories. So much is this a story town that it's an obstacle to writing about Venice. How do you say anything new

---

[2] Where the perpetrator of the first great stock swindle, John Law, is buried.

about a town where you can use a four-hundred-year-old map to get around?

The sort of permanence this suggests is the sort Alfonso Gatto drew on for his little poem on Giotto. The hands, the evening, and probably the houses Giotto painted are gone; their reality exists only in his painting; and we know it only as he did seven hundred years ago. (As for Gatto's twenty-five or thirty words, they too hold us for a minute or so, gattoize us as Giotto giottoized us.)

Even now, something like this is happening. A small part of me is becoming a smaller part of you, and for these moments, anyway, we are both somewhat altered, courtesy of a thirteenth-century painter, a modern poet, an ex-queen, and an eighty-year-old lady whom I have simplified into caricature.

2. A week later. I'm in Dôle, a small town on the Doubs River in the Jura. The town is best known as the birthplace of Louis Pasteur, whose house is sixty or seventy yards down the street where I write this. The house is darkened by a large sixteenth-century church on the hill above. Its darkness reminds me of the especially dark darkness of Thomas Edison's house in the little town of Milan, Ohio. (When I saw it last year, it occurred to me that the inventor who transformed the nights of the world must have been especially conscious of the old helplessness of human nights.) Pasteur's town suggests an analogy which comes to me at the table in the dining room of my little hotel, the Pomme d'Or.

Three hours ago, I was heading for Dijon, a gastronomic Jerusalem for Crusaders of the Belly. But the train stopped a few extra minutes at Dôle, and I (mistaking it for another town I'd enjoyed seeing and eating in several years ago) got off. It's turned out to be a sad little place, but one which conceals—at least contains—an (as far as I know) unsung artist who converts trout, bean, potato, and other earthly goods into culinary marvels. These direct me to my analogy.

Men and beasts share the chemical/mental complex called hunger and erase it with whatever they recognize as food. The recognition is infinitely more complex in men than beasts; so the jellied roaches which delight the gourmets of Osaka do different things to the hungriest Westerner. Already the basic reality, hunger, has been rerouted over a complex map. If we compare a tiger's devastation of a gazelle's ribs with the average Westerner's restrained arrangement of his appetite into breakfast, lunch, and dinner, or his conversion of a meal into occasions of reunion, domesticity, thanksgiving, intellectual exchange (à la Plato's Symposium), or religious communion, we see how that basic reality, hunger/food, is only a plank in the architecture of human consumption.

So stories convert the data of event into a coherence which doesn't just transform actuality, but creates it. That is, it makes sense out of sensation. Consciousness depends on storied notions. We say of a described character, "Ah. That's the way I feel. That's what I want to do." We alter by inventing new stories about ourselves and others. Between the—let's call it—life force which brings X to Y, and the decision to "go with" (let alone "marry"), falls story. "Is X the sort of person I want to spend a week with? A lifetime with?"

We're all story makers, constant inventors of the realities we call *our life*. Story-making pressure is so great, it continues in that nightlife of dreams which work to order unresolved, that is *unstoried* tensions, fears, hopes, desires, hatreds, sensations.

October 1979 addendum: A recent American visitor displayed the power of story. A gray-haired man in a white dress went through the streets transfiguring the energy of millions of people. The pope, no different physically from a bench-sitter tossing nuts to a pigeon, is nonetheless a kind of human Venice, a package of stories. So he became part of millions of American story-makers.

3. This essay of three cities continues in Paris. I arrived September 19, thirty years to the day after my first arrival. I'm saturated with nostalgia, real and phony. I walk the street where a girl I was to marry lived and cross the bridge where I got the idea for the first story for which I was ever paid. Melancholy rapture takes over: "So much not done, so much gone wrong." An orgy of self-impeachment, controlled by a little fund of self-satisfaction.

Two days later, reading *Le Monde* over a beer at the Café de la Marie, I find myself interrogated by a large-bellied gentleman in an old tweed jacket and orange turtleneck, the top of which looks like a neck brace. I've noticed him because he's used his cane to open the door for a spaniel whose master sits at a corner table. The old fellow croaks, "*Sont-ils indiens?*" "They" are a young Vietnamese woman and her small son. They've come in with an armful of packages and sat down on my right. They speak English, although the woman orders ice cream in good French. I tell him the woman seems part Vietnamese, part French, the boy American. I have

[371]

overheard them saying they were going back to Dallas. The man says I needn't whisper, then invites me to consider history, in particular the history of Rome (pronounced "Rrum"). Was I aware that that community was brought low by mongrels: "*les barbares*"? I tell him I understand his point. Well then, I should look about me. I should regard the menacing presence of the Portuguese in Paris. Then there was Washington, D.C. Was I aware of the enormous percentage there of *nègres*? He touches my newspaper. And what are we doing about this ebony swine, Bokassa, so-called emperor of Central Africa? "The government has been cuddling this mongrel for years. Now it's reduced to restricting his landing rights at Orly and Bordeaux. In my time," he says as if from the grave, "we'd have sent in a battalion of paratroopers. Now we can't afford to send in a gendarme with a revolver. All our money went into the swine's coronation."

Well, this is certainly better than *Le Monde*. It's been a while since I've encountered views like this in the flesh. I pass my time in precincts where tolerance and enlightenment are scarcely violated in jokes.[3] So I encourage the swinish historian, offer him a cigar, nod as his insights open tunnels in my ignorance, and supply only those responses which will keep his golden spigot open. Twenty minutes later, I've had it. "*Au 'voir, m'sieu.* It's been a great pleasure." Here I notice the spaniel's master regarding me with loathing. It's clear he sees me as co-sponsor of my neighbor's repulsive views. Doesn't he know I'm only a literary provocateur, that this is research?

The next day I drink coffee at another café with another gentleman. I don't know him well—this is our second meeting in two years—but like and respect him enormously. He is one of the few writers who's invented a type of person and experience so different from others that his name and theirs have become labels.

He too is somewhat melancholy. "I hate nine-tenths of everything I've written," he tells me. He has none of Madame Incognita's theatrical pessimism. He is personal, but not egotistic. She was comical, farcical; he is humorous and affecting. "I'm ashamed of my life," he says quietly. "The world's so full of misery. And what have I done? Words." Despite a surge of fellow feeling, I think of Hamlet's "And like a whore unpack my heart with words." But of course that unpacking is just one thing you do with

---

[3] Of course he was right about Bokassa, about whom I knew little or nothing when I was in the café.

[372]

words, and the creator of Godot, Lucky, Pozzo, Hamm, Malone, Murphy, Winnie, and Watt has not only unpacked his own but millions of hearts. He tells me his fiction came out of the dark. "I never had a plan for it. Never knew where it was going." His plays were written for relief. "They were all out there, in the light. Much easier. But the call comes from the dark." Now he'll write but not publish. "Just finishing translating a ten-thousand-word piece I wrote in English. I call it *Company*. Because I wrote it to keep myself company. Then I found the company even worse than my own.[4]" The words of the constant story maker keep coming: despite the misery out there, the—what?—energy within gets to the page, and the septuagenarian inventor of the Beckett world continues making it.

Like any manufacturer, an artist creates not only to satisfy a want—his own, his patron's—but to create wanters whom only he can satisfy. (Even if he is his own chief wanter.) Can we separate the producer from the product?

A nonpublishing Beckett will still be Beckett, but will a nonwriting Beckett? (If there is no web, shall we call the bug a spider?)[5]

Or is this the wrong question? There is the *Iliad*-Homer and his older self or careful successor, the *Odyssey*-Homer. There is the *Watt*-Beckett and the *Godot*-Beckett. What counts are *Watt* and the *Iliad*. Without them, or rather, without their successors, the invention of the real would stop and human beings would, each year, become less human.

---

[4] He changed his mind. *Company* is published. [1993. I hope the reader will forgive the repetition of this conversation; it seems to belong to this essay as well as the one on Beckett.]

[5] Yeats's poem wonders about telling "the dancer from the dance." How about an ex-dancer? Well, that's what he is then, an ex-dancer.

[59]

UNDERWAY[1]

I doubt that there's ever been a totally naive literary act. The very manual energy involved in the transfer of thought to paper is at some point entangled with awareness of the process of transference. To some degree, then, there's always been "the story of the story." *How did this poem come about? How or why did I— or he— write this? What is the relationship between the words and the actualities or images to which they seem to refer? In what ways are this text and this author products of economic, political, social, sexual, linguistic, literary, and other ventriloquial powers?*

The twentieth century may be the great promoter, distributor, and advertiser of such questions and their answers. That so many modern writers make their living teaching alongside scholars and critics has not impoverished the literature of narcissism.[2]

2

I'm going to add my bit to it now. There's some danger here, I know: "Never seek to tell thy love/ Love that never told can be." There's a law of diminishing returns at work when a force retracts for self-regard. Mine will be partial, a "modified, limited hangout."

One alert. I'm not going to put much psychological pressure on myself. That deep fears and desires determine the shape and content of books is no secret. It's probably best, though, that they remain secret to the author-sufferer.

One guess: work which involves complex choice is best done by

---

[1] 1992. Some of what is talked about here emerged in "Shares. A Novel in Ten Pieces," part of *Shares and Other Fictions*. (Delphinium books. 1992).

[2] That it may have impoverished literature is another matter.

people whose selves are up for grabs, people, that is, whose egos need lots of bolstering. I don't know if the author of "When in disgrace with fortune and men's eyes" had a fragile ego, but I suspect his extraordinary work was not just the spume of a cyclonic personality. His famous sweetness and just as famous litigiousness are, I think, signs of an exceptionally tender psyche. (Now I'm going far beyond the caution I intended; it's clear my own tremulous ego will go to any length to armor itself.)

3

> *Die angefanen Skizze zum Roman-mit der Kindheits-geschichte voran—ähnelt im Schema den Verwirrungen.*
> (The early sketches of a novel with their infantile history resemble the schemes of a madman.)
>
> Robert Musil, *Tagebücher* (Rowohlt, 1983), p. 71

Autobiography is a particularly deceptive form of deception.
-R.S.

It isn't easy tracing the origin of any fairly complex complex. One of my weaknesses makes this particularly difficult. In the past ten years, I've had trouble screening out what belongs and what doesn't to the work in progress. I think I've felt that with time growing short, I'd better deal with everything I know.

I write this piece three months after dispatching the galleys of a work which I mistakenly thought I'd finished in 1983 and again in 1984. In Regenstein Library there are several thousand typed and scribbled pages, a monument to this literary sickness of excess, indecisiveness, and bad judgment.

Now I'm engaged in another literary civil war. When did it begin?

4

Beginnings. Much tougher to describe than endings. All right, you get the idea—I won't bother working over this complexity—an idea that looks as if it'll stick. (Again, I won't analyze the thousand whys of that.) Even one of Poe's ideal lyrics is made up of more than one idea. Pinning ideas—or inspirations—down is not easy. The road to Slobovia—the motel version of Xanadu—doesn't pass through gorgeous country, yet it's every bit as tortuous a road.

Every discussion of beginnings is more or less arbitrary. One just says, "Here."

This discussion is different from most in not being after the fact. Not only has the trip to the novel hardly begun, its destination is uncertain. All I can say is that it's novel-bound. I'm sure I'm carrying too much baggage for a short story, even a long one, and my gifts exclude epic-writing.

5

In the spring of 1982, my friend and former student, Jim Schiffer, invited me to talk at Blackburn College in west-central Illinois. I took a prop plane from Meigs Field on the lakefront to Springfield. Jim met me there and drove me sixty miles through corn-heavy prairie to Carlinville. This small town, the site of one of the Lincoln-Douglas debates, centers about the college. Its outstanding building is a Greek Revival courthouse which in 1870 had cost a million dollars and caused a scandal. Early in the century, a seven-foot seam of coal was discovered under the town. It was bought by Standard Oil of Indiana, which then purchased through the Sears, Roebuck Catalogue fifty or sixty pre-fabricated houses for the mine workers. Seventy years later, these gave Carlinville a little burst of publicity.[3] There is little else to draw national attention here.

By the time Jim put me on the Springfield plane the next day, something about the town had started to work in me. The people who came to my reading, mostly Blackburn students and faculty, were so pleasant and intelligent that I felt as if I'd come upon a new link in the great chain of human culture. Out here on the prairie there was this eagerness which, a century and a half earlier, had brought out a Lincoln.

There was another feeling, reminiscent of one I'd had more than thirty years earlier when I'd first driven through Europe. Driving through Spanish villages I'd felt Zeus-like. Zeus moved at will through a static world, picking up, then returning whatever charms and goods he wanted before moving on again. Somewhere between the sense of the great transmission belt of culture and a feeling about Carlinville's small, manageable remoteness was a desire to

---

[3] *Smithsonian Magazine*, November, 1985.

write about it.

I grew up in New York City and have lived most of my life in Chicago. I've written mostly about city people. Even when my characters live in small towns—as I have now and then—they are in retreat, or exile from the city. Now, I thought, there's something I can do with a small town. The fact that I know very little about living in one is, if anything, an advantage. It'll allow me, it'll force me, to invention. The danger is that I'll fall into the inventions of other writers. I have to be careful to avoid the versions of Anderson, Faulkner, or Flaubert.

I needed my own handle.

In the summer of 1982 I found one. In Venice, I met a middle-aged American who, unlike most Americans there, was neither an artist, a scholar, or a millionaire. Jim had grown up in a small Iowa town and fallen in love with Europe through reading Hemingway and Fitzgerald. He quit high school, left home, and got a job in a shoestore. At eighteen, he was drafted and sent to Italy. Immediately he knew it was where he wanted to live. He also knew that a foreigner with no degree and few skills couldn't survive there. He decided that after his discharge he'd go home and save enough money to retire in Italy. Back in America, he worked in shoestores all over the country, California, Arizona, New York, Ohio. Then, with a fifteen thousand dollar loan, he opened his own orthopedic store in Flint, Michigan. In ten years he sold out, repaid the loan, and invested his money in tax-free municipals. Then he took off. Later, back in Italy, he realized that he'd miscalculated inflation by two-and-a-half percent. Now in Venice, he counters the shortfall by renting rooms to visiting American graduate students, professors, and artists. It's turned into a double boon, for it's given him the sort of company he prefers.

Jim is the basis for my character, George Share. George doesn't live in Venice or want to. George does work ten months a year in his own shoestore, but his life there is shaped by something else, something I came upon a few weeks after I met Jim.

I was driving in the Jura. It was a wonderful day. I kept getting out of the car to smell the mountain air. In a village, I picked up a hitchhiker, a girl of nineteen or twenty who worked for a jeweler in Les Chaux-des-Fonds. I asked her about her life—she was too polite to ask me about mine. She said she loved movies. I said that people had been telling me to see a film called *Tre fratelli*; I'd tried to see it in Chicago, Rome, Venice, and Munich; just that morning I'd read the paper in Basel to see if it were playing there.

"I've seen it," she said. "We have a *Ciné-club* at home." (The population was eleven hundred.) Her high school history teacher had started it five years ago and showed its members the best European, Japanese, and English-language films.

In Willsville, George Share starts such a club. At home, he has a library of classics and good new books. There, too, he hangs reproductions of paintings, sculpture, and buildings. For twenty years now, Willsvillians—mostly young ones—know they can see films, borrow books, look at paintings and discuss them while they drink Chablis and eat good cheese. For twenty years, George's house has been the social and intellectual center of the county, and for twenty years, George has taken the brightest and prettiest county girl to Europe as a kind of graduation present. The novel opens in Venice during the summer of 1982. George is living in Campo San Margherita with Bug—real name June, nickname "Junebug"— Venerdy, who discovers in the course of the novel that the first Willsville girl awarded this European diploma was her mother.

6

Every once in a while, somebody in search of a lecture topic berates American writers for not dealing with great public subjects and men in public places. There is, they say, no American equivalent of Asturias's *El Señor Presidente* or García Marquez's *Autumn of the Patriarch,* of *War and Peace, The First Circle, Lucien Leuwen,* or *The Charterhouse of Parma.* The only American writers who write about men in high places are popular writers like Upton Sinclair, Herman Wouk,[4] and Allen Drury. As for the Latin-American works, they derive from a political and literary tradition of grotesquerie and farce. (Farce is a traditional way of handling grotesquerie. American writers from "Sut Lovingood" to the authors of *Macbird* and *The Public Burning* have responded to their sense of political grotesquerie with the same weaponry.) There are,

---

[4] Incidentally, I prefer Wouk's versions of Hitler and Roosevelt in *War and Remembrance* to Solzhenitsyn's Stalin or his Lenin (in Zurich). The reason may be that, lacking imaginative power and a dominating thesis, Wouk leaned on good documentary material.

however, no American versions of the political characters in Stendhal, Tolstoy, or Trollope. That's the vacuum I'd like to fill.[5]

Like most people, I've spent most of my life far from the corridors, let alone the seats of power. Men and former men of power come to the university, and now and then I meet and talk with them, but that's about it. In that same summer of 1982, the secretary of state who replaced Alexander Haig was a former colleague of mine. I'd not exchanged more than a few words with him but I did know his new deputy and many of his friends. At last, a foot in the door of the mighty. I felt an itch. Even though I think the point of fiction is to make the "unimportant" "important," I thought, "Why not relate the man I know to the public product of which he is an ingredient?"

Until a novelist like me fuses personality and theme, there is no fiction. As for me, personality almost always requires setting. As if to aggravate the new itch, my daughter moved to Washington. Her husband actually works for the State Department. Things were conspiring in a fictional direction. As for Washington, unlike Willsville, it didn't have to be invented. Its actuality is so rich it's as much as a writer can do to handle a thousandth of what he sees there.

In the spring of 1984, then, I went to Washington.

When I went into the deputy's office in the State Department, I saw him looking at the television news broadcasting the first electoral returns from El Salvador. He said U.S. observers would be flying back to Washington at three, they'd report to the president at four, and a statement would be prepared for the media at five. "It's not the world I worry about," he said. "It's Congress and the media."

It struck me that he had a problem similar to mine. He had to make sense of a large complex of events for somebody else. He is a

---

[5] I speak of a literary vacuum. American films and television dramas are full of presidents, generals, senators, and cabinet ministers. The usual dramatic strategy is to make a political step personally costly to the protagonist. So a president's wife will be in the town he has to bomb. Movies have done better with farce (*Dr. Strangelove*), as the theater did with musical comedy (*Of Thee I Sing*). The basic message is, "You think this is crazy? Go read the *New York Times*."

Then there's the treatment of great men by greater men. For Sophocles and Shakespeare, the rules were different. Oedipus and Hamlet have personal problems, which means that the states they rule—or should rule—have them. This was the case in early novels as well (*The Tale of Genji, The Princess of Clèves*). In the last two hundred years, the state has outgrown personal britches. (This was true even in Stendhal's little Duchy of Parma.) The novelist should treat a public figure as he'd treat a grocer. The type of business counts—competition from a supermarket or a superpower—because it transforms the protagonist's life, not vice versa.

charming, witty, and intelligent man, obviously at home in the world which reduces the pains and pleasures of several billion people into manageable abstractions. (I want my "man of power" to have some of his range and charm.) He and his wife took me on a brief tour of the seventh floor. Much of it is a museum of American art and artifacts. There are American versions of the great furniture makers, Sheraton, Hepplewhite, Chippendale, and the Adamses. There are Philadelphia highboys, Shaker chairs, satinwood commodes, teak porcelain jars and tea seats of Lowestoft and Wedgwood, beautiful paintings by Marin and Childe Hassan; there is the double-tiered desk at which an upright Jefferson wrote the Declaration of Independence. The rooms breathed symmetry, reason, and beauty. I imagined diplomats from Zaire and the Seychelles walking to appointments here and sensing the America which grew not out of intolerance and mass murder but out of the eighteenth-century Enlightenment, an America of equity and beauty. Whoever surrounded American power with such works of art had done something wonderful.

The deputy secretary's dining room is called the Livingston Room. We ate under a portrait of this diplomat who'd nearly haggled away Napoleon's gift-sale of the Louisiana Purchase. (There's a marvelous account of it in Henry Adams's great history of the United States.)

I asked my friend if anyone in the State Department had time to actually think about foreign policy. He said that there really were a couple of people around who did that. I said I'd been reading about Spain—I was going there that summer—and was struck by what had happened to it in the centuries following the discovery of the New World. Gold poured into the country, prices were inflated, human energy went into speculation, into ideologies of national purification, and then aggressive armament. There was also the cultural flowering of the *siglo de oro*, but this marked the end of Spanish greatness. Ruinous engagements were followed by a four-hundred-year slide into parochialism, strife, tyranny, and a long national snooze. I wondered if there were a lesson there for us? My friend had neither time nor inclination to discuss this. The most he ventured was that our Central American policy had a great deal to do with fears of Americans in the southwestern states that they'd be overrun by Latin immigrants.

To get to the point here: I was fascinated by the literary possibilities of men like my friend, the deputy. And soon I saw a connection between their international world and George Share's *école des femmes.* George too had foreign affairs. Now he was going to have something else: a brother who like him had left Willsville, but by another route: the local college, then the University of Chicago Law School, a Wall Street law firm, and, finally, the State Department.

7

I began doing more political reading than I usually do, and it was through a book that another element of the novel's matrix entered. The book was Daniel Ford's *The Button*, a discussion of nuclear strategy which reinforced the feelings of dismay and farcical *je-m'en-fichisme* which grips me when I try to understand large-scale politics.

More importantly, the book generated another character. Ford describes the strategic notion of decapitation, the policy of eliminating enemy leadership in the initial nuclear strike. The Soviet Union and the United States take various measures to deal with it: they have alternative headquarters within easy reach of their capitals (though nobody has figured out a way of communicating from them in an atmosphere of nuclear explosion). The Americans also have Looking Glass, planes in the air twenty-four hours a day commanded by general officers supplied with communication codes to unleash the counterstrike.

My counter to decapitation was this: the National Security Council assigns some general officers to various parts of the country. They bury themselves in little towns accompanied by the codes which enable them to destroy the other half of the world. My character ranks number thirty-two in the hierarchy of succession. He is sent to Willsville, where he buys the town's grocery store. A hundred feet below its crates of tomato juice and crushed pineapple is a concrete room containing the communication system which will insure that a half-incinerated America will incinerate its incinerator.

As I read the Ford book, I also read a story in the newspaper about several owners of midwest pizza parlors who turned out to be Mafia moles. They'd been placed in small towns years ago as drug distributors. My grocer-general, now in his ninth year in Willsville, is a good friend of the local pizza parlor operator.

So the theme of the double life, already present in George

Share's ambivalent tutelage, is reinforced[6]

Now I don't want to write a Jules Romains novel, one in which, say, a town is dominated by a single phenomenon. (Romains called such domination *unanisme*.) My interest remains the psychological and dramatic pressure which makes individuals go different ways. So my decapitation hero's wife disintegrates under the duplicity of her life, and one of his two daughters becomes Bug Venerdy's successor.

There are many other things which I see going into this book. I'll mention only one. My wife worked as a rental agent in a large apartment complex. Her colleague was a fine young black girl who was unjustly accused of stealing a master key, threatened with prison, and made to take a lie detector test. The girl resigned and so did my wife. In my book, I make someone like my wife a daughter of the State Department official. (Which makes him older than my friend, the deputy.) He is used to—and occasionally charmed by—his daughter's letters of protest about foreign policy. Her views are as changeable as mine often are. In life, this is awkward. In fiction, it's a godsend. (Any continuity full of ups and downs is a dramatic and psychological goldmine.)

A few words about literary considerations which indirectly shape this novel's matrix. I've grown tired of the domestic subject matter and sedate prose which have been my stock-in-trade. I've read work by such writers as T. Coraghessan Boyle, Barry Hannah, and Thomas Pynchon. I like their energy, allusiveness, obliquity, obscenity, and—looking at all of them—the range from articulate mumbles to Joycean polylingualism. I don't know how much I can alter but I hope this novel will be invigorated by my new admiration.

Some recent French critics indict most American writers for textual naiveté. They claim that Americans don't make linguistic and narrative subversion the center of their work. For me, narrative naiveté is essential, and, at least until revision, stylistic naiveté is essential also. My energy goes into the construction of a story which seems beautiful and moving to me. Language is, of course, a powerful component of the beauty, but I do not engage it immedi-

---

[6] I could not manage either the general and his family or the mafioso. Their pages are part of the novelistic slag.

ately as Mishima claimed Japanese writers engage Japanese and Italo Calvino claimed Italian writers engaged the problems of their dialects and Italian. Nor do I wish to make such engagement the center of my work.

8

A final note. Over the course of writing a book, one's feelings go all over the map. The relationship of extra-literary to literary feeling is a wonderful subject. Here I only want to say that the feelings which dominated my life before I started thinking about the book were a sense of waste and a sense of dangerously pleasurable comfort, both of which I consciously related to preparation for ceasing to write (and, for that matter, ceasing to live). Feelings pivot on very small happenings. Think sadly of X, and nostalgia socks you. A dream brings you a voice, unheard for years, and you are overcome with feeling. The novel-in-progress is affected by such events and feelings, but more and more, it acquires an emotional life of its own. More and more it's insulated from other events, other feelings. It has its own rhythm, its own principles, its own range of thought and feeling. This novel is not advanced enough for that. My fear is that it may be dying even as I write this. That is, it may not yet be an "it." Of course my hope is that this abstract preview will not be its epitaph but part of a fructive matrix.[7]

---

[7] 1993. The novel never became the envisaged "it." It swelled, it diminished, it swelled again. Many trials, many errors, a few successes. Finally, I found what I thought was a way of making it. The result, *Shares. A Novel in Ten Pieces*, is supposed to "suggest" rather than be a complete novel. Yet it is not a novella. Only three readers whom I know think that it succeeds. (I am not one of them.)

[60]

THE NOVELIST ON HIS WORK:
A PARTIAL AUTOBIOGRAPHY[1]

You have, as I understand it, been considering the role of the Jew in contemporary fiction, both as subject and as writer. Jews should perhaps subdue their joyous pride[2] at the astonishingly disproportionate place they have occupied on the world scene in the past century, for it is of course fatally easy to exempt oneself from activity by pointing to the success of those with whom one identifies. But who, Jew or non-Jew, can be anything but amazed at the prominence of Jews in the twentieth-century worlds of intellect, art, and affairs? Everyone aware of his own partial identity as a Jew considers in his personal development the large measures of possibility to which these men point. And today a Jew who is a writer, particularly a writer of fiction, no longer measures fellow Jewish writers by the touching but sporadic brilliance of a parochial literature, but by the books of perhaps the finest active writers of prose in the Western world. Even when the subject matter of a novel by Saul Bellow, Bernard Malamud, or to a somewhat lesser degree, Norman Mailer or J.D. Salinger is Jewish, the treatment of that matter is not private; it takes root not only in the minds of Jewish readers but in readers everywhere. Their achievement is comparable to that of the American Southern writers of the previous genera-

---

[1] A talk for a synagogue series on Jewish writers (about 1961). 1993. I leave this thirty-two year old piece. It was the way I thought and felt then. Later thoughts and feelings will show up in *Quickly, Quickly. A Sistermony*, the book I'm finishing now.

[2] Jewish modesty has a tough time of it in the tide of post-Hitlerian analysis of the "Jewish problem." One of the noblest analysts was Karl Barth:

We find it uncanny that the Jews live among us and move like shadows through world history with that unmatched historical permanence, yet without roots, without security; without roots because they are sustained by the free grace of God. . . . ("The Jewish Problem and the Christian Answer," *Against the Stream* [New York: Philosophical Library, 1954].)

tion and that of the nineteenth-century New England writers.

Any man who talks of work he presents to the public as an objective exhibition is somewhat presumptuous; for a writer whose work has an almost nonexistent public, the presumption is immense. Nonetheless, the twentieth-century public has been intrigued as much by the process of creation as by its results. As more and more of the human interior has been mapped, interest in the man whose strength consists in his ability to exhibit his own weaknesses is as great as it used to be in those men of an earlier age whose greater deeds were not accounted for by their perversities. The saints and heroes have yielded the stage to what Kirkegaard in *Fear and Trembling* called the least of the three types of significant men, the witness, the artist-writer whose significance consists in abstention from the action he reports and endurance in the publication of diaries, letters, autobiographies, notes, first drafts, and numerous other droppings from creative lives.

"Autobiography" is a fairly new word; according to the New English Dictionary it was coined in 1809 by Robert Southey.[3] Of course, there were many books written by men about themselves before Southey's day, but the invention of the term does bespeak an increased self-consciousness of the art, practice, and significance of writing about oneself. By the end of the nineteenth century, autobiography, either unadorned or in more or less fictional form, was very common and the subject of quite a number of essays, the most famous of which may be Sir Leslie Stephen's in the Cornhill magazine in April 1881. The famous progenitor of the *Dictionary of National Biography* and Virginia Woolf wrote:

> The autobiographer has ex officio two qualifications of supreme importance in all literary work. He is writing about a topic in which he is keenly interested, and about a topic upon which he is the highest living authority. It may be reckoned, too, as a special felicity that an autobiography, alone of all books, may be more valuable in proportion to the amount of misrepresentation it contains.

---

[3] Southey was the poet whom Lord Byron fixed in acid with the epigram "Southey will be read when Homer is forgotten, but not until then." In 1830 he was again the victim of comic savagery when Macaulay reviewed his *Sir Thomas More; or Colloquies on the Progress and Prospects of Society*. This may be the most brilliantly funny, destructive book review in the language.

I suppose that Sir Leslie meant by the last sentence that when one knows how a man lies and what he lies about, one knows something special about his needs and character.

I do not propose to lie here, perhaps because I am not going to unload a full autobiography on you. I restrict myself to the way my writing may have been affected by my being a Jew. If it turns out that I discuss work too inconsiderable to be called even minor, I can only plead that nearly as much can be learned about rocketry from an analysis of the missile which melts on its own launching pad as from one which joins the universe's own comets.

2

Every case is special, so I will not begin my description of the assemblage and launching—or attempted launching—of my work by pleading my difference from other Jewish writers of our day (as if they could be lumped together as a cake on which I preened as the birthday candle). Yet my case is quite different from those of the Jewish writers whom I know, and these include the most brilliant, Saul Bellow (probably the most important prose fiction writer now active), Bernard Malamud (the finest bloom of the parochial school), and Norman Mailer. I am going to approach my "case" via Rilke's poem "Archaic Torso of Apollo":

> We'll never see that wonderful head
> in which the eye-fruit ripened, but the
> body glows like a candelabrum
> where, way down deep, the glance, retained,
> shines. Otherwise the curve of the chest
> wouldn't blind you, the soft spin
> in the loins couldn't shift smiles
> into the genitals which hang there;
> otherwise the stone would seem defaced,
> a lucent plunge from the shoulders,
> not aflame like the coats of wild animals,
> not bursting out of its borders
> like a star: for there's no place that
> doesn't see you. You must change your life.

This poem applies to me in the following way: my work is the headless torso which in some fashion glows the way the eyes of a head glow. My Jewishness—so attenuated a fact in my life and

[386]

consciousness—I analogize to the lost head of the poem. Perhaps the Jewishness is the source of the glow. Who knows the source? Here is a book [*Golk*] which unlike many of the works of writers I've mentioned does not deal with a Jewish scene or background, yet it may well be that there is much in it that can be thought Jewish in quality, in tone, in things which its author—less than anyone—can see.

A reader may caution me at this point about the subject matter of *Golk*. Aren't two of the leading characters, Hondorp and his father, Jewish? I have to give a peculiar answer, namely "Probably." I say "probably' because on looking over the novel, not while I was writing it but after, it occurred to me that Poppa Hondorp is—*of course*—a Jew. A character in fiction is not like you or me a composite of many identities. I am a teacher, a Jew, a native New Yorker, a father, homeowner, Ph.D., a bad tennis player, big eater, a member of this, writer of that, etcetera. You may be a Chicagoan, Anglophile, Methodist, plumber, wife beater, Elk, stamp collector, manic-depressive, and so on. A character in a novel or story exists only in those identities for which the author needs him, although the author may also be filling in other identities which are not important to his scheme but more important than he may know at the time to the energy of his work. Now for Poppa Hondorp I wanted (1) someone who was a fanatically devoted and domineering father, (2) someone who was maniacally absorbed in television, (3) a comic prop whose growing deformity—a lipoma—would be a laugh every time it showed up and thus could be used to vary the tone of episodes, and (4) a man who so much wanted something that its not being granted him by his son would be a telling point against that son. These are Poppa Hondorp's functions as seen in retrospect by his inventor. That he has an accent which I think of as a German Jewish one is due to my desire to achieve an effect of warmth, for my own literary standard is both near and far enough from Henry James's so that what James in the New York ghetto called "the torture-rooms of the living idiom" is for me at least a source of comic warmth.

At any rate, as far as characters are concerned and as far as the narrative idiom is concerned, my novel is not Jewish. In what ways if any, then, is it Jewish and can it be identified as the work of a Jew? I had best preface an answer by saying what my own status as a Jew is, and see if I can draw from the novel certain characteristics which may be related to that status.

[387]

I suppose that I knew I was a Jew about the time I knew I was an American, which was probably a few years after I knew I was a boy. Yet my Jewish-consciousness has been an impoverished one. I went but a little while to Sunday school; I was not "bar-mitzva-hed," and although I more or less respected things Jewish as a boy, there was no tradition I observed which was Jewish except staying home one day for Yom Kippur and Rosh Hashanah. This impover-ished Jewishness was part of the atmosphere in which I and almost all of my friends lived. In my own case, I can only ascribe it, first, to that paternal grandfather who was orphaned early in Austria and who spent much of his energy getting to America and making his way in the world and, second, to a maternal grandfather who was an assimilated German whose energies were also largely devoted to being "comfortable." Jewishness, like hair color, was an accepted part of our house, but though it was more important than that physi-cal trait insofar as it helped shape, say, the liberal politics of my father, I cannot see that it particularly enlarged my own religious, intellectual, or moral consciousness. When I went to the University of North Carolina, I was sixteen, and there, happy in a very differ-ent sort of environment, I became both conscious of my Jewishness and afraid of it. I did not join a fraternity because at that time I did not wish to be thought of as a Jew more than, say, someone from the North. I also tugged at my past to the extent of being attracted by manners, habits and characteristics which did not seem "Jewish" to me. Although I always had Jewish friends, my closest friends then, both men and women, were not Jewish. By the time I graduat-ed from college and went to work in a number of places around the country, I had lost most of my self-conscious embarrassment about Jewishness. I was now so involved in other things that it was almost never a factor in my life, and when it was, I accepted it as a minor, even a comforting fact. In part I attributed what I thought of as my artist's disposition to the displacement from ordinary life which being a Jew allowed me, just as I attributed my distaste for what I thought of as the mundane affairs of my family to my artist's disposition. I liked being an outsider, not a penalized but a glam-orous one, and my three years in France and Germany as a college lecturer and government worker were in part consistently pleasur-able because I enjoyed my identification as that least penalized of outsiders of the early 1950's, the American Abroad. When I came back from Europe in the spring of 1952, I came back to become a writer and professor.

My early writing was done under the influence of those fiction writers who had been established as The Masters by such textbooks as Brooks and Warren's *Understanding Fiction*. The principles of such writers are (1) to secure your effects with a polished style, (2) to integrate all the materials of your story, and (3) to suspend the meaning of the story in the action as "naturally" as orange bits in jello. I wrote about ten stories between 1952 and 1954, more or less under such guiding principles, but more and more I was dissatisfied with the results and with some of the principles behind them. In 1957 I started the novel *Golk*. This novel was written in the midst of writing another novel which I'd been working on since 1952 or 1953.[4] A month or so after I actually started writing the new novel, I met Saul Bellow, who at that time was writing his novel *Henderson, the Rain King,* the first of his long works which was not about a Jew. Now Bellow did a number of things for me: his own energies and regal view of the writer's life helped confirm my pass across the borders of well-tailored fiction. Although *Golk* may still be thought of as a careful book as far as construction goes, its freedom seems big to me, and its explicitness and occasionally rich prose seem to me to stand for fictional liberty. Bellow did more as well, although he had started to do that before I'd met him. He was the first major American novelist who was a Jew, and it seemed to me that his books were already as good as Hemingway's and the other American idols of my literary Pantheon. Of course, my favorite of all novelists, Proust, was a half-Jew, but Proust, like Tolstoy or Dante, is a man too great to be of help to other writers. If anything, such men hinder you as a writer as much as they help you as a man. But of the second rank, of a rank that might just possibly yield a Proust, Bellow was someone who spoke intimately to me about his work and plans. Now his life was much closer to a traditional Jewish life than mine was, and I learned from him some of the convolutions of that life and its language—Yiddish—a language from which I had been cut off by assimilation. As I met other Jewish writers, notably Malamud and Mailer, and got to know my colleague at the University of Chicago, Philip Roth, I became conscious of my place not as a Jewish writer but as a writer who was also a Jew even though his material had never been explicitly Jewish. Now there were and are dangers here: think of yourself as a member of a school and you'll flunk out; think of yourself, or

---

[4] *Europe, or Up and Down with Baggish and Schrieber* (New York: McGraw-Hill, 1961).

rather forget yourself, and do your job, and you may come to something. At no point did I seriously consider writing a work which would spring not from my feelings but from a school of fictional fish. I have written only one story[5] in which a leading character is specifically a Jew, and that's because the character's life is determined by his Jewishness. (He's a refugee from Nazi Germany.) If I look at *Golk* now to find out in what way it might be "Jewish," I'm stumped. Perhaps such scenes as the knockdown fight—or as it turns out, apparent fight—between Hendricks and Golk can be classed with others in "Jewish" fiction. One scene in the book was spurred by Bellow after he read the first version of the book, the scene in which Hendricks and Hondorp have it out before they separate. Before I wrote the Bellovian version of that scene, the breakoff between them was oblique and muted. Now they yell at each other, and the atmosphere is what I think of as Russian—open, frank, or to the point here, Jewish. Anything else? Perhaps. People have noted a certain coldness about the characters in the book, people who do not regard me as a particularly cold fish. There is, I think, a reason for this, perhaps a Jewish reason.

There are Jews who accept and Jews who deny. Marx, Freud and Trotsky are famous examples of denying Jews. In literature Mailer is one whose coldness may stand in part for a rejection of Jewish schmaltz. Much as I consciously deny this denial in my own work or life, something tells me this is my case. Hondorp is a conscientious denial of that notorious warmth and marvelous tradition of ethical accountability which I think of as Jewish. For me, there is perhaps a ray of hope: at the end of *Golk* Hondorp renounces his chilly way.

Perhaps I too, in my way, am renouncing my denial. At least I am now writing a book[6] which is about a man who is trying to reclaim what he has thrown away; and I am having emotional trouble with the book. My agent says that it doesn't sound like me. A colleague says that it is a sentimental book. I know something is wrong, but I have a feeling that I am both going to continue and to pull myself up to the tone I want without faking it.

But one never knows. In the Rilke poem it says that if the body did not glow with the power reserved for the head, the statue

---

[5] 1993. There have been more since.

[6] *In Any Case.*

wouldn't seem to burst out of its borders like a star. In German this goes

> und bräche nicht aus allen seinen Rändern
> aus wie ein Stern

Stern meaning "star." I shall conclude by saying that this *Stern* feels there's some chance he could not have broken out of his literary borders if the glow of his Jewish past had not somehow or other been transferred into the body of his work.

[61]

ON REPRINTING GOLK

Phoenix Books is living up to its name in republishing this novel thirty years after I began writing it a few blocks from where I'm writing this now in Hyde Park, Chicago. I began the book in April, 1957 and finished it nine months later. It's the only book of whose writing dates I'm sure. My son Andrew was getting born that summer, and I felt a connection between the two gestations.

I'd been writing short stories; a novel was a big leap. (The novel may be short but looked immense to me.) There were pains as well as pleasures in opening up, letting go, inventing more or less ad lib, sending people anywhere I wanted. What relief, what freedom. Short stories in my writing blood, I wasn't worried about closure or shape. (Then.) My big problem was discipline of another kind: the long form called for a different sort of energy. To get it, I remember forcing myself to stay up every night until I'd written at least four pages. I sometimes woke at 4:00 am, head on the typewriter.

Does this show? I still can't chance finding out. I haven't reread the book in twenty years, don't dare discover it's not what I hope.

Books come out of many things. I remember a few which fed *Golk*. The most obvious is Allen Funt. I'd first heard his spontaneous "sketches" on the radio. (Candid Mike.) Then he made movie shorts. Don Justice remembers my laughing so hard at one that I fell into the aisle of an Iowa City theater. (I remember the sequence, a lady buying flowers from a Broadway florist, the ubiquitous Funt, who played it fairly straight because the lady was a natural comedian.)

What interested me about Funt's show—something other than being amused by it—was Funt's gift for discovering the gift and power of "amateurs." There was something god-like about this.

Out of it came my protagonist, Hondorp, the "golk", because I felt power should be approached gradually. I thought of three books which did this: *The Sun Also Rises, Anna Karenina*, and its parent, *Madame Bovary*. An image for it was looking at the sun by way of a reflector.

As for Hondorp and his father, their relationship was a burlesque version of my father to his father and mine to him. I believe that all the other characters were invented out of the unassignable material of such invention, although I also remember certain programmatic controls. So the plan was to subvert conventional associations. There'd be no "drunken Irishmen" or "tight Scotsmen" in the book except for outright farce. (The subversion of the character Hendricks was secured by *The Second Sex* and *Lamiel*.)

Then there was television, new in my life back then and felt as its power is felt in those first weeks (like a hick's first week in New York). Poppa Hondorp became *homo televisionus*. Inventing comic turns around him was one of the pleasures of writing.

2

When I first published stories in 1953 and '54 (in the *Western* and *Kenyon Reviews*), editors wrote to ask if I were working on a novel. I wasn't, but said I was and started right up. I worked from one of the short stories, "The Sorrows of Captain Schreiber," joined it to several others and tried making good connections among them. In 1957, I was stuck. Only after I finished *Golk* did I see how to bring off the other book, *Europe, or Up and Down with Baggish and Schreiber*. *Golk* was comparatively easy. When I finished it, my agent, Candida Donadio, sent it to the editors who'd written me. All turned it down, some with praise, some with suggestions for revision. In all, eighteen publishers rejected the book. It wasn't until the summer of 1959—I was in Weekapaug, Rhode Island— that I heard Candida tell me over the phone that Sydney Phillips of Criterion Books had accepted it.

Criterion was a small house with—what was called—"a distinguished list." Phillips's friends were *Partisan Review* editors and writers; his closest friends were Jackson Pollock and Clement Greenberg. His list was made up of books I treasured, among them one of my favorites, *The Collected Stories of Isaac Babel*. His senior editor, Murray McCain, had fallen for *Golk*, and it was Murray who saved it when Criterion went belly-up the week it was published. Murray was—is?—smart, energetic, gentle and courteous; he greatly impressed my dear wasp in-laws who had not made very much of me.

Criterion was counting on *Golk* and its other spring book, Leslie Fiedler's *Love and Death in the American Novel*, to pull it out of the drink. Too late. Murray hand-carried *Golk* up and down New York. He wrote a hundred letters to editors around the country. What attention the book got was due to him. (Wherever he is, I thank him again.) The book was reviewed widely, not always well. The *Times Book Review* gave it to a television producer who'd written "a television novel"; he didn't make much of it. In Chicago, the papers and local programs made a fuss because "a professor had written a dirty book." It may have sold five thousand copies.

When it came out a year or two later in England, the reviews were exceptionally good. Penguin reprinted it, and Aaron Asher's fine new series, Meridian Books, reprinted it here. There were Italian and Danish translations, and it was scooped up by the new critical rubric, "black humor."

All this seems fairly remote, as does the interest taken in it by movie comedians—I remember Steve Allen and Alan Arkin—who talked of making a film of it. Here they ran into a wall. The wall was Funt.

When I was finishing the book, I wrote him a letter telling him I'd enjoyed his show so much I'd written a book about a program based on it. He wrote—or called—to say he was excited about that, he was looking for a script about the program, could I send him the manuscript when I finished it? (This was a year or two before his program went national and became the country's most popular.) Candida was against his seeing it. She said he had a reputation as a very tough cookie; she felt he should be ignored; the book wasn't really about him or his work: why make trouble? I wanted him to read it, though. I thought he'd be amused at what I'd made of what he'd made. He and Candida made arrangements: he was allowed to see the manuscript for twenty-four hours. He came into New York, took a room at the Pennsylvania Hotel, and read the manuscript overnight. The next day I got a phone call from him. It began: "This is going to be one of the hardest calls I've ever made." My heart skidded across the room. I thought, "He's going to make trouble. Candida was right." He went on, "You got into my brain. I've never had an experience like this. Richard, you seem like a nice fellow, why do you have to write about such awful people? Baudelairean people." The adjective was more surprising than his feelings about the characters, though that too surprised me. (I liked them.) Anyway, the point for Funt, the "hardness," was that he could never in a million years base a film on such a book.

What a relief. I didn't give a damn about a film, especially one made by Funt. (I respected him, but we worked different sides of the street.)

Criterion's lawyer drafted a letter for Funt to sign. He called me up, read me the jargon-heavy letter and said he couldn't sign it. I said, "I don't blame you. How about this?" and rolled out a sentence or two which took account of his wish that no film be made until he'd made his own. In return for that, he'd do nothing to interfere with the book's publication. Funt signed it, and that was that.

Or almost. Fifteen or twenty years later, he called and asked where the statement "we" signed was. I didn't correct the "we." (I'd signed nothing.) Nor did I ask if Funt had heard that someone wanted to film it. Every once in a while, such rumors drifted my way. Nothing ever happened. I suspected that people had heard that Funt might make trouble. That didn't trouble me. For me, the chief good of a film would have been further interest in the book.

I didn't like, though, remarks Funt made about me which were reported in a profile published in *The New Yorker*. He'd said that this Chicago professor had done him in after he'd given him all this help with the book. I wrote him angrily about that. He wrote back gently saying I wasn't to pay attention to anything *The New Yorker* said. Decent enough advice. I preferred to remember the Funt who'd given me hours of pleasure.[1]

---

[1] In November 1991, he called again. He couldn't find his copy of the book, could I send him one? I referred him to the Phoenix reprint. He called a few days later to say he'd bought it, I'd be hearing from him soon. As of May 1, 1993, I haven't.

[62]

GAPS

A Rilke sonnet begins "How far it is between stars / But the gaps are even larger way down here."

1) February, 1987. A train going from Shanghai to Wuxi. My wife, Alane Rollings, and I, sit in the "soft berth" coach on old green and yellow upholstery, a lacy fern in a blue vase on the table beside a thermos of tea and two cups. There are a dozen people in the coach, mostly foreigners. A gray day with gleams of silver. We pass muddy farms, people in fields, paddies with green shoots, court-yards of wooden houses where children chase each other, then the enormous Yangtzee, a freighter unloading at a pier. At a barred crossing, bicyclists and a loaded cart wait for the train to pass. The cart is pulled by a man stretched almost horizontal by the strain; a leather thong on his forehead bears much of the weight; his mouth is bared to gritting teeth. Our eyes meet; his register nothing I can make out. He seems a flesh extension of the cart.

2) September, 1987. An office on Sunset Boulevard, Los Angeles. My cousin has made an appointment for me with one of Hollywood's "most literate agents." It's hot. The agent is amiable, apologetic, thirtyish, dressed like a teenager in jeans and sport shirt. On the walls, clients' books in multiple copies. He asks about my work. I tell him about books that have been optioned by movie peo-ple and about one which I think might make an interesting film. 'It's about someone whose life is a bit like Ezra Pound's." He asks, "Who's Ezra Pound?"

3) Chicago, Spring 1985. I'm having lunch with an up-and-coming television newscaster. [1] I want to do an article on the odd, one-way relationship between viewers and those they view. The broadcaster is blonde, blue-eyed, bright, candid. She's telling me about her family of sisters all living near each other in the town in which they were raised. I say she makes them sound like something out of Jane

---

[1] Deborah Norville.

Austen. A square of blankness fills her beautiful eyes.

4) Chicago, November, 1988. I'm in a municipal courtroom ready to testify against one of the two young men who broke into our house last summer, ate, drank, went around with candles dripping green wax on rugs and couches, emptied drawers and took off with what they thought saleable before being spotted and caught by the police. I look at the young man. (The other has broken bond.) He is solid, tight-haired, dark, impassive, dressed in a sport shirt, jeans and sneakers, much like the twenty other young black men who have been before the bench this morning. I lean forward to draw his look to mine. I succeed: he looks at me. My look says, "I'm the person into whose house you broke, whose food you ate, whose typewriters, television set and father's watch you stole." His look says, "You are a white nothing. I took you once and will again."

5) Chicago. Spring, 1989. I work with a small class of men and women aged 18-22. It's a relaxed, free-wheeling group; we have a certain amount to tell each other. I have learned about "death chicks" (girls who talk of suicide as a "life-style") and such sub-groups of "Punk" as "Death" and "Gothic." I hear about such bands as The Bauhaus. I ask if they know about the original Bauhaus Group. They don't, and I tell them about Gropius, Klee and Mies van der Rohe. I mention the "little madeleine" episode in Proust's novel. None has heard of it, so I promise to read it to them. I tell them of Joyce, of Rimbaud, of Vietnam, of Twain and James. It is my job.

Every year it's harder; the gap between what we know seems wider. Some of this is inevitable, but a small fear trembles in me that this gap's a gulf. "Just the door ajar that oceans are." Too much about television programs, rock bands, singers, drugs. Most read a lot also, but here they are late starters and show less ability to distinguish excellence from—what I think trash. I tell myself that mine is the standard complaint of age, but then don't convince myself. Which is the scariest gap of all.

[63]

AN OLD PROFESSOR SPEAKS

I write this at the end of April, 1990, a few minutes after reading a proposal to establish a Humanities Institute at the university I've taught at for thirty-five years, the University of Chicago. The proposers

> believe that humanistic learning is going through a period of fundamental transformation . . . [with the] outpouring of new models, theories, research questions, technologies and archival materials . . . The humanities are, in the words of Thomas Kuhn, undergoing a 'scientific revolution' that does not merely 'advance' learning in a linear, quantitative fashion, but transfigures the questions we ask and the objects to which we address them . . . Words like 'text,' 'author,' 'representation' and 'intention' that could, a few years ago, be taken for granted, are now undergoing fundamental rethinking, in both theory and practice.

For what it's worth, my own life as a professor and writer of stories, novels, poems and essays has been a "prerevolutionary" one. The Proposal tells me that the revolution has been going on for twenty-five years, During these years, I have worked at writing stories about largely invented characters, stories charged with as much mental brio as I could summon up at the time of invention or revision. I don't much favor the notion that I was writing texts; to me texts suggest matter for a limited audience of students, scholars or parishioners.

As a professor, I spent much time, of course, with students and scholars. I thought my chief job there was to evoke in students the same love for the books we read, as I had. This involved all sorts of things: a close reading of the book so that most of us would be reading it more or less the same way, that is, the way our common sense of the words and their relationship to the conventions of life and literature led us; a study of the context in which the book was

[398]

written, so that many of the juices which flowed in its original audience might flow in us; a study of questions which flowed from the book, its relationship to the author's other work, the relationship of the work to other works and the relationship of the work to the shape and meaning of our attitudes, our feelings, our lives. Almost always I felt that I was engaged in highminded work, work that was as meaningful as any I could imagine. I felt that my students would be able to have experiences which were deeper, higher, finer than they had known before, that their lives would be touched, and perhaps transfigured, by sublimity, that they would themselves be able to tell others of these sublime experiences, and that they and all those to whom they talked about them would constitute a sort of society within society, a reasonably benevolent, reasonably beneficent, minority.

I knew, of course, that my own knowledge, experience and intelligence were small, but I hoped it was clear to my students that what I was doing was but a sample job of work; there was a much bigger and juicier pie outside my classroom, and they should head for it. I hoped I displayed my limits in showing which works I preferred. To students I suggested certain other books, professors and procedures which travelled other roads, to other fountains of artistic bliss.

I had another serious job of work, in and out of class. It had to do with the use of the language itself. I told students that even if we weren't capable of supplying artistic bliss ourselves, we were obliged to talk, and particularly to write about it in an attractive way. "You don't go to a great feast with filth caking your hands and clothes, because you would disgust others if not yourself and ruin their pleasure if not your own." Teaching students to write coherently, clearly and concisely has been increasingly difficult. Part of the reason for the difficulty is, I believe, the revolution about which the proposal for the Chicago Humanities Institute speaks.

Does this revolution make the tasks which have occupied so much of my life superfluous? It would be too easy to accept the sentimental response to this question: how can the transmission of the sublime and the writing of stories be superfluous?

Most people, including those who write and teach books "in the new way," like most of us, are at their best when their intellects and spirits are fully engaged[1] in interesting tasks. It is the task which interests many of these new scholars which has changed, for many reasons, one of which, of course, is that the world has changed, that certain things which were ignored can no longer be ignored.

My tasks were those of an interpreter, a stage director. A more or less unique intelligence had created something which needed to be transmitted. You believed in the fineness of the work, and you did everything in your power to transmit it as you understood it.

Many of the new tasks are quite different. Though the work may be regarded as more or less the product of an exceptional intelligence, the work and the intelligence are seen as parochial. The work treats certain things, it does not treat others. It reflects the equities and inequities of its time in its conventions, its vocabulary, its meanings, its meters and rhythms. To treat the work without acknowledging its defects is to be naive, and to be naive is to perpetuate its inequities. The text is a subset of an author, an author a subset of his or her time, and there is no excuse for being ignorant of these facts. The reader, too, is a creature of his time, his situation, his parochial nurture. Every reader not only reacts to a text in ways which are similar, he reacts to texts in ways which are different. Texts about subjects close to your prejudices or your heart are the most obvious example of this. Everyone must learn how to spell out a special understanding of the text. Our understanding of the variety of the approach is what links us together as a society within a society. We will be a less naive, less gullible society, ready to spot the devices of seduction which paralyze our intelligence and administer or perpetuate inequities. A text's devices, a text's omissions, are of great importance. The student is no longer the interpreter of the text, he is its policeman, its judge, its rival. The old relationship, in which the audience sat in the dark and the text was illuminated on a raised stage, no longer obtains. No longer is the professor the virtuoso performer or the inspired preacher, drawing on the sacred text for his inspiration. We are all on the stage together, rather like the people in the recent revolutions in Eastern Europe, calling out as inspiration gripped them, and, if they had a powerful voice or access to a microphone, getting heard, and helping form the revolution on the spot.

As these democratic revolutions have their crises of authority, so does the humanistic revolution. The democratic revolutions call

---

[1] *Docere est opus activae vitae.* (Teaching is the work of an active life.) Thomas Aquinas. *Summa Theologica*, II. 11

forth certain figures tested by their resistance to the powers that jailed them. So the humanistic revolution has drawn first on old professorial practitioners to be its gurus and shamans. The democratic revolutions have their slogans and phrases, the humanistic revolutions—because they are revolutions of language—have new vocabularies and analytic techniques as well as slogans.

It's interesting that revolutions for redistribution or realignment of power frequently develop habits, vocabularies and institutions which create schisms and estrangements. So the rise of general literacy led to a contempt for the newly literate masses, and to intellectual formations, publications and institutions from which they were excluded. As John Carey wrote in a recent *Times Literary Supplement*, "Intellectuals believe in giving the public what intellectuals want. That is what an intellectual means by education." A group of undergraduate majors is not "the public," but at a recent meeting on undergraduate curriculum for English majors, I had the impression the undergraduate was regarded like a goose in Gascony—something to be stuffed until a certain organ— his "major"—swells into proper material for intellectual *foie gras*.

In some ways it is unfair to indict the thoughtful men and women who are one's colleagues with such a charge. One risks sounding like Ronald Reagan's Education Secretary, William Bennett, whose bully manner in his bully pulpit adulterated his charge that humanistic scholars had forfeited their responsibility as teachers and were intoxicated with intellectual fads.

The richer a culture, the more fads, the more groups, the more elites, the more specialties there will be. It's like an immense oak tree, with branches begetting smaller branches, yet the whole seeming, to an outsider, a marvel of natural architecture and splendiferous foliage. Here is where both the writer and the intellectual faddist coining his vocabulary for his own group are, in a sense, allied. The artist counts to the extent that he finds a way of expressing what has never before been expressed in his way. The further his individual expression is from the common expression of the time, the more he'll need the assistance of a group of supporters who understand his novelty, usually having been trained to understanding by the writer himself. The Joyce of *Ulysses* and *Finnegans Wake*, the Rilke of *The Duino Elegies* and his coterie of sympathetic women, the Eliot of *The Waste Land*, with Pound as his flugelman, the Proust who wrote reviews of his own book and who educated his

[401]

friends in its complexities, are examples of cult artists who became culture heroes.

It has been more natural for artists to become part of common life than their intellectual counterparts. The artists work with the situations and emotions of common life. The intellectual cultist deliberately estranges himself from common life, even when he is crying against the inequities of old elites, say, the "belletrists" who "unselfconsciously sustain traditional hierarchies, traditional, social and cultural exclusions."[2] As these intellectuals frequently examine their own procedures and methods, their debate is internal, and feeds on itself. If common life is the trunk of the tree, they are far up in a distant branch.

Or that is the way it seems when they begin. But it comes about that they can turn the educational wheel—no point in continuing the arboreal metaphor—and have a powerful influence on the direction of society. Fortunately, in humanistic revolutions, interests change, vocabularies stale, fashion alters. If there is puzzlement about where to go, it usually returns to the center. And that center is common life and those beautiful works which have shaped, interpreted and transfigured it.

I have briefly and metaphorically described some of what is happening in the profession I've practiced for over forty years. Now I'll end with some questions for the new revolutionaries.

1) Is there a fit substitute for the artistic bliss which both carried us individually and bound us as a group? (The response may be that the excitement of group practice, the wielding of a special vocabulary, the pointing out of old inequities is exciting enough to carry us individually and bind us together.)

2) Is the general excitement of the revolutionary sect a substitute for fusion with a fine work of literary art?

3) Is the revolutionary guru an adequate substitute for the great artist?

4) Is the old hierarchy of great artist, professorial interpreter and student intrinsically bad?

5) Will we still need poems, stories and novels?

6) If so, will they be written? (If authors are no longer honored and books are to be seen more as collections of omissions than vital

---

[2] George Levine, Peter Brooks, Jonathan Culler, Margerie Garber, E. Ann Kaplan and Catherine Stimpson, *Speaking for the Humanities, published by the American Council of Learned Societies.*

presences, will authors have sufficient incentive to write? Or is the group expected to write poems as well as manifestoes?)

Coda 1: There is much good to be said about our new Alexandrian Age of criticism, but I believe that I and my kind will die without access to the bliss of the great works of art, transmitted more or less as they have been transmitted, in East and West, for most of recorded history.

Coda 2: January, 1993. I just read my colleague Gerald Graff's book on debates about multi-culturalism, political correctness and other agitations in the American university (*Beyond the Culture Wars*, W. W. Norton, 1992). It's a sensible counter to recent hysteria about the ruination of the university and its students. Graff says that the methodological debates flow from important cultural changes. He suggests that making the conflicts explicit in team-taught courses would free the students from the confusion of the universities' "cafeteria curriculum."

This makes some sense to me, although I think professorial debate, whether it's bellicose or deferential, will succeed only if the debaters are first-rate teachers. Despite Graff's uneasiness about curricula based on "virtuoso" professors or "inspired" teachers, I remain convinced that the best way of transmitting the sublimity of fine work is the course-long interplay between such teachers and their—one hopes—inspired students.

I was shocked to read that Graff himself was in his late teens before anything but sports books and magazines meant anything to him. He associated reading books with being a sissy. ("I disliked and feared books.") Graff, was roused from his unbookish sleep when an instructor in American literature discussed the critical controversy about the last part of *Huckleberry Finn:*

> It was a revelation to me that famous authors were capable not only of mistakes, but of ones that even lowly undergraduates might be able to point out . . . I gained confidence from recognizing that my classmates and I had had thoughts that, however stumbling our expression of them, were not too far from the thoughts of famous published critics. I went back to the novel again, and to my surprise found myself rereading it with an excitement I had never felt before with a serious book. Having the controversy over the ending in mind, I now

had some issues to watch out for . . . [This] made it possible not only to concentrate, as I had not been able to do earlier, but to put myself in the text—to read with a sense of personal engagement that I had not felt before. Reading the novel with the voices of the critics running through my mind, I found myself thinking of things that I might say about what I was reading . . .

In his *New York Times* review of the book (December 21st, 1992, C-16), Christopher Lehmann-Haupt wrote that this account worried him. He wondered "if Mr. Graff is capable of reading books for the stories they tell rather than the issues they raise. After all, in the greatest works of literary art, political issues cancel one another out."

I don't believe that "political issues cancel one another out" in works of art,[3] nor did I *worry* about Jerry's autobiography. I was, however, astounded at it. I've read and told stories to three, four and five year olds, and watched them totally enchanted by what they were hearing. I remember the same enchantment listening to my father tell bedtime stories, and when I learned to read, I was so "over-excited" by the fairy tales I took out of the library that my mother tried forbidding me to go there. So I've thought delight in stories was universal. Could it be that some people are "tone-deaf" to them? Graff's claim is that some are. If so, I suppose those of them who are intelligent might come to "enjoy literature" through such indirections as intellectual controversy. (After all, the great Helen Keller was able to appreciate something of the beauty of song by putting her hands on the singer's vibrating throat.)[4]

---

[3] They are vital parts of a larger whole.

[4] The day after I wrote this I asked Jerry Graff about his pre-school feelings for literature. As I should have expected, his mother read him nursery rhymes and tales and he was "a great fan" of *Let's Pretend*, a radio program which featured story-telling.

[64]

THE WRITER ABROAD

Some of my pals spend much happy time at conferences. The scholar pals read and discuss papers at scholarly conferences; the writers exchange flattery at writers' conferences, read their own work and the work of ambitious writers, young, middle-aged, ancient. I've been invited to very few conferences and have attended fewer. In June, 1982, there was a rare and scarcely resistible invitation to a conference in Rome, sponsored by UNESCO and the Italian Ministry of Foreign Affairs. The conference had to do with the fate of Italian literature in the United States. On June 1, I flew to Rome and taxied to the American Academy, the site of the conference.

Every expedition forms itself in several ways. For the attentive fiction writer and journal keeper, expedition-time bunches into themes. The taxi driver from the *Stazione Termini* to the Janiculum supplied the first one. A young, thick-necked, aggressively comic fellow, he was fond of very little. His chief antipathy was the Italian football team—the *Azzuri*—that was now on its way to Spain. They were, he said, certified losers, cripples who couldn't pass the ball to each other. It was clear that Italy was finished. In fact, Europe was finished. World football was in the hands of savages, the Africans and South Americans. For the next month and a half, I followed the fortunes of the *Azzuri*, watched them tie the Cameroonians in a hotel at Foligno and cheered their amazing victories over Brazil and Argentina in the knickknack store below our apartment in Campo Santa Margherita in Venice. The night they won the championship, I left a Gatsby-like party at the Hotel Cipriani on the Giudecca to go to San Marco and watch the town burst with joy.

It had been a summer of wars. Mrs. Thatcher and Prince Andrew took on Argentina over the 100,000 sheep in the Falkland Islands. Iranians and Iraqis killed thousands of each other in the hundred-

and-ten-degree heat along the Euphrates, and General "Caliban" Sharon risked the soul of Israel in his punitive strike beyond the announced forty kilometers of southern Lebanon toward the streets of Beirut.

While Tardelli, Rossi, and the other *Azzuri* practiced maneuvers in Madrid, and the armies lunged for each other's throats, I was ensconced on the first floor of the Villa Chiaraviglia across the street from the American Academy. In a bathing suit, I sat in the garden, feet up on a fallen classical capital, head shaded by cypress and oleander, drinking white wine. A couple of times a day, I dressed and walked up the hill to another villa, where the conference meetings were held. There, in hot rooms, Richard Wilbur talked about taking up translation as a relief from lyric poetry, Anthony Burgess—who, it turned out, shared a birthday with me—talked about the impossibility of translating *The Waste Land* into Malay, Italo Calvino described "every Italian writer's struggle" with the problem of language. The rest of us, poets, critics, novelists, translators, chimed in with our *interventi*. An Italian conference is organized like an opera. The main speakers sing the arias, and the minor ones sign up for the equivalent of recitative: interventions. There is little give-and-take. People do not face each other at a round table; everyone comes up to the front, faces the audience, and lets fly.

The audience consisted of well-bred, at least well-dressed and well-titled, people, in search of guests for their own parties. In the intermissions, there was much bowing, kissing, exclamatory recognition: *"Principessa." "Ammiraglio." "Ambasciatore." "Professsore."* There were also journalists, a few students, and some young scholars and painters from the American Academy. A speaker's success was judged by applause; the audience applauded most for anecdote, rhetoric, wit. My only success, a very small one, came when I told a Fernandel story about a whorehouse and a dentist.

One man held the conference together, supplied the connections between arias and interventions, made sense of everything, praised everything, touched all bases, massaged all egos. Diplomat (Italy's ambassador to UNESCO) and scholar (Ph.D. in Romance languages from the University of Chicago), he was one of those perfections with which Italy supplies the world. His clothes were a marvel, cuffs, flaps, lapels, and pockets so beautiful that even a clothes-blind slob like me thought of visiting a tailor. The Ambasciatore's black hair and pink nails, the gold of his cufflinks

[406]

and watch flickering through the hairs of his wrist, spoke more elo-
quently of art than any of our speeches. He summarized in English
and Italian. His French, too, was perfection, and one felt that if
Bulgarian, Finnish, or an African click language were needed, the
Ambasciatore would supply it. The only oddity was that his felici-
tous summaries omitted everything which interested me. Still,
never had banality sounded so beautiful.

In the evening, some of us went across the Tiber for dinner
under a golden moon in the Campiello Lancelotti. This was life.
And then there was the Pauline Chapel.

The third day I played hookey from the conference and went to
see the two great Michelangelos there, *The Conversion of Paul* and
The Crucifixion of Peter. Alone in the papal chapel with these stu-
pefying works, I never looked so hard at paintings or felt their
instruction so strongly. The painting about Peter was, I thought,
about the miserable consequences of human work. It is full of
picks, lances, hoes, rakes, and shovels. In its center is a magnificently carpentered upside-down cross to which Saint Peter is
nailed. (Still, his old head is raised, and his mouth is open, instruct-
ing, to the end, a group of mourners.) To the right, shivering in a
diaphanous garment, is—I think— Michelangelo. He's full of
despair. The despair is—I *knew*— of man's work, his work of tools
and weapons, of making and doing, of warfare, carpentry and,
eventually, the crucifixion of the Word.

The other painting centers on another old man, Paul. He's tum-
bled from his horse and is half-supported by a tough soldier. His
head has been struck with light. The light has come from the hand
of God at the top of the painting. Everything in the painting but
God's hand and Paul's face is closed. The soldiers' muscles are
taut, their faces are hidden; the hills are closed; a suit of armor
looks empty until you see an arm and hand coming out of it; the
horses' rumps face us. As for Paul's face, it is contorted with the
pain of conversion. God's work.

As the third—and only living—Jew in the chapel, I felt that
every would-be Pope should have to write an essay on these two
great—and final—paintings of Michelangelo.

Nothing at the conference came up to them. Though it was full
of delights. The last day, the Ambasciatore gave a marvelous lun-
cheon at his duplex penthouse in old Rome. I sat with Shirley
Hazzard, author of one of my favorite novels, *The Transit of Venus*,
and her delightful husband, Francis Steegmuller, whose book,
Flaubert and Madame Bovary, had spelled out for me the impor-

tance of artistic agony. On the Roman terrace there was none of that, though now and then helicopters flew close to our heads, and, down below, the streets were full of marchers and soldiers with submachine guns. (President Reagan was in town to see the Pope and President Pertini.) Above it all, we ate strawberries, quiche, prosciutto and melon, drank wine and told stories. I shook hands with my fellow *conférenciers* and walked Mary de Rachewilts to the apartment in which she was staying. She'd come up to me after one of my *interventi* and said "Do you remember me?" While I fought the cobwebs, she gave me a clue. "I last saw you in my father's house." Light broke. I kissed her. It was Pound's daughter, and I'd last seen her twenty years ago. Later that summer, my wife and I went to see her in her beautiful castle outside Merano, saw her children and grandchildren, the furniture Pound made, the history of China which he'd used for the *Cantos*, the antique farm equipment his grandson Walter collected for the little folk museum established in case a Communist government came to power and threatened their tax exemption.

I saw something else that summer. A few days after leaving Merano, we were driving out of Munich. We went to see the enormous palace of Nymphenburg, and then, driving out of that pink and white nightmare of symmetry, found ourselves on Dachaustrasse. Could it be? Yes, an actual street with the actual name. On the right was the Dachau Shopping Mall and there was the Dachau Housing Project. We began looking for signs to what was really Dachau, *echt* Dachau[1] and sure enough, small wooden plaques with arrows pointed us off the main streets and into a sort of suburban vacuum. A back road and here, a few kilometers outside of charming, *gemütlich* Munich, was a long long stretch of barbed wire, three or four strands of it with the dull damp thoughtless silver of suburban air showing through, and then, every couple

---

[1] 1992. I've since learned how much has gone on behind these shockingly innocent names. (See Tymothy Ryback, "Report from Dachau," The New Yorker, August 3, 1992.) When the Nazis selected an abandoned gun factory near Dachau as the site of the first concentration camp, they were to pin an invisible yellow star on its inhabitants that would not be easy to remove. The citizens of this 1200 year-old town have been trying to remove it for almost half century. They want the town remembered for its famous landscape and the painters who lived here (Corinth, Emil Nolde, Spitzweg), for the writers who were attracted to its artistic colony (Thomas Mann, Rilke), for its rejection of the National Socialist Party in the March 1933 election which preceded by a few weeks the establishment of that which has made the two syllables of its name an historic curse. This local struggle with memory is an intensification—a concentration—of what Germans of this half century know as the effort to "deal with the past" (*Vergangenheitsbewältigung*).

of hundred yards, a beautiful watchtower, bare with the two colors of Nymphenburg. A tremendous quiet. A quarter of a mile down was an entrance. No tickets required. Inside, a few buildings, and then bare acres. Not quite bare: there were eighty-foot-long rectangles filled with stones. Here the barracks had stood. One was preserved. We went in. Again, remarkable human carpentry. On the wall, a few pictures. The neat wooden bunks, stacked in empty perfection, were, in the pictures, packed with human beings. Heads, eyes, faces, limbs, human beings in striped jackets or bare to their fatless bodies. A washroom with wooden tubs, and was there a dining room? (I can't remember.) Past the rectangles was a stream with a bank of wildflowers. Beyond that was a grove with a lovely weeping willow, and then a kind of cottage, Hansel and Gretel style, except longer. On it were three chimneys. Inside were not one but three large ovens. Also a shower room. The sign said *Krematorium*. There was more. Memorials, Catholic, Protestant, Jewish, all beautiful and bare. On a dais a book, where many signed their name and wrote messages. A sculpture, humans caught in barbed wire; a museum. Here one saw a map of Europe. By a couple of hundred cities whose names spelled out the culture of the West were black squares with other names. I didn't know that so many cities had had these anti-cities, these death cities. Inside was the display of books and proclamations which charted the intellectual genealogy of insanity. It had all begun fairly reasonably, with some notion of purity and renewal. Then there were the photographs of what these notions had become, hills of bodies, the terrible faces of the lost, the faces of human beings in extremis, gouged, whipped, starved. Like a thousand thousand Grünewalds, Guernicas, or Francis Bacons, but art had not encompassed what's here. Only facts could, documents, black-and-white movies of the pits filled with bodies, eyes trying to escape their faces.

I knew, but didn't know. As I know now and don't know. Leaving, one tried to understand. Did the Michelangelo painting help? Only a little. It was too grand. It breathed redemption. This memorial did not breathe redemption.

A couple of weeks later, in some sort of reflex, I drove for the first time to Freiburg im Breisgau on the edge of the Black Forest. My mother's grandparents had come from here. Her father had been born here and had come to the States to marry his first cousin who'd been born in New York. I went to the beautiful, rebuilt City Hall (Red Army Faction slogans were sprayed on the walls) and asked if I could see the records of my great-grandparents. The

[409]

young archivist said they'd probably be in the cathedral. I said, "I doubt it. They were Jewish." "Ah," he said, flushing a bit. "I'm afraid that all the Jewish records were *vernichtet.*" *Vernichtet.* Nothinged. (Destroyed.) "I'm very sorry," he said.

He was a young man. It was not his fault. Perhaps one of his uncles had come in one day with an order to search out the records of local Jews and remove them from the files. Who understands the logistics of hatred? Did the pieces of paper infect those near them?

There was more to the summer which began with the *Azzuri* and the drive for the World Cup and went on through General Sharon's and the other wars, past the Michelangelos in the Pauline Chapel, but for me the summer ended there in this beautiful town on the edge of the forest where undoubtedly the men and women who'd passed their leg shapes and eye colors down to me had gone for walks and swims and bicycle rides, but had not left any paper trace of their births, marriages, and funerals.

[65]

STATEMENT FOR THE AMERICAN ACADEMY AND INSTITUTE OF ARTS AND LETTERS (MAY 15, 1985)

> ". . . a short statement on your work in which you might describe your working methods; plans for future project; your thoughts on the current award; autobiographical anecdotes; or any topic you find appropriate."

Work. It's unfair to call some of it work. Work is what you do. In the best times, something is done to, or within, or maybe even despite you. It often happens in that no-place hallway between sleep and waking.

Then there's the time of perfect liberty. Alone in the small room with the dictionaries, the typewriter, the shell ashtray, and the rectangle of Chicago sky, you leave all this for the Great Boundlessness. It's there you meet the choices which become your work.

That these choices have been so paltry is the worst disappointment of this retrospect. That all you've seen and felt and been, all that you've pretended to be, all that you've imagined, all the nuttiness and wildness have come to so little seems pathetic now. The inefficiency. The waste. The dumbness. The cemetery of pages. Typed, inked, penciled, arrowed, x'd, hexed, piled. Each other's tombs. (Yet kept, for who knows when you'll find a gold filling there.)

What isn't buried, what's on show, is a couple of thousand pages, a dozen books or so which testify as much to fatigue and abandonment as triumph. Awfully small potatoes for those thousands of hours in the field. (Was the soil punk or were you?)

The prize. Totally unexpected. Out of the unblue blue. Strange, beautiful, heartrending, disturbing. The last because you'd settled into a version of yourself which excluded such acknowledgment. You protected your vanity by telling yourself you'd renounced it.

Better to be an anchorite than a constantly rejected suitor. (After all, deep down, you knew you didn't deserve the girl.) What kept you going? The going itself, the pleasure of telling stories, of setting things straight, of praising, punishing, surprising, laughing and making *them* laugh and cry. Making sense and nonsense out of everything, disentagling life from bad words, making it clear in your words.

The prize has been given to some of the marble statues in your pantheon; yet you know there's nothing marble about you. Unless it's a mistake, a joke, you've got to deal with that. You look at biographies to see how the statues received the award. A bit surprising. In 1949, Thomas Mann wrote "Dear Archie" (MacLeish): "It has been said. . . that I, more than any other writer, consider myself 'worthy of any distinction, received from the contemporary world.' Nothing, dear Archie, can be farther from the truth. I've just muddled through. . ." and "This is the greatest honor my American colleagues. . . " and so on.

Dreiser, Auden, Odets, Hemingway, Huxley, O'Hara.

Hemingway's plane cracked up in Uganda, he'd read his obituaries, but, months shy of the summons from Stockholm, he's thrilled, delighted, enchanted, as he spends the award money over and over with epistolary pals.

As for that tough guy, John O'Hara, he bursts into tears; he's been denied so often, been belittled, ignored, shunted aside. This is "the climax of my life."

Can it be? Are there marble tears? Or is the stock of human reaction so small that tough guys and tender ones, giants and pygmies, feel the same way?

So what do I do? What do I make of the award? Use its fine, small music to make a graceful exit? Or, since what's outside that exit looks like the Great Boredom, can I somehow buckle myself into this armor and see if it won't give me a little more courage to go further into the Boundlessness than I've gone? That would be a prize.

[412]

INDEX OF PERSONS

[413]

[418]

Lindon, Jerome, 47
Lippmann, Walter, 201
Liston, Sonny, 56
Longfellow, Henry Wadsworth, 184, 316
Lovett, Robert Morse, 61-62, 305
Lovingood, Sut , 380 (see Harris, George Washington)
Lowell, Amy, 270
Lowell, Robert, 49-53, 56, 274-276
Lu Binyan, 115
Lu Wenfu, 114, 121
Lu Xun, 115
Lubbock, Percy, 134
Lucid, Robert, 119
Lucilius, 150
Lytle, Andrew, 36

MacArthur, Douglas, 127
Macaulay, Thomas, 387
Macdonald, Dwight, 220
Maclean, Norman, 286
MacLeish, Archibald, 353, 412
Maeterlinck, Maurice, 185
Magnani, Anna, 304
Magny, Claude-Edmonde, 213
Mailer, Norman, 4, 28, 54-56, 82, 84-86, 95-96, 98-100, 108-109, 111, 119-120, 122, 137-138, 166, 342, 384, 386, 389-390
Malamud, Bernard, 92-94, 166-167, 231, 257, 384, 386, 389
Malatesta, Sigismundo, 11
Mallarmé, Stéphane, 67-68, 71, 253
Malraux, André, 185, 313-315
Malvaux, 330
Mandelstam, Nadia (Nadezhda) 224, 292-295, 309
Mandelstam, Osip, 292-295
Mann, Thomas, 209-212, 229, 231, 258, 260, 304, 338, 408, 412
Mao Tse-tung, 70, 185, 315, 319, 321
Mapplethorpe, Robert, 58
Marceau, Marcel, 259
Marco Polo, 191

Marin, John, 380
Markov, 131
Marlowe, Christopher, 285
Marsh, Jean, (189)
Marshak, Alexander, 198
Martin, David, 168
Marx, Karl, 94, 138, 390
Mason, A. E. W., 215
Mason, Bobbie Ann, 257
Masters, Edgar Lee, 171, 179, 195, 256-257, 283, 328, 351, 389
Matthau, Walter, 270
Maugham, William Somerset, 187, 190, 333
Maupassant, Guy de, 45
Mauss, Marcel, 68, 70-71
Mayakovski, Vladimir, 292
McCain, Murray, 393-394
McCarthy, Mary, 27-28
McDaniel, Dr., 88, 90
McGovern, George, 85, 136-137
McGuane, Thomas, 245
Meltzer, Françoise, 71
Melville, Herman, (240)
Mencius, 115
Mencken, Henry Louis, 177, 337
Merrill, James, 50, 272
Merwin, W. S., 272, 310-312
Michelangelo Buonarroti, 23, 208, 407
Mies van der Rohe, Ludwig, 397
Milano, Paolo, 343
Miles, Jack, 252
Milhous, Grandma, 316
Miller, Arthur, 94, 103, 120, 122-123
Milosz, Czeslaw, 136
Milton, John, 65
Mishima, Yukio, 383
Mitchell, Thomas, 67, 69-70, 73
Moles, Abraham, 142, 381
Mondrian, Piet, 208
Monroe, Harriet, 61
Monroe, Marilyn, 342
Montaigne, Michel de, 151-152, 159, 250, 293

Pope, Alexander, 165, 185, 371, 407-408
Porter, Cole, 118, 161
Pound, Ezra, 8-12, 43, 60-61, 63, 97, 207, 258, 270, 275, 278, 283, 351, 355-359, 396, 401, 408
Powell, Padgett, 257
Powers, J.F., 46, 207, 219, 257, 259, 264, 325, 334, 374, 401
Price, Richard, 50, 136, 237, 331
Prior, Matthew, 185
Proust, Marcel, 70, 125, 152, 156, 158, 171, 182, 185, 201, 213-219, 231, 233, 237-238, 345, 351, 389, 397, 401
Prozio, 80
Purdy, James, 166, 181
Pynchon, Thomas, 131, 382

Quinn, John, 357-358

Rabelais, François, 185, 254, 355
Rachewilts, Mary de, 408
Raditsa, Bogan, 81, 117-118
Ramjerdi, Jan, 245
Ransom, John Crowe, 51
Rapaport, Herman, 68
Raphael, 214
Rau, Santha Rama, 6
Read, Forrest, 355-356
Reagan, Ronald, 98, 117, 120, 137, 324, 401, 408
Redford, Robert, 309
Reich, Wilhelm, 231-232
Reisner, Larisa, 222
Renan, Ernest, 314, 336-337
Reynolds, Mary, 47
Reynolds, Myra, 62
Rhee, Syngman, 319
Rich, Adrienne, 272
Richardson, Hadley, 239
Richardson, Samuel, 151, 184
Richter, Conrad, 35
Riefenstahl, Leni, 103
Rilke, Rainer Maria, 273, 299, 386,

390, 396, 401, 408
Rimbaud, Arthur, 62, 184, 397
Rio, Sanz del, 336
Robbe-Grillet, Alain, 131, 163, 256
Roberts, Elizabeth Madox, 57, 61
Robison, Mary, 256, 261
Rodgers, Richard, 118
Roethke, Theodore, 279
Rogers, Thomas, 181
Rollings, Alane, 277-278, 396
Rollings, Cynthia, 89
Romains, Jules, 382
Romney, George, 325
Rong, Shen, 115
Roosevelt, Franklin Delano, 51, 182, 189, 378
Rosenberg, Isaac, 274
Ross, Cudden, 37
Ross, Harold, 304
Ross, Jean, 57, 285
Rosset, Barney, 47
Rossi (of the Azzuri), 406
Roth, Henry, 168
Roth, Philip, 20, 22-26, 93-94, 108, 129, 131, 166, 181, 183, 236-238, 257, 264, 389
Rousseau, Jean-Jacques, 216, 311, 318
Royko, Mike, 178
Rubens, Peter Paul, 108
Rudge, Olga, 8-9, 11-12
Ruggles, Carl, 285
Rushdie, Salman, 110-111, 124, 252-255
Russell, Bertrand, 337, 349
Ryback, Tymothy, 408

Saint-Saens, Charles Camille, 112
Salinger, J. D., 131, 166, 342, 384
Sample, Albert Race, 299-303
Sample, Emma, 299-301
Sanchez, Sonia, 199, 281
Sandburg, Carl, 61, 183
Sang-Deuk Moon, 80
Sappho, 276-277

[424]